AF540207

# *Lokavidya* Perspectives

A Philosophy of Political Imagination
for the Knowledge Age

# *Lokavidya* Perspectives

## A Philosophy of Political Imagination for the Knowledge Age

Edited by
Amit Basole

AAKAR

*LOKAVIDYA* PERSPECTIVES: A Philosophy of Political Imagination for the Knowledge Age

*Edited by* Amit Basole



First Published 2015

ISBN 978-93-5002-332-7 (Pb)



*Published by*
**AAKAR BOOKS**
28 E Pocket IV, Mayur Vihar Phase I, Delhi 110 091
Phone : 011 2279 5505 Telefax : 011 2279 5641
aakarbooks@gmail.com; www.aakarbooks.com

*in association with*
**VIDYA ASHRAM**
SN 10/82A, Ashok Marg
Sarnath, Varanasi 221 007
vidyaashram@gmail.com

*Printed at*
Sapra Brothers, Delhi 110 092

# Contents

## II. *Lokavidya*: Epistemics and Politics



## III. Economics of *Lokavidya*

# Preface

In our youth we worked with received theories. Philosophy, science, politics, everywhere one sat on a mountain of scholarship. Much was known and something more was to be found. This constituted the milieu of research and political activism. But mid-way through our lives the mountain started crumbling. Philosophy took a leap from Kant (back?) to Socrates, and from Marx to Gandhi and Kabir; science lost its place of absolute command in the world of knowledge, and people everywhere stopped looking to politics for a better future. The world changed through the 1990s.

The people of the Global South started facing a new world-in-the-making that uprooted and displaced them afresh from the activity and resources with which they were managing to live. The philosophy, science and politics that had reigned through the 20th century no more came to their rescue. This turned out to be a great opportunity for activist-thinkers of the former colonies to intervene in the ideological world with knowledge perspectives of their own people. New ways of thinking started coming into existence that did not resort to European reference, and instead rooted themselves in the ways of thinking and doing of the people. *Lokavidya* is the generic name of such ways of thinking and doing of people who have not gone to the university. *Lokavidya* is their knowledge; in it is embedded their worldview—philosophy, politics, economics, genius, what have you. *Lokavidya* perspectives are thus the new and emerging knowledge perspectives that pave the way for a political imagination which can deliver the people from the traps they are in since the beginning of imperialism.

These new ways of thinking are embedded in the new movements of *adivasis*, peasants, artisans, women and the small retailers who have been called in this book the *lokavidyadhar samaj,* the communities of *lokavidya*-bearers. Seen from a *lokavidya* perspective, movements for people's control of water, forest and land, as well as movements against forcible acquisition of and consequent displacement from land and forest or from daily artisanal and retail activity are companions of a knowledge movement in India which seeks equal status for *lokavidya* in the world of knowledge, claims equal returns on it, and calls for the secure right of everybody to live by the knowledge she or he possesses. Rights of Nature (Ecuador), Rights of Mother Earth (Bolivia) or food sovereignty (*via Campesina*) are fraternal knowledge movements in other parts of the world. These movements are inaugurating a new philosophical niche that seeks its criteria in the knowledge, initiative and well-being of the people, that is in *lokavidya.* In so far as these movements are pitted against the new capitalist order, the corporations and the State, they are preparing fragments and grounds for a new political imagination, again based on *lokavidya.*

Lokavidya Jan Andolan (LJA, http://lokavidyajanandolan.blogspot.com/) represents the idea of this knowledge movement of the people in India at present. The writings collected here are by those in LJA who could write in English and did write. Many of them have worked together since the mid-1970s and have come through a long course of activism and radical ideological debates. Vidya Ashram (www.vidyaashram.org) is the latest organizational form that they have adopted with the understanding that a radical intervention in the world of knowledge is now a precondition for politics of change. The flux in the world of knowledge today is providing the double occasion for such an intervention. For one the epistemic order of the industrial epoch is crumbling and in addition there is the rise of *lokavidya* with new found dignity and political propensity.

The articles in this book may be seen as a kind of response to the demands on thinking that the new world places before the people of the Global South. They have attempted to handle the emerging reality and issues in the world of knowledge related to changes in hierarchy, command, controls, criteria of legitimacy, paradigm, commercial importance, technology, place of knowledge activity, and also the appearance of the new sciences as well as the recognition now coming to *lokavidya*. And this time the South prepares to respond bringing its own knowledge traditions back to life, traditions of knowledge that have always been alive among the people, among those who have not been to the university, and who earn their livelihood and serve this society based on their own knowledge.

Amit Basole, the youngest amongst us who teaches in a university, agreed to edit this volume. He has attempted to weave a pattern and introduce a running thread in this set of articles written by different people on different occasions, between 1998 and 2013. Through this collection, we hope to disturb the reader to such an extent that he or she is ready to rethink the world again from the first principles rooted in ordinary life, the life of the people.

Varanasi, January 2015 **Sunil Sahasrabudhey**

# List of Contributors

**Sunil Sahasrabudhey** is founder president of *Vidya Ashram*. He has done studies in the philosophy of knowledge and politics with the Gandhian perspective and has been active in the New Farmers' Movement in India since the late 1970s. A founder participant of the *Lokavidya* Movement, he lives in Varanasi.

**Avinash Jha** is librarian at the Centre for the Study of Developing Societies. He is a philosopher and a major participant in the Dialogues on Knowledge in Society. He has contributed greatly to the development of the *lokavidya* perspective and the knowledge standpoint in the era of the Internet. A close associate of *Vidya Ashram*, he lives in Delhi.

**B. Krishnarajulu** was Professor of Physics at Osmania University, Hyderabad and has been part of the New Farmers' Movement in Karnataka. He is a close associate of *Vidya Ashram* and a core member of the *Lokavidya* Movement. He lives in Hyderabad.

**J.K. Suresh** is Principal Knowledge Manager, Infosys Technologies. A close associate of *Vidya Ashram*, he has studied in depth the contemporary changes in the world of knowledge and has brought that understanding to the *Lokavidya* Movement. He lives in Bengaluru.

**Chitra Sahasrabudhey** turned to lifelong social activism after receiving her Ph.D. in Chemistry. She has worked primarily to organize women and artisans with focus on *lokavidya* as their source of strength. She is the National Convener of *Lokavidya Jan Andolan* and Coordinator of *Vidya Ashram* and lives in Varanasi.

**Ananya Vajpeyi** is a writer and social historian, presently on the faculty of the Centre for the Study of Developing

Societies, Delhi. She lives in Delhi.

**K.B. Jinan** has had a lifelong engagement with art and education, critiquing the formal and written word, and experimenting with learning and creativity among children with a naturalist's perspective. He lives in Thrissur.

**K.K. Surendran,** a physicist and philosopher, is founder of Dialogues on Knowledge in Society. He is a close associate of *Vidya Ashram* and has insisted on moral rigour and spiritual content in the *Lokavidya* Movement. He lives in Pune.

**Vijay Kundaji,** an Electronics Engineer, has travelled extensively in India engaging with ordinary people and ordinary lives. He is a close associate of *Vidya Ashram* and lives in Bengaluru.

**Amit Basole** holds Ph.D. degrees in Neuroscience as well as Economics. He teaches Economics at the University of Massachusetts, Boston. He has explored artisanal economics from a *lokavidya* knowledge standpoint. A close associate of *Vidya Ashram* and contributor to the Dialogues on Knowledge in Society, he lives in Boston.

**Lalit Kaul** is an Electronics Engineer and has been in the R&D division of Bharat Heavy Electricals Limited (BHEL). He has had lifelong social concerns. A close associate of *Vidya Ashram* and a core member of the *Lokavidya* Movement, he lives in Hyderabad.

**Girish Sahasrabudhey** is Professor of Physics at B.R. Engineering College, Nagpur. He has been actively involved in the New Farmers' Movement in Maharashtra. A close associate of *Vidya Ashram* and a core member of the *Lokavidya* Movement, he lives in Nagpur.

**Gigi Roggero** is a founding member of the edu-factory collective (www.edu-factory.org) and teaches at the University of Bologna, Italy. He has written extensively on the new students' and informal workers' movements in Europe and is an active participant of these movements.

**Ritu Priya** is a medical doctor and Professor in Social and Preventive Medicine, Jawaharlal Nehru University (JNU), New Delhi. She is a keen participant in the discourses on society and healthcare. She lives in Delhi.

# Introduction

*Amit Basole*

The myriad ongoing popular struggles against displacement and dispossession, inequality and imperialism will acquire a new civilizational significance as well as a sense of solidarity with each other if they are seen as knowledge struggles, struggles for restoring legitimacy to people's knowledge or *lokavidya*.[1] The coming of the Knowledge Society in the past two decades has destabilized the established hegemony of modern science by recognizing the knowledge of peasants and artisans. In the process it has created a space for building a new politics of *lokavidya*. These are the principal claims of the present volume, a collection of articles by associates of *Vidya Ashram* located in Sarnath, Varanasi. Among the contributors to the volume are activists, scientists, social scientists, and a knowledge manager. They have been all participants or close observers of people's movements in India.

## The *Lokavidya* Standpoint

Radical social and political movements of the 19th and 20th centuries challenged every oppressive structure of the capitalist social order except one: the hegemony of modern science and modern knowledge over other traditions of knowledge. In particular, knowledge traditions of the "uneducated majority," those millions of peasants, *adivasis*, artisans, small retailers, and women all over the world who are outside the modern economy,

1. Words and phrases that come from languages other than English have been italicized and defined in the Glossary.

were considered inferior. The result was that even when the masses participated in these movements, they only constituted the "mass-base," never the intellectual command. And often they ended up fighting someone else's battle; a just world remained elusive.

In Gandhi and in Marx is found the political insight that we cannot begin a struggle that moves in our favour if we base it on a foundation which is not ours and that we do not understand. The cognitive foundation of a people's strength in the ultimate analysis lies in the knowledge they possess to organize their lives, to understand the world, to resist the oppressor. This is knowledge produced in ordinary life from which all knowledge (including science) originates and to which, in a just society, all knowledge must return. This knowledge is *lokavidya*.

The essays collected together in this volume are born from the belief that till the people's struggle against imperialism is carried to the knowledge plane, counter-revolutions will be inevitable; that unless the University is challenged alongside the State, restorations will recur. The authors articulate the position that ordinary people the world over are knowledgeable, and that they know it to be so. The "uneducated masses" are on the move everywhere in struggles across the world, forming not just the mass base of these movements, but also the intellectual motive force. They supply not only the bodies but also the brains. That they can construct a new world based on their knowledge is the claim of the *lokavidya* movement.

The modern university, instead of recognizing *lokavidya* and seeing that society is knowledge abundant, sees itself as being located amidst knowledge scarcity. The hegemony of modern science and its allied knowledge traditions such as liberal and radical social thought originating in Europe has meant the denigration of other ways of seeing, knowing, and doing that belong to the ordinary people in the colonized countries. The political implication has been clear: a movement cannot be organized on the basis of *lokavidya* because the so-called "traditional societies" are incapable of challenging imperialism or of removing their own unjust structures without help from outside. It is this pervasive belief that the present volume challenges by calling for a knowledge movement (*gyan andolan*) based on *lokavidya darshan*.

When we view Indian society through the lens of knowledge traditions, new solidarities emerge, which are not visible through a class or caste lens. The majority of the people, those 90 per cent whose worldview has not been shaped by the University, whose skills have not been acquired in colleges, appear on one side. The small minority who is in command of the public sphere, the State, the media, the corporate sector, appears on the other side. The majority society is the *lokvidyadhar samaj*, the society of *lokavidya*-holders. In economic terms they constitute the "informal sector," in social terms they are the *bahishkrit samaj*. Their success and progress is measured by the extent to which they give up their own ways of thinking, knowing, seeing, and doing. The *lokavidya* standpoint is that their struggles which they wage daily, in organized and unorganized fashion, will be sharpened if they stake the claim that their knowledge, *lokavidya*, is not inferior to any other knowledge tradition.

This book argues that the moment is ripe for engaging in the above task because we are living through a period of momentous changes in the world of knowledge. Global capital is attempting to shape a new world order. It is known by many names depending on the point of view adopted: Globalization, Neoliberalism, Cognitive Capitalism, Information Society, Network Society, Knowledge Age and so on. An entirely new vocabulary is coming into existence around the concept of knowledge: knowledge management, knowledge worker, knowledge economy, knowledge parks, knowledge divide, etc. The technological impetus for the creation of this new world order has come from the Information and Communications Technologies (ICTs) and the new connectivity through the Internet.

From the perspective of those who are on the other side of the digital divide, the paradigm shift from the "Industrial Age" to the "Knowledge Age" (see Chapter 9 for a schematic look at this shift) has brought unprecedented dispossession, loss of livelihood, and an absolute impoverishment in the material standard of living. But at the same time it has opened up possibilities for a new type of politics based on *lokavidya*. We believe that the moment is ripe for the construction of a new vocabulary at the people's end. Why is this so? In the new Knowledge Society, the *vidya* of the peasant and the artisan, their knowledge of production, processes, designs, and their skill, is commanding new attention. Local healthcare, knowledge of natural resources, water management, house building, everything is being recognized as legitimate knowledge. Through our educational system we have been trained to see ordinary people, those who have not gone to school, largely as ignorant. We have been trained to see them as doing what they do in the way they do it because modern knowledge and facilities have not reached them. But if we make an effort to see ordinary people, peasants, artisans, women, *adivasis*, as knowledgeable persons we would realize that with them lies that huge store and variety of knowledge that may far exceed the total knowledge content produced and accumulated by the universities so far. This process has started, albeit under the compulsions of the globalized market that extracts value wherever it is produced, no matter which knowledge is used in the value creation process.

The language of *lokavidya* has the capacity to transform ongoing struggles in India and elsewhere. The preeminent conflict in the neoliberal era has been over displacement and dispossession of people from their lands and livelihoods. Till peasants and artisans stake the claim that their knowledge traditions are in no way inferior to any other, their struggles against displacement will appear to be rear-guard defence of meagre livelihoods at best or anti-development and anti-progress at worst. The popular slogan that "another world is possible" would have a clearer message if we take the language of *lokavidya* seriously. The new indigenous movements in Latin America which have thrown up concepts such as Rights of Nature and Rights of Mother Earth, the numerous *jal-jangal-zameen* struggles against displacement and dispossession in India and across the world appear to be coherent and in solidarity with one another when seen from the *lokavidya* standpoint. Can we see these as part of a *lokavidya jan andolan*, a knowledge movement of *lokavidya*-holders?

It is becoming part of common wisdom now that the same knowledge tradition that created the multiple social, economic, and ecological crises we face, cannot be expected to transcend these crises. It is the contention of this book that a *lokavidya*-based society offers one way forward.

## Overview of This Book

The articles collected together for this volume were originally written for diverse purposes such as political pamphlets, World Social Forum booklets, journals, seminars, online discussion fora, invited lectures, and conference presentations. As such the essays vary widely in length as well as depth, but are bound together by a common set of concerns that have already been articulated above. The writings have been divided into five major themes; Transition to Knowledge Society, *Lokavidya*: Epistemics and Politics, Economics of *Lokavidya*, *Lokavidya* and the University, and *Lokavidya Jan Andolan*, which roughly match the core concerns of *Vidya Ashram*.

A founding concern of *Vidya Ashram* has been to construct a theoretical understanding of the changes that Indian society and the world at large are undergoing with the advent of the Internet, and the information and communications revolution. Which are the new classes that have come into existence? What have been the effects on the working majority? To this end, members have been writing from the earliest period of the founding of the *Ashram*, on the nature of the transition from the Industrial Age to the Information/Knowledge Age. Section One of the book, "Transition to Knowledge Society" contains nine essays on this theme. Some of these are explicitly from the perspective of the bearers of *lokavidya*, while others take a more general view of the transition. The principal claim in this section is articulated thus by Sunil Sahasrabudhey:

> For over a decade and a half now the world of knowledge has been experiencing an extraordinary flux. The Internet has created a new virtual world of knowledge activity and knowledge management and the place of the university as the undisputed command in the world of knowledge has been challenged and there is an atmosphere of a new recognition to the knowledge in society, *lokavidya*.

In several of its political pamphlets published in Hindi, the *Ashram* has presented the ongoing transition and its impact on various classes in society, in schematic terms easy to understand by all. An English version of these schematics is presented in the chapter titled "Jaipur Lectures on the Knowledge Society." This material has been adapted from slides prepared for a series of lectures to B.Tech. students at the Lakshmi Narayan Mittal Institute of Information Technology, Jaipur, as part of a Technology-Philosophy course. The principal concern, reflected in all the pieces, is to create a new political imagination that will serve the people in the Knowledge Age. Altering the current, unjust, relationship between *lokavidya* and organized knowledge (as presented by Science, capital, the State, and the Internet) is a core component of this new imagination.

A second major concern at the *Ashram* has been to develop a new language to effectively work towards a knowledge politics in the Internet Age. The idea of *lokavidya* has been continuously with us, getting substantiated and theoretically fleshed out with every intervention in society. Section Two, "*Lokavidya*: Epistemics and Politics" contains pieces which focus specifically on the *lokavidya* viewpoint. Essays in this section interpret modern social movements such as the indigenous people's movement in South America, the international farmers movement (via Campesina), farmers' movements of India, *adivasi* movement in India, the *jal-jangal-zameen* struggles led by the National Alliance of People's Movements in India, and the women's movement from the *lokavidya* perspective. The readers will find here fresh takes on long-standing issues such as imperialism, oppression of women, dispossession and loss of livelihoods. Other articles explore a specific *lokavidya* world, such as the iron-smelting *vidya* of the *Agaria adivasis* of Chhattisgarh. On the philosophical plane, articles in this section are concerned with developing a theory of *lokavidya* and its relationship to ordinary life (itself a philosophical concept developed in Chapter 18).

The *lokavidyadhar samaj* is characterized by material deprivation. Hence the economics of this *samaj* has always been a particular concern. Section Three, "Economics of *Lokavidya*," contains four essays that focus on the economic significance of *lokavidya*. Here the starting point is the well-known fact that the vast majority of the Indian people sustain themselves on the basis of knowledge that is not gained in colleges and universities. In economic parlance, this so-called "informal economy" runs largely on the basis of "informal knowledge." The essays in this section try to go beyond categories of informal knowledge, traditional and indigenous knowledge, etc. and posit *lokavidya* as the knowledge-basis of the economy. Two articles specifically investigate the emancipatory potential of the local market and the *karigar samaj* (artisans). The local market is seen as a location where emancipatory ideas of Marx and Gandhi can come together. The article on the *karigar samaj* analyses the extensive reorganization of manufacturing in the period of globalization, the exploitation of family labour by finance capital, and the possibilities of constructing a new society based on artisanal production. The other articles in this section theorize the connection between knowledge production and the world of work. They investigate the contemporary development discourse on "traditional and indigenous knowledge" (TK/IK). The argument put forth is that while the increasing visibility of TK/IK in development theory does create a space for articulating the *lokavidya* viewpoint, there are strong limitations imposed by the TK/IK framework which sees "non-scientific" knowledge as a "bag of tools" to be incorporated into conventional development models or as a set of practices that need to be validated scientifically. These articles also investigate the dangers posed by online digital archiving of TK/IK.

*Vidya Ashram* considers the re-casting of the relationship between the University (broadly interpreted as the various colleges, universities, research establishments, etc. which embody modern science and its allied knowledge traditions) and the world of *lokavidya* as a central task in constructing a new emancipatory politics. Since the ascent of modern science, the University has been conceptualized as a knowledge producer standing amidst a world of knowledge scarcity. The *lokavidya* standpoint instead sees the University as one location of knowledge in a world of knowledge abundance. A recent *gyan panchayat* organized by the *Ashram* in Varanasi had the theme "The Walls of the University Must Come Down." What would a university that is not walled-off from society, and that respects the *lokavidya* traditions look like? This question is raised in Section IV.

The fifth and final section of the volume contains blog posts written as part of an online dialogue conducted in preparation for the First International Meeting of the *Lokavidya Jan Andolan* (LJA), held in Varanasi in November 2011. The LJA, as the name suggests, is a people's knowledge movement, a knowledge movement of the majority of people, who have been dubbed as the ignorant masses by the science establishments, the universities and the modern state. LJA is the realization that only if politics is based on the people's own knowledge can it be on their initiative, can it serve their interests. No longer can "educated" women claim to speak for all women or "educated" workers for all workers.

The following pages greatly expand and elaborate on the key ideas outlined above. While some amount of repetition is inevitable in a collection such as this, we hope that together the pieces offer a comprehensive introduction to *lokavidya darshan* and *gyan ki rajniti*, the philosophy of *lokavidya* as well as the politics of knowledge based on this philosophy.

# I

# The Transition to Knowledge Society

# 1

# Knowledge Management versus Knowledge Production*

*Sunil Sahasrabudhey*

The unfolding reality of the last fifteen years is seen by us as a historic opportunity for the oppressed classes of the world, not because the Internet or the computer and communication technologies have appeared with a promise, but because they have unleashed a historic destabilization of world capitalism, concomitantly destabilizing both the university and the nation-state. The take over of the university by the corporations and of the national state by a trans-national state in the making, also called the Empire by American theorists, are the immediately visible phenomena. These have tended to put many of us on the defensive and if we are not careful we start defending the university and the state that capitalism had produced of which we are dissenting products.

The Internet has divided the world afresh into those who manage knowledge and those who produce knowledge. Conflicts in the knowledge domain constitute the gateway to an understanding of this phenomenon. These conflicts constitute the bed for the production of new theories that can produce new alliances, a new politics in the interest of the oppressed of the world. These conflicts of the knowledge domain are there in the fields, the workshops, the factories, in the riverbeds and forest terrains and also in the universities where people produce

---

* Originally written in 2007 for edu-factory.org online dialogue on Conflicts in Production of Knowledge

knowledge. The organization and manipulation of these knowledge-production activities is now managed over the Internet.

That the university is the chief location of the production of knowledge is the Euro-centric view. Theories of human emancipation, particularly emancipation of the oppressed, must see every human being as a knowledge producer.

Ordinary life in fact is that vast bed where knowledge is produced hourly, daily. Ordinary life is the life without condition. It presupposes no technology, no religion, no state, no university. People constantly produce new knowledge based on their genius, experiences and the needs of everyday life. There has perhaps never been a greater source of knowledge than ordinary life. I live in one of the most populous regions of the world. Here the life of the majority is just ordinary life. No air travel, no Internet, no electricity for half the day. Cities and towns are places of household artisanal production and small shops; the countryside is full of very small farmers. I trust different regions have different concepts of ordinary life and the majority everywhere is part of ordinary life. If we see this in a deprivation framework, we will be led to development theories; if we see this in an exploitation framework, we will be led to theories of radical social transformation.

Broadly speaking there are four locations of knowledge in contemporary society—University, Monastery, Internet and ordinary life. Science, religious knowledge, knowledge management and *lokavidya* are the chief occupants of these sites. Knowledge management is in the process of assuming the command of the knowledge domain as much as information economy is assuming command in the domain of economics and a transnational state is situating national states as its subordinate and serving partners.

Production of knowledge in the monastery is minimal. Production of knowledge in the universities is in the process of splitting into two halves. One will become part of the activity in the Network Society and the other will be pushed down into the world of production, the world of technicians, artisans, farmers and forest dwellers. So part of the university will be gobbled up by the world of knowledge management and the other parts will move to populate the already populated realm of ordinary life with its infinite variety of production of knowledge. What will happen to the university as an idea or as a campus reality I do not know; however, what appears to be staring into our faces is not the hitherto known division between managers of knowledge and producers of knowledge. The producers of knowledge are the oppressed classes and their seeing themselves as such is the condition of the politics of emancipation.

Knowledge management redefines what is knowledge: it aspires to be the knowledge itself. It does not represent only a new form or practice of management; rather it is primarily a new form of knowledge. We may deny it this status, and many do so, but knowledge management does occupy the top slot in the new knowledge hierarchy of the information age. It occupies the command position and rules from the virtual domain. Sitting at the eye of the cyclone in the epistemic world it sucks in everything of substance. All knowledge that is produced anywhere feeds into it and all knowledge at the site of production stands emaciated and alienated. Knowledge producers thus enter into a fundamental conflict with knowledge managers. The transnational state develops primarily to manage this conflict. The recent American wars appear to underline the inherent irreconcilability of the situation. Only when producers of knowledge start understanding that their knowledge is turned against them in the new dispensation, the possibility of a new radical politics is born.

# 2

# Dialogues on Knowledge in Society*

*Sunil Sahasrabudhey*

The sweeping changes occurring in society seem to demand a fresh and radical return to the first principles today. The human engagement must grapple again with the fundamental question of where lies the strength of the people. Dialogues such as these may be expected to contribute to the logic of this rediscovery. A first stretch of thoughts is given below to start a discussion. It is an exploration of the place of knowledge, its role, function, content, organization, methods of production and communication, etc and its relationship with everything that there is both in the world of thought and in the material world.

## 2.1. Society

The modern society has been divided into two worlds named differently by different ideological pursuits. Some of the names are rich and poor, West and East, Centre and periphery, industrial and non-industrial, capitalist and pre-capitalist, imperial and colonial, etc. The emergence of Information and Communication Technologies (ICT) has given birth to a further new language perhaps reflecting a new reality, the two worlds now being those of netizens and citizens or the two sides of the digital divide.

Discussion of knowledge in society seems to require liberation from the framework of the industrial society and

---

* Occurs as the opening statement in the bulletin *A Dialogue on Knowledge in Society*, published for a workshop in the World Social Forum, Mumbai 2004.

development of new paradigms in accordance with the emerging realities of the knowledge society.

### 2.2 Exploration

Since we are at a transition from the industrial to knowledge society and not only that it is not known what future holds in store for human kind but that the future is a matter of what and how men and women build it, define it, imagine it and actually shape it, therefore the exploration in the sphere of knowledge, the dialogues themselves must constitute a mode of transcendence, a method of incessant booting theoretically. This is to say that the exploration is not towards a known ideal but itself constitutes an ideal dynamic. It is not to build theories of present and future but to assist individual, collective, social, etc. transcendence from one's own theoretical constructs.

### 2.3 Science

The industrial society created in 'Science' the new God. It was, with its method, the supreme form of knowledge and also the only legitimate source of knowledge. It was declared value-independent and culture-free; these characteristics tending to assume the status of criteria of legitimacy, universality and even absoluteness. Method of production of knowledge and its content assumed singular importance. The world of the poor and the colonized seldom mustered enough strength to question all these in the public domain and therefore they developed ways of not accepting any of this in their own world. The processes of real life still give them enough opportunity to practise their own methods and develop their knowledge further in an integral relationship with their culture and their system of values. This was survival with an intrinsic strength, which would some day serve a challenge. Gandhiji was that phenomenon in India.

With the emergence of the knowledge society, from within the first world itself there is a questioning of the absoluteness of science. The characteristics of value freeness and culture independence may not enjoy the same status now. Sanctity of 'the method' may go overboard in due course; production of knowledge is not the chief concern of the knowledge society.

ICTs are methods of organization and communication of knowledge. It perhaps does not matter now how knowledge is produced and who produces it and the status as knowledge may be determined by its organizability by ICTs. So knowledge society transforms the relationship of man's epistemic activities with truth. Science in the industrial society was imagined as a pursuit of truth. Knowledge-related activities now have an explicit connection with pragmatism. Not that industrial society did not have such a connection but then it was part of truth-seeking whereas now, at least at present, it is part of management activity.

The last quarter of the 20th century witnessed a method of challenge to science with a new critique based in a fresh appreciation of the logic and content of traditional knowledge, living traditions of knowledge among peasants and artisans, the colonized and the poor. Such basis seems now to require the inclusion of the method of organization and communication of knowledge among the people which may be reflected in various institutional forms and methods of struggle in the other domain.

### 2.4 The Shift

The shift from content to organization and production to communication has taken the world of thought by storm. For all philosophy hitherto (from Descartes to Popper and Chomsky) survival is at stake. The world of things and forces is being replaced by a world of representation, structure and meaning. The world (ontology) of the natural sciences may become one of the many possible worlds. The ICTs may know how to organize the knowledge content of different social formations legitimizing their ontologies in the process and carrying out an epistemic reduction, a price that the diverse civilizations shall pay. Dialogues on knowledge in society must recognize both the new spaces that this shift creates and the epistemic reduction that the other domain suffers. The new spaces are structured against the industrial society and therefore in a definite sense also against the forms of domination in the old world. These spaces on their own are not emancipatory and are favourable to building new structures of domination and deprivation. However in so far as the shift must dismantle the old world, it must provide space for organization and communication of knowledge from a people's standpoint also. Dialogues on knowledge in society may clearly focus on the nature and type of this space and the kind of initiatives that enhance the strengths of people and their capacity to wage a battle against (the price of) epistemic reduction being thrust upon them.

### 2.5 *Lokavidya* Standpoint

What is generally referred to as people's knowledge, people's standpoint, etc. are partial ways of referring (prevalent in the old world) to what is a wholesome epistemic stand of the other domain. This is the *lokavidya* standpoint. *Lokavidya* philosophy is a comprehensive understanding of knowledge in all its aspects, functions and relationships which is the genuine subject matter of dialogues on knowledge in society. However given below are a few distinct points strongly relevant in the present discourse.

*Lokavidya* means those methods (philosophy, etc.) of organization and communication of *vidya* which place *vidya* in the midst of the people. Being in the midst of the people means (a) the strings of control should be among the people that is in their social organizations, (b) the values of the other domain should actually be the guiding principles, (c) it must measure upto the criteria of ordinary life and (d) ensuring its role in the processes of construction and reconstruction of truth.

Thus *lokavidya* provides a different meaning to knowledge than provided by the knowledge society. It is completely opposed to the epistemic reduction by the ICTs and further provides a wide enough aperture to comprehend the emancipatory aspects of knowledge in the net-domain. Dialogues on knowledge in society may develop tools of disaggregation and hedging of knowledge in the net domain and the domain of ordinary life. It can develop, with the help of the *lokavidya* standpoint ways of meshing the knowledge in the two domains in the interest of human life, both contemporary and future.

The *Lokavidya* standpoint helps us understand people's

initiatives and possible initiatives in practically every sphere, economic, social, cultural, etc. *Lokavidya* pervades the activities that sustain a sphere of economic exchange in ordinary life, it is there in how people combine with their brethren to produce desired forms of solidarity, it provides the criteria for social values governing the cultures of people's lives and in most palpable form it is seen in the improvements and innovations by the people in their practice according to need and based on their experiences and genius.

**2.6 The Dialogue**

Drawn into this dialogue are people who recognize, often not explicitly, the centrality today of organization and communication of knowledge, and this in both the domains, the net-domain and the domain of ordinary life. At one end therefore are ICTs and at the other *lokavidya*. These dialogues are not just theoretical or philosophical; they can be on very concrete issues like market, solidarity among the people, energy, industry, organization, administration, communication, education, healthcare; in fact, on anything.

# 3

# Internet and the Shifting Grounds of Knowledge*

*Avinash Jha*

One way of looking at the Internet and its effects is to see how the traditional (meaning, modern!) activities and institutions make use of the Internet to augment and advance their traditional activities. How through the use of Internet certain activities are facilitated, made faster, cheaper, easier and so on. When we look at the immense amount of information that is available on the Internet and round the clock access to this information for millions of users, we are looking at the Internet as a set of tools and techniques which we can apply to perform tasks and fulfil functions that we were doing earlier, but which can be done better now.

It is comparatively more difficult to discern the significant qualitative changes that may occur on account of the Internet. With the growth in electronic connectivity and development of increasingly more sophisticated handling and manipulation of information, we may need ways to discern precisely such qualitative and epoch-making changes. Since we are ourselves in the throes of change, we do not have at our disposal a method, or a well-rounded perspective, which can be applied in order to understand how our lives and societies are changing. This is especially true with regard to the question of knowledge. How

---

* Paper presented at a conference on "The Emerging Organization of Knowledge and the Future of Universities," December 2008, 32nd Indian Social Sciences Congress, Jamia Millia Islamia, New Delhi.

do we judge the claim that the grounds of knowledge are shifting in the Internet era, which indeed is the claim we are advancing in this paper? And, why is it important after all?

### 3.1 The Idiom of Knowledge

We can perhaps begin by noting that it is now possible to talk and frame our questions in terms of 'knowledge'. A certain language, or idiom, is available to us so that we can talk about production of knowledge, ownership of knowledge, power and knowledge. Social discourses are full of references to knowledge economy, knowledge society, knowledge management, and so on. Earlier, when we discussed questions of knowledge we discussed questions of science—questions of evidence, argument, justification and scientific discovery, or we discussed the philosophy of social science. Questions of knowledge were specialized questions to be dealt by epistemology or the philosophy of science. Their effort was to establish and refine the foundations of knowledge and guard the boundaries of valid knowledge to protect it from pseudo-sciences and other unscientific intrusions. In the last few decades, we have come to see knowledge everywhere. It is in marketing, it is in forests among tribal communities, it is in machines.

We are emerging from an era where the grounds of knowledge were secure in the foundations of science. Science, or the university, as an institution authorized what was the right kind of knowledge and the rest of us didn't have to worry about the criterion of knowledge. We have now moved to an era, where knowledge is everyone's concern. Each one of us worries about having access to and possession of valuable knowledge that would increase our chances of survival and success in the emerging knowledge society. Companies are worried about the control, management and possession of their employees' knowledge and the knowledge possessed by other companies. The whole idea seems to be to untie knowledge from its context, render it as existing something outside of us, and free it for circulation, organization, application and possession.

### 3.2 Knowledge Activities on the Internet

It is in this context that we can speak of the 'explosion of knowledge' on account of the Internet. Whatever knowledge is to be found, there is a rush to 'digitize' it and put it on the Internet. 'Digitization' here can mean just a conversion of information in other forms into digital form—for example, books into electronic documents, or video cassettes into DVDs. Or it may mean something more—an incorporation of that knowledge into digital routines and organization that would make possible further development and use of that knowledge. For example, digital recording of a musical piece may merely serve as a record, like the older varieties of tape. But when this digital recording becomes a part of a larger database and the various elements of this recording are organized according to different logics of representation and used to make other music, something new is happening. What is happening is a new kind of knowledge activity. Even the traditional activities like music editing become transformed. The editor does not necessarily edit the music based on hearing but by looking at the visual representation of the sounds on the screen. This knowledge activity is taking place within the domain of the Internet.

But why call the activity of making music a knowledge activity? Here we can see a shift in the understanding and evaluation of knowledge, grounds for which were being prepared in the transition to a post-industrial economy. The industrial economy was characterized by assembly lines where the workers performed a series of simple, repetitive tasks. Workers were not required to have any knowledge. All knowledge was embodied in machines and routines. There were many changes in the industrial economies after the Second World War. The service sector grew to much larger proportions, increased competition led to quicker obsolescence of products and incorporation of high technology in products, symbolic value of products became more important leading to the growth of advertising and image building. These changes required that a larger proportion of workforce be more knowledgeable. In fact, 'knowledge economy' is understood to be characterized by the mobilization of diverse human faculties in the work process, including the social skills. As Nicolas Guilhot summarizes:

> It is a commonplace in the organizational literature to point out

> that, while the subjectivity of the worker was suppressed in the assembly line model, it is now at the centre of the work process: interpretation, creativity, autonomy, flexibility and decision capacity are the qualities required from workers, even in the most industrial or menial settings.[1]

Economy is central to the organization of modern society. This new perception of the economy summons a new perception of the work process, which in turn requires that the role of knowledge be seen anew in all activities. All activities are in some sense knowledge activities. In the age of scientific method, knowledge that existed in society, among people, was not considered knowledge at all. Knowledge economy is not concerned with how the knowledge is acquired; whether by scientific method, or through some other means. This broadening of the definition of knowledge is to be welcomed. It allows us to see the richness of knowledge that exists in society and how this knowledge can play a role in the reconstruction of society.

### 3.3 The Cybernetic Turn in Sciences

Apart from the changes in the economy, there were changes taking place in the domain of knowledge activities itself—in science, and in the university. The period before, during and after the Second World War saw the appearance of a new set of research programmes in various sciences which differ in their organization, conceptions, content from the classical science paradigm. These new programmes, associated in that period with the name of cybernetics, have as their fundamental categories related to control, communication and information. This current has influenced theories in physics, biology, linguistics, economics, etc. Donna Haraway has examined the incursion of this paradigm in biology and cultural theory. With regard to fundamental conceptions of biology, she says:

> Nineteenth century scientists materially constituted the organism as a labouring system, structured by a hierarchical division of labour and an energetic system fuelled by sugars and obeying the laws of thermodynamics. For us, the living world has become a command, control, communication, intelligence system in an environment that demands strategies of flexible accumulation.[2]

The genetic theory incorporates the concept of information in a fundamental way when the genes are defined as carrying information from one generation to another, which results in the reproduction of the organism. Philip Mirowski has produced extensive documentation to show how the cybernetic vision has come to be incorporated into the science of economics over past decades. [In his words, 'how economics became a cyborg science', which is a word in vogue among some historians of science like Donna Haraway to indicate this new paradigm]. One can say that there is a transdisciplinary formation in the sciences, which increasingly employs the concepts of information, communication, and control in fundamental ways. The computer—as an idea, as an artifact—plays a crucial role in these conceptualizations. Peter Galison writes that:

> At first no more than a faster version of electro-mechanical calculator, the computer became much more: a piece of the instrument, an instrument in its own right, finally (through simulations) a stand-in for nature itself.... In a non-trivial sense, the computer began to blur the boundaries between 'self-evident' categories of experiment, instrument and theory.[3]

These cybernetic conceptions disturbed the hierarchy of sciences with physics as the most fundamental science and also the strict divisions between natural and human sciences. Another thing to be noted is:

> It is a historical fact that each of the cyborg sciences traces its inception to the conscious intervention of a new breed of science manager, empowered by the crisis of the Second World War and fortified by lavish foundation and military sponsorships.[4]

As we can surmise, the development of the Internet itself is a part of this same history. Military purposes were extremely important in the origins of the computer and the Internet. The university and the utopian ideas of free knowledge have played their role too. Conceptually, the Internet is of course dependent on the information sciences or cyborg sciences. But in an exemplary cybernetic feedback process the Internet is now itself reconstituting the domain of knowledge in society. It is the advent of Internet that has enabled the idioms of knowledge society, knowledge economy, etc. to take centrestage and made knowledge central to the post-industrial, globalized world.

### 3.4 A New Kind of Knowledge?

Let us ponder on why Information Technology Parks are called 'knowledge parks' or why the plans for making knowledge society always translate into building better computers, achieving better connectivity, and enhancing computer learning. Presumably the activities taking place in these places are considered knowledge activities. This is jarring to our university educated ears and sensibilities. We can understand activities being carried out in a physics laboratory with its equipment, wires, dials, and readings as a knowledge activity, which would result in the affirmation or discovery of a law, or a new application of such a law. But activities in a room full of computers, connected to each other and connected to the Internet, how are these knowledge activities? Especially because these activities are not geared to producing a new representation of reality.

We are arguing that the Internet is a domain of knowledge activities of a different kind. We witness different kinds of structuring of knowledge in the physics laboratory and in a cyber workstation or a control room. A physics research laboratory might seem disorderly to a non-initiate. The laws of order that apply here are derived from the laws of matter as discovered by physics. These laws are representations of reality. In a computer room the situation is different. Laws of physics are taken for granted. They are relevant only as far as the proper functioning of the computing machines is concerned. Interest here is not in going into the 'depth' of reality and wrest exact representations, which take one closer to truth. The interest is in organizing information and its flows in ever-new ways for ever-new domains. Physics takes apart the world to reorganize it in an orderly and exact manner. In contrast, knowledge itself is taken apart and reorganized in computers. Knowledge finds a new representation here.

Taking articles, books, pictures, songs and putting them on the Internet after digitizing them is only the preliminary form of representation of knowledge on the Internet. Even this is much more than a mere copy. Texts can be easily broken up and reorganized. They can be hyperlinked to other information in many different ways. These are just the basic features that are routinely employed by everyone using the computer. We have also referred to more sophisticated activity of music making on the Internet. Internet also makes real time collaboration possible where spatially distant agents come together to make something new. Extensive open source software is developed in this fashion.

We should note that even the music performed by flesh and blood artists that we enjoy listening to, whether through cassettes and CDs available in the market or even in live performances, are assembled together digitally. The 'knowledge' that the artist has, which is realized in his or her performance, is just one part of the knowledge activity that is going on in producing that music. If we take any domain of activity, be it culture and art, or finance, or scientific research, or management of workers, or just travel—the computer and the Internet play an important role in their organization. The more cutting-edge the activity is considered today, the more sophisticated the digital management systems would be.

What is cutting-edge to a computer enthusiast may sound like very superficial stuff to people who grew up with models of a quest for knowledge, whether in science or elsewhere. J. David Bolter in this book *Turing's Man: Western Culture in the Computer Age* contrasts the emerging paradigm of knowledge in this manner:

> The man on a quest had to go to the ends of the world to learn his difficult lesson; in general he changed in the process. Not so for the computer programmer. He remains in the confined logical universe of his machine, rearranging the elements of that universe to suit the current problem. The programmer remains the same, and the world changes around him. Self-knowledge is not particularly his goal; self-improvement may be a goal, but this is understood in practical terms as increased efficacy. The programmer reworks his logical world to make it more efficacious or more comfortable, and he proceeds till he comes up against the ultimate electronic limitations of time, space, or logic. In the process, he learns nothing more than he put there himself, for he does not discover his world so much as invent it.[5]

In the new technological forms of life, the emphasis is on creating self-correcting human-machine systems. This is the basic cybernetic problem situation. The more knowledge that can be wired into the system, the better such a system functions. This requires advanced forms of knowledge representation and ontological engineering. A lot of the trading in premier stock exchanges are performed automatically by such systems. A lot of military manoeuvers by advanced armies are conducted by human-machine systems where the knowledge is coded into the very architecture of these systems. Massive experiments involving hundreds of researchers are designed in this fashion.

If we look at the Internet as a new domain of knowledge activity of a new kind, then we may be justified in saying that in this domain of knowledge: knowledge = (digital) representation of knowledge. This equation of knowledge with knowledge representation might sound logically odd (mixing up entities of different logical types) but it is nothing more than an Internet age commonplace: digital information = knowledge. What it means is that the premium, most well-paid, and 'coolest' knowledge activity is the knowledge activity carried out in the domain of the Internet and knowledge that does not or cannot find digital representation on the Internet is of little value, except when it represents a surmountable challenge for the activity of representation.

### 3.5 Data, Information, Knowledge

There is a common way of articulating the relationship between knowledge and information. It is represented in the form of a series: Data, Information, Knowledge, Wisdom. In this conception, knowledge is meaningful information. This might give the impression that knowledge is a higher order entity compared to information. This would be true if 'information' is understood in the everyday sense as a bit of knowledge tied to a medium. In this case, knowledge is the fundamental concept through which the series data-information-knowledge is interpreted. All the terms in the series are defined in terms of knowledge.

But the information that is in information technology, the information that flows through the worldwide networks and in and out of our computers, cannot be understood as a bit of knowledge. This technological information can be understood only within a cybernetic conception. The basic principle of cybernetics is self-regulation and the basic interest is in building self-regulating or self-correcting machines.

In 1782 James Watt patented the fly ball governor for the steam engine. When properly functioning, this device would keep the engine running at a particular speed. If the speed increases, this increase of speed itself results in activation of a mechanism to bring the speed down. Similarly if the speed decreases, the speed will be brought back to the mean value which has been set.[6]

There are two important aspects to this mechanism:

1. A part of the output energy is redirected to the controlling apparatus further back in the causal order of the system—Feedback.
2. Feedback is such that it counteracts the action of the machine. It is corrective, not reinforcing.—Negative Feedback.

Target-seeking torpedo is a paradigmatic example of the self-correcting system. A torpedo follows a moving target. This means the torpedo has to adjust its direction whenever the target changes its position or course. This is not simply a result of a force that is exercised by the target on the torpedo. Torpedo is powered by another device within it. Torpedo is not attracted but is steered towards the target—in response to an influence emanating from the target. But this influence is not a force, but of the order of a "message".

The dominant aspect of the industrial revolution was power engineering. The pilot function of the governor was merely to ensure the steady functioning of the engine. In the middle of the 20th century, certain developments in various fields came together in the context of wartime efforts to push the creation of self-correcting systems or servomechanisms to the top of the agenda. Let us also remember that the idea of self-regulation was central to the conception of the economy in the industrial capitalist stage. Economy was conceived as a self-regulating system of markets. Labour market, consumer market, the market for raw materials are supposed to work in a self-regulating system, which does not require outside intervention. Karl Polanyi describes this beautifully in his book *The Great Transformation*.[7] Actually, some also see the cybernetic idea of self-regulation in Hobbes's conception of the state.

Now the stage is set for Shannon's mathematical theory of communication and the concept of information that can be computed. What is a computer and communication system doing? It takes sounds, shapes, colours, and breaks them into bits of information—zeroes and ones. These are converted into signals. An ordered procession of signals is transmitted and then reconstructed into the meaningful information, sounds, shapes, etc., that we can read or understand. Shannon looks at information as the computer does. There is no doubt that this technical concept of information employs the commonplace concept, which was and remains the dominant meaning of information in discourse. The epithet 'information explosion' was in fact used first in the context of the exponentially growing number of documents, articles and papers, preprints, reprints that were circulating among scientists, policy makers and others. Documentation (in the library sense) was a method of handling this information.

Shannon uses information as a metaphor and generates a computable formula for its measurement in terms of a probabilistic equation. As is always noted, this information is without meaning. What happens is that now there is a concept of 'information in general'. Some of it is carrying meaning and some not. This generalized information functions in exactly the same way as the 'message' in a target-seeking torpedo—as negative feedback in a cybernetic system. So the information that is not meaningful in our terms is not necessarily noise. It may be doing the job of self-regulation or self-correction. Here truly the meaning is the message itself.

This conceptual development would have had limited significance, but for the technological developments leading to convergence of media and the concurrent development of the notions of information society. When it became technologically possible to convert 'all' forms of communication to the single digital platform, it became possible to think of information as independent of the medium. Information from any medium—

texts, sounds, images—can be separated from the original medium and converted to digital form.

So we have a double concept of information associated with the digital revolution. The information which is pure meaning or representation, supposedly independent of any medium. And the information which is a message in a cybernetic system functioning as negative feedback, without any meaning. We have a world of meanings and representations which floats above, and is apparently independent of the underlying medium—the virtual world.

If we were to reinterpret the series data-information-knowledge in the light of this conception, we note that information is the more general concept in the light of which all other terms are to be understood. Some information could be meaningful and the rest would not be meaningful. Knowledge is merely the meaningful information. In a fundamental sense, knowledge is seen as being made up of information.

## 3.6 Reconstituting the Domain of Knowledge

We have been trying to articulate the way Internet constitutes a new domain of knowledge in society and how the conceptions of knowledge and knowledge activity here are differently constituted. There is no meaning in opposing the constitution of this new domain of knowledge and the associated new conceptions. What is alarming and eminently contestable is the fact that in the light of this knowledge activity, all knowledge in society is seen now in a different light and cast in a new hierarchy. Digital domain now becomes the arbiter for deciding the value of knowledge of all kinds. This is so because virtual domain or the digital domain is becoming the commanding domain. As the *Vidya Ashram* call for contributions for a workshop stated:

> The activity, development, interaction, formulation, transaction, creation, invention, discovery, collaboration, criticism, etc. in the virtual world have taken the lead and tend to give direction to human activity everywhere, ...finance, science, art, entertainment, name any.[8]

Society, economy, culture are being reconstituted in the process of the development of the global knowledge society and the domain of knowledge that is Internet plays a central role in this reconstitution.

The whole domain of knowledge in society is being reconstituted. We have noted the broadening of the field of knowledge which accompanies this reconstitution in the sense that all activities are seen in some way as knowledge activities. Various kinds of knowledge which exist in society among tribals, peasants, women and others are also accorded the status of knowledge. Then we also noted the contraction in the understanding of knowledge that follows from this reconstitution and the resulting hierarchy of knowledge when knowledge is reduced to digital information.

The effects of the reconstitution of the domain of knowledge on the university are only too evident. In the industrial society, the university was the dominant place of legitimate knowledge activity. It was accorded an independence and authority which could not be challenged. Now the university is subject to a different logic of knowledge and is undergoing deep restructuring. What seems paradoxical is that as the economy is becoming post-industrial, knowledge activities of the university are subject to a process similar to that of industrialization. While the process of production in general is becoming more knowledge based and less Taylorized, Nicolas Guilhot notes that:

> ...the core activities of knowledge production and transmission—research and teaching—are subjected to an inverse trend, as the pervasive use of ICTs allows for the rapid Taylorization of these activities. Where teaching and research were still, till recently, "crafts" indissolubly attached to the person performing them, scholars are now regarded as a "bundle" of functions that can and should be "unbundled", desubjectivized, and broken down into as many discrete tasks that can be fulfilled more efficiently, and on demand, by interchangeable operators—a development made possible by the pervasive introduction of ICTs as instruments of coordination.[9]

Knowledge factories take on a very literal meaning here.[10] Taking apart of knowledge and putting it back together is happening at an altogether different scale here.

It is neither possible nor desirable to go back to the older forms of university now. What is needed is the construction of a new perspective on knowledge, which sees a role for all kinds of knowledge in reconstructing the society. Development of such a perspective is possible only through dialogues.[11]

## REFERENCES

1. Nicolas Gulhot : Paideia 2.0. http://www.ssrc.org/blogs/knowledgerules/2008/03/10/paideia-20/.
   This is a contribution on the blog 'Knowledge Rules' [http://www.ssrc.org/blogs/knowledgerules/], a good site for reflections on our theme.
2. Philip Mirowski: *Machine Dreams: Economics Becomes a Cyborg Science*, Cambridge University Press, 2002, p. 5.
3. Quoted by Mirowski, p. 15.
4. Ibid.
5. J. David Bolter: *Turing's Man: Western Culture in the Computer Age*, Penguin, 1986.
6. Hans Jonas: "Cybernetics and Purpose" in *The Phenomenon of Life: Towards a Philosophical Biology*.
7. Karl Polanyi: *The Great Transformation: The Political and Economic Origins of Our Time*, Beacon Press, 2001. First published in 1944.
8. New Command and the Knowledge Question, Invitation for Contributions to a Workshop on "Virtuality and Knowledge In Society" held at the World Social Forum, Karachi. [http://www.vidyaashram.org/dialogues.html].
9. Also see the World Bank report to which Guilhot also refers: Constructing Knowledge Societies http://www-wds.worldbank.org/external/default/WDSContentServer/WDSP/IB/2002/11/01/000094946_02102204203142/Rendered/PDF/multi0page.pdf.
10. See the Edufactory website www.edu-factory.org for contributions to the extended round of debates on the 'conflict and transformations of the university'.
11. See a set of attempts at such knowledge dialogues at the Vidya Ashram Website www.vidyaashram.org.

# 4

# The Current Conflict in Knowledge Societies*

*B. Krishnarajulu*

## 4.1 Technology and Society

The advent of IT heralds a new phase in the history of mankind and the changes it has wrought in the social and economic fabric are as, if not more, far-reaching and decisive as those that modern science, engineering and technology ushered in at the beginning of the $19^{th}$ century.

The changes of that era were marked by concerted efforts to free nations and peoples from foreign rule (decolonisation) and/or despotic rule. Those changes were also marked by migration of labour from agriculture, a large-scale expansion of centralized factory production and the creation of industrial classes-workers and capitalists. They signified new freedoms—from restricted production and markets to large-scale production for markets, from localized labour based on hereditary occupations to skills acquired in new training institutions—the workshops, technology schools, etc. The overall belief among social scientists was that that transition was progressive, in that they seemingly marked a forward step in societal development through increased degrees of freedom of man. The contradictions and conflicts that were thrown up such as loss of identity and large-scale deprivation; were to be resolved in the struggle, for newer freedoms, between the main

---

* Originally written for the bulletin *A Dialogue on Knowledge in Society*, published for a workshop in the World Social Forum, Mumbai 2004.

contending classes, namely, the rich-industrial capitalist-control class and the disinherited-industrial proletariat-oppressed class. The resolution of the contradictions were seen leading to a better, freer society—economically in terms of better terms and wages for labour, socially in terms of equality of labour, politically as democracy versus oligarchy/despotism and a challenge to archaic authority.

### 4.2 Knowledge Society

The society that is emerging is a knowledge society, i.e. it is characterized by new structures in the organization of knowledge, new methods of dissemination and a technology that permits and sustains seemingly unrestricted access to knowledge and control over it. Therein lies the basis of the classes constituting this society. The dominant classes constituted by those that have understood and have access to this technology and would want to rule and guide the destiny of the world and the subservient classes who are marked by their limited access and control over this new technology and knowledge, in short, those seen to be on the other side of the digital divide.

If knowledge (the different kinds and their organizability) constitutes the basis of the emerging class division, and, since every class does inherently possess and use knowledge, then class hegemony is based on quality marking of knowledge. By quality marking and promoting some (forms of) knowledge to the detriment of other forms, a hierarchy of knowledge-categories has emerged, characterized as structured/ordered versus fragmented, patented versus open/free, universal/global versus localized and so on; and class hegemony is built on this categorization.

Since all human activity is based on and uses and creates knowledge; the rural, semi-urban societies (the so-called traditional societies) are also, in this sense, knowledge societies. Each society would be characterized and identified by its knowledge-base (*lokavidya*) and the structure of this knowledge-base, the methods of its dissemination, its development, the societal forms required for its efficient propagation would be—recognizably—a unique feature of each society. In short, a society draws its identity from its *Lokavidya*.

### 4.3 Indicators of the Hegemonistic Process

The advent of globalization, since the late 1980s, saw the emergence of new political formations such as the Confederation of Independent States (CIS), European Union (EU) to name a prominent few. These formations were not militaristic, they were more economic and partly social. They however, gave a go-by to the old concept of nation states based on national identities. The new identities were based on the emergent techno-scientific knowledge base of the post-industrial era. It was as if their *lokavidya* had given way to a new identity.

On the economic front too, changes in the knowledge arena, perforce led to various organizational changes. In order to manage the emerging global market new organizations were put in place-G8, WTO, etc. These organizations were transnational and largely comprised the developed nations who could take advantage of the new marketing possibilities in the underdeveloped and developing world thrown up as a result of the opening up (liberalization) of their economies. New standards were put in place—ISO, IPR, Patent laws, etc.—to safeguard their control. International (World Bank, IMF) and direct monetary assistance was tied to adherence to these standards. Intellectual Property Rights (IPR), in particular, assumed a crucial role in subjugating and undermining the genius of native knowledge.

The stranglehold on the agricultural sector—in seeds, pesticides, fertilizer prices has led to the almost total destruction of native knowledge and practices in agriculture. The monopoly of genetically engineered seeds has been ensured through dubious ways. The massive protests of farmers in the underdeveloped countries (and even in some developed ones) mark this aspect of globalization.

The Internet is the largest self-governing organization—it is all pervasive. Even those opposed to the adverse effects of globalization depend on it to exchange ideas and mobilize support. While the Internet facilitates exchange of ideas, access to knowledge, communication between diverse peoples, etc. it also prescribes the modes of knowledge exchange and proves advantageous to those who have better access to it.

### 4.4 Information Technology in Prospect

The question now being posed is—does the advent of IT signify a progressive phase leading to increased degrees of freedom, throwing up its own contradictions—the resolution of which can lead to, what we may call, a New Democracy or is it just an adjunct to the industrial revolution phase?

We notice that information—its access, dissemination and control—is at the core of this technology and has led to a digital divide. While there is perceptibly more centralization and control of production, production itself appears much more decentralized. Though unbounded access to information through increased communication facilities is, in principle, an accepted hallmark of the IT revolution; this does not automatically imply betterment for ordinary people.

As human knowledge increases, i.e the knowledge-base expands, the space available to *lokavidya* will get restricted, if the current trend continues, by disuse and through constricted or limited dissemination. This process is marked by the withering away of traditional societies. Modern life steps into the space vacated by traditional society and often appears as new found knowledge based on new standards. Lifestyles are sought to be altered to meet the requirements of this knowledge-base and concomitant social demands. [The Internet has also largely influenced the culture of its users—netspeak, netslang, advertisement spam, online trading, etc.]

The destruction and de-legitimization of such *lokavidya*; through hegemonistic assimilation/supplantation is a very visible process today. And we are supposed to be heading towards a global village and a seamless society.

### 4.5 What is To Be Done? *Lokavidya* as the Basis of a New Democracy

The revalidation and legitimization of *lokavidya* is therefore the need of the hour. The imposed hierarchy on knowledge should be dismantled. Some concerted action needs to be initiated on the following:

(i) A movement in academic and intellectual circles for giving due recognition to traditional knowledge and practices.

(ii) A movement to bring about legislation for the protection of traditional knowledge and practices by curbing the jurisdiction of international IPR and patent regimes.

(iii) A cultural movement to show the incongruity of modern lifestyles and consumersim.

(iv) A movement to enable, through legislative action, and sustain local markets so that the economic support for the above movements is ensured.

(v) Efforts to confederate with other similar (*lokavidya*) movements worldwide.

# 5

# Towards a New World of Ideas

*J.K. Suresh*

*The Mind Precedes Dhamma*– The Buddha

## 5.1 Introduction

In the context of empires, it seems plausible to venture that few ideas that ruled the world in the pre-modern era were capable of enforcing a wide spread or a consistent understanding of their essence amongst large sections of the populace in establishing their legitimacy or practice. Accordingly, their domination was usually considered both effective and comprehensive once they were imposed in their core economic and social forms, usually structured as systems for public and revenue administration and justice, together with a cultural form representing the reflective self-images that define the stereotypes and standards of a given epoch. Several reasons may be ascribed for this. For one, the conceptual representation of societies as aggregations of rational actors pursuing independent goals as individuals did not by itself have the strength to significantly influence either statecraft or the meta-theories of man and the world till the 17th and 18th centuries, a period that saw the initial stirrings of the idea of the nation state. For another, the intent as well as the ability of empires to develop a reliable theoretical and interpretative groundwork for the practice and management of these ideas as they operate on the world, acquire new meanings and produce varying effects over the course of time seems to have been rather limited. So perhaps were the means to reach, convey and instil diverse flavours of the sense and purpose of ideas into sufficiently large numbers of people distanced, both cognitively and physically, from the centre of the empire. Perhaps as a consequence, ruling ideas of the past appear to have been less concerned with, or successful in, dominating the inner mental world of the subjects than with the establishment of interfaces that enforced subjecthood through the worldly means of the market and the society. This also meant that, irrespective of their size and sense of grandeur, few empires could deeply affect the ideas and visions about man, life and the world of a large fraction of their subjects across their dominions; at any rate, for long. In fact, the legitimacy of the empire in this period often seems to have been derived by its professed or actual alignment with belief systems exogenous to the context of power, as for example with Christianity in Europe or the idea of *Dharma* in India.

### 5.2 A World of Many Ideas

In the times before the modern, such circumstances enabled the emergence of a diverse array of customs, religions, sciences, technologies, communities and economies across the world; these in turn were embedded in a rich and tacit framework of languages, symbols, meanings, interpretations, theories about man and the like; when viewed together, they define a range of traditions and cultures recognizable as a complex tapestry of human civilization's achievements and progress over millennia. Over the ages, most societies, in the process of operating within and on the world around them, seem to have relied on the creative relationship between these explicit and implicit assets to develop an extraordinary assortment of practical and conceptual instruments, customized to their material and mental environments. For example, even as late as during the 1980s and 1990s, the people of India seem to categorize themselves into no less than 4,635 distinct communities, many spanning across wide parts of the geography, traditionally pursuing hundreds of specialized occupations (associated with agriculture, industry and the services) since antiquity and possibly till the beginning of the 20th century, with around ten per cent of them claiming to follow more than one faith or religion.[1] Until as late as the early parts of the last century, a village or town was typically constituted by many communities and its affairs managed in line with the recognized rights and duties of both entities.[2] Accordingly, while the principles of village or town administration would equally apply to all its constituents, the former could neither appropriate greater power for itself nor drastically alter a community's rights to manage its own affairs. This ability to accommodate multiple dimensions of beliefs, world views and practices perhaps laid the foundations for the extraordinary resilience of the society over the millennia before British rule and formed an integral part of the self-image of ordinary people as well.[2] It is this self-image that Gandhi possibly invokes while describing the people in pre-British Indian society in the following terms:

> They saw that kings and their swords were inferior to the sword of ethics, and they, therefore, held the sovereigns of the earth to be inferior to the rishis and the fakirs... This nation had courts, lawyers and doctors, but ... (e)verybody knew that these professions were not particularly superior. Moreover, these vakils and vaids did not rob people, they were considered people's dependents, not their masters. Justice was tolerably fair. The ordinary rule was to avoid courts...The common people lived independently and followed their agricultural occupation. They enjoyed true Home Rule.[3]

In the language of the present times, the foregoing seems to indicate that the ideas, standards and norms situated in the locality—as represented by individuals in relation to the community, or communities in relation to the village, or villages in relation to the town, or towns in relation to a kingdom—would usually be expected to prevail over those situated in a *global* setting (the second part of each relationship above) in most circumstances.

The oft-painted picture of a somewhat static society in India since antiquity, bearing little influence of the concerns of even large empires, whether of the Chalukyas and the Vardhanas of the 6$^{th}$ century, or of the Mughals, the Marathas or the Rayas of Vijayanagar of the 15$^{th}$ to 17$^{th}$ centuries, too appears to reinforce this hypothesis. While disruptions, occasionally spread over long periods, often followed the vigorous processes of empire building during these times, the sense of continuity of life appears to have been relatively unaffected for major sections of the society. In other words, while war and diplomacy shaped and re-shaped these empires constantly, the rich diversity of customs and practices, cultures, economic relationships and the like, as well as the sense of relative well-being in large parts of India, seem to have persisted, even if sometimes under stress, well into the mid-19th century.[2]

### 5.3 The Ideas of Colonization

It is with the colonization of a large part of the old and the new worlds that a striking change in the character and dynamics of the ideas that define an empire may be observed, beginning perhaps in the 16th century, although they are likely to have been latent in European society since much earlier times.[4] With colonization, the core ideas—till then largely limited to the continent—driving trade, money, finance, credit, insurance, technology, warfare and the like in Europe soon established their rule over much larger domains; and, over time, developed deeper interconnections between themselves to aid their further growth on a larger scale. More significantly, the underlying ideas of humanity's relationships with itself and with the world seem to have undergone fundamental shifts during this phase of history with wide ranging consequences for both, as described in the subsequent parts of this section.

It may be appreciated that the ideas and practices of colonialism were dynamic of essence and therefore subject to continuous change in the centuries since the 16th. For instance, the indigenous people inhabiting the Americas (estimated to have numbered between 90 and 112 million around 1492. Europe in contrast had a population of around 60 to 70 million at the time) were almost completely eliminated within a few hundred years after they were colonized, possibly as a result of consistent failures in converting the native population into productive uses for their colonial masters.[2] As the process of subjugation of the native population through the sword, musket and the cannon continued, the logic of colonialism appears to have evolved, as for example through the unearthing of the potential of pestilence to decimate the colonized, the discovery of new strategies for enforcing subjecthood within Europe (e.g. through the brutal treatment of Scotland and Ireland by Britain), the development of systems (such as surveys and studies, reconstructed objective histories, ethnographies and mythographies of annexed territories) to provide rational criteria for justifying the imposition of oppressive political and economic policies for colonies, or the expansion of slave trade from Africa into the Americas.[5] True, this version of early colonialism provides very little discursive space to reason about the rule of ideas; however, it does provide a definitive indication of its notable adjunct—the pursuit of massive and coordinated violence in the face of extensive resistance to subjugation. A point to note here is that in distinction from earlier empires, colonialism—when viewed through this prism—seems to have continually experimented with blending ideas and coercion in various proportions in the building of the empire all through its evolution. In this sense, its practice for instance in the Americas or parts of Europe in the early years of the modern era could be seen as a precursor to its more nuanced expression over time in other regions.[6]

Not surprisingly, large sections of European society do not seem to have fared much better than the colonies during the period of its conquest of the rest of the world. The opening up of the colonies indeed offered many opportunities for its people to migrate, trade and partake of a frenzied transfer of raw materials and bullion as booty from across the world into Europe. However, these very factors enabled a vigorous development of mercantilism and its able counterpart, war, whose control came to be swiftly concentrated in the hands of powerful classes such as the merchants, politicians and the like. Ironically, therefore, the rigid social hierarchies and economic inequities of the middle ages came to be further accentuated even as the wealth of the colonies continued to be efficiently transferred to Europe for centuries thereafter.[2] During the course of a hundred years from the mid-1600s, this led to the beginnings of a successful development of systems for managing taxes and debt (for example, through bills and bonds) that would reliably divest common people of their resources in order to finance wars and also safeguard the process of limiting the accumulation of the proceeds of mercantile enterprise to a few privileged sections of the society.[7, 8] Periodic failures of these new and volatile instruments via bubbles and collapsing banks[9], which inevitably affected the commoners most, did little to check their growth.[10] Clearly, the 21st century notion of capitalism as being primarily about privatizing profit and publicizing losses seems to have a long and distinguished history! Building on such humble ideas as of banks, joint stock companies and national debt, nationalism as a core concern of Europe during this period appears to have provided an additional rationalization for erecting the framework for a strong state which—in the name of equity and collective good—in turn developed more and more sophisticated mechanisms in the areas of taxation, warfare, markets, finance and commerce to enable the periodic destitution and unsettlement of large sections of the society; these together facilitated the atomization and easy marshalling of labour in the service of the empire and its ruling classes over the course of time.

In the case of India, colonialism marked the first widespread effort to wholly recast not only existing social and economic structures and relationships but also the ideas and theories that drive their balance in the society.[2,11,12] With the benefit of hindsight, it might be said today—especially after the experience of more than six decades of freedom from colonialism - that the strategic transplantation of a new model for education in India was to prove more effective than the tactical imposition of the Indian revenue settlement in the extended and systematic destruction of the economic and cultural fabric of the society. For, the new model ensured the evolution and continuity of ideas, during this period and beyond, not with the pre-colonial society, but with one whose economic and social reins were firmly in the grip of its new masters. The results of this change were momentous: a large number of people, perhaps for the first time in the history of humankind, began perceiving themselves through the eyes of their victors; and thereby came to view their pasts, their customs, their social and political organizations and their ideas of man and the world as either shameful signs of primitivism or pathetic examples of unmanliness and cowardice;[13,14] worse still, these attributes came to be regarded as serious impediments in achieving a commanding strength enabled by a nationhood built on the ideas of scientific progress, liberty and equality—presumably the very qualities that empowered the new masters of India to rule the world. In a transformation that lasts to this day, a significant part of the attention of this section came to be focused on continuously discovering innumerable examples of, and thereafter bitterly critiquing, the backwardness of their society, and enthusiastically supporting those institutions and practices of the empire which were believed to help make India strong and progressive. In a complex and multi-cultural society where a process of militating against social ills was widely accessible and energetically utilized across the ages, these developments which cast the individual and the society in relation to the world through a wholly new language seem to have constituted a fundamental departure. The age of ideas of the empire ruling the world may now be recognized as having truly begun. Nonetheless, that even such heightened deprivation and breakdown could not eliminate the cultural memories of a dignified life and its core principles amongst large sections of its people—perhaps constituting an important reason for the groundswell of support for Gandhi all through the Indian freedom struggle—points to the scope and limitations of colonialism as an idea in the history of the world.

In line with these developments, fuelled by major advances in the sciences and engineering—with its vast dominions across the world ably supporting its consequent increase in appetite for capital and resources—Europe in the 19th century seemed poised to build on its successes of the previous three hundred years along at least two dimensions, viz. the growth of the state that ostensibly aimed to promote the well-being of its people through freedom and equality, and the development of the sciences to decipher the principles that drive worldly phenomena in order to provide a firm basis for their application on the world, in turn enabling the former goal to be achieved. Critical reasoning blended with a spirit of scientific inquiry to aid the exploration of all human and natural phenomena of the world was not only seen as the defining characteristic of the age, but also as a recipe for moulding the ideal society of the future where rationality and order reigned supreme. Thus it is that the dominant ideas of social emancipation and scientific and technological growth converged to captivate, if not rule, Europe during these years.

In respect of its citizenry, statecraft as an idea as well as a practice in Europe continued to strengthen itself all through the 19th century at the expense of the people whose interests it claimed to represent, and it is only near the end of a series of extraordinarily violent conflicts spreading well into the next century that it seems to have successfully broken down the last vestiges of public resistance to its authoritarian prescriptions for the organization of life in the society; and, thereafter, provided a modicum of universal literacy, material and emotional well-being to a significant fraction of its citizens, albeit at the expense of the former colonies—thanks to the development and optimization of global supply chains that provided raw materials at minimal expense to feed large-scale industrial and agricultural production in the continent.

Meanwhile, the seemingly well-grounded expectation that all of nature's laws were within the grasp of humankind and that it was only a matter of time before the few remaining enigmas of the physical universe were resolved was to unravel by the 1930s through two major developments: first, the discovery of quantum phenomena that unsettled long held notions of what constitutes the material reality of the world through the foundational work in this area by Bohr, Born, Planck and Heisenberg,[15,16,17] and others; and second, the establishment of the limits of mathematics, and thereby the boundaries of understanding the world through the application of formal principles of reasoning and logic, primarily through the works of Gödel, Church and Turing.[18]

As if in consequence, subsequent decades witnessed an acceleration of the process of unshackling of technology and engineering from the constraints, as it were, of a rationalist science of previous centuries whose exalted social status and essential puritanism often made out the former to be a somewhat addled and poor cousins of the latter. In contrast to the pursuit of the sciences, it may be noted that the disciplines of technology and engineering[19] were less concerned about eternal truths and unifying principles than with practically operating on the world usually within an empirical framework. In the ensuing decades, between the call of the empire and their own internal dynamics, the two disciplines developed well enough to support an often touted claim, at least till the end of the 20th century, that mankind has entered a new age of technology-driven progress holding out an unparalleled promise for the betterment of lives across the world.

In summary, it appears that colonialism can be considered an extraordinary phenomenon in human history purely from a consideration of the effects it brought in the course of the establishment of a global empire unlike any in the past, viz. the widespread and systematic disruption of societies, cultures and their material and spiritual wealth, as well as of the physical universe and its various life forms. Its uniqueness, however, stems from its capacity to develop the conceptual teeth to support the building and sustenance of a global empire, comprising a network of complex, inter-related and compelling ideas that define what the human and the physical world are, what human enterprise is, what life and its norms are, and what denotes imagination, meaning and dreams and what does not, etc.

Some effects of these ideas were to prove to be long lasting. For example, a central idea that seems to characterize the modern era—the Cartesian separation of the mind from the body—was predicated on the construct of the supremacy of the mind over the physical world. Over time, the latter therefore came to be considered as mere raw material at the disposal of the former, which in turn not only equipped humanity at large with the power to regard and manipulate the external physical world with a feeling of absolute sovereignty, but also provided it with the ability to create and deal with abstractions of the world that helped discriminate and distance both nature and animals in the exercise of this authority. Over the centuries, this seems to have become so deeply ingrained in humanity's approaches to understand the world that it may today be said to form a part of our "intuition", thereby lending influence to the basic epistemic and ontic aspects of human thought; for example, through imposing a method and structure for justification and reliability of propositional calculus[20], or in prescribing specified ways of understanding and classifying what there is in the world. One consequence of this was the development of a mechanistic view that found it expedient to understand the physical world purely in terms of objects and forces that act upon them. Thus, for example, rocks and trees—which according to this view had no soul—could be legitimately considered inanimate and therefore capable of being characterized principally through their physical, chemical or other properties; and because they are inanimate, they could be manipulated and dealt with in any manner that suited the interests of humans, who had souls. Moreover, animals did not have souls either, and therefore it "gradually became all right to use them as so much dead matter, or to subject them routinely to painful scientific experiments"[21,22]. A great paradox that this view of the world entails is seen in the great enthusiasm with which societies over this period unquestioningly accepted, and even welcomed, the devastation of nature in the name of development, while simultaneously denoting the destruction of manmade artifacts as tragic, evil or criminal.

This newborn ability to represent the world through powerful abstractions, superimposed with the dualism that the Cartesian view enabled, seems to have provided a novel instrument for mankind to act upon the world and develop theories and practices that truly distinguished the modern from previous ages. Propelled by this new undercurrent, the natural sciences developed at a scorching pace during the few hundred years after Galileo, and so did other areas of inquiry and practice, e.g. medicine, technologies, warfare, the social sciences, philosophy and the arts. While defining a critical inflection point in the history of mankind, this phenomenon may also be considered to constitute an expression of the unity of ideas underlying the colonial empire.[23,24] Accordingly, the visible end products of the age—forced atomization and mobility of labour, displacement and accumulation of capital, the restructuring of the economics of wage, rent and profits, development of ever more efficient instruments of war, the setting up of global supply chains for the production and consumption of goods and services on a large scale, germination of a uniform global subculture of internationalism sans diversity and the growth of large imbalances between the poor and the rich—can also be equally legitimately seen as outcomes of the core ideas of colonialism. When integrated with mechanisms such as media,[25] education, technology, politics, banking and finance, taxation and markets, these factors have contributed to the progressive strengthening of the interests and the authority of the state while also redefining the cultural and social foundations of the meaning and purpose of life as understood and practised by its subjects. As we shall see in the following sections, the power of this fundamental transformation may be gauged by the fact that its underlying ideas have not only served the epoch of colonialism well, but also seem to have laid the groundwork for the next.

### 5.4 Ideas of the Post-colonial World: The Initial Years

The foregoing suggests that events of the last few hundred years have had the effect of permanently changing the conceptualization as well as the construction of empires; accordingly, be it in the building of contending empires, as attempted most recently by the Germans in the early part of the 20th century, or in professedly constructing alternatives to the empire, as exemplified by the former Soviet Union, most attention seems to have been directed towards either replicating colonialism or taming capitalism, its more genteel expression in the continent and other civilized parts of the world. Was this because the fascination for the instruments and ideas of colonialism proved to be irresistible when balanced against the revulsion towards their effects on the world? At least in the context of the Indian struggle for freedom, it does appear so, given that a tacit consensus seems to have emerged during the 1930s and 1940s amongst its leadership that Gandhi's vision for a free India was not merely retrogressive, but also impractical and unachievable;[2,26] and that European technology and institutions, combined with a paternalistic democracy,[27] and a sprinkling of socialist intent,[28] were the inescapable means to nudge the country onto the road of progress and prosperity while avoiding their hazards.

For a period of perhaps thirty years after the Second World War, such beliefs in the newly liberated colonies across Asia and Africa led to the dutiful development of a set of modern systems for administration, industrialization and education—often under the benign supervision of their former masters and other enlightened and supportive nations in Europe and America—that were soon to be recognized as being high in spirits and low on sustenance and performance; in other words, as pathetic caricatures of the original. That they seemed to provide some succor to people for a short period of time is certain. What is also certain is that the conviction that the former colonies could somehow leapfrog into the league of developed nations through institutions and practices modelled after the West has been comprehensively falsified, as evidenced by the fact that most post-colonial societies seem to have entered a period of internal strife and decline starting from the 1970s. A host of elaborate explanations has been devised for explaining these failures, ranging from the supposed unwillingness of the citizenry to enter the modern world—tied as they are to sloth, ignorance and primitivism sustained by stubborn and unscientific beliefs of an earlier age—to the venality of the state apparatus, the ruling classes and the bureaucracy. Be that as it may, a singular result of the transplantation of the ideas and practices of Europe has been the strengthening of the state as the arbiter of human destiny in all former colonies, accompanied by a corresponding reduction of the freedom, initiative and expression of people all across Asia and Africa. In light of this, in terms of its dealings with its internal domain, as well as with the external world, the state seems to have become congruent with the empire in both theory and practice in the 20$^{th}$ century.

### 5.5 A New Understanding of the World

In retrospect, it is possible to consider the thirty years after the Second World War as a period of crisis and change for the ideas and practices of the modern state that were painstakingly constructed over the previous centuries. During this period, even as a degree of relative calm and prosperity was achieved in significant parts of Europe and the US, the widespread rhetoric of the Cold War within and frequent military interventions abroad seem to have had the effect of alienating influential sections of society such as the youth and the intelligentsia from the mainstream. New or intensified vehicles for managing the society—widespread manipulation of public opinion through media, increased assaults against individual liberties, demonization of the enemy through sophisticated propaganda and suppression of independent opinions through endless witch hunts and scare mongering, forced conscription and the like—came into being during this time to create an environment of mistrust in the laity about the professed intentions of the state to promote individual freedom, well-being and equity.[29] Moreover, the harmful effects wrought by the processes of modernity on the physical world and on humans came to be widely understood and appreciated in this period. Further, new ideas about man's relationship with the world and the state began influencing large sections of people across the world, e.g. that there are limits to growth imposed by the finite nature of the resources of the world; that the disruptions created in the complex connections between various forms of life and non-life on the planet may not only be irreversible but seem to have the potential to quickly snowball into ecological disasters of great magnitude; that the destructive aspects of the sciences and technologies of the modern world appear to be foundational and not capable of being explained away through traditionally accepted and simplistic explanations of their being intrinsically value-free, with the outcome of their use being purely dependent on the context of the users; that powerful commercial interests combining together to form influential alliances with the state (e.g. the so-called military-industrial complex) were successfully working against public good; and that the state[30] itself, being beholden to such interests, had become progressively more intolerant and intrusive as a result of expropriating more power to itself. Perhaps as a consequence, the relationship between the logic of the ideas of man and the world, born of the experiences of the past few centuries, and their continued application to the real world came to be increasingly questioned in this period.

On the other hand, the state, both in Europe and the US, seems to have been confronted by challenges along two important fronts; externally, the prospect of falling behind in the costly political-rhetorical-military race with the Soviet Union or China in the grand conflicts of the Cold War, potentially leading to a serious erosion of the global reach of its actions and ideologies; this, coupled with the distrust of Euro-American capitalism and militarism in the former colonies, did appear for a time to seriously threaten the supply chains (of materials as well as of ideas) set up over centuries to serve the interests of the empire; internally, the problem of estrangement of the intelligentsia and the middle classes whose continued hostility to, and growing awareness of, the machinations of the state threatened to disrupt the management of the empire.[31,32,33,34]

From today's vantage point, it may be possible to hypothesize that the extraordinary transformations witnessed in the world in diverse areas of human endeavour since the 1970s indeed constitute an ongoing response to the challenges for the empire outlined above, which of essence demanded a radical re-organization of the physical and mental models of the world. Two important manifestations of these developments may be recognized at this point in time, viz. the development of a new global framework for economics, politics and culture whose foundations intertwine with the information and communication technologies (ICT), and the newly emerging theories of the human and the world which aim to transcend the limitations of Cartesian dualism. In the following, an attempt is made to depict some of the facets of these developments from a standpoint of understanding their basic motivations and effects.

## 5.6 Knowledge and Society in the Age of the Network

In recent years, it has become fashionable to characterize the world as being information and knowledge driven in all its dimensions—economy, society, media, warfare, industry, governance and even cities. In line with this, knowledge has been ascribed a pivotal role in the supposed achievement by global economies of increased productivity, effective resource utilization, greater efficiencies in manufacturing and services, better governance, reduction of information asymmetries in markets and the like. The ability to effectively harness and use information and knowledge networks is also said to help the journey towards what is called the knowledge society—an advanced form of human organization whose principal means of production is knowledge. An expectation following from this is that a focused application of knowledge in all spheres of life now would lay a broad foundation for a just and equitable society of tomorrow. From manufacturing to entertainment, and from medicine to capital markets, the radical changes witnessed in recent decades across significant parts of the world in both process and output are often proposed as evidence for the progress made in realizing such an expectation in practice.

At this point, it is possible to postulate that a predominant focus over the last two decades on the organization of information and knowledge has significantly influenced the corresponding development of new concepts for the organization of the world, and vice versa; of these, the idea of networks seems to be central[35], especially in its new form of realization as a virtual entity and built on a large scale through the instrumentality of the Internet, the World Wide Web (WWW) and the like. Virtual networks have made distance irrelevant[36] in establishing speedy connections and communications between people across much of the world and have thereby profoundly impacted the process of creation, dissemination and consumption of information. Not being subject to much control by governments or businesses, networks in their initial years were considered a disruptive development due to the essentially egalitarian nature of the platforms they provided for the use of all humans, independent of their political beliefs, economic status or geographic location; and as emancipating, due to their potential to help people across the world to benefit through their collective knowledge to better understand and act upon the world; and also, when understood as communities with a common purpose, to act as effective pressure groups to counter errant governments and delinquent businesses.

However, the rapid insertion of new models of commerce, coupled with the power of governments and businesses to subtly, yet firmly, control and package the information consumed by people, has led to the progressive subordination of the networked world to these interests. As a result, through a combination of channels such as television, movies, websites, on-line media, books, games and software apps, governments as well as businesses seem to have grown from strength to strength during this period: the former in extending an increasing degree of influence and control over large sections of the populace through curating and disseminating vast amounts of information, statistics and propaganda[37] in proportion to their relative power and status in the world; and, the latter in developing geographically widespread markets that by their very nature have more to do with influencing, creating and fulfilling demands by developing a uniform and sterile culture of consumption than with integrating the global production systems with the diverse systems and traditions of knowledge, skills, arts, languages, and literatures, etc. of the world. Coming to the composition of the networked world, it is true that only a relatively smaller section of people outside Europe and America—usually from the more privileged classes of a country—has directly been a part of this transition to the so-called knowledge society. However, it is important to recognize that the economic, social and political processes as well as the idioms of the networked world have in the meantime come to constitute the dominant framework within which all other processes—even of the non-networked world—necessarily have to find the space to operate in today's world; accordingly, from commodity trading to money markets, and from media spins to twitter campaigns, the rich possibilities entailed by the network have progressively been assimilated into the powerful arsenals of commercial and political interests.[38]

In the interim, the language of discourse and the framework of human actions have also changed significantly during this period. Not merely in the sense that every epoch in history creates its own language and metaphors for describing itself and others, to convey its purpose, to define and illustrate its normative principles, to disseminate doctrines for its brand of reasoning and logic, to paint a picture of the future, and the like. Rather, in the sense that the new focus on information and knowledge[39] has led to a radical redefinition of long cherished perceptions about the self as it relates to the world—and in the process, profoundly altered established notions of life, progress, freedom, health and community; which in turn has resulted in changes to the structure and form of thoughts and actions of our times.[40]

For instance, the information and communication technologies provide a seductive means for the inner world of individuals to transcend the mundane world of the local and achieve a free communion with a (potentially) global set of others; in turn, this has led to the development of what may be termed a virtual self that is capable of connecting with similar entities across geographical boundaries with few of the limitations of the physical self. It matters little that such communities often are not really global in terms of membership and access, or that many amongst them are dysfunctional, chaotic or perhaps even senseless. Nor does it matter that they indeed frequently act as channels for the distribution of useful information as an aid to our understanding of, or operating on, the world. What is of significance here is that their virtual nature provides an agency to represent ideas, interpretations and actions in an idiom that is perforce global and therefore subject to its standards—of structure as well as content. Such an edifice, under the influence of powerful commercial interests, has the effect of moulding opinions, preferences and tastes largely outside the constraints of the proximal physical networks of family, community, customs or the culture of a place; and in alignment with a narrow set of principles that are highly de-contextualized. When coupled with an ethic, or an imperative, to consume ever more goods and services as an accepted means to attain greater happiness in life (itself another global idea gaining high currency for example in India as in other parts of the world), it is not difficult to see that a cycle of actions towards self-fulfilment naturally follows this.[41]

The same is perhaps true of our notions of freedom, for example in situations such as in the conflicts of the last two decades between the West and parts of the Middle East, where a global standard for freedom—obligingly pushed by media through large scale blitzkriegs of opinions couched as news, analyses or reports—seems to have progressively influenced significant sections of people across the world, including some within the troubled areas, to form beliefs largely in line with it. Once such beliefs are formed, and the rationale for the removal of a tyrannical ruler of a benighted state is established, they endure for long periods even in the face of evidence that such interventions have caused greater long-term damage to the societies being liberated than the depredations of ruthless dictators. It does appear that in the brave new world of the 21st century, while violence is unavoidable sometimes to protect freedom, not all its forms are equal; that of despots, being arbitrary, primitive and illogical, is of essence condemnable and inhuman; and that of the liberators, being rational, technologically sophisticated and cool headed, is quintessentially laudable and human.

In yet another dimension, virtual networks have served to expand the space for one-way communication to dominate the inner lives of individuals in a manner that a largely physically networked world of earlier times was not capable of doing. This is perhaps a result of the increasing preference for the consumption of ever larger amounts of information—in the form of news, opinions or evident truths that are available on the WWW, or are presented through television and other media, for example—by individuals in (largely) anonymous settings.[42] In such a context, in the absence of socially intermediated interventions in the form of real-world discussions, debates and similar exchanges, individuals are likely to be predisposed towards seeking biasing inputs and data from this large mass of information in order to deduce connections between ideas and actions in the world that are in alignment with their own overt as well as repressed beliefs, preferences, desires and fears.[43,44,45] While its consequences are not very well understood, it seems likely that this process tends to reinforce a tendency to rationalize actions, thoughts, beliefs and opinions through an appealing set of context-free and universal arguments, rich in data while being removed from the immediate environment of the individual. In this background, based on clinical studies, it might be possible to speculate that these are essential consequences of equipping the individual's mind with a new set of standards and norms that help her override hitherto accessible modes of normalization to local customs and practices via physical interactions with embodied other minds.[46]

In summary, the new capability acquired by Global capital

and the state to manufacture consensus and impose homogeneity across vast parts of the world provides a space for a new form of universalism of ideas that makes possible the manipulation of the tastes, values, beliefs and patterns of consumption of people on a scale unimaginable even twenty years ago.

## 5.7 Manifestations of Change

There has been an intense effort in recent decades, both in popular discourse as well as in academic literature, to arrive at an understanding of the emerging new world around us in terms of its various manifestations. In the ensuing section, we turn our attention to some of these.

**(a) The Locus of the Knowledge Society:** A central aspect of the notion of the networked society seems to be the dilution, if not the abandonment, of the premise of a clearly identifiable spatial-temporal locus (or a "home ground") in imagining a post-modern and post-industrial age for mankind. At the conceptual level, this is driven by a mental model of virtual communities—essentially a network of stakeholders with common interests and usually functioning across geographies —that operate on productive resources using knowledge in order to communicate and interact or produce and consume goods and services. In a manner of speaking, the virtual community, or the network, today may be said to have acquired the semiological prerogative of providing the symbols, structures and the meaning of economic, social and cultural organization of our times. From a political economic perspective, such models of cooperative enterprise tend to be viewed as equitable, partly because the networks prima-facie appear to be value-free and contract driven, and therefore as mere tools for improving the effectiveness of collaborative work; and partly because they work like supply chains, where control over resources and their transformation determines their efficiency for given market conditions of supply and demand, which in turn regulate the assignment of the fruits of labour in proportion to its degree of specialization, demand and availability—parameters that usually are understood as being somewhat extraneous to the network itself. The formation of the G-20 group of nations (which includes China and India as members) to represent the economic concerns of the world in 1999 may be seen in this light as a first step taken towards establishing a distributed and networked knowledge society within a networked global economy.

The social lives of individuals meanwhile are also steadily being organized around the network to form spaces for communication and interaction that not only drive opinions and ideas about the attributes and actions of the world, but also mould the norms and ethics of consumption of the members of the networks.[47,48] In this background, it is possible to view the network as progressively developing into a new locus of power, not merely in the aggregative sense of representing the collective will, as it were, of the people (the nodes in the network), but also in the sense of providing the semantics that drive the behaviour of the nodes in the network.

**(b) Knowledge as a Good:** The changing role of knowledge in human enterprise seems to have led to a redefinition of its status, from being largely considered a public good in economic terms, to being regarded more as a positional or a private good[49], thereby empowering it with the potential to extract value from the market with a reduced danger of immediate commodification. Two important trends have contributed to this development, the first being an ability to create protected enclaves of knowledge which are continuously, often incrementally, enhanced through blending varying proportions of newly generated knowledge within a network to publicly available knowledge. One result of this process appears to be the gradual sequestering of public knowledge for the purposes of commerce and trade, ostensibly for its eventual redistribution to the public at some point in the future, or to governmental bodies for strengthening policy regimes. In practice, however, while knowledge in the form of intellectual property, viz. trademarks, patents and the like has become an eminently tradable commodity, the rush to protect markets, growth and profits has only led to much publicized and protracted patent wars amongst competitors, in turn inhibiting innovation and imposing high social and economic costs on consumers. Meanwhile, public knowledge—possessed by governments and people at large—continues to lag the knowledge within the walled gardens[50] (in a sense that goes beyond software systems), thereby making regulations more complex and difficult to create, understand or administer, as well as rendering public vigilance against the ill-effects of misapplied knowledge infructuous, as for example in the case of the wrongdoings of the multi-trillion dollar pharmaceuticals industry.[51,52] Another example of the effect of a widening gulf between specialist knowledge of corporations and that of regulators or people at large is the lack of the means to control or prevent an event like the melt-down of global finance seen in 2008 in the wake of an unchecked application of sophisticated, and deeply flawed, instruments of financial engineering[53], underlying which were the familiar attributes of greed, manipulation and unethical conduct on part of the architects of the crisis.[54,55]

Yet another result of the above is the ongoing attempt by public and private interests to comprehensively harvest, categorize, classify and encode traditional knowledge of various regions of the world in areas such as agriculture, medicine and the manufacture of goods. In theory, such an organization of knowledge is supposed to ensure that different systems of knowledge of a given field are treated as valid and equal elements in the cataloguing or classification process and captured in an exhaustive fashion to eventually form a corpus of knowledge of the world in every conceivable area of human enterprise. Potentially, once the corpus is well populated, an objective comparison of various knowledge systems can be carried out in as many dimensions as is required—economic, cultural or social—to arrive at the most adequate choice which meets the objective criteria for solution to a problem at hand. It is reasonable to assume that such a process would not only help the continuance and sustenance of traditional knowledge systems in the world, but also contribute to better solutions to some problems that for example, modern systems of medicine, metallurgy, or dietetics have only approximately solved; or in some cases, provide new solutions even.

However, in practice, this process operates somewhat differently; for instance, in the case of, say, a Chinese herbal medicine for a specific ailment, its body of knowledge needs to be normalized (i.e. de-contextualized from its original setting of application and re-contextualized in line with the categories of modern system of medicine) and standardized (wherein the protocols related to input and exit criteria of its extraction and usage, together with its effects and results, are described in terms of the principles of the modern system) before comparisons can be made with other bodies of knowledge in the corpus that specify medicines for the same ailment. Correspondingly, the language, means and conventions of encoding, storage, extraction and processing of the resulting collection of facts and relationships from the body of knowledge are designed to ensure compliance with the demands for reliability and verifiability in accordance with the scientific method of the West. Not surprisingly, such a process of normalization, standardization and comparison can only result in either the replacement of a traditional remedy by its modern version—of course well branded and packaged—that totally excludes the eco-system and the tenets of usage as defined in its original environment, or its elimination from further consideration based on an assessment of its overall effects and commercial viability in relation to other alternatives.

Similarly, current debates about genetically modified (GM) crops are no longer about the pros and cons of introducing a high yielding and pest-resistant food grain vis-à-vis preserving the diversity of traditional varieties or lifestyles centred on the rich assortment of age-old practices of cultivation across the world; rather, they are being formulated purely in terms of the economics of GM as if it is simply a matter of making a rational choice from a set of candidate practices sanctioned by the formal criteria established by universities and laboratories through their extensive knowledge of agriculture acquired over a hundred years or more. It must be recognized here that the principles that drive such decisions have very little to do with the economics or socio-cultural norms governing the lives of people; they are mere instruments of markets that are designed to aid the protection of the interests of the global supply chain while directing its optimal functioning. In this background, the encoding of traditional knowledge, although pursued with great passion in countries like India to preserve, rejuvenate or increase its application in society, has little chance of success given the need for it to submit to the realities of market economics or the methodological imperatives of the sciences of the West.[56]

The second trend is the growing specialization of processes to collect, collate and analyse data related to consumption of goods and services by people in order to derive insights about the fundamental drivers of human behavior such as motivations and preferences that influence consumption; such processes also aid the creation of new goods and services that understand and fulfil new or unmet aspirations. Some of these processes operate in an overt manner by explicitly soliciting inputs from consumers regarding their needs, wants, preferences and tastes in respect of commercial goods and services as well as attitudes and opinions regarding social, cultural and economic issues and governmental policies and actions. Many others, however, operate in an unobtrusive fashion by tracking people's behaviour within virtual networks along various dimensions such as the types of goods and services they (desire to, or actually) consume, the pathways through which they navigate the virtual networks, their preferred channels for consumption of content and their outlook and political leanings.[57]

While it is considered that knowledge, especially of the specialist variety, has always conferred power to those who possess it, it was believed in the pre-Internet era that a greater access to knowledge was a key element in reducing the distortions that arise from its ownership being restricted to a small group of individuals and organizations. Ironically, however, even as the last two decades have made information and knowledge more accessible, the asymmetries of their deployment have not only continued to persist but also appear to have deepened. An attendant issue is that, as these processes for data analysis and synthesis have continued to acquire greater sophistication, they have also become less explicit; this has led to a further deepening of the asymmetries between the interpreted knowledge that organizations have of consumers—obtained from interactive media, surveys, polls, user behaviour tracking on the WWW, etc.—and the ordinary knowledge of individuals who have no access to such tools of analysis or interpretation. No wonder that this has resulted in a sense of deep insecurity and significant loss of control over privacy for a large number of people in the networked world today.[58]

When combined together, the two trends described in this section appear to strengthen the development of monopolies and oligopolies with an increased potential to convert knowledge into an enduring competitive advantage, almost always at the cost of the consumer. Moreover, the heightened ability of technology to provide an extensive array of mechanisms for governments to spy on its citizens or for prosecuting military actions against foreign states has led to a convergence between the interests of businesses and governments in the process of developing ever more sophisticated instruments for acquiring, mining, analysing and deriving insights from data and information on a scale considered impossible even 20 years ago.[59,60]

**(c) Technology for the New World:** From a technological perspective, the years since the 1990s constitute a period of profound change for planet earth. Merely a decade before, in the 1980s, computers—those venerable and complex tools of trade considered the preserve of a select group of scientists, academics and a few businesses—had rapidly become "personal" and affordable, largely as a result of fundamental advances in digital micro-electronics and a briskly evolving ecosystem comprising the theories and applications of computer systems. The 1990s witnessed a swift transition to a highly connected world based on the revolutionary development of the World Wide Web (WWW), radically redefining the economics and culture of business and society. The past decade appears to have further extended these shifts by completely recasting the way significant sections of the world live, think, communicate, undertake economic activities and govern themselves. In many ways, these developments may be legitimately interpreted as constituting the underlying foundations for the ongoing reorganization of economies, politics and cultures on a global scale.

An interesting outcome of the demonstrated success of professionally managed and technology-led societies in recent decades is the impact it has had on the basic sciences. Although the sciences continue to be an important component of the education system and academic research, their progressive co-option into the processes for application of knowledge for commercial and military purposes seems to indicate that the days of projecting science as an unfettered inquiry into the nature of the world or of the human being—the *zeitgeist* of the 19th and (much of) the 20th centuries—are long since over. Perhaps as a result, the grand projects of earlier centuries, e.g. unification of the theories of the natural world, play little part in the expectations of the mainstream regarding science anymore. Meanwhile, perceived methodological insufficiencies[61], or a belief that the end of the Cold War was responsible for a shift in focus towards the economic competitiveness of, e.g. the US, with a consequent reduction of emphasis on science[62], also seem to indicate a shift in the relative position of science in the overall priorities of nations in recent years. In line with this, a prevailing view amongst large sections of the public as well as planners seems to be that the sciences ought to be regarded as systems of thought whose raison d'être is to help perfect the application of technologies for the betterment of society, or as independent efforts that sometimes lead to meaningful advances after being duly assessed as being practical by the world of technology, or as enablers of the approaches and practices of inquiry necessary for further technological progress, etc. Of course, the ability of science to discover the wonders of the world does continue to elicit occasional popular interest, as witnessed in the case of lasers, semi-conductors, silicon chips, nano materials, graphene, or in considering the future prospects of quantum computing.

Another development in the area of technology is its role in strengthening the tools for the management of the internal and external environments for the state. As described before, through a network model that has come to define the substratum for understanding and structuring human interactions and exchanges, technology has played a fundamental role in transforming economies and societies in this period. Given that the model entails a rich and complex set of connections between large numbers of people, it has also stimulated the development of powerful tools in the service of the interests of businesses and the state to amass large amounts of data about people's behaviour, thoughts and ideas; such data in turn is used in building extensive profiles of individuals to enable deductions to be made about their beliefs, intentions and interests and inferences to be derived about their future behaviour. As described in the previous section, this has given rise to serious concerns of abridgment of privacy, dangerous and mindless algorithmic profiling, stereotyping, extra-judicial and intrusive conduct and retaliation by powerful interests.[58-60]

As regards the external environment, technology has provided a force multiplier unheard of in the history of mankind by enabling Euro-America to quickly project its power through its land, air and naval armies across all parts of the globe to protect its interests. Meanwhile, military expenditure across the world reached the same levels as in 1991 (when the Cold War ended) by the end of the next decade and has continuously risen thereafter.[63] The increased sophistication in integrating information and communication with military hardware—made possible by the new technologies developed since the 1980s—has vastly improved the ability to inflict enormous damage to adversaries[64] while reducing the vulnerability of Euro-American forces.[65]

In summary, these developments seem to indicate that the world of technology has come to dominate the content of discourse as well as the idioms and methodologies of inquiry for humankind in much the same way as the sciences had a couple of centuries ago. In the process, it appears that we have entered a new era of imagining and acting upon the world through a largely utility-oriented approach that is theoretically less demanding and methodologically more loosely structured than was demanded by the scientific method since renaissance; in light of this, the term 'techno-science' may perhaps be more appropriate to describe it, with a caveat that it should not be interpreted as a simple aggregation of the concerns or methodologies of the technology of today with the sciences of the old. In a subsequent section, we will have an opportunity to investigate this change more deeply.

**(d) The New Age Organization:** Building on the developments since the 1960s, the 21st century business organization is expected to be both global in thinking and capable of operating in an environment of continuous technological change, increased competition, market volatility, geographically dispersed operations, heightened consumer awareness, rising workforce diversity and stringent regulatory regimes.

An important reason for these changes seems to be the developing trend towards outsourcing parts of the production of goods and services to countries outside Euro-America, marking a departure from the centuries old practice of channellizing raw material (and selectively, labour) flows into the latter, with some of the finished goods being exported back into the dominions. The consequences of this new design of the supply chains of Euro-America are twofold: firstly, the empowerment of countries like Japan, China and India as important actors in the value chain, which—while developing interdependency through economic means—in turn has affected the political and cultural contexts as well as the balance of power between the individual states in the combine. Secondly, it has led to a new model for organizing capital, labour, ideas and other resources around the value supply chain through a highly networked commerce which is driven by the new technologies of information and communication. The apparent success of China and India (and to a lesser extent of Brazil and Russia) and the complete recasting of the principles for the design and development of markets and organizations in line with a collaborative, cooperative and networked model are indicators of these developments. It is perhaps in this vital sense that globalization, although a process that has been underway over the last five centuries in another sense, ought to be considered a new phenomenon.[66]

Meanwhile, changes to the nature and purpose of organizations have driven, and in turn have been driven by, a growing degree of complexity of products and services that require knowledge-infusion and knowledge-based decision making across many more productive activities and numbers of people than ever in the past.[67] The central position that today's organizations accord knowledge for its role in the transformation of resources seems to be an important consequence of this. From the standpoint of the value supply chain, it has also forced a deeper reassessment of the role played by various factors of production, hitherto defined primarily in terms of land, labour and capital. A corollary to this is the growing acknowledgement that the means of production reside at least partly within the minds of all employees in the organization.

In a period of perhaps thirty years, knowledge has swiftly acquired the position of being the representative idiom of capital, as evidenced in areas as diverse as property rights, agriculture, entertainment and global sourcing for manufacture and services. In this background, all human enterprise seems today to be subject to the context defined by the new age organization, irrespective of whether an organization is local or global.

**(e) Intellectual Property:** Intellectual property (IP) is a term that has acquired popular currency in recent years as the principal legal means to bring the products of the mind into the market.[68] While the instruments for the exercise of IP rights (IPR) such as copyrights, patents and trademarks have been in existence for long, the increased development of knowledge-infused products (e.g. computing and sensory devices and electronic and communications equipment) over these years seem to have brought to the fore an important issue, that of monetization and control of intangible assets. Compared with older notions of property that provided control of resources through the primary means of ownership by physical possession, it may be appreciated that the idea of intellectual property is fundamentally different: for example, because their originality, non-obviousness or uniqueness cannot be easily established; or, because it is not easy to detect infractions, or because they can be replicated speedily across geographies and markets at little, or no, cost (e.g. computer programs or music). This then appears to have been an important motivation for the development of a legal framework for IP applicable perforce to the entire world.[69,70]

Guided by a compelling need for unhindered access and comprehensive control of markets across the world—including rapidly developing markets such as China and India—the speedy encoding of punitive laws to protect intellectual property was initiated in the late 1980s. Soon enough, multilateral frameworks were defined and enacted as international covenants through intense lobbying by the US, EU and Japan, leading to the replacement in 1994 of GATT (General Agreement on Tariffs and Trade) by TRIPS (Trade Related Aspects of Intellectual Property Rights), which is being administered by the WTO (World Trade Organization). In the guise of providing a level ground for all nations, these agreements appear to have laid the foundations for the development of a worldwide network powered by ICT, which in turn forms the basis for a new form of organization of capital, labour and resources driving the world of commerce and trade as we see today. Meanwhile, the power of Euro-American interests in refining the legal frameworks governing trade and commerce has led to an inevitable reduction in the ability of less developed nations to preserve their sovereign legal structures and traditions, notwithstanding weak attempts such as the Doha Round[71] to protest against the new forms of dominance that such frameworks have led to.

An unaddressed challenge related to intangible assets during these years is regarding the economic implications of the exclusivity of rights on intellectual products, e.g. the potential to convert many economic goods, for long considered public or common, into private or positional goods. A related problem to this is the absence of reliable models for assessing the value of intellectual property vis-à-vis other resources employed in economic activity, as a result of which its management continues to pose important challenges for markets.[72] The paradox of the conflation of IP as a good (which is non-rivalrous from an economic view-point) with material goods (which are generally rivalrous) is of course, more enduring and indicative of the power relationships that have enshrined IP as a stellar example of economic progress in recent decades.

**(f) The State and Ideology**: It was with the rise of European nationalism more than three hundred years ago that the power of ideology in organizing people came to the fore in the process of building, developing and nurturing societies in the image of the nation state. As the devastating effects of statecraft led by ideologies grew over the subsequent centuries, so did the opposition to its rule. The period spanning approximately a hundred years from the middle 1800s saw widespread opposition to the increasing authoritarianism of the state, articulated not only through mass struggles but also by theories of liberation that repeatedly attempted to muster the strength to provide humane alternatives to counter the pernicious effects of capitalism, e.g. through various flavours of Marxian thought. However, the experience of the Soviet Union, the first large-scale experiment in socialism, indicates that the failure of Marxist ideology is perhaps rooted in an acceptance of the instruments of capitalism such as its Cartesian ideas of the world, its sciences and technologies and its methods and frameworks for inquiry which in turn seem to have outweighed the effects of a rejection of its consequences—inequity, exploitation, authoritarianism and servitude. So it was that, even when possibly tended by genuine socialist aspirations, the road to communism was wont to ultimately produce results similar to that of capitalism.

In any case, it appears that the tendency to accumulate ever greater amounts of power and control over its subjects has resulted in a situation where the state itself seems to be transformed into a super class that can, at will, determine and dictate class relationships, resource ownership and distribution, interpret equity and justice as well as define their practice. Accordingly, it is only in the degree of violence and crudity that the manifestations of these characteristics differ across the world. As a consequence, irrespective of the variety of political denominations, ideological manifestations and records of success through which it projects itself to the laity in its progression, the state as a class seems to be in profound conflict with its raison d'être—the exercise by humanity of freedom, equity, liberty, justice and the like. Warmongering in foreign parts is only one part of the story; what the state seems to do to its own citizens is often equally frightening. It is increasingly becoming apparent to many even in the first world that the true character and motivations of the state as witnessed in its actions against its own flock are not fundamentally different from that encountered in underdeveloped parts of Asia and Africa, even if perhaps not to the same extent.[73]

**(g) Globalization:** Globalization, while not a new

phenomenon— given the history of trade and industry under Euro-American supervision and control over the last few centuries—appears to have entered an age of fundamental change in character and scope in recent decades. A new phase of globalization perhaps began in the 1960s through the steady shift of steel manufacture away from the USA to Japan, followed by that of goods manufacture to China in the 80s.[74] Interestingly, these developments—usually projected as measures to cut costs, increase efficiencies of capital deployment and usage and improve the competitiveness of businesses—were not considered a matter for much, or bitter, debate across Euro-America as outsourcing today is. This period may be considered from today's vantage point as a logical harbinger of its next phase—the ongoing globalization of communications and information as the primary means to integrate commerce, business and politics on a scale never before conceivable.

On the other hand, globalization as it is understood today may be said to have taken off in a big way with the ICT boom of the 90s. As the premise of globalization started taking deeper roots, some striking results followed. For example, the ability to partition productive tasks effectively—largely made possible through ICT—helped the development of a global and reliable assembly line of goods and services, as it were, through a process of outsourcing and offshoring spanning the developed and the developing world (notably China, South Korea, Brazil, Russia and India) with relatively efficient cost structures. The setting up of global value chains was assisted in no small measure by the parallel development of capital and financial markets, investor friendly governmental procedures for the deployment of land, labour and capital, new norms and policies for international trade and commerce (e.g. TRIPS) and infrastructure to support industry in the backwaters of the world. These in turn helped speed up the expansion of globalization. That in the course of 20 years, China and India have grown at a sizzling pace to respectively become the second and the tenth largest economies in the world, is a testimony to the forces unleashed by globalization.

It must be noted that globalization is of necessity a two-way street. Since trade and commerce constitute the heart of globalization, its progress depends decisively on continuous and efficient flows of capital and goods across countries. Such flows can sustain themselves only through driving consumption which in turn is propelled by promoting a desire in humankind for more and more of material and virtual goods, thereby constructing a world where money, labour, materials and goods chase each other in an endless loop. An assured way of promoting consumption therefore is to develop values that support it, and a means to instil them is to provide high levels of exposure to the cultures of the exemplars of consumption, i.e. Euro-America, or perhaps Japan, and occasionally, countries like China after the recent Olympics.

That global networks—like global capital—are not very tolerant of diversity is easily understandable; for example, over the last 20 years, the question of what constitutes an ideal life has become far simpler for a large fraction of humanity to answer than in the past, e.g. through some or all of the following: financial wealth, travel, leisure, shopping, physical love and food.[75] New notions of freedom, happiness, responsibility, relationships with other humans and the world have meanwhile come into existence and intertwined themselves with this concept of an ideal life to help legitimize actions designed to attain it. Once these views begin to crystallize, it appears that individuals tend to become increasingly conscious of a new set of unfulfilled aspirations that in turn drive their behaviour in totally new ways. The astonishing power of the new media and entertainment industry in initiating and sustaining this process can be gauged by its spread in recent years.[76]

Another effect of globalization witnessed in recent years is a new type of vulnerability of economies manifested in the form of frequent market failures. For instance, capital flows—conditioned to take advantage of small perturbations in market valuations, trends or sentiments—have an inherent potential to magnify financial market instabilities through their near instantaneous reactivity. However, because of the depth of participation in such markets, bets and counter bets on e.g. stocks usually cancel out leading to a relatively stable market in ordinary times with an attendant result of low returns on the deployed capital. Investors, especially high net worth individuals, on the other hand seek returns that beat the market averages; in recent decades, although many companies do continue to operate on markets through traditional routes (e.g. value investing), this has resulted in the phenomenal growth of large hedge funds[77] and private players who aggressively deploy hundreds of billion dollars into the market, often taking risky or rash bets.[78] Consequent to this, two important trends are developing in recent years: the first being the increased ability of large funds to apply relentless pressure on businesses to show revenue and profit growths consistently every quarter, based on the considerable leverage they acquire through owning significant fractions of the equity capital of organizations. The relative elevation of finance functions within the organization, speedy CEO turnovers, hostile take-overs and an unyielding emphasis on the performance of individuals in recent years are some indications of the power of capital to enforce a strong alignment from within organizations to support its constant search for returns. Either because of this, or because of the compelling need for some individuals to pursue financial rewards regardless of consequences, the temptation to manipulate data and cook books appears to be on the increase in the last two decades.[79]

The second trend seems to be the coming of age of complex financial products—many of which ignore, discount or hide current and future risks—that are designed to be sold and resold in multiple steps, each to a different class of investors, after adding spreads that benefit the intermediary. When the fundamentals of a product are bad, its widespread distribution can lead to sudden and catastrophic effects on the market once its weaknesses come to the fore. In this background, the crisis of 2008 may therefore be recognized as being engineered not only by corporate greed and malfeasance, but also by the utter incapacity of regulatory bodies to deal with or understand the issues at hand before it became too late. What this means for structuring economies and markets of tomorrow is not well understood now, but it is increasingly becoming clear that unfettered and unregulated (or under regulated) markets can only result in more and more disasters.[80,81] Possibly as a result of these and other developments, many countries today experience a high degree of economic difficulties and uncertainty through recession, high levels of inflation and joblessness on a much larger scale than in previous decades.

In light of the foregoing, it may be possible to argue that the world economy today is susceptible to frequent cycles of growth and collapse largely because the network model within which it operates produces effects that are not always predictable or controllable.[82] Parallel to this, the management and control of networks have come to be concentrated in the hands of a few large and influential entities (typically the corporate and political elite of the state) in recent years.[83] As a sequel to this, there is a growing trend towards imposing controls on the network in order to tame it in the service of commerce, business or the politics of the state. The rising inequality in many countries across the world may well be a result of these developments.

## 5.8 The Idea of a New World

The foregoing suggests that the last few centuries have seen a singular phenomenal rise and gain supremacy in the imagination of the human civilization: the power of ideas to objectify the physical world, and thereby humans, in the process of creating a universe seemingly captive to the inescapable logic of thought, action and belief entailed by them. There are two dimensions to this: the first being the power to either subsume and control, or alienate the individual from, the fruits of human effort through an extensive process of reification[84] of the concepts and attributes arising from humanity's relationships with, and actions on, itself and the world. The second is the extraordinary capability of modern societies to instil the belief —through media, education and other institutions—that such reification is foundational and indeed critical for the continuance of human life and the survival of civilizations and their products, themselves reified concepts in turn. The relationship between labour and capital lies between these dimensions, as a consequence of which the labourer is confronted by capital as a category different from the capitalist, and the capitalist is empowered to deal with labour as separate from the labourer. Spanning these two facets lie the rationalizations for war, peace, liberation or conquest through the ideas of nationhood, democracy, socialism, secularism, progress and civilization; as well as the operative concepts of justice, fairness, equity, liberation and happiness. The marvels of technology, the magic of the big cities of the world and the conquest of outer space or the deepest oceans are all results of the subjecthood of man to these very dimensions. So are the material and spiritual poverty and sufferings of humanity, characterized by a frenzy of unquenchable desire that propels an endless search for its fulfilment for some, and the often futile seeking for vectors of thought and deed to sustain a dignified life, albeit at the margins of existence, for most others. Together, it may be hypothesized that these two dimensions comprise the "what and the how" of "things" which take the form of knowledge of the world and actions upon it, and the "why" of "things" which assumes the form of faith. In an important sense, this denotes the imagination of the modern man whose operations on the world with knowledge and belief sourced from the reified ideas of humanity have shaped the empire in this era; and through its workings, created a strange symmetry that binds together the haves and the have-nots, the oppressor and the oppressed, the rational and the irrational and the like. In time, the reified ideas of the world have come to acquire a life of their own as the fundamental principles that order the world, and have progressively appropriated for themselves the power to mould humanity through an extraordinary inversion of the subject and the object of thought,[85] discourse and action. For now, it appears as though nothing can come in its way, neither the voices of sanity and suffering nor the wisdom and the experiences of the world.

In light of the above, a question might arise as to whether this represents the views of all societies and as to what means the empire may be countered through. In answering this, we first make a useful distinction between the centre and the periphery of the empire through the simple device of gauging the nature and extent of people's relationship with the virtual network. From this standpoint, most of Euro-America and parts of the developing world may be considered a part of the core of the empire, even if the latter obtains in a subsidiary relationship with the former. Whereas, although influenced by the network in all spheres of life, much of the world outside Euro-America does not determine the empire's dynamics except in its role as a subject and therefore may be said to constitute the periphery. With this distinction, it may be hypothesized that the preceding account seems more likely to represent the view of the world from its centre. On the other hand, the periphery, while initially somewhat ill-prepared to respond to the wave of changes in recent decades, seems to be slowly cognizing the new ordering of the empire as a new form of colonialism, as being designed to exclude it from the new order and as a process that threatens to disrupt its already weakened structure of social and cultural relationships.[86]

However, in spite of its misfortunes and misery, the periphery appears to have been culturally less alienated or dehumanized as compared to much of the West over the centuries. Perhaps as a result, in the age of the network, it seems that the poverty of the soul of the core of the empire not only drives greater individuation and apathy, but also severely constrains its potential to imagine worlds that are substantively better than the existing; whereas poverty of the material kind in the periphery appears to continue to provide a locus of resistance through a collectivism of ideas if only as a means to preserve human dignity through a common search for meaning and reason supported by native concepts and idioms rooted in its culture—however irrational, superstitious and backward they might appear in the eyes of the empire.[87,88] And, ignorant of the nuances of the workings of the empire, it preserves its inherent potential to imagine new worlds different from the current. Stated another way, for the core, the empire and the world are congruent, while for the periphery, they are not.

In this light, if indeed the periphery can be reasonably expected to constitute the locus for a new imagination of the world and derive the strength to dialogue with or resist the empire, what are the likely sources for its ideas? While there are no clear answers currently, three trends appear to show promise, as briefly discussed below.

**(a) The Continued Relevance of Gandhi:** Among the many that shook the empire to its foundations in the last hundred years, the greatest challenge to the empire has been that of

Gandhi, notwithstanding the reverses that his thoughts have suffered in reshaping India after independence.[2,23] It is through the adopting of his ways by disparate movements of people across the world that his thoughts continue to live during this period,[24,89] and not just in India.[90] A reason for the enduring appeal of Gandhian thought could be that it does not easily fit into the scheme of an ideology, at least not as it is understood in the West.[3,91,92] For example, for Gandhi, mental constructs about the world as well as actions on it are not fundamentally distinguishable; in other words, instrument and deed are of essence inseparable; and, because they cannot be completely specified a priori, they do not have invariant meanings even when they satisfy his criteria of *Satya* and *Ahimsa*, which in turn are also not considered by him to be absolute. The principle of received consciousness therefore does not appear to form a part of Gandhian thought, since the consciousness that inheres in the human—irrespective of disposition, knowledge or socio-economic status—seems to be the only qualifying criterion he lays down for accepting or adopting his path. It is in this fundamentally different conception of the relationship of ideas with agency, teleology, agents and actions that Gandhi's thinking appears to diverge from the conventional ideologies of the West. Moreover, he seems to have had little enthusiasm or interest in representing or understanding either societies or history through definitive and discriminating categories such as classes, systems, oppressors and the oppressed, base and super structures, development, backwardness, progress, etc. Perhaps because of this, his magical abilities in rallying people together probably had less to do with moving them with rational arguments of individual liberation than with persuading them to restore the order of things in the world by changing themselves; and this only in the seemingly ordinary process of discharging their responsibility as humans, which perforce included acting on behalf of all living and non-living beings in the world.[93]

A theory that eliminates, or weakens, the distinction between the self and the other, and proposes that man's journey within is perhaps superior to the one without, can only be characterized, if at all, as a civilizational view—not as an ideology. And the resources it demands from the individual are a morality that is innate, beyond the grip of ideology, and self-directed; and a bias towards action that is informed by compassion, humility and inclusion; in other words, his definitions of *Satya* and *Ahimsa,* which provide large spaces for individual agency in a manner that organized ideologies such as socialism and communism do not permit. In a world whose new organization is rapidly creating novel forms of disruption and uncertainty in the world—including within geographies near the very centre of the imperium—it does appear that the appeal of Gandhi can only increase in the coming decades.

**(b) The Problem of Knowing and Doing:** Centuries after Descartes and Newton, mechanistic notions of the relationship between reasoning and practice are under retreat, thanks to recent developments in fields as diverse as economics, biology, social and behavioural studies and neurosciences. In the context of the modern society, some of these propose a resolution of paradoxes stemming from "self-reference, meaning, communication, contingency, reduction of complexity, truth, (or) cognition"[94] through a rejection of the idea that it is the individual or the individual psychic system who knows; this not only leads to a denial of the central role of humans in social theory, and of their autonomous agency, but also results in a conclusion that "the individual not only does not form the basic element of society but is excluded from it altogether, situated instead in the environment of the social system."[95] Some others, in investigating assumptions about the process of discovery of knowledge, posit that all scientific methods are delusions in pursuit of theory, and that the mind's ability to create self-consistent accounts of itself, or a belief in the certitude of causal reality, is born of the very act of observation. Therefore, the theories and ways of thinking about the world are of essence distinct from the reality being observed.[96]

Behavioural studies on the other hand provide disturbing evidence that upsets long cherished notions of humans as rational, autonomous and moral beings—attributes that are widely believed to establish a special place for humanity, in distinction from other beings in the world.[97] For example, our notion of human rationality is seriously undermined by the finding that a large majority of human actions are caused not as a consequence of the deliberative processes of reasoning (that are consciously initiated and slow), but by automatic processes (that are unconsciously initiated and fast);[98] and that even in those cases where deliberative processes are invoked, reasoning is fallible because of its high susceptibility to biases (e.g. confirmation, hindsight and omission), heuristics (e.g. representativeness, availability and anchoring) and constraints (e.g. framing).[99] Likewise, the assumption that we are autonomous because we can distance ourselves from our beliefs and attitudes and evaluate choices objectively before proceeding to act is weakened not only because we are less rational than we assume (as we saw above), but more significantly because of agencies such as hyperbolic discounting and ego depletion.[100,101] Similarly, a vast body of studies (investigating, e.g. the role of personal and impersonal dilemmas or emotions on our moral decisions) seems to suggest that our reasoning in the course of moral judgement is often mere rationalizations, that the presumption of morality being accessible to reason is incorrect and that the belief in moral argument leading to moral progress is baseless.[97]

Moreover, advances in the brain sciences suggest that customary assumptions of rationality in understanding the logic of thought—based on the Cartesian separation of the mind and the body—are incommensurate with actual human cognitive processes.[102,103,104] In addition, various studies indicate a widespread bias in humans in choosing logical forms for analysis, e.g. in showing a preference for the *modus ponens* form (affirming the antecedent) against the *modus tollens*[105] form (denying the consequent) in syllogistic reasoning. Other investigations suggest that when reasoning tasks are overlaid with orthogonal considerations such as beliefs, serious errors of deduction can result.[106] Yet other studies show that biases (such as of confirmation) have significantly impaired, and continue to affect, our understanding as well as approach to science, medicine, judicial reasoning, policy rationalizations and the like.[107]

Meanwhile, in recent years, investigations of complexity have attained a better understanding of how large-scale, complex, organized, and adaptive behaviour materializes from simple interactions among myriad individuals across a broad variety of phenomena, ranging from ant hills to the stock market, from viral videos to Web searches, and from epidemics to popular uprisings. A study of the characteristics of such systems, such as agent autonomy, networked structure, profuse experimentation, emergence and the like seems to suggest that most social, cultural and biological processes of the world—hitherto considered simple—are in fact extraordinarily complex,[108] e.g. the exercise of common sense.[109]

What do the aforesaid ideas entail? For one, an understanding that the process of operating on the real world is more complex than we commonly tend to believe; and that retrospective narratives presuming imperative connections between reason and action are almost always flawed—not merely in the sense that they have the character of confabulations, but also in another, that there cannot be a single or true representation of the relationship between the two. This also means that logic as a tool is far more tenuous in its connection to practice than is often assumed; and regarding the world, more pithily, that it might not perhaps be really knowable. As a consequence, the rational models of the world, the histories of the world and the analyses of societies and phenomena either lose their sense of objective universality, or at best appear as hypotheses informed by a lingering and irreducible subjectivity innate to all epistemic quests.

**(c) *Lokavidya*:** Viewed from the perspective of the present times, it increasingly appears reasonable to conjecture that the misery of humanity today owes as much to the devastation of material lives wrought by the empire as to the destruction of its spirit. It may be therefore inferred that, while rapaciousness and violence played a significant part in damaging the resilience of the spirit of the dominions, the assimilation of the ideas of the empire seems to have ensured their complete demolition. Of course, in circumstances where a dialogue between the cultural structures of the territories and their masters could not be established, as for example in the Americas, physical elimination of the populace inexorably followed; on the other hand, in situations where it could be, as in India since the mid-

1800s, the constructs of the victors of the notions of freedom, liberty, progress, man and his relationship with the world and the like—carefully re-packaged to appear to be in continuity with the traditions of the vanquished society[2]—slowly subjugated the mental spaces of the defeated civilization and acquired wide currency through the new educational systems that replaced the old. These practical and ideological thrusts of the empire in India led to two important consequences over a period of a hundred and fifty years, the first being the complete restructuring of the public spaces in the society to exclude the practices of the old and thereby aid the process of organizing them through new principles, and the second being the development of new theories of the subject societies which rationalized their misery as arising from, unsurprisingly, their own ignorance, backwardness and retrograde economic and social structures. While the former led to a continuous reduction of the possibilities of organized resistance to the empire, the latter led to a spiritual crisis that could only be resolved by an alignment with the ideology and practices of the colonizer, or alternately, in opposition to them; the first option provided an opportunity for a section of India to eke out a tenuous life in service of its master, while the second usually meant a banishment to the margins of life, an unavoidable eventuality for much of India. In time, however, the first section has come to acquire the exclusive political and economic means and privilege to not only drive India in line with ideas inherited from the empire, but also to imagine, represent or plan the future of the country in line with what are understood as legitimate needs of the 21st century; the two sections, both in terms of their status and the ideas they represent, may be denoted respectively as *India* and *Bharat;*[110] it may however be noted that the distinction is made here purely to serve the argument below, given that all Indians continue to be simultaneously influenced by the ideas and lives of people on both sides of this division.

For *India, Bharat* as a set of ideas is indubitably responsible for the enslavement of the country by the British through its subscription to the insidious practices of religion, region and caste, through its technological and scientific backwardness, or through its ambivalence towards those attributes which are considered vital for building a nation, viz. order, consensus and authority. However, it is *Bharat* as a mass of people which is the theme of much lament in *India*, seen as unchanging in its retrogressive and superstitious ways and obstinate in clinging to its own outdated theories of life and the world. Increasingly, this creates an imperative for *India* to exorcise itself of the *Bharat* hidden within it, and simultaneously do its best, with a missionary zeal, to enable the *India* in *Bharat* to bloom and thereby enable the country to confidently march ahead and take its rightful place in the comity of nations.[111] That it has, in the sixty-five years of independence, neither achieved an iota of progress towards realizing the *Swaraj* of Gandhi's dreams nor managed to provide relief from hunger for a vast majority of its people does not seem to dilute its enthusiasm for chasing the chimera of development through the same instruments of thought and action that have enslaved and impoverished the world materially and spiritually over half a millennium.

In this background, the idea of *Lokavidya*[112,113,114] (derived from the Sanskrit, *Lok*: people, *vidya*: knowledge, meaning people's knowledge; the meaning is the same in almost all Indian languages) provides a promising set of conceptual vectors and a sound practical basis to understand as well as to develop a locus of resistance to the dominant ideas of the empire. *Lokavidya* as a concept goes beyond today's notions of appropriate technologies, old conventions and practices, and traditional, non-Western and folk knowledge in several important ways, as summarized below:

In simple terms, *Lokavidya* may be understood as knowledge that is integral with and inseparable from human agency, and vice versa. In other words, it is knowledge which is—subjectively as well as objectively—inextricably bound to the context of human thought and action, along all its dimensions, viz. its nature and scope of applicability, the extent of control over the outcomes of its use, a view of the world, feelings, an ethical framework for its operation and a logic to determine responsibility for its consequences, etc. Moreover, *Lokavidya* as an idea implicitly assumes and unequivocally asserts that the value of knowledge is inevitably realized through the interplay of all these dimensions, including in circumstances where it has been grafted on to a social or an economic process outside its origins. Understood thus, *Lokavidya* is essentially incommensurate with the norms for standardization, normalization and aggregation that form the basic methodological tools of the modern knowledge systems (e.g. sciences, economics and humanities).[115] In line with this, *Lokavidya*[116] also takes a normative position against the separation of knowledge systems from their context which has an attendant potential for the development of knowledge hierarchies that are usually correlated with power structures (as is apparent in the case of the modern conceptualization of knowledge)—which it considers to be a primary basis of an exploitative framework for the society.

The separation of *Lokavidya* from the people (or alternately, knowledge from its human and social moorings) seems to form an important beginning point for the alienation of the products of human effort and the first step for the reification of relationships that together lay the basis for an exploitative system. In this process, the devaluation of the various dimensions that form its background becomes a necessary precondition for the de-contextualization of knowledge; this in turn creates an appropriate setting for it to be isolated from its original tenets of usage in order to aid its further refinement and enhancement, perhaps in laboratories or universities and possibly employing specified methodologies and conceptual frameworks that help in investigating, understanding and modifying its attributes and areas of application; subsequently, the resulting new knowledge can be readily re-packaged for introduction into the world of practice in alignment with, and in the service of, specific and pre-determined interests and not necessarily with those of prior beneficiaries of the practice in the same social setting.[117] In the hands of power structures, such a process of dealing with disembodied knowledge not only provides it with an apparently independent and objective (and an almost supra-human) status but also eases the further division of economic and social activities into smaller fragments which can be transformed into marketable entities whose value can in turn be determined from *secular* criteria such as demand-supply, significance, efficiency and the like.[118] The foregoing suggests that the successes of the empire in the present times primarily arise from its unchallenged ability to encode the primacy of de-contextualized knowledge into the formal political and economic processes of the world, resulting in the spread of iniquity and injustice on a large scale. The subjecthood of much of the world to the ideas of the empire, moreover, therefore may also be interpreted as a consequence of the loss of centrality of *Lokavidya* in the public spaces of thought and action of these societies.

In terms of its location, *Lokavidya* is situated within the society, that is, in its people, institutions and various expressions. In its public manifestation, it facilitates various types of economic and social activities through a collective intentionality[119] and shared agency which are in consonance with its own norms and values as well as with those of individuals. In its private expression, it enables the strengthening of individual agency through its ability to bridge and enrich the relationship between the inner, intensional context of the individual and the outer, extensional context of the society. Its potential power therefore may be gauged not merely by postulating the immanence of *Lokavidya* in every living being, but by its capacity to enable a constant connection and communication between the private forms of *Lokavidya* and its public versions.

Furthermore, *Lokavidya* is not merely about economics, sciences and technologies, or social organization—it entails a loose, undogmatic and inclusive integration of concepts such as justice, aesthetics, health, happiness, emotions and interpersonal relationships within the framework of knowledge in developing a picture of life and society that holds out a promise for restoring balance and harmony to a world weary of dominance and inhumanity. In summary,

> *Lokavidya* means those methods (philosophy, etc.) of organization and communication of *vidya* which place *vidya* in the midst of the people. Being in the midst of the people means (a) the strings of control should be among the people, that is, in their social organizations, (b) the values of the other domain should actually be the guiding principles, (c) it must measure up to the criteria of ordinary life and (d) ensuring its role in the processes of construction and reconstruction of truth.[120]

As may be seen from the foregoing, *Lokavidya* can be considered an important step in conceiving an epistemic and ontic break from long established traditions of knowledge of the empire.

## 5.9 Concluding Remarks

A new structure and organization of the world appear to be emerging in recent years as drivers, as well as outcomes, of the current phase of globalization that has been underway for a few decades now. Characterized by a radically new model of the world with a seemingly fresh approach towards understanding human knowledge and society, the principles that underlie the new structure declare an intent to distinguish themselves from the old by reducing inequity in society and violence on nature—acknowledged to be among the principal negative consequences of the concepts and practices ruling the world since the time of the Industrial Revolution. Correspondingly, the ideas that underlie the new organization of the world aim to redefine the relationship between knowledge and its operations on the world in two important ways: by effectively harnessing the distinctive potential of supply chains to widely distribute the fruits of development equitably across geographies, and by encoding the new ethic of efficient and responsible use of knowledge into global supply chains so as to enable sustainable development of societies. In line with this, the new technologies, economics and politics of the age have come to constitute a set of critical tools for developing robust linkages, both physical and virtual, between the major sources of labour and raw material in the world which in turn has led to the establishment of a globally connected society, economy and culture. A principal expression of this emerging structure is found through the means as well as the symbolism of the network—as witnessed by the increased currency of terms such as networked economies, networked societies, and the like in all major discourses about the world in recent years.

In its progression, however, the emergent structure seems to manifest a principal tendency to exclusively serve the interests of the empire—exemplified by its control over global commerce, culture and politics—by facilitating a small section of the world to efficiently extract value from global supply chains to the detriment of the rest on a scale previously considered inconceivable. This is aided in no small measure by the new technologies for manufacture, management and distribution of goods and services as well as the global trade pacts and agreements of recent decades which together provide the means for effective cost arbitrage, easier development of new markets, reliable connectivity between economies, smoother financial flows and the like; they also broaden the scope of commerce to include the domains of knowledge labour and intellectual property. In this light, the networked world may therefore be considered an essential expression of the imperatives of the political economics of the empire in extending its global reach through the development of a uniform culture of consumption and a homogeneous set of world views and belief systems across all societies.

Meanwhile, the early successes of such efforts directed towards reorganizing the world may be ascribed to the steady induction of elites from different geographies into a global elite that is structured in the form of real and virtual networks—perhaps an indication that the empire of the 21st century may have transcended traditional notions of race and geography in determining its composition. In as much as these developments compel an alignment of the cultural, economic and social bases of societies across the world with the requirements of the networked world, they also simultaneously dilute hitherto dominant notions of nationhood and sovereignty. Together, these factors appear to be leading to increasingly severe disruptions in the lives of major sections of people through the accentuation of inequity and imbalances in societies across the world.

Over the past two decades, many attempts to develop a meaningful opposition to these processes have met with little success. It is possible that this might be either due to the inadequacies of the ideas that underlie such resistance, or the ineffectuality of individual acts of resistance in promoting the development of such conceptual means as may nourish their rapid growth and spread. Nonetheless, the uncertainty experienced in many societies over this period due to the frequent failures of markets, periodic crises in economies and recurrent and horrific armed conflicts seems to have created a significant opportunity for the development of new ideas of the world with a potential to counter the essentially anti-human ideologies and actions of the empire; and, alongside, an opportunity for humanity to revive and restore sanity, stability, harmony and equity for itself and the world around it through the cultivation of a grounded practice of these new ideas. In this struggle for reversing the relentless downward spiral of humanity in our times, three themes—the rediscovery and reinterpretation of Gandhi, the evolving new understanding of the world and the ideas that underlie *Lokavidya*—appear to hold a great promise for enabling dialogue, moulding resistance and imagining a just and equitable society of tomorrow.

## REFERENCES

1. In many ways, these communities represent the traditions—unbroken over millennia—that have produced the diverse means for sustaining the civilizational development of the sub-continent, ranging from the drill plough to muslin, from literature to the arts, from mathematics to the sciences and from the Buddha to Gandhi. For data on the survey of communities in India, see Singh, K. Suresh, *The People of India*, Vol. 1, Oxford University Press, New Delhi, 1994.
2. Dharampal, *Collected Writings*, 5 Vols. , Other India Press, 2000.
3. Gandhi, Mohandas K., *Hind Swaraj*, Navjivan Publishers (1938): 49.
4. Epstein, Steven A., *An Economic and Social History of Later Medieval Europe, 1000-150*, New York: Cambridge University Press, 2009.
5. Less than a century after the church granted to Christians the right of taking pagans as perpetual slaves through papal bulls such as Dum diversas (1452), it was taken away through the bull Sublimis Deus in 1537, which unambiguously stated that the indigenous peoples of the Americas were beings with souls and condemned their enslavement while calling for their evangelization. Nonetheless, it had no effect on the ultimate fate of the natives, whose elimination set the stage for the slave trade originating in Africa to flourish. For details of the Deus, see http://en.wikipedia.org/wiki/Sublimus_Dei.
6. The notion of the American native as a noble savage is very old,

beginning with Bartolomé de Las Casas's "Apologética Historia Sumaria," of the 1530s. Over time, this possibly helped fortify the indifference towards their mass elimination as well. For example, as late as in a 1987 edition, a standard high school textbook by three well-known historians summarized Indian history as follows: "For thousands of centuries—centuries in which human races were evolving, forming communities, and building the beginnings of national civilizations in Africa, Asia, and Europe—the continents we know as the Americas stood empty of mankind and its works." Accordingly, the story of Europeans in the New World "is the story of the creation of a civilization where none existed."For these details as well as for a fascinating account of the Americas before 1491, see: Mann, Charles C., *1491: New Revelations of the Americas Before Columbus*, Knopf, 2005. For details of the textbook, see: Current, R.N., Williams, H.T. and Brinkley, A., *American History: A Survey*, New York: Knopf, 7th ed., 1987.

7. For example, Britain's national debt rose from £12m in 1700 to £850m by the end of the Napoleonic Wars in 1815. (http://www.debtbombshell.com/history-of-national-debt.htm.)
8. "From the Glorious Revolution to the French Revolution, Britain's taxation system operated to provide its navy and army with the indispensable monetary means required to combat the kingdom's foes and to maintain the military forces and the credit of the central government in conditions of readiness for the next war." O'Brien, P.K., "The Political Economy of British Ttaxation, 1660-1815," in *The Economic History Review*, 41: 1–32. 1988.
9. Banks were not a new phenomenon in Europe, having been in existence since at least the 13th or 14th centuries. However, their spread seems to have been largely limited to the mercantile and royal classes for many years thereafter. The removal of restrictions on usury by the church in the later middle ages seems to have led to a rapid expansion of banking and a steady development of the ideas of credit and insurance.
10. Ferguson, N., *The Ascent of Money*, The Penguin Press, 2008.
11. Dutt, Romesh Chunder, *The Economic History of India in the Victorian Age: From the Accession of Queen Victoria in 1837 to the Commencement of the Twentieth Century*, Routledge & Kegan Paul, 1956.
12. The Indian economy amounted to an estimated 24% of the world's GDP in the early 17th century (that of Britain being around 2%) and over the course of the next two hundred years came to

account for less than half a percent of global GDP. See, for example, Dirks, N.B., *The Scandal of Empire: India and the Creation of Imperial Britain*, Cambridge: Belknap Press of Harvard University Press, 2006.

13. Nandy, Ashis, *At the Edge of Psychology: Essays in Politics and Culture*, Delhi: Oxford University Press, 1980.
14. Nandy, Ashis, *The Intimate Enemy: Loss and Recovery of Self Under Colonialism*, Delhi: Oxford University Press, 1983.
15. Cushing, James T., *Quantum Mechanics: Historical Contingency and the Copenhagen Hegemony*, University of Chicago Press, 1994.
16. Capra, Fritjof, *The Turning Point*, Flamingo, 1982.
17. Mehra, Jagdish and Rechenberg, Helmut, "The Quantum Theory of Planck, Einstein, Bohr and Sommerfeld: Its Foundation and the Rise of its Difficulties, 1900-1925" in Vol. 1, Part 2 of *The Historical Development of Quantum Theory*, 1982, Springer-Verlag New York, Inc.
18. For an accessible introduction to the works of Gödel and Turing, see for example, Petzold, Charles, *The Annotated Turing: A Guided Tour Through Alan Turing's Historic Paper on Computability and the Turing Machine*, 2008 by Wiley Publishing, Inc., Indianapolis, Indiana.
19. Even the term "engineer" seems to have been coined and gained currency only in the early parts of the 19th century, as much perhaps to name the adherents to a growing profession as to seek legitimacy for it, something that the term "scientist" had enjoyed for centuries.
20. It appears that the ascendance of propositional knowledge to an exalted status was also a part of this transformation.
21. http://facultyfiles.frostburg.edu/phil/forum/Descartes.htm
22. For an argument that 17th century science is implicated in today's ecological crisis, the domination of nature, and the devaluation of women in the production of scientific knowledge, see, Merchant, Carolyn, "The Death of Nature: Women, Ecology, and the Scientific Revolution," No. 42, *HarperOne*, 1990.
23. Nandy, Ashis (ed.), *Science, Hegemony and Violence: A Requiem for Modernity*, Delhi: Oxford University Press, 1988.
24. Sahasrabudhey, Sunil, *Gandhi's Challenge to Modern Science*, Other India Press, Mapusa, Goa, India, 2002.
25. For an examination of the role of mass media in the construction of social reality, see Luhmann, N. and Cross, K., *The Reality of the Mass Media*, English translation, © Polity Press, 2000.
26. Interpreting Gandhi's role in the Indian freedom struggle as

being tactical was perhaps an unavoidable device through which the makers of independent India could overcome the contradiction of having to build a state which approved his means while denying his ends. That such a sterile interpretation is now an integral part of middle class public consciousness—even if not always acknowledged explicitly—indicates the grip of statism on India's elite. See, for example, Guha, Ramachandra, *India After Gandhi*, HarperCollins, New York, 2007.

27. It does appear that by the 1940s the peculiar schizophrenia that characterized Europe's constructs and self-images of its alleged democratic traditions had replicated itself within a substantial section of India's intelligentsia as well. For a modern version of such triumphalism, see for example, Patapan, Haig (ed.), *Westminster Legacies: Democracy and Responsible Government in Asia and the Pacific*, University of New South Wales Press, 2005.
28. Kopstein, Jeffrey and Lichbach, Mark (eds.), *Comparative Politics: Interests, Identities, and Institutions in a Changing Global Order*, Cambridge University Press, 2005.
29. The developments in the former Soviet Union during this period, except for the relative difference in the crudity of propaganda or the amount of force involved in oppressing its citizens, indicate a perfect symmetry of thought processes and actions in this so-called war of ideologies between the protagonists.
30. At this point, it might be useful to clarify that the term state has been used in two senses in this paper: sometimes to indicate an entity that usually, although not always, represents and acts on behalf of the collective will of the ruling elite, and at other times an entity that represents and acts on behalf of many sections of a society either to recast the collective will of the elite or to determine its composition in new ways. The co-option of new ideologies into the language of the state and the induction of new classes into the ruling elite probably owes more to this latter sense of the state's character.
31. Chomsky, Noam, *At War with Asia*, AK Press, Oakland, CA, USA, 1969.
32. Chomsky, Noam, *Towards a New Cold War: Essays on the Current Crisis and How We Got There*, Pantheon Books, 1982.
33. Marcuse, Herbert, *One-Dimensional Man: Studies in the Ideology of Advanced Industrial Society*, Beacon Press, Boston, 1964.
34. Baran, Paul A. and Sweezy, Paul M., *Monopoly Capital: An Essay on the American Economic and Social Order*, Monthly Review Press, 1966.

35. See for example, Galloway, Alexander R. and Thacker, Eugene, *The Exploit: A Theory of Networks*, University of Minnesota Press, 2007.
36. Drucker, P. "Beyond the Information Revolution," *The Atlantic Monthly*, 1999, 284 (4): pp. 47-57.
37. The Gulf War and the financial melt-down of 2008 provide interesting vistas into the workings of the networked world. Despite the surfeit of information on the war that was constantly provided by a hyperactive media, neither the excessive civilian deaths nor the use of tens of thousands of tons of depleted uranium shells elicited a strong domestic opposition as it did a few decades ago in response to the extensive use of toxic defoliants and napalm in Vietnam. As regards the latter crisis, suffice it to say that no serious effort seems underway to prevent such a mishap from recurring; meanwhile, the nearly 30 billion dollar annual bonus largesse that Wall Street grants for itself continues as a tradition broken for just a short time after the financial collapse. Evidently, the reduction of information asymmetry has not helped mount an effective opposition to the machinations of the state or of business.
38. What challenges this new culture poses for preserving individual, family, local, linguistic, micro-cultural and religious freedoms of the world is not well understood today. That it does challenge them, though, seems to be clear.
39. The terms information and knowledge seem to have become indistinguishable in lay usage, perhaps as a result of the ICT revolution of the last two decades. While academic literature often strives to clearly distinguish between the two, the proliferation of definitions in either sphere makes it difficult to adopt a common standard and uniquely describe them. In most parts of this paper, the term information is used to indicate data in a context, while the term knowledge is used in this sense as well as in the traditional sense of true and justified belief.
40. For a study of some of the effects of the Internet on the human psyche, see Gackenbach, J. (ed.), *Psychology and the Internet: Intrapersonal, Interpersonal, and Transpersonal Implications*, Academic Press, 2006.
41. That the conquest of minds is likely to prove more lasting than acquiring dominions seems to have become increasingly evident from the rapid homogenization of tastes and preferences across the world in recent years. Is it possible that this provides a wider play for the economics and psychology of consumption of

positional goods than is suggested by Hirsh? See for example, Hirsch, Fred, *The Social Limits to Growth*, Routledge & Kegan Paul, London, 1977.

42. Or, in non-overlapping private groups that networked individualization promotes. See, for example, Wellman, B. and Hogan, B., "The Immanent Internet," http://homes.chass.utoronto.ca/~wellman/publications/immanent/immanent.pdf.
43. It is not being suggested here that one-way communication is either new, or that it is harmful in itself. Books, the theatre and newspapers of the old world have been exemplars of such communication for centuries in the past.
44. Funk, Jeanne B., et al., "Violence Exposure in Real-life, Video Games, Television, Movies, and the Internet: Is There Desensitization?", *Journal of Adolescence* 27 (2004) 23–39.
45. For an argument that the internet should be monitored to filter out the promotion of violence, see Cohen-Almagor, R., "Why Monitor Violent Websites? A Justification," *Beijing Law Review*, 2012, 3, 64-71.
46. Doidge, Norman, *The Brain That Changes Itself: Stories of Personal Triumph from the Frontiers of Brain Science*, Penguin, 2007.
47. Interestingly, unlike in the case of e-mails that enable communication with a relatively higher degree of privacy, social platforms such as Facebook or Twitter provide spaces largely meant to be used for public, open and multi-way communication; over the years, this seems to have resulted in the development of a new type of behaviour that disregards traditional distinctions between the notions of the personal, the private and the public in the process of self-expression. While this does indeed provide immense opportunities for commerce, politics and media to radically influence networks of people, an unanswered question it raises is regarding the consequences of the psychological forces unleashed by such platforms through their ability to equip people with the capacity to create multiple personas by suitably blending anonymity, impersonation, avatars and verifiable true identities in projecting their individual selves onto them.
48. In the first half of 2012, the multi-country advertisement revenues of Google, a 14-year-old company, surpassed that of all other US print media (which have been around for the last hundred years and more) put together. See, for example, http://beforeitsnews.com/financial-markets/2012/11/google-ad-revenue-surpasses-all-of-print-media-2468096.html.
49. In theory, public goods cannot (or will not) be produced for

private profit and are considered an outcome of market failures, requiring governmental interventions for providing them. A positional good is one whose enjoyment is affected by the number of others consuming it; the more this number, the less the enjoyment, and vice versa. A private good can be divided into parts to sell on the market, because it is excludable and rivalrous. Each type of good can change its status over time due to a variety of influences, e.g. technological progress. Pure public goods are rarely encountered today, e.g. national defence and property rights systems; education and a private jet are examples of positional goods, while a loaf of bread is a good example of a private good. See, for example, http://en.wikipedia.org/wiki/Public_good.

50. For a definition, see, for example, http://en.wikipedia.org/wiki/Closed_platform
51. Goldacre, Ben, *Bad Pharma: How Drug Companies Mislead Doctors and Harm Patients*, Fourth Estate, 2012.
52. Pharmaceutical companies have been repeatedly found guilty of profiteering from falsification of data in drug trials, dumping useless drugs, and conducting unethical trials on unsuspecting people. In the USA alone, the pharmaceutical industry has paid more than $30 billion as fines for misdeeds over the past 20 years. See for example, (http://www.burrillreport.com/article-4978.html).
53. The steady dilution of the operative principles of the Glass-Steagall Act over time, ultimately leading to its repeal in 1999, seems to have strengthened the transformation of the nature and scope of global capital, ably supported by world-wide networks of people and computing devices enabled by ICT. Given that it almost immediately led to a frenzy of innovative packaging of financial instruments of doubtful value, it is not surprising that within the next eight years, the toxic consequences of the marriage between banking and the securities industry became manifest through a global tsunami whose effects are yet to subside. The much acclaimed 2010 documentary, *Inside Job*, by Charles Ferguson on the 2008 financial crisis provides an excellent account of how the greed and socio-pathic tendencies bred by the initial successes of Wall Street companies in financial engineering emboldened them to develop even more complex instruments that were not only conceptually questionable but unethically pushed to unwary investors through deliberate misrepresentation and falsification (http://www.sony

classics.com/Insidejob).

54. Ritholtz, Barry, *Bailout Nation, with New Post-Crisis Update: How Greed and Easy Money Corrupted Wall Street and Shook the World Economy*, Wiley, 2010.
55. Taibbi, Matt, "Why Isn't Wall Street in Jail?" *Rolling Stone Magazine*, February 16, 2011. http://www.rollingstone.com/politics/news/why-isnt-wall-street-in-jail-20110216.
56. In this background, patenting traditional products can also be interpreted as a legally sanctioned process of developing a validated repository of information that provides a sense of inclusiveness and respectability to traditional knowledge while simultaneously denying it the space, both physical and conceptual, to operate within its own assumptions or in its traditionally defined social, cultural or economic domains.
57. Cavoukian, Ann, et al., "Privacy: Front and Centre", *Security & Privacy*, IEEE 10.5 (2012): 10-15.
59. That privacy concerns are growing by the day is gauged by the spate of regulations implemented over the last few years by governments across the world, including the Indian, to limit the tracking of individual behaviours in the service of businesses. However, it is a moot point if any legislation would be effectively able to address this problem. See for example Russom, Miriam Berhane, "Concepts of Privacy at the Intersection of Technology and Law", Dissertation, Politecnico di Milano, 2012 (https://dspace-prod-lib.cc.uic.edu/bitstream/handle/10027/9566/Berhane%20Russom%20-%20Miriam.pdf?sequence=1); also, for a report on consumer tracking and profiling practices in the US, see http://repositories.tdl.org/tdl-ir/handle/2152/ETD-UT-2012-05-5679.
59. Governmental snooping on individuals and groups as a response to threats of networked terrorism is increasingly being justified by a suggestion of imminent and apocalyptic devastation which in turn promotes extensive paranoia and a mentality of siege not very different from that experienced in the USA of the 1950s and 1960s. How extensive and routine such intrusions have become of late can be seen, for example, in http://online.wsj.com/article/SB120511973377523845.html# printMode.
60. In recent years, ordinary people increasingly seem to be reconciled to the conclusion that the threat of constant surveillance is not easily countered. Especially with the increased availability of inexpensive tools for spying, this phenomenon has become so widespread and effective that it qualifies today

as an area of study on its own. See, for example, Ball, Kirstie, Haggerty, Kevin and Lyon, David, (ed.), *Routledge Handbook of Surveillance Studies (Routledge International Handbooks)*, Routledge Press, 2012.

61. For an argument that the methodology of the sciences of yesteryears is not relevant any more, see for example, http://www.wired.com/science/discoveries/magazine/16-07/pb_theory.
62. The shift towards techno-science is sometimes justified as a measure to enhance the overall competitiveness of, e.g. the US economy. See for example, http://www.joachimschummer.net/books/discovering-the-nanoscale/johnson.pdf.
63. Of the 25 trillion dollars spent across the world on defence since the end of the Cold War twenty years ago, approximately 40 per cent has been the contribution from the US. In contrast, the United Nations and all its agencies and funds spend about $30 billion each year. See, for example, http://www.globaliss ues.org/article/75/world-military-spending.
64. And in recent conflicts, long lasting damage as well. The massive amounts of depleted uranium used in the extensive bombing of Iraq and Afghanistan are likely to ravage the countries for millennia to come. See, for example, http://www.guardian.co.uk/commentisfree/2012/oct/25/fallujah-iraq-health-crisis-silence, http://rense.com/general64/du.htm and http://www.presstv.ir/detail/223986.html.
65. For example, in contrast to the war in Vietnam that resulted in around 58,000 casualties for the US between the years 1955-1975, the Afghan and the second Iraq war have resulted in approximately 6,500 deaths of US personnel till 2012. See, for example, http://en.wikipedia.org/wiki/United_States_military_casualties_of_war.
66. It is often said that the Iraq war is about the control of oil and thereby of the world. See for example, http://www.chomsky.info/interviews/20050131.htm and http://www.chomsky.info/articles/20050704.htm. Is it also likely that the politics of Euro-America was heavily biased towards applying disproportionate force over the last two decades as a strategy for strengthening, in the interim, the new model and practices of a networked world.
67. Drucker, P. F., "The Rise of the Knowledge Society," *The Wilson Quarterly*, Vol. 17, 1993.
68. http://en.wikipedia.org/wiki/Intellectual_property.

69. How this restricts freedom in the field of software and enables oligopolies to thrive by excluding non-commercial interests while exercising complete control over its development and usage is well articulated in this popular essay: Raymond, Eric. "The Cathedral and the Bazaar", *Knowledge, Technology & Policy* 12.3 (1999): 23-49.
70. That laws protecting IPR can have draconian effects on the freedom of individuals and economies of less powerful countries in the world has been realized for long. The open source movement has been an important opponent of the laws of IPR especially through the work of Richard Stallman and his team of thousands of co-workers dispersed across the world. In addition to developing freely distributed software, they have been consistently militating against software patents, extension of the scope of copyright laws and digital rights management. See, for example, Wikipedia entries on the open source movement and Richard Stallman.
71. http://en.wikipedia.org/wiki/General_Agreement_on_Tariffs_and_Trade.
72. Drozd, F. Anne, "The Components of Value Measurement", *Journal of Accountancy*, 198, No. 6 (2004): 79-82.
73. Debates that underlay the recent Occupy Wall Street (OWS) protests in the US seem to clearly illustrate the lack of access to fundamental conceptual as well as practical mechanisms for opposing the growing inequity and injustice in society in the supposedly most advanced nation in the world. Its inability to sustain momentum is difficult to understand, given the widespread recognition that a small number of people (constituting a much lower fraction than the 1% portrayed in the slogans) determine the fate of the rest, and the growing awareness of the perverse role of the state in sacrificing the interests of the majority while strengthening itself. The long-term implications of such a decline in the legitimacy of the institutions defining the new world order in the very heart of the empire are not clear at this point in time, though. See for example, http://en.wikipedia.org/wiki/Occupy_Wall_Street and http://www.criticalglobalisation.com/issue5/110_113_OWS_AND_IPE_JCGS5.pdf.
74. Another form of globalization that began in the years after the Second World War—not considered here—is characterized by the new found use of Asia and Africa as dumping grounds for hazardous and toxic wastes in the face of mounting resistance to

their disposal within Euro-America. Some of it is done in the guise of technology transfer, e.g. the export of paper plants from Europe to India a few decades ago after their continuance in Europe became environmentally unsustainable. Export of mislabelled pharmaceutical wastes and antibiotics, poisoning international waters with hazardous waste and illegal experimentation with unlicensed drugs on unsuspecting patients in the Third World are of course more recent innovations of Euro-American industry. For an account of dumping as practised till the early 1990s, see James, Valentine Udoh, (ed.), *Sustainable Development in Third World Countries: Applied and Theoretical Perspectives*, Praeger Publishers, 1996, and http://www.multinationalmonitor.org/hyper/issues/1984/12/braithwaite.html. For more recent developments, see http://www.i-sis.org.uk/FDAinDrugTrial.php and http://www.culturalsurvival.org/publications/cultural-survival-quarterly/brazil/medicinal-drugs-third-world.

75. Curiously, the insecurity bred by the developments of the past few years seems to have produced a counter to such definitions of life from within the centre of the empire, although its outer reaches do not seem much impressed by such considerations. See, for example, Robbins, John, *The New Good Life: Living Better Than Ever in an Age of Less*, Ballantine Books, 2010.
76. While not by any means a new phenomenon, the culture of consumption in Euro-America has accelerated in recent decades. Moreover, for countries like India and China, the adoption of this new ethic has been surprisingly rapid in the past 20 years. According to Wikipedia, China, USA and India are the top three consumers of cable TV services in the world. More than half of USA has 3 TVs or more per household while close to half of the homes in India and China own TVs. Remarkably, the order of the top three is the same for users of the Internet: approximately 500, 250 and 120 million users respectively. As regards mobile phones, China, India and USA are the top three consumers, with nearly 1050, 900 and 330 million mobile phones respectively (Data sourced from the Internet and Wikipedia).
77. Dixon, Lloyd, et. al., *Hedge Funds and Systemic Risk*, Rand Centre for Corporate Ethics and Governance, 2012.
78. The strategies and operational styles of a hedge fund are usually very different from those of other funds because the former is not required to conform to the same levels of transparency, regulatory compliance or risk avoidance as the others. In addition

to distorting the market's character, they have been implicated in the increased volatility and potential for heightening systemic risks of the market. However, it is generally believed that their effect is secondary, such as through amplifying instabilities, rather than primary, such as through deliberately creating toxic assets like CDOs and CDSOs as witnessed in the collapse of markets in 2008. See for example, Lysandrou, Photis, "21 Hedge Funds," *Handbook of Critical Issues in Finance*, 2012.

79. For a list of recent corporate frauds involving (mostly) various types of financial malfeasance, see http://en.wikipedia.org/wiki/List_of_corporate_scandals. The term creative accounting may be 45 years old, but it is only in the last 20 years that its practice seems to have reached scandalous proportions.
80. Krugman, Paul, "How Did Economists Get It So Wrong?," *The New York Times*, September 6, 2009, as reproduced in: http://coin.wne.uw.edu.pl/lhardt/How%20Did%20Economists%20Get%20It%20So%20Wrong_%20-%20NYTimes.pdf.
81. Krugman, Paul, *The Return of Depression Economics and the Crisis of 2008*, W.W. Norton & Company, Inc., New York, 2009.
82. Some analysts suggest that the world will soon be without a centre of gravity, not amenable to domination by any system. See for example, Kupchan, Charles A., *No One's World: The West, the Rising Rest, and the Coming Global Turn*, Oxford University Press, 2012.
83. War as the means to force globalization, of course, is another matter altogether. See Barkawi, Tarak, *Globalization and War*, Rowman & Littlefield Publisher Inc., 2006.
84. Simply put, reification is the identification of an abstract concept with a concrete reality that, in the age of the empire, has transformed all social relations into the appearance of relations between things. "... (T)he concept of reification ... describes a situation of ... individual producers whose relation to one another is indirect and realized only through the mediation of things (the circulation of commodities), such that the social character of each producer's labour becomes obscured and human relationships are veiled behind the relations among things and apprehended as relations among things. In this manner a particular (historical) set of social relations comes to be identified with the natural properties of physical objects, thereby acquiring an appearance of naturalness or inevitability—a fact which contributes, in turn, to the reproduction of existing social relations." See, Burris, V., "Reification: A Marxist Perspective,"

*California Sociologist*, Vol. 10, No. 1, 1988, pp. 22-43.

85. Through reification, "...attributes (properties, characteristics, features, powers) which exist only by virtue of a social relationship between people are treated as if they are the inherent, natural characteristics of things, or vice versa, attributes of inanimate things are treated as if they are attributes of human subjects. This implies that objects are transformed into subjects and subjects are turned into objects, with the result that subjects are rendered passive or determined, while objects are rendered as the active, determining factor." Reproduced from: http://en.wikipedia.org/wiki/Reification_(Marxism).
86. That a significant part of the discontent against globalization originates from within Euro-America can also be taken as an indication that the new empire is progressively transcending traditional notions of race or geography in determining its composition. See, for example, http://en.wikipedia.org/wiki/Anti-globalization_movement.
87. Nandy seems to suggest that the changing conceptions over time of the village and city in India actually constitute attempts by a dislocated and disoriented society to cope with the dissonances produced by an exogenous, impersonal and distanced power structure through a constant recalibration of their own accounts of themselves and their pasts in relation with others. See Nandy, Ashis, *An Ambiguous Journey to the City: The Village and Other Odd Ruins of the Self in the Indian Imagination*, Oxford University Press, 2007.
88. Nandy, Ashis, *Bonfire of Creeds: The Essential Ashis Nandy*, Oxford University Press, 2010.
89. Sahasrabudhey, Sunil, ed., *The Peasant Movement Today*, Ashish Publishing House, 1986.
90. Some recent examples of struggles inspired by Gandhi's thoughts are Nelson Mandela's in South Africa, Ibrahim Rugova's in Kosovo, the Dalai Lama's in Tibet, Aung San Suu Kyi's in Myanmar and Rigoberta Menchu's in Guatemala. That the Occupy Wall Street should adopt Gandhi as the model for resistance may also be interpreted as a recognition of the spreading decay of institutions at the very centre of the empire.
91. Gandhi, M.K., *Hindu Dharma*, Diamond Pocket Books, 2010.
92. Gandhi, Mohandas K., *An Autobiography or The Story of My Experiments With Truth*, Translated by Mahadev Desai, Navajivan Publishing House, 1948, (1927): 90.
93. It is quite possible that such notions about the self and the other—

deeply interwoven with the social, economic and religious lives of Indians—are not easily deducible from displaced contexts such as of the West. Part of the problem may lie in the categories employed by the observer in portraying the observed society. For example, an assumption that underlies Western descriptions of Indian religions—that religion is a cultural universal—may have more to do with the Western culture than with what human cultures are. See, for example, Balagangadhara, S.N., "The Heathen in His Blindness: Asia, the West, and the Dynamic of Religion," Vol. 64, Brill, 1994.

94. González-Díaz, Emilio, Paradox, Time and De-Paradoxication in Luhmann, *No Easy Way Out*, http://www.unizar.es/sociocybernetics/congresos/CORFU/papers/egonzalez.pdf.
95. Luhmann, Niklas, *Theories of Distinction: Redescribing the Descriptions of Modernity*, Stanford University Press, 2002.
96. Angell, Ian and Dionysios Demetis, *Science's First Mistake: Delusions in Pursuit of Theory*, Bloomsbury Academic, 2010.
97. Levy, Neil, "Introducing Neuroethics," *Neuroethics* 1.1 (2008): 1-8.
98. For an account of automatic and deliberative processes, see Stanovich, K.E., *Who is Rational? Studies of Individual Differences in Reasoning*, Mahwah, NJ: Erlbaum, 1999.
99. Kahneman, Daniel, Paul Slovic and Amos Tversky, (eds.), *Judgment Under Uncertainty: Heuristics and Biases*, Cambridge University Press, 1982.
100. Kahneman, Daniel, *Thinking, Fast and Slow*, Farrar, Straus and Giroux, 2011.
101. For an excellent summary of the work in this field, see Kahneman's Autobiography, http://www.nobelprize. org/nobel_prizes/economics/laureates/2002/kahneman-autobio.html.
102. Damasio, Antonio, *Self Comes to Mind: Constructing the Conscious Brain*, Vintage Books, 2012.
103. Damasio, Antonio, *Descartes' Error: Emotion, Reason, and the Human Brain*, Putnam Publishing, 1994.
104. Ramachandran, Vilayanur S., *Phantoms in the Brain: Probing the Mysteries of the Human Mind*, Harper Perennial, 1999.
105. In syllogistic reasoning, Modus Ponens is of the form: If P, then Q. P. Therefore, Q. Modus Tollens is of the form: If P, then Q. Not-Q. Therefore, Not-P.
106. Dube, C., Rotello, C.M. and Heit, E., "Assessing the Belief Bias Effect with ROCs: It's a Response Bias Effect," *Psychol Rev.* 2010 July; 117(3):831-63.

107. Nickerson, R.S., "Confirmation Bias: A Ubiquitous Phenomenon in Many Guises," *Review of General Psychology*, Vol. 2, No. 2. (1998), pp. 175-220.
108. Mitchell, Melanie, *Complexity: A Guided Tour*, Oxford University Press, 2009.
109. Watts, Duncan J., *Everything is Obvious: Once You Know the Answer*, Crown Business, 2011.
110. Sunil Sahasrabudhey's thesis of Paschimikrit Samaj and Bahishkrit Samaj in the late 1970s may be seen as a precursor to this categorization. See, for example, http://www.vidyaashram.org/mkn.html.
111. A constant obsession of the Indian middle classes during the last few years with the predictions of the West that India, with its new found political and economic determination, is poised to leverage its demographic dividends to overtake Euro-America by 2050 is perhaps a good indication of a their new found belief in a planned and well-engineered future; such optimistic visions of their prospective fortunes have also propelled an increasing distaste for the affairs of Bharat, except in terms that would meet with the approval of Euro-America, e.g. through involvement with not for profit organizations in the areas of sanitation, health, literacy, education, and the like. Evidently, India's elite seems increasingly determined not to any longer allow Bharat to come in the way of the exciting future possibilities for India.
112. http://www.vidyaashram.org/.
113. http://lokavidyajanandolan.blogspot.in/2011/07/with-lokavidya-lies-solution.html.
114. Sahasrabudhey, Sunil, "Taking Democracy to the World of Knowledge," http://kicsforum.net/kics/KD/012-Democracyto knowledge-sunil.html.
115. While the death of various knowledge systems of the world during the colonial period may be seen as a fait accompli, India's disinclination even after independence towards rejuvenating its great traditions, for example, of iron and steel making—known for millennia to be highly evolved—seems rooted in an unquestioned acceptance of the commensurability of these systems with that of the West, predictably leading to their complete extinction. For a discussion on this theme through the example of the Agaryas of India, see Sahasrabudhey, Sunil, "LOKAVIDYA," Session 11. http://multiworldindia.org/wp-content/uploads/2010/05/SESSION-XI.pdf.
116. Is *lokavidya* a reified concept? The answer is a qualified yes,

because *lokaviḍya* resists reification (in the sense of Marx or Lukacs) essentially through its deep bonding with its context and location, as well as through its non-universal scope of operation and effects.

117. A reading of Dharampal (see footnote: 2) provides several instances of this in the colonial period. An example of this in recent years may be found in the slow death of the Indian systems of medicine even as medical formulations swearing provenance from Ayurveda or Unani have cornered a sizeable share of the Indian market.
118. Can we hypothesize here that the economic activity of a society based on *lokavidya* would be predominantly structured through considerations of use value while, in contrast, the principal logic of economic activity in a society based on a separation of knowledge from its context would be that of exchange value?
119. Taken together with the set of non-representational capacities that underlie intentional phenomena. See, for example, Searle, John R., *The Rediscovery of the Mind*, MIT Press, 1992. Ch. 8, "Consciousness, Intentionality, and the Background".
120. Sunil Sahasrabudhey, "Dialogues on Knowledge in Society," http://www.vidyaashram.org/papers/1Dialogues.pdf.

# 6

# Knowledge Flux and the Demand on Thought*

*Sunil Sahasrabudhey*

## 6.1 Introduction

For over a decade and half now the world of knowledge has been experiencing an extraordinary flux. The Internet has created a new virtual world of knowledge activity and knowledge management and the place of the university as the undisputed command in the world of knowledge has been challenged and there is an atmosphere of a new recognition to the knowledge in society, *lokavidya.* All this seems strongly related to what is being called the neo-liberal global economy and the beginnings of a situation in which sovereignty of the nation-states is seriously in jeopardy. Mobility, connectivity, modes of employment in the modern sector, the new media and entertainment have all changed life so much that the ideas of politics, resistance, mobilization and culture developed through the previous two centuries are struggling to maintain their relevance. Poverty elimination, brotherhood, equality, liberty, *swadeshi*, *swaraj*, non-cooperation, *satyagraha*, class-struggle and many more concepts of political significance radically concerned with the essential human condition are struggling for a restatement of their meaning in the new contexts. It seems that the task now first relates to the world of knowledge to secure the new meaningfulness to be useful for

---

* Paper prepared for an invitation lecture at the Indian Association for Cultivation of Sciences, Kolkata, 15 April, 2008

humanity. Let us therefore first very briefly go over the kind of economic and political changes that are taking place for the last two decades to locate the issue of knowledge in the reality for which its resolution must in turn make sense.

**6.2 The Changing World**

It is less than 20 years that the world has moved into a new era. A virtual cyclone has been building up through the marriage of the Internet and the Neo-Liberal Economy. The new dispensations, information technology, media, entertainment, market, management, higher education and so on are lifting away both knowledge and wealth that people produce in the course of their lives. The peasants, artisans, informal workers and their households again constitute the other side of the divide, this time it is the digital divide. The digital divide is also a knowledge divide of a certain type, knowledge management helping the virtual cyclone lift away everything of significance from across this divide. What is left behind even after being taken away is the knowledge with the people which is their last bastion of strength.

The changes since 1990 resulting from Globalization, the Internet and the American Wars have taken the world by storm. Every department of human life has been shaken. The Internet and the Mobile have not only given new and high connectivity but have led to entirely new lifestyles. Industry no more occupies the place of command. In that place now sits Information. Machine is no more the chief expression of capital. Finance and information have moved into its place. They call the shots now. The workers of organized industry have suffered successive defeats. The trade unions are at an all time low. Industry seems to be in the process of being externed from the capitalist social formation. So with the workers. With the rise of capitalism, industry had moved to the centre stage and industrial workers constituted that slot into which large parts of humanity moved to become part of the new society, albeit an oppressed part. Even this is being lost, workers being pushed out into the world across the digital divide to become an informal worker, an artisan. This has the interesting result of pushing all production outside the dominant social formation.

This is the Neo-liberal Economy financed by banks and financial agencies and managed by the Information Technologies.

The city of the industrial epoch was the place which housed industry. The Information Age is rebuilding the city as the marketplace. Large and dominant social sectors of health and education are now in the private domain and constitute integral parts of the market. The market is assuming a new quality and extent every day. At one end there is a huge corporate sweep to capture the retail market and at the other capital and management reach the farthest and remotest corners to lift revenue from whatever may constitute economic activity there. In the globalized world now there shall be no exchange even in the private domain from which the corporations do not take away their 'share', legitimized by the new order, law, politics. Media, entertainment, games, art, everything has joined the race in the market up-front. The so-called social sphere is also in step. Education, healthcare, water management, rural development, poverty alleviation, everything has queued up to be listed in the stock market. All this is being called the development of knowledge economy. Software giants and their lucrative employment rationalize the new idiom.

The new conflicts in their express forms since the First Gulf War, in 1990, seem to have inaugurated a new phase of politics and law. There is talk about the building of a new empire, at present America leading the show. National parties and people's institutions like the parliament are becoming less and less important in making the national policy. Shots are being called by the emerging institutions of the new international order. Nations are no more sovereign the way they used to be in the later part of the 20th century.

The whole thing is going on as if without challenge. Islam and communism still remain the foci around which resistances have built up. But neither seems to be giving a new imagination for a different and just world. The World Social Forum is a secular worldwide phenomenon which is generally anti-America and anti-globalization and which talks about another world being possible. But the participation, the methods and the debates fail to carry conviction. The world is in need of a new politics to move minds across the globe on issues of fundamental human concerns like poverty and autonomy with conviction.

It is our conviction, that promise for change towards a better and just world can only be based on mobilization of people's strength. This strength in the ultimate analysis lies in the knowledge they possess to organize their lives, to understand the world, to resist the oppressor. The changes occurring in the world, the failure of science to deliver and the appearance of the virtual world as the new place of organization of knowledge and the ruling classes, tend to convince us further that *lokavidya* must be taken on board to solve the challenging problems that humanity is increasingly facing. It is this argument that this dialogue tries to unfold. We shall for this purpose first talk about the flux in the field of knowledge, then about the disturbance that science is experiencing and about the internet, the new hub of knowledge, and finally about *lokavidya* as a just and promising resource for everybody.

### 6.3 Knowledge Flux

Practically every knowledge activity is experiencing big changes in content, method, organization, values, place in knowledge hierarchy, place in society, remunerative potential, etc. We can see this happening in education, production, healthcare, science, arts, agriculture, media, management, etc. These changes as we know are located in the larger changes in life guided by the new global economy, the development of computer and communication technologies and the new wars with the realignment of forces all over the world. Since science has been the centre piece of the world of knowledge, a look at what is happening to it should take us to the heart of the matter. Needless to say that an understanding of what is happening to industry, media, arts, or agriculture as knowledge activities is also very important but this would be a very large exercise beyond the scope of this attempt.

An indication of the flux in the world of knowledge may also be seen in the spread of the knowledge terminology. Phrases like knowledge society, knowledge economy, knowledge work, knowledge management, knowledge production, knowledge dialogue, knowledge partnership, knowledge collaboration and so on are being used extensively and also indiscriminately. One cannot enumerate the list because it is a new idiom and these phrases are produced anywhere in the expanding sectors of the economy and activity. Both the concept of knowledge and the politics of knowledge are changing. Knowledge of different peoples has assumed a new movement. Monasteries have become active again and knowledge with the people, *lokavidya,* is on the path of greater recognition though not yet politically assertive. Even the media is claiming to be a place of knowledge activity. A new way of life and thinking, a new imagery of the world is in the making. Received ways of understanding and comprehending changes are failing to serve. With the institutionalization of science and growth of industry in the 19th century human activity had come to be comprehended by scientific ways through economics, political science, sociology, history and even philosophy. With the destabilization of the place of science in the world of knowledge all this stands shaken. How do we go about reconstituting our understanding in times of such knowledge flux?

**6.4 Science is Disturbed**

Science now has less money than it had before. It also has less attraction than it had before. Those storming higher education are more evenly divided into streams of law, management, computers, medicine, etc. Engineering colleges still attract very large crowds. In fact, this crowd is growing. But the output of these colleges in a way splits into two. One is like the products of erstwhile polytechnics and the other ready to join the software stream. The science of engineering seems to have taken a beating. Products of the best known engineering colleges go to software and management irrespective of the specialized stream they may come from. It is notable that knowledge activity with high value in the market does not presuppose knowledge of science. Management, software, media are the instances. This response of the state and the market is not unconnected with the position of science now in the world of knowledge. Its place in the position of command, its function on the frontiers of knowledge and its philosophy with strong realist and positivist orientation, have all been disturbed. This wave of disturbance is too large not to be noticed or even not to be a matter of serious concern, not from the vantage point of defence but from the point of view of truth seeking.

### *6.4.1 Science Loses its Command Over the World of Knowledge*

Every human activity is a knowledge activity. Scientific research, production of new knowledge, teaching, design, explanation, comprehension, creative arts, management, writing software, collection, organization and dissemination of information, religion, spiritual enterprise, artisanry, farming, collecting food in forests, hunting, bringing up children, health-care, organizing communities, name any human activity and you will find that it is a knowledge activity. Other than may be those which are performed purely on instruction like in rituals or by a worker on the assembly line, purely mechanically, human activity in general is knowledge activity. The age of science, as we know, weaves a pattern in this world of human activities from a standpoint of knowledge known as the scientific point of view. It had developed wide ranging criteria and methods to allocate any of these activities their 'rightful' place in the world of knowledge. These involved the ideas of experiment, testing, verification, reproduction, analytical content, systematic organization, universal applicability, value-independence, etc. This cluster of ideas constituted the general basis for producing a structure in the world of knowledge. Farming, food gathering, local healthcare, etc. would not be called knowledge activity at all but a simple application of knowledge which may have been handed down through generations. The arts were strictly distinguished from the sciences and placed lower down in the order. Writing for newspapers, making films or collecting information for reporting would hardly be considered knowledge activity. Computing would be a service and so would writing programmes be. Economics, market or public finance were all tuned to this understanding. Is not all this changing in a big way? Science no more seems to order the world of knowledge.

Science had given a new understanding of nature and

produced great riches by providing the basis of new technologies and new industry. However, as it has come to pass, this same technology and industry is destroying nature in unprecedented and irrevocable ways. This shakes science from inside. Can humanity's best knowledge be destructive towards nature and side with the propertied classes to keep the poor always poor? This adds to the breakdown of the position science has enjoyed for so long. Philosophically too therefore science ought to cease to occupy the command of the world of knowledge.

### *6.4.2 New Sciences and the Loosening Grip of Physical Sciences*

Certain sections in the Euro-American world find information technology, biotechnology, nano-technology and cognitive science at the frontier and see that unstoppable forward movement in them which was once seen in the steam engine. These four taken together have come to be known as converging technologies. Starting around 2003 there has been an attempt to build a debate around the leading nature of these technologies in the present-day world (Ref. : http://www.wtec.org/ConvergingTechnologies/ and http://www.converging-technologies.org/cyberconference). Unlike science whose prime object was an exact understanding of nature and development of methods of manipulating it, the converging technologies programme has understanding of human being in material terms and developing methods of manipulating them, their behaviour, performance, etc. at the centre of its concerns. In line with this, the programme has major participation of philosophers and social scientists in it. The cyber conference in May 2007 had put out Eight Opening Statements which essentially talked about 'improvements in the performance of human beings' through the use of new techniques like 'prosthetic limbs, silicon chip implants and nanobotic medicine', which are supposed to 'redefine the human condition in fundamental ways'. For them "Short of total annihilation of Homo-sapiens, it really does not matter if the converging technologies agenda ends up having substantial negative consequences." The programme is arguing for fundamental changes in science policy such as to free research in these technologies from control of 'national governments and international agencies' and says that "the actual pace and direction of research should be left to specialists in the relevant sciences and technologies".

It cannot be anybody's case that all these can be done without science or even without science prospering but one could surely argue that it may not require physics, chemistry and even biology to share space in the frontline. The new technologies are likely to demand new types of scientific formulations. And these four themselves are so very different from one another that there is no way to tell at present if at all there is going to be a common epistemic framework which would tie them all together.

### *6.4.3 Science and Philosophy*

Philosophy since the Kantian enterprise had accepted the pre-eminent position of science in the world of knowledge. Slowly science attained an absolute position. Not just philosophy but no social movement could question this for a long time. The feminist and the post-modern movements of America and Europe of the 1970s-80s question the absolutist position, they question certain philosophical assumptions and implications. And these can even be seen as precursors to what has been happening to Western thought since the early 90s, though not as causes.

India too has seen an alternative science movement questioning the absoluteness and value independence of science and arguing for the validity of knowledge traditions of different civilizations. Though marginal, this movement led in the 1990s to the organization of three national congresses of traditional sciences and technologies of India. It is this stream which has brought to the fore the idea of *lokavidya* and the question of rightful place in the world of knowledge for different streams of knowledge present in society. All these, feminism, post-modernism and the *lokavidya* standpoint, do not accept the downright positivist scientific ontology.

The idea of ontology itself may be undergoing a major change. Science had given birth to realism, as if there was a reality waiting to be discovered through progress in science. The progress in the world of computers and Internet and coming into existence of the virtual world has also shaken the scientific ontology. It has no use of 'realism' and the activity on it does not favour thinking in terms of things and forces. The world of communications has greater concern with ideas of syntax, meaning, representation, etc. If they are asked about what this world consists of, they might even say: human (epistemic) beings who communicate with one another. Philosophical debates born in the wake of scientific advances may soon make way for new debates in a world of different concerns. Philosophy once again needs to recreate itself in relation to the new flux in the world of knowledge.

## 6.5 Internet: The New Hub of Knowledge

New criteria seem to be emerging which now stake their claim to order the world of knowledge. The world of computers and communications, the world of Internet is, as if, saying that there is no use and that there is no great point in reserving knowledge and knowledge activity to the secure places of science, the universities, the research institutions, the laboratories. They seem to be saying that all that is organizable by the new technologies, all that can be processed by a computer, all that can be networked through the new means of communication, deserves to be called knowledge. And the science and art of doing this is called knowledge management. The personal computer, its lightning speed and for all practical purposes unlimited storage, the new connectivity through the Internet and the principles and practice of software have made possible in the name of knowledge management an entirely new type of activity which is as much knowledge activity as it is an act of management.

### *6.5.1 The Knowledge Terminology*

Internet is the new location of human activity. You send letters, chat with friends, partners and collaborate with other agencies, retrieve data and information, do scientific research, strategize experiments, run personal blogs, access the market, design new products, indulge in artistic activity, entertain yourself, carry out educational programmes, see films, enter into critical dialogues, create dialoguing groups, form virtual communities, form and run institutions, and do many more activities on the internet, the world wide web. Obviously, as you can see, the list is not completable, because, one, it may be too large and diverse and two, it may be essentially not completable, in the same sense in which a complete list of human activities cannot be made. Most of these are referred to as knowledge activity. The software that makes all this possible are called knowledge products. We should ask the question why these activities are called knowledge activities now? They were not called knowledge activity when the Internet was not there. And now when these activities on the Internet are called knowledge activities, when they are performed without the Internet also they are called knowledge activities. The same is true with knowledge products. Now that the knowledge product terminology has come into existence through the expanding sector of software, people tend to call many other products in the field of education, health, art, media, science, etc. knowledge packages or knowledge products.

Is the knowledge terminology being increasingly accepted because the software sector and online management have emerged as the most remunerative in the market or is there more to it in terms of meaning and philosophy?

### *6.5.2 Information and Knowledge*

The Internet works on the basis of a huge storage of information and a very fast movement of pieces of information from one site to another by the computer and communication technologies. The question that has seriously come up is whether what is being organized through this new technology is just information or can it qualify as knowledge too as the popularizing terminology suggests? The question of where to use 'information' and where to use 'knowledge' is an older one. Computers brought to bear new dimensions on this question and after the appearance of the internet its scope further increased because a wide range of human activity became possible in and through the new virtual realm.

Often information is considered part of knowledge but there

are strong objections to identifying information with knowledge. In the context of the new technology information is mathematically defined, knowledge is not. But in the ordinary usage the term 'information' has much greater scope and one can easily find cases where the use of 'information' and 'knowledge' could justly be interchangeable, and cases where it would be difficult to decide whether to use one or the other more correctly. So there are disagreements and confusions ranging from everyday use to philosophical interpretation. What is most commonly said is that understanding and even points of view are part of knowledge, whereas information is neutral to these human qualities. This debate between knowledge and information is rich, it has philosophical content and it has value also in day-to-day work. It is unlikely that the public domain will see a resolution of the issues involved. What is likely to happen is that words and concepts which find wider and wider use would tend to stay and others with their meanings will get marginalized. Similar phenomenon may be said to have happened before when the mechanical science appeared on the scene in Europe around $16^{th}$-$17^{th}$ centuries. There were already present in society various knowledge traditions. These knowledge traditions often couched in religious terms had their own values and a relation with human concerns and interests. The new science was value independent and was based on mechanical interpretation of worldly phenomena. So it could not have been easy to accept it as 'knowledge' in the then existing context. However, with the passage of time it spread worldwide and claimed universal and sovereign status for itself in the world of knowledge.

Internet has created a virtual world where information constitutes the representation of all that can be represented, knowledge included. There is no doubt that such representation of knowledge differs from knowledge itself, for example, values, social interfaces, aesthetic command, etc. of any body of knowledge in the real world may not get transferred to the virtual world in which such knowledge may be associated with different values, social interfaces and aesthetic qualities. Even a change of place of such knowledge in the world of knowledge is certainly expected to occur when it reconstitutes itself through informational representation in the virtual world. However as the virtual world grows bigger and bigger, as it becomes richer and richer and more and more activities of consequence from all the fields, economic, cultural, scientific, political, etc. start locating themselves on it, the arguments underlining the difference between knowledge and information as we understand them now may tend to become less and less important. In theory the validity of arguments distinguishing knowledge from information may remain as it is but in reality the focus of interest and also the nature of theory building may change so much as to rationalize the shift.

But this is arguing for the ascendant. What happens to that and those on whose backs this new ascendancy is constituting itself? What happens to art and *lokavidya* for example? And what happens to the artists in the real world and the ordinary life, the great house of *lokavidya*? The ascendancy of informational representation and its claim to being knowledge itself has given a new lease of life to popular art and *lokavidya* but not without a heavy price, namely the distortion they undergo in this process of representation.

### *6.5.3 Management and Knowledge*

The ICTs changed both the quality and the extent of the market and made possible the present global economy. As we know this globalization does not pertain only to economics, which though many may view as being the central phenomenon. Today irrespective of their location in the world, finance, management, knowledge, production, ownership are all related to one another in a manner which was not possible earlier. Previously production and knowledge on the periphery was related to the centres of management, knowledge and finance only through trade and the revenue apparatus of the state (this is leaving out the governance part). Now this relation has developed two new aspects of management and learning-teaching directly. So generally speaking in addition to exchange and revenue two new dimensions of management and knowledge have come into existence across the socio-economic divide. Similar changes seem to have occurred in the relationships of different sectors like media, science, art, entertainment, development, welfare, etc. with one another. Knowledge and management are those two aspects which have got added to the existing relationships between various human activities.

The emergence of the management aspect in these relationships ties the world economy very closely and tightly. Autonomy of different activities has reduced considerably making them vulnerable to influences emanating from apparently distant sectors. And these may be very often planned influences. This has therefore pushed up greatly the importance of management in all the activities and departments of human life.

The development of the knowledge aspect in the relationships between different sectors seems to give birth to new legitimacies in the world of knowledge to a great variety of activities. Activities on the media, art works, entertainment, design, agriculture, local healthcare, handicrafts, women's work at home and with children all now tend to seek recognition as knowledge activities and they seem to have traversed a fair distance on such a road.

The sufferers of the industrial epoch would be right if they say that the excesses of science in the field of knowledge are getting corrected. Art, design, agriculture and craft were always legitimate knowledge activities, the turn of events ought to be very welcome. However the correction of this excess will remain mainly semantic if other excesses of the period of science and industry are also not corrected.

Whether the reordering of the world of knowledge is based on the recognition that different fields of human activity have it in them to be equals in the realm of knowledge or whether it is because of an expansion in the meaning of knowledge required by the neo-liberal economy or cognitive capitalism as certain sections of the European Left call it? If it is only the latter then in the ultimate analysis the change will only be cosmetic and no actual advantages will accrue to the vast population of the world.

The management and knowledge axes that have emerged with the information technology between the various sectors of human activities have actually not emerged independent of one another. The two are strongly enmeshed with each other in fact to the extent that knowledge management has taken a new and distinct form. Although the term Knowledge Management first came into existence for management of knowledge within corporations, it is now being used extensively almost everywhere.

### *6.5.4 Knowledge Management (KM)*

It is not that management of knowledge did not take place before. Schools and colleges are popular places where knowledge management means constituting various departments and disciplines of knowledge, imparting knowledge to students, distinguishing between practical and abstract knowledge, learning to connect practical knowledge with processes of production and organizing dialogues and conferences for clarity and communication in the abstract arena, etc. Libraries and research institutions are places too of such management of knowledge. Peasant and artisan communities too have their ways of managing their knowledge. Learning from one another about techniques, implements, processes, new discoveries and about raw material, market or policies of the government and training of new generations through communitarian processes involves management of knowledge and information. But knowledge management in the age of computers and communications has a totally different meaning. It is shaping itself as a new kind of knowledge placing itself at the top, for it manages all types of knowledge which includes also the earlier methods of management of knowledge. In this process an extraordinary new world, the virtual world, is created which tends to become the new location not just of epistemic power and proceeds to redefine society, humanity, nature. In one word a new world and a new philosophy are born. It is just the beginning so we too can take only a preliminary view of it.

Knowledge management makes possible handling of information on computers in a great variety of ways. One can enter information, organize it in desired formats, systematize it in different ways, retrieve it from wherever it is in the virtual domain, dialogue, cooperate, fight or work together with anybody sitting anywhere in the world. It deals with information as written word, visuals and sounds. (I do not know whether touch, taste and smell are also candidates on the list of possibles and whether a virtual community can in any real sense be a replacement for a face-to-face community.) Somebody doing all this need not himself be a knowledge manager, just as users of telephones need not be communication engineers and drivers of cars are not mechanical engineers..

Today KM is more remunerative than most other knowledge activity, it gives high returns in the market. KM personnel get very high salaries and enterprises where it plays a crucial role earn great profits. It cannot be said that in society and in the world of knowledge it has the highest place as knowledge but it is constantly moving upwards. Our question is, what kind of reordering of the world of knowledge is on the cards. What are the principles, criteria, methods and values that emanate from the virtual world to reorder the world of knowledge? Some straight answers could be the following:

All information that is organizable by the ICTs shall be called knowledge.

Knowledge that is visited more on the Internet is more important, better or higher knowledge.

Methods of investigation, research that use KM are superior methods compared to those which do not. So also a grading on the vertical scale according to the extent of the use of KM.

Utilitarian values are the leading lights of the world of knowledge. Market competitiveness provides the quantitative measure of utility.

Not that all this has already happened but this is how it seems it has been happening. It is too large a phenomena and too close to the eyes to see it with high resolution. A huge and epoch-making conflict is underway in the world of knowledge for contention for the place of command and therefore on what would hence forward order the world of knowledge.

This shift of command in the knowledge domain from scientificity to the virtual realm tends to break the hierarchies of the old house of knowledge. Arts, management, design and software activity fetch greater value and have high esteem in the public realm than scientific and industrial activity.

Knowledge content of these activities therefore, refuses to occupy a lower place in the world of knowledge. But their moving up inevitably changes the concept of knowledge we have become so familiar with through the age of science. Are language and creativity superior knowledge habitats than the scientific experiments and the theories of nature? Are we mistaken in thinking that the world in the ultimate analysis consists of things and forces? Is it a better way to think that the world is created and recreated every moment, incessantly? Is building theories the way science did, after all, a very limited exercise and has run its course of usefulness to humanity? What happens when traditional knowledge, the knowledge of peasants, artisans, women, *adivasis* and small businessmen no more remains one of an inferior variety? What happens if we think that the idea of the university as an island of knowledge in a sea of ignorance is incorrect and universities ought to be places of specialized knowledge activity in a world of abundance of knowledge?

## 6.6 *Lokavidya*: A Just Resource for Everybody

### *6.6.1 A Historic Opportunity*

However this entire show is being played out within a minority which thinks that the rest of the world, those on the other side of the digital divide, peasants, workers, artisans, women and *adivasis* do not know and even if they do what they do, they are suppliers of sorts and not players. It is our contention that this historic destabilization of the house of knowledge gives a great and historic opportunity to those who love truth, who love nature and who love people, to enter this game of reordering the world of knowledge to shape it in the interest of what they love: truth, nature and people.

### *6.6.2 The Case of Lokavidya*

The house of knowledge has been disturbed by one more factor. This is the inclusion of *lokavidya* (people's knowledge, knowledge in society, different knowledge traditions) in the world of legitimate knowledge. The knowledge of the peasant and the artisan is commanding new attention. Their knowledge of production, processes, designs and their skills have started earning recognition again after a gap of several generations. Local healthcare, knowledge of natural resources, water management, house building, everything is getting an attention which they did not get for a long time. Through our educational system we have been trained to see ordinary people, those who have not gone to school, largely as ignorant. We have been trained to see them as doing what they do in the way they do because modern knowledge and facilities have not reached them. But if we make an effort to see ordinary people, peasants, artisans, women, *adivasis*, the ordinary middle class as knowledgeable people we would realize that with them lies that huge storage and variety of knowledge which may far exceed the total knowledge content produced and accumulated by the universities so far.

Huge populations all over the world have either never gone to schools or are early drop outs. And even those who continue for a few more years hardly take home any knowledge that they can effectively use. All these people acquire their knowledge in society, in the community, in the family, at the worksites through informal training, trial, apprenticeship and so on. They use their knowledge to serve their life needs and in the process serve the larger society. It is this knowledge which is called *lokavidya*.

### 6.6.3 The Nature of Lokavidya

The nature of *lokavidya* is totally different from organized knowledge systems, in particular science. Its organization, values, logic, method, philosophy, everything is different. When one refers to *lokavidya*, one is not referring to any particular value, method or even logic, philosophy or organization. As nature and social organization varies from one place to another and from one time to another, friendship with nature and harmony in society assume different expressions, forms and contents.

So for example, the knowledge, methods and values of peasants in Bengal, Rajasthan, Kenya and Argentina for that matter may be expected to vary greatly from one another, but one can expect that an expert farmer from Bengal will with some experimentation be able to grow rice also in Rajasthan or Africa or even America. He can perhaps do this because his knowledge expressed in very site-specific parameters is not local or limited as knowledge. He may have a great knowledge of soil, water conditions, climate, seeds and also the tastes of the people of his area. But when taken to another place with different soil and water conditions, different climate and even different seeds, he may resort to deeper layers of his knowledge of rice cultivation, design experiments and change factors so as to be able to produce the result. I do not know of any such experiment conducted. But we know about the extreme change in input conditions and factors that he has braved through at least two centuries now. Also the every voluminous and famous *Voelcker Report of the Late 19th Century on Agriculture in India* concludes by saying that Indian agriculture is optimal everywhere and as if best suited to the conditions, that there is little that the Indian peasant can be told from outside to improve upon his practice and that if he should improve, it is through inter-regional interaction alone that it is possible (Review of Voelcker Report in *PPST Bulletin*, 1982, Chennai). And this is about a full century after the introduction of the *zamindari* system and half a century after the Rothamsted Experiment and the NPK theory of fertility.

I, had an opportunity to investigate the practice of traditional ferrous technology of this country. *Agaria*, an 'untouchable' tribe of central India preserves this tradition to date. They smelt iron ore of relatively low metal content in a small furnace (outer dimensions dia 50 c.m. x height 1 metre) made by local mud mixed with rice husk. It is a vertical shaft cylindrical hole ( dia >15 c.m.) in which ore is charged with locally made charcoal. No slagging material is used and about 3 kilograms of iron bloom is pulled out from the bottom after about 3 hours of firing which requires constant manual pumping of air. The product is beaten to expel mainly air and extraneous matter. This is malleable iron which contains less than 0.3% carbon. As the region changes, the furnace and the methods change slightly. In our experiments a master-fireman from Wardruffnagar successfully produced the metal in Varanasi and in Mumbai. He had to use different and low grade charcoal and work under different humidity conditions but each time after a couple of experimental runs he could optimize the process to produce the metal. Let us remember that producing the critical temperature for iron smelting at atmospheric pressure is a demanding task. His knowledge, call it science or not, is of a type which can take into account charges in all input conditions to optimize the process for successful smelting. I do not know whether it is possible to do a knowledge engineering task to software all experimental and alternate paths that he may have to suggest with change in input conditions. I think it is unlikely, not because the permutations and combinations would lead to far too large a number but because perhaps the knowledge may not lend itself to discrete classification and may involve continuums and depths of understanding which unravel only on demand.

I would like to take one more example. Dr. Winnin Perriera of Mumbai had conducted a small experiment with the *adivasis* in the adjacent district of Thane. He said they brought certain plants from the eastern part of India. The *adivasis* of Thane had not seen these plants before. In two years time they were using this plant for healthcare purposes. One can get into the details of the possibilities involved and produce a socio-scientific analysis of how it may have happened. However, let us grant that there is something more in such knowledge which delivers on fresh ground which is not all captured by the analytical tools that science provides us with.

These examples can simply be multiplied for thousands of social and geographical segments of the world and for thousands of types of activity that human beings do and are capable of. We are talking about knowledge in society. This is all *lokavidya* in its great variety. Every combination of a social segment, a geographical segment and an activity may give us a different combination of values, logic and method with fresh philosophical imports. It would be uninteresting to look for such values and methods of *lokavidya* which are universal in the sense of being applicable in the whole world of *lokavidya*. But *lokavidya* is universal in the sense that it is present everywhere. Where ever there is man/woman there is *lokavidya*. A slight investigation would show that even the most 'ignorant' parasites possess knowledge which has the capacity to do and deliver in everyday life. The best of scientists and professionals also have a large part of their knowledge derived from society or from sources other than the institutional frames in which they work. So, *lokavidya* is universal in this strong sense too that whether individuals are equipped with any formal organized knowledge or not, they always possess *lokavidya* of which they make a significant use in daily lives, in building relationships, in designing and strategizing their work and in understanding the world around them.

### 6.6.4 Logic of Lokavidya

As said above there is no single logic of *lokavidya*. However, since we are familiar with the logic of science it will add to clarity if we tried to look at some possible general features of understanding, explanation and structure in *lokavidya*. For example a modern scientific understanding of soil or plants demands knowledge of the chemical constitution of these things and then the observed qualities need to be related to the chemical constitution in a causal way. But a peasant's understanding is not based on analytical reduction into constituent simple parts but factors like colour, seasonal behaviour, uses it can be put to, etc. are part of it. Now, these factors are external for a scientist. It is not that the peasant's knowledge is more empirical and less grounded in universal theories but that his understanding is not based on isolating the subject matter from the rest of the world. On the contrary, things are seen as an integral part of a larger world in which relationship with other things, phenomena, human uses, etc. is not secondary to something which may be called its intrinsic or essential nature. In line with this, such knowledge is not amenable to a hierarchical structuring, so *lokavidya* also appears unorganized which it is if organization of knowledge can be done only on a deductive model, the way science is organized. If we want to use a modern term we can say that *lokavidya* follows the network logic of organization, nothing is above or below and there is no beginning or end even in principle. Knowledge of agriculture, water management, forestry, architecture, healthcare, industrial activity and everything else should all be related with one another, any one of these drawing understanding from many other areas without looking up or down to it. *Lokavidya* traditions are very large traditions of knowledge encompassing gradually all that there is while granting great autonomy to every aspect of it. The oft resorted practice of providing a rational scientific explanation to a peasant's knowledge or to an *adivasi*'s understanding or to a metal worker's method or even to the use of local plants in healthcare practices is an exercise which turns the epistemic humanity upside down, explains the living in terms of the dead.

### 6.6.5 The Dynamics of Lokavidya

Unfortunately even those who recognize the great fact of *lokavidya* see it as leftovers of the traditional knowledge or just as traditional knowledge which is drying up by the day. This understanding is alien to *lokavidya*. Man's epistemic capacities may withdraw, may become dormant because of oppressive external conditions, but to think that it is in some sense becoming leaner or drying up in some absolute sense is to be completely in error. It is in the nature of man to think, to innovate, to improve upon, to create according to his genius and according to the needs. In this process he seems to use both his theoretical understanding and his experiences. *Lokavidya* is born with man and conversely. In *lokavidya* theory and practice merge, knowledge and life become one. Changes in lifestyle, technology and ways of thinking are routinely assimilated in *lokavidya*. The greatest fact about *lokavidya* is that it resides in the *loka*, among the people.

Organized knowledge, its systems and methods come into existence in different times, their importance waning with the change of times. Whether it is *Yoga samhita* or *Nyaya vaisheshika* or whether it is *Navya nyaya* or modern logic, they are all subjected to such change. Science is not going to be an exception. All knowledge starts from *lokavidya* and must return to *lokavidya*. Aspects of organized knowledge that do not return to *lokavidya* lose all reference to humanity and turn *asuri*, where after they have no option but to perish. If science insists on the atomic bomb and if it insists on violating nature then its days have to be numbered. The world of knowledge needs to be reordered according to the values of *lokavidya*. But this demands transformation also into a society where there is no exploitation of man by man.

The Internet with its ever expanding virtual world gives an impression of according social dignity to what it calls traditional knowledge. Traditional knowledge may have more entries on the Internet than any other type of knowledge. The knowledge managers have set their eyes on the knowledge outside the university, with communities, with individuals, on informal knowledge. Media, entertainment, drug industry, food industry, the world of design, art products are all in it in a big way. The word is being spread that the new world recognizes knowledge with the people. It is not *lokavidya* that they are interested in, they only want pieces of knowledge which can be worked further to fit into their economic schemes. People's values, way of thinking, method of work, social accountabilities, nothing interests them. So whereas, the university had refused to recognize that there is knowledge at all with the people, the virtual world recognizes that there is knowledge with the people but brings it into the public domain in a completely truncated form.

These processes have just begun, they are not in any accomplished state. The fact that traditional knowledge has become a matter of public debate in a world when the house of knowledge is without a clear command is a condition of great significance. *Lokavidya* must find ways to assert and claim the place of command in the new dispensation.

### 6.7 Bauddhik Satyagraha

Let us look back in very brief and try to construct an arrow for the future. We first noticed the sweeping changes occurring in the world since the beginnings of Globalization, the Internet and the first Gulf War (1990) and in this context discussed the flux in the field of knowledge, the breaking of the received order in the world of knowledge. Our discussion covered the disturbance that science was experiencing, the emergence of the converging technologies, the rise of knowledge management from the virtual domain to increasingly claim the place of command in the world of knowledge and *lokavidya* the perennial source of strength of the people which ought to be seeing a historic opportunity to make a bid for a proper place for itself in the world of knowledge. Converging technologies embed knowledge in the technological endeavour. Knowledge management from the virtual domain weds knowledge to management. Science is unable to rise above its institutional framework. *Lokavidya* embedded as it is in practice finds the theoretical challenges from organized knowledge somewhat tall to handle. Knowledge that has been produced cannot be eliminated by corporate manoeuvre or by government decision or by decision in professional bodies however large and powerful they may be. The need of the times is a knowledge movement that apportions a just and rightful place to all streams of knowledge in society, a knowledge movement that reorders the world of knowledge and erects afresh the society-knowledge interface which has been so badly bruised and disfigured by the ever pushing economic powers and economic criteria. Will the dissenters of the university, social activists, political activists, constructive workers and all those working for emancipation of knowledge in their own ways like those engaged in struggles against the patents regime and activists from the Free and Open Source Software (FOSS) movement make a common cause to build such a knowledge movement? Should this knowledge movement take the form of a knowledge *satyagraha* whose basic set of values could be :

No method of production or management of knowledge to be accepted as superior to others. The world of knowledge ought to be free of hierarchies.

- To oppose privatization of knowledge.
- To oppose restrictions on peasants and artisans in the use of their knowledge for their life purposes.
- To give *lokavidya* the respect that any proper knowledge deserves irrespective of its market value under the present circumstances.
- To support struggles aimed at improvement of the economic value of *lokavidya*.
- To understand and oppose the expropriation of *lokavidya* by the corporations. Let us remember that all ex-situ storage and preservation of natural processes endangers its in-situ existence.

- To recognize and underline the limitations of the virtual domain as a location of knowledge activity.
- To oppose the false propaganda about the potential and capacities of the new technologies.
- Knowledge that destroys nature be refused the status of legitimate knowledge.
- Knowledge that creates a supra-natural realm be it through religion or through a virtual dispensation, be refused the status of legitimate knowledge.

# 7

# Towards a Gandhian Approach to Knowledge Politics*

*Sunil Sahasrabudhey*

## Introduction

This year (2008) the political atmosphere in India has warmed up due to the debate on the nuclear agreement with America and the proceedings in the parliament on the related confidence vote. Not only the larger parties but small political formations have also become active. There are issues of energy security, price of energy, fallout of nuclear enterprises and American designs and the ruling political establishment giving in to their strategic designs, this last also leading specifically to complicating this country's relationship with Islamic militancy, etc. On each one of these, sufficient arguments have appeared in the popular press both for and against the nuclear deal.

However it is important to note that in spite of the intensity of this debate, no serious questioning took place from a fundamental standpoint on the question of acceptability of nuclear energy from a human civilizational point of view. It is true that this question does not perhaps have the pressing nature of political or strategic questions. But the level of debates on climate change, bio-diversity, preservation of natural resources, renewable energy, etc. should have been expected to provide a reasonable context to raise this radical question.

---

* Paper written for a seminar on The Moral and Political Philosophy of Mahatma Gandhi, October, 2008 at the Department of Philosophy, University of Hyderabad.

The nuclear debate allows us to raise the question of technology and science in a somewhat bare form. Sixty-three years ago the United States dropped the atom bomb on Hiroshima and 'told' the world that what has taken shape in the name of human civilization in hundreds of thousands of years could be erased from the surface of the earth instantly. And that they are capable of doing it. Nuclear technology only poses in extreme form the question that all modern technology poses. Modern technology destroys nature in absolute terms. And let us not keep man out of nature, for countless men, women and their families have been eliminated in the course of mopping up of the natural resources from across the globe for this industry to develop and expand and in the course of capturing markets for this industry to sell its products.

Modern industry is power driven. It presupposes organization of energy at lightening speed. This is where the root of the evil seems to lie. Now we have organization of information and knowledge at lightening speeds. Should the destruction let loose by industry therefore be expected to assume radically new dimensions in the Information Age? The human question, properly speaking, is not about energy or information, it is about people and their lives. The energy and information concerns flow from lifestyle interests, class interests and interests of domination. And these interests express themselves in and through the market and the political arena. This is why across the market there is a common understanding of the energy crisis and need of advancement in the information technology. In the world of politics too there is convergence on both these and one will have to search hard to find a dissenting voice.

If the dead of Hiroshima are martyrs, then:

- What is the Gandhian polity of this era which addresses the issues of lifestyle, class interests and domination?
- How is the question of *lokavidya* relevant for such a polity?
- Is this a knowledge politics based on a people's knowledge movement?
- Will this politics bring man's relation with nature to the centre stage?

Since about 1990 the entire world is engulfed in a storm of change. Internet and the development of information technologies, privatization and liberalization of economies, international market, the new media and the entertainment industry, bio and nano-technologies, the reorganization of the cities and the American wars starting with the Gulf War underline the nature of this change.

Somewhere it seems that the information technologies are producing and reproducing the thread that weaves this change together. It is being claimed that a new era has begun, a knowledge era just as there was an industrial age. It is also being said that this change is shaping what may be called a knowledge society just as there have been in past industrial societies, religious societies, etc. Science no more seems to lead this knowledge show. Internet and along with it knowledge management seems to assume the command. *Lokavidya* also is on the way to recognition in the public domain.

At one end there are windfall profits and unprecedented accumulation of wealth. But at the other end, knowledge and development seem only to prepare the way for further pauperization of artisans, peasants, workers, women, the middle classes, small business people and the *adivasi* communities. All these people possess a great variety of knowledge and skills. But on the one hand such knowledge is being captured into the computers making it available to financial powers and on the other, commodities produced on the basis of such knowledge by its bearers fetch little in the market.

All political parties follow a model of development in which there is no place for eradication of poverty. There is a clear and distinct need of a new politics of change which keeps the interest of the poor and the outcast above everything else. Humankind is in need of a new political imagination. Is Gandhi, the greatest source of ideas for such a political imagination?

This article discusses the developing social logic of knowledge through a critical appreciation of the social locations of knowledge and the relations thereof, then takes a brief look at the resistances against the new order and then proceeds to investigate what could possibly be a Gandhian approach to a new political imagination.

### 7.1 The Question of Knowledge

Many people these days use the word 'knowledge' often apparently in ways in which it was not used before. These are mainly educated people, politicians, NGOs, finance managers and those active in the IT (Information Technology) sector. They talk about a 'knowledge-based society' and say that increasing use of IT, mainly computers, internet and the mobile leads to a 'knowledge-based society'. The extensive use of the word 'knowledge' and calling software knowledge products seems to take the idiom of 'knowledge-based society' into a tautological realm. The new terminology of knowledge industry, knowledge product, knowledge dialogue, knowledge platform, knowledge partnership, knowledge collaboration, knowledge management, knowledge bank, knowledge city and even a knowledge university and so on indicates a proliferation of the use of the word 'knowledge' such that it is almost compelling to think that a central role of knowledge is being accepted in methods of work and conceptualization. That, societies be knowledge-based is a welcome idea, but to go about it in a manner such that knowledge becomes inseparable from computers and internet, meaning 'where there is no computer there is no knowledge' is beyond one's imagination.

Modern society has all along been divided into two worlds—which have been named differently by people of different concerns and theoretical pursuits, for example rich and poor, West and East, centre and periphery, industrial and agricultural, urban and rural, the world of capital and the world of workers, imperialists and colonies, *pashimikrit* and *bahishkrit*, etc. Everybody accepts that two such worlds are there in this Information Age too, popularly understood through the phrase 'digital divide'. Alternatively the naming goes as netizens and citizens, network society and civil society or the virtual world and real world. In one there is wealth, connectivity, fun, entertainment and the support of the state. And in the other there are uncertainties, physical labour, unemployment and starvation deaths. One has access to IT and the other has no such access. So the new machine decides the nature of the new division. This time it is the 'knowledge machine'.

The industrial society led by science in the realm of knowledge did not recognize other forms of knowledge as legitimate knowledge and the ideologies of that period saw the world of capital as based on exploitation of labour. But now the Information Age is doing all its activity in the name of 'knowledge'. Society is being divided afresh in the name of knowledge and along with exploitation of labour, systems of exploitation of knowledge are shaping themselves. Ideologies of social change must now, therefore, confront the question of knowledge squarely. Liberation ideologies need to develop an understanding of the nature of relationship the paths of change should have with this knowledge question. This article makes an attempt at this.

To discuss the question of knowledge it is necessary that one frees herself or himself from the theoretical frameworks of the industrial society. These include both the bourgeois ideologies and the ideologies of social change. Not that we should not learn anything from them but only that their theoretical frameworks be avoided, that is, our thoughts need to be radically free from the logic and the conceptual apparatus of the Industrial Age.

Industrial society created a new god in the name of science. It was claimed that science is the absolute form of knowledge and methods of science are the only legitimate ways of acquiring and producing knowledge. It was said that science is independent of social values, culture, history, etc. In this manner with the help of science, industrial capitalism captured and cornered all power based on knowledge into its own hands. Knowledge in society, knowledge of peasants, artisans, workers, women and *adivasi* communities was simply denied the status of knowledge. Having made them an 'ignorant' lot, the idea of 'dignity of labour' was pressed into service to resurrect their humanity, if and when it was deemed necessary. Owing to exploitation, poverty and enslavement these people could not muster the strength required to publicly claim for their knowledge the status of genuine knowledge. Thus even ideologies of people-oriented societal change could not raise the question of knowledge.

In the last decades of the $20^{th}$ century, critiques of science started developing from many angles. Often the basis of such development was in the movements of women, peasants, artisans and other outcast communities. The ideas mostly derived their backing from *lokavidya,* the knowledge of the people in movement and the logic and values of such knowledge. However, by then the house of science was on its own moving towards a historic destabilization. Internet, its growth and spread, starting in 1990 quickly provided the basis to raise questions about science housing all the criteria of legitimacy of knowledge.

The Information Age refuses to acknowledge the absolute status of science in the world of knowledge. The industrial society had presented science as the 'search for truth'. Now utility and commerce appear more directly related with knowledge activity. Not that science was not related to commerce, in fact it had a deep relation with capital and commerce. But it was also related to 'search for truth'. Now there is no talk about 'truth'. Knowledge activity across the board is governed by a management standpoint.

Search for truth and production of knowledge are not the chief concerns of this so-called knowledge-based society. The technology of information and communication is mainly concerned about organization and communication. Now it does not matter who produced knowledge and how, whether it was done in a laboratory, in a university or in a distant village or in some community outside the pale of modern life. It does not matter whether the confirmed scientific methods were obeyed or not. For anything to be given the status of knowledge it is enough that it be organizable by the computer/internet. This indeed seems to be fast becoming a necessary criterion too.

The transition from content to organization and from production of communication has brought about a veritable storm in the world of knowledge and thought. Modern Western philosophy seems to have run its course. Information and communication technologies have the capacity to organize the stores of knowledge of different communities and this has opened a gateway for public recognition of such knowledge. However it is not difficult to see that this process can lead to fatal editing of the knowledge of these communities.

This way, new opportunities are there for the dignity of knowledge but these opportunities have their price tags. The logic of *lokavidya* is forced to adjust according to the logic of computers/internet, the logic of software and the unbound connectivity. In the process of being transported from the real world of people to the virtual world it may simply become something else. Also through storage in the computers and availability on the internet, it is placed at the disposal of others, companies, who have no interest in it other than using it for their purposes. Is this a new development in the relationship between *lokavidya* and organized knowledge or is humanity familiar with this dialectic in the historical course of the relationship between *lokavidya* and organized knowledge? History may be witness that from time to time parts of *lokavidya* get assimilated in organized knowledge according to the space-time specificities and then overtime return to the fold of *lokavidya* bringing with it more and in a more evolved form. So, one may expect that society is at least partly familiar with this dialectic and metamorphosis in the world of knowledge. However, this process today places the software form of knowledge in the control of persons and institutions, who have no concern for the larger society, there by making it distinctly possible that *lokavidya* is used against the people whose knowledge it is. Through such transformation of *lokavidya* into the virtual domain, it suffers further erosion due to the limited interest and viewpoint of the companies. This control and ownership of knowledge by somebody else, this alienation of knowledge, is born with the birth of the Information Age. That knowledge be free from such control and alienation is a condition for society to be free from exploitation and inequality. The struggle for emancipation of knowledge thus has twin starting points of public dignity of *lokavidya* and freedom of knowledge from the control of companies. This article is an attempt at laying bare the social logic of knowledge as it is developing at present with special focus on emancipation.

## 7.2 Types of Knowledge

Everybody knows that there are many types of knowledge. For example knowledge of healthcare, agriculture, chemical processes, physical sciences, solar system, mathematics, methods of teaching, organization, tradition, values, belief systems, etc. This is just to illustrate, for the list can be extended almost at will.

Any specific type of knowledge has a variety of people who specialize in it, the methods of understanding also exhibit a variety. For instance, peasants possess knowledge of agriculture and so do agricultural scientists. But both of them have very different methods of understanding. Modern doctors, *vaidyas*, homeopaths, *hakims* and many ordinary people possess knowledge of healthcare, cure and nutrition. They all have different ways of knowing and doing, their effectiveness varying with the nature of problems. Spiritual knowledge has a great variety toc. *Adivasi* communities living in and near forests seem to have a wider and finer spread of knowledge about forests than those specializing in botany or forestry. The two have very different approaches too. Art and architecture also lend themselves to a huge variation depending on geography, cultural heritage, etc. So, just as there are various types of knowledge, each type exhibits a variety of approaches, paradigms, concerns and values.

All types of knowledge do not command equal respect in society, nor are they seen as equal even from the prevalent philosophical standpoints. Compared to a peasant, an agricultural scientist earns several folds more and also commands much greater respect in society. The social and economic condition of forest specialists is incomparably better than that of the *adivasis*. The engineers earn much more money and respect than artisans or mechanics. Spiritual teachers also exhibit extreme hierarchy. Those teaching the deeper aspects of life to businessmen and the English-speaking world have a five star lifestyle. Who does not know the conditions of life of the spiritual teachers who move through the villages and often live in *ashrams* in remote areas? Why is there so much social inequality between various types of knowledge, methods of understanding and persons commanding these?

May be for clarity on this we need to understand the relationship that knowledge has with capital and political power. Is it true that knowledge which is closer to the people, which has widespread existence in society and which is available and accessible to a great majority, commands both less respect and less earning? Knowledge and methods of understanding that pave the way for and help in increasing the profits of business and those that concentrate power in the hands of a few, command social respect and economic returns.

Modern social development has incessantly tried to eliminate methods of knowing and doing which are closer to the people and generally belong to the people. In Europe and America where capitalism prospered at all costs, the great variety of knowledge traditions were almost completely eliminated. Science alone commanded respect as knowledge and now it has turned into a Frankenstein, witness the nuclear bomb and Climate Change. It seems that a variety of knowledge in society is a pre-condition for continued human existence with equity and respect. This requires a radical redefinition of the relationship of knowledge with capital and political power.

With the arrival of the computer and the internet the idea that all types of knowledge deserve public dignity is reborn. A claim is spreading that all types of knowledge are genuine knowledge and in a fundamental sense equal to one another. But the present economic system governed by vested interests does not let these paths to dignity open. For example-

a. Enterprises centred on computer/internet belong to corporations and/or are regulated by financial agencies, therefore they allow to open only those paths which serve their interests. Further, as the diversity of knowledge makes itself felt in the public domain, it also suffers destruction because the world of capital tends to monopolize whatever proves useful for them and in the process also works to remove it from its natural erstwhile locations.

b. Secondly, the computer-internet businesses require certain proficiency in English and this narrows severely the opening for the great majority of knowledgeable people.

To remove these economic and cultural obstacles is one of the central tasks of knowledge politics. In this alone lies the regeneration of social and economic dignity for all types of knowledge and methods of understanding.

### 7.3 Locations of Knowledge

There are four chief locations of knowledge in society. These are ordinary life, religious orders, university (modern educational institutions) and computer/internet. Broadly knowledge at these locations is respectively called *lokavidya,* religious or spiritual knowledge, science and knowledge management. Knowledge at these four places is different from one another, different in form, content, object, dynamics and philosophy. Understanding the challenges before a knowledge politics requires that we understand the mutual relationships of these locations of knowledge.

Society witnesses a variety of competitions, claims of being one up or a step ahead, all the time. In politics and in economic and religious spheres such competitions are a common place. Similarly the world of knowledge also houses a competitive atmosphere. Different locations of knowledge keep making claims of being higher or more true as compared to others. However just as in religion, economics or politics, such competitions are not in the interest of the people and are generally guided by personal, narrow and vested interests. Similarly such competition in the world of knowledge too does not serve the interest of society, rather creates a vicious and demeaning atmosphere. This discussion of locations of knowledge and their mutual relationships is intended to produce an understanding of how these relationships be based on cooperation to lay a wider knowledge basis to live up to the challenges of the new age.

*Lokavidya* is the knowledge spread in the entire society. Peasants, artisans, women, *adivasis,* small business people, healthcare workers, all have their knowledge and their teachers, social leaders, saints and mahatmas keep giving them the philosophy of their knowledge too. Peasants do not get their knowledge from an agricultural university or artisans from a college of engineering. *Adivasis* do not undergo a forest training. The small business people may not even know that management and entrepreneurship have formal trainings. Do women learn cooking or bringing up of children in some school? All these people do their work with a degree of competence without ever going through any formal training. They are simple folk not having any animosity towards other locations of knowledge. Those from the university think that these people are ignorant. But these people when they come into contact with those from the university take from them whatever is useful or worth taking from their point of view. Is it not possible that the university accords *lokavidya* the same respect that ordinary life accords to the university?

Religious orders are somewhat isolated from the point of view of knowledge. They are not able to build a positive relationship with either the university or the ordinary people. People's religious thinking is mixed with *lokavidya* and is somewhat distant from the religious orders. People's religious beliefs and practices (*lokadharma*) seem to have the same qualities as *lokavidya*. *Lokadharma* like *lokavidya* is guided by need, experience, logic and wisdom and its windows are always open for fresh winds. The knowledge of religious orders is communal too like their social philosophies. So, this knowledge generally remains isolated from ordinary people and their lives making it especially suitable for serving the anti-people forces and communal practices. There should be pressure on the religious orders to test their knowledge on the criteria of *lokavidya* and bring about desired changes.

As a location of knowledge universities command the highest respect. These are the most widespread formal centres of knowledge activity, mainly production and distribution of knowledge. Reaching a university is a high point of the aspirations of the youth. However, there is not enough place there for most. The idea of knowledge too in the university is under an all round influence of science. Departments of engineering, arts, social science, history, all the departments, claim for their knowledge activity the status of science. As a result students acquire values which accord a rather low status to *lokavidya*. However, the spread of the Computer-Internet and the newly acquired dynamics of *lokavidya* have erected a challenge before the university to redefine its place in the world of knowledge. The university needs to develop positive relationships both with *lokavidya* and the new media. These would help end the narrowness in the activities of knowledge.

Computer-Internet is the new location of knowledge. A new science is growing in the name of knowledge management (KM). The self-acclaimed status of KM and the support it receives from the world of finance and political power has produced great turbulence in the world of knowledge. Three things are especially worth noting—

- It does not accord to science the highest place in the world of knowledge and does not accept the university as the chief location of knowledge.
- It gives status of knowledge to *lokavidya*. People declared ignorant by the university thus acquire a new status as those possessing knowledge.
- It does not adopt the standpoint of truth towards knowledge but develops and elevates to a new high the utilitarian standpoint.

These three are connected and the consequences are there for everybody to see. The university and the knowledge activity there seeks assistance from the state and is guided by the modern lifestyles. Now the transnational corporations also have explicit relations with the university. A huge store of knowledge has been created on the internet in the name of traditional knowledge and there is a debate on who is and should be the owner of this knowledge.

The big question is how should the youth from the households of *lokavidya* respond to this situation? There is pressure from the market to develop competencies to make a place for oneself in the evolving situation. And there is 'demand' from the larger society to serve its interests and develop forms of struggle that change the relationships between different locations of knowledge. There is inner falsehood in thinking that spending time on the computer or in a laboratory is something great compared to the life of a peasant or an artisan. One has money in it the other does not. That is all the difference. And this difference too is not natural in any sense, it is entirely artificial. It is a historic task before the youth from the households of *lokavidya* and before all those well meaning people who wish to stand for justice that the relationship between various locations of knowledge be altered radically. This is the task of a knowledge politics which emancipates knowledge from the clutches of the state, capital and the English language.

## 7.4 Production of Knowledge

Social change and production of knowledge are two faces of the same coin. New knowledge causes new situations and development of new situations demand production of new knowledge. Locations of knowledge in society are also the places where production of new knowledge takes place. Changes in climate, raw materials, technique, market, patterns of ownership or any other aspect of the economic system demands new methods of production, new arrangements and production of new knowledge and when new knowledge comes into existence it demands changes in various factors and components of the economic system. This is not true only about economics. The political, the cultural or any other social arena would also reflect a similar dialectic between changes in the area under consideration and production of new knowledge related to it. Broadly speaking production of new knowledge which spans the full spectrum from marginal changes to radically new knowledge is strongly related to four types of human mediations—needs, experience, wisdom and rational inference.

Peasants, artisans, scientists, teachers, political and cultural activists, all engage in production of new knowledge in response to given needs, based on their and other's experiences and by using their faculties of wisdom and rational inference. This involves adding something new and removing or dropping what may have become irrelevant.

Universities are the well-known places where new knowledge is produced. According to the needs of the nation and based on certain expertise and political commitments the government prepares policies which often require knowledge which is not readily available. Such demand is placed before the universities, and resources are allocated so that scientists and researchers may produce the desired new knowledge on the basis of the experiences of the world of science (generally published work) and their faculties of rational and scientific inference. Needs of the nation could relate to any area like agriculture, energy, irrigation, textile, defence, electronics, software, anything. According to the need, the knowledgeable get at work and produce new knowledge.

In a certain sense peasants and artisans also do the same. If the wood changes the toy makers change their methods. The advent of plastic, created new methods of production. When fuel changes, the construction of the furnace changes to produce the desired temperature. If irrigation facilities decrease or increase, patterns of crop rotation change. If the seeds change, a number of components of agricultural production change in detail. According to the market demand agricultural produce is even managed totally out of season. New practices do not sustain without a knowledge basis. That is practices that are time-tested must be based on sound knowledge. It will be a great mistake to see production by peasants and artisans only as practice, technique or accumulated information. Such propaganda greatly lowers the position of the peasants and artisans in society. It is important to understand that agriculture and household industrial production are both knowledge-based activities. And those who engage in these activities constantly renew their knowledge basis and produce new knowledge based on their needs, experiences, concerns and methods of rational inference.

Production of knowledge has two chief components, experiment and cooperation. Universities and research institutions have laboratories. Those who command similar and relevant knowledge cooperate to do experiments. Both these activities are lifted to a new high with the advent of computers. The computer on the basis of its speed of computation is often able to tell in advance which experiments are not likely to give results. Results of an experiment cannot of course be known in advance by the computer but it surely helps in identifying experimental courses that are likely to give results. The internet has made possible cooperation and collaboration on the world scale.

Experiments, by the way, are done by peasants and artisans too. Mutual cooperation is also common. Although neither is easily visible to the outsider because these activities by them take place within a household, village or community. Because of these limitations their experiments and the extent of co-operation is also limited. However, their process of knowledge production in a definite sense integrates within itself the interest and concern of the poor. Mostly these experiments and collaborations have a defensive orientation and occur as activities to save or protect from the aggression of the larger players, corporations and the global market. If the process of production of knowledge in the fields and domestic enterprises can transcend the boundaries of family, village and community then a revolutionary process of expansion and growth of *lokavidya* can come into existence. Thus the tall but specific order is to break on the one hand, the forcing conditions of capital, market and profit and on the other transcend the boundaries of the village and the community.

Knowledge management is the new knowledge that is being produced in the green rooms of the computer-internet businesses. It tries to connect in one link all the locations and types of knowledge. It gives an impression that it is free from the compulsions of capital and market. May be for a small part of it, it is truly so. It has the capacity to help peasants and artisans to transcend the limits of village and community but that requires localisation (of software) on a big scale. If the computer is in people's language (Hindi, Marathi, Telugu, Bengali,... etc.) and a correct knowledge politics is given shape to, then the production of knowledge in villages, in fields, in household industries, in forests, in a variety of social activity and in the universities and research institutions can all be connected with a positive approach leading to innovation that interests the entire society, poor included.

## 7.5 Organization of Knowledge

Organization of knowledge has been at the centre of discussion since the advent of computers. Computers organize huge amounts of information which is accessible to very quick retrieval. Over the years almost everything under the sun and beyond it has found a place in the storages the computer has created. The difference between knowledge and information as a result, has been a subject of serious discussion. Information found a theoretical place for itself mainly owing to the post-war theories of communication. These are mathematical theories and information has been mathematically defined too. Naturally there is a serious problem if the difference between knowledge and information is not underlined. Ordinarily information is part of knowledge but to say that it itself is knowledge is surely problematic. The common objection is that in knowledge there is an element of understanding, values and a point of view, whereas information is closer to being neutral to these. The debate is both philosophical and of consequence to daily life. Such debates probably do not go to a conclusion and the meanings in which the words are used more and more extensively mostly stay and other takes are forced to back seats. May be it has happened before when science appeared on the scene with a claim to a mechanical explanation of the movement in the universe. There were a variety of knowledge streams already present in society which had an explicit relation with human beings and had explicit social values. The new science was theoretically value neutral and indifferent towards human interests. Therefore, it must not have been easy for it to ascend to a status of knowledge. However, over time it spread worldwide and also claimed the status of the highest form of knowledge. In this age of information, information is pressing to spread over the entire world of knowledge. The situation must be taken seriously and the challenges accepted by those who wish to build a just world.

Organization of knowledge in the computers opened a way for recognizing the variety of knowledge in society which was treated as outcast and strictly not up to the mark in the age of science. Knowledge of agriculture, forestry, industry, healthcare, design, art and management, etc. which is there with the people is slowly getting loaded on the computer. A speciality of such knowledge has been that those who possess such knowledge have a value-laden understanding of the world and therefore their knowledge activity kept environmental and ecological considerations as first concerns. When such knowledge is organized in computers as information accessible to anybody, values associated with their use earlier, shall cease to be respected. In one word, traditional knowledge will be available on a large scale for use by the capitalist enterprises. This has opened new ways for exploitation of knowledge. What ideas are there in society today which can face up to this situation.

Knowledge was organized before the advent of the computer too. Science and earlier traditions had found written expressions. Knowledge was organized in books, in research journals, through the medium of publication, in hand-written manuscripts and if we go further back by writing on copper plates or stones and in oral traditions. The written material was made available by building libraries. Even today however, writing is not a precondition for organization of knowledge. For example, *lokavidya* is largely unwritten but if the knowledge of peasants, artisans, *adivasis* or women was entirely unorganized then how is it that it has been taught to the following generations and how is it that it improves constantly in the face of new demands and new conditions? The local society seems to have a different concept of organization. As it is the written word unlike Europe did not dominate the knowledge scene in our society. We did not write our history and even major commercial agreements used to be based on the word of month. Thinking in the context of *lokavidya* and the society which lives by it, we need to avoid the organizational traps that the modern world has laid. *Lokavidya* is in need of an organization which is situated among the people and belongs to the public domain. Caste, community, family, even village in a certain sense are not the public domain. Whereas *gram-panchayat* is and so is the rural market. *Lokavidya* for its organization requires a new institutional form, say a *Gyan panchayat* in a locality. This would be a serious beginning of the knowledge politics of the people.

## 7.6 Privatization of Knowledge

Right from the beginning of the Information Age knowledge is taking the form of private property. It may appear strange to those who are not familiar with the new trends because no popular ways of thinking or social ideologies have place for conceptualizing knowledge as private property. How can knowledge be unto oneself? It used to be said that knowledge flowers with sharing. But now it is being said that if knowledge is private property, there is incentive for improvement and innovation. Privatization of knowledge, however, forecloses options and spaces that are otherwise available for growth and progress of knowledge but on the other hand it is becoming a source of great accumulation of wealth in a few hands. Privatization however is facing challenges from within the world of information itself. The campaign of Free and Open Source Software (FOSS) challenges such privatization in a definite sense.

Patent laws provide the juridical arrangement for privatization of knowledge. Almost all the countries have such patent laws now. Commodities, methods of making them, knowledge of these processes and all kinds of software from those of scientific research to entertainment are covered by these laws. Anything that has been patented is available for use by others only in a format prescribed by those who hold the patents. Often strictly personal and private use is also prohibited. You cannot make a copy of such software or give it to somebody else to use, nor can you improve it even for personal use. Without getting into the technical details of the law, one can perhaps say that this is the policy in vogue to limit all knowledge that can fetch reasonable returns into the hands of a small rich minority.

There is a big debate on whose property should *lokavidya* be considered. It is called traditional knowledge and there is competition to lay hands on it. Patent debates on *Basamati* rice, *Neem* and Turmeric have reached most of us. International companies make small changes in the knowledge in society where it makes sense from the point of view of the competitive edge in the market and claim that it is their discovery to bring it into the purview of the patent laws and go ahead and patent it. When they do such a thing, it is not easy to challenge legally. The struggle against turmeric patent had to be carried to the courts of law in France. It is beyond ordinary people and their organizations to acquire patents in Europe and America and fight legal battles in those lands. The chief question is whose property should traditional knowledge be considered. There is a definite view that the community possessing such knowledge should be the one whose property it is. But such communities do not have legal identity. So, should such knowledge be beyond patenting? It is also possible to create a legally identifiable organizational identity for these communities to enable them to enter the world of patents. 'Patent' is the chief weapon of privatization of knowledge and it is not possible to face up to it on grounds of international law and the world market. What is called traditional knowledge is actually *lokavidya*—a source of imagination for a new world altogether. It is the struggle for a new and just world which will include fighting privatization of knowledge as one of its constituents.

Privatization of knowledge has become so important due to the new networks of worldwide communication and connectivity. It is more than 200 years ago that the idea of patent took shape in Europe. With it came into existence the theory and practice of the private ownership of means of production. Then it became the source of exploitation of labour and accumulation of huge properties. Socialism erected a challenge and the world was engulfed in struggles against private property, revolutionary changes took place, new systems of society were inaugurated. Now computers, communications and the internet have started building a new world which has added exploitation of knowledge to the already existing exploitation of labour. The new patent laws are giving a concrete and secure form to the privatization of knowledge. Emancipation of knowledge is the central conception around which struggles opposing privatization of knowledge can take place.

Universities and research institutions across the world are undergoing major changes. Higher education everywhere is being so organized that the graduates will not be knowledgeable persons but knowledge products to be used by the corporations. Reform in education means only this. Privatization of schools, colleges and universities leads in a big way to privatization of knowledge and this in turn prepares the principles and basis for privatization of education. Teachers, researchers and students who see knowledge as a natural quality of man should be in the forefront of a movement for emancipation of knowledge.

Emancipation of knowledge is a key idea in the knowledge

politics of the people. Peasants, artisans, activists of free and open source software, those fighting against patents and patent laws and those opposing privatization of schools, colleges and universities all need to come together to shape the idea and practice of emancipation of knowledge.

## 7.7 Control on Knowledge

Knowledge and activity related to it are not free today. We are not free to use our knowledge as we might wish. It is natural to think that there should be social controls on such freedoms so that they cannot be used to give trouble to others or to exploit others. But the control today is not guided by any such thoughts. On the contrary there is freedom of exploitation but if you wish to use your knowledge for livelihood purposes or to help others then you may face various obstacles resulting from laws of the land. For example if you have obtained your knowledge of healthcare from your elders or from others in the community then you cannot use it for health security of others, not even for your own livelihood. If you do so, you will be violating certain laws and your actions shall be punishable by the courts of justice.

There are detailed laws pertaining to the use of knowledge and resources. Some laws straight away stop you from using your knowledge and some put constraints on the use of resources. Constraints on the use of resources amount to constraints on the use of knowledge because the knowledge of use of such resources becomes lame in the absence of permission to use those resources. For example, there are detailed laws governing the use of minerals. Those *adivasi* communities who have the knowledge of processing these minerals have been denied the use of their knowledge for their own livelihoods by such laws. The *Agaria adivasis* of Central India have kept alive as their knowledge the very famous ferrous technology of this land. Their techniques, involving mini-furnaces, can extract the metal from ores which are too low grade for the blast furnaces. But the laws of the land forbid them from carrying out their smelting exercises which are on a very small scale and this in spite of the crushing poverty they live in. This is the situation with a variety of minerals and forest produce. Agriculture in this period of globalization is increasingly becoming the target of such restrictions. The seed law has been widely debated for the restrictions it imposes on the farmers in respect of production, use, sowing and marketing of seeds. Tomorrow there will be laws relating to the system of irrigation. Further, agro-processing too suffers from a host of restrictive bye-laws. If we are not allowed to operate a small cane crusher to make jaggery (*gur*) in the vicinity of a sugar mill then it amounts to restricting the use of knowledge of making jaggery and promoting the knowledge of industrial production of sugar. Knowledge in society related to forests, minerals, agriculture, artisanry and healthcare suffers from wide ranging legal restrictions. Such restrictions are spreading their tentacles in newer and newer areas in the Information Age. But this is only one way of controlling the use of knowledge. There are other ways of exercising such control. Very often even if there are no legal restrictions people are deprived from using their knowledge because of artificial and commercially created unavailability of resources. For instance, absence of power leads to uprooting of household industries and unavailability of water or fertilizers leads to very restricted agricultural practices. Such is the case also in the areas of education, market and information.

The educational sector in so organized that only those reaching higher education acquire knowledge. Simple competencies involving counting, multiplication tables, correct use of everyday language and elementary knowledge of one's surroundings which should be imparted to everybody are also not there in the lot of a very large number. So the national debate heavily relates to the quality and quantity of primary education. The question of control of knowledge is more explicit in the arena of higher education. Just as the buyers of flats in the high-rise buildings are those who already own residences in the cities, similarly the entrants to the good universities, medical and engineering colleges are mostly such students who come from families of the higher educated and the English speaking with mostly at least upper middle class status. This is how knowledge flowing from higher education has been circumscribed. If in the 1950s and 60s children from the rural background could go for science education, why is it not possible today? There are no laws stopping them.

But the entire system through competition, etc. has taken such a turn that children from poor households and rural backgrounds can hardly ever reach genuine higher education. Now, the sky-rocketing fees have further tightened the interstices that were sometimes mapped by some with a poor background. Those coming out through this higher education walk straight into a world of high salaries. They are free to use their knowledge to build institutions, enterprises and consultancies, bring finance from wherever they can and invest to exploit whoever and whatever they can. The high knowledge of science, computers, communication, media, law and medicine and some other domains has started defining a new class. A system has been developed such that this knowledge stays within this class.

The market strengthens those processes of control on knowledge, which take shape as a result of government policy, laws and the educational system. If the malls multiply then the knowledge and art of textiles and food products will be greatly controlled by the businessmen at the malls. Most people will be out of work and only a small number of artisans will be in business. If all the commodities in a rural market, metal, oil, cloth, rope, cold drinks, soap, biscuits, everything comes from distant places the local industries will be uprooted. It has already come to pass. There are two chief consequences of this. First, income of the artisans takes a beating and second, the related knowledge becomes static and loose. One affects physical life and the other has a spiritual and psychological effect. The two are of course strongly related. If our knowledge becomes useless because of strong control and restrictions then our lifeline starts drying up. We do not only become unemployed we become useless and idlers.

The Information Age has made great advances in the world of knowledge. New techniques of organization, communication and management have come into existence. A new science seems to be in the making. So far it is the tip of higher education. Very few people reach there. There is propaganda that there will be computers in every village and in every market, however, those sitting on these computers will only be serving others and since everything will be in English, there will be very limited scope for them to use their imagination. It is one thing that the computer reaches out and another that the science of computers reaches out. We will become new technicians, typists and clerks. We will do photo, e-mail and railway bookings. Tasks will multiply but we shall remain workers or at best a very small business person. The new science will remain out of reach and we will only be a cog in the machine that creates a new class of consumers. Information science is something that many even in higher education do not know anything about. It is the knowledge basis of the new transnational order. Any knowledge politics of the people will have to take the sting out of this new snob.

### 7.8 Knowledge Management

Knowledge management is a radically new idea. With the advent of Computer-Internet and development of new connectivity which establish contact at lightening speed, a situation has developed where very quick access to desired knowledge has become possible. Knowledge management has made its entry to make this possibility a reality. Knowledge management as will be explained shortly needs to be distinguished from management of knowledge. Management of knowledge has occurred all along and happens today too everywhere. For example:

1. Schools and colleges are the obvious places that come to one's mind. Management of knowledge here involves its division into various disciplines, imparting knowledge to students, distinguishing between abstract and applied knowledge, connecting abstract knowledge to research activity and application-oriented knowledge to production processes, etc.
2. Peasants and artisans too indulge in management of knowledge. Cooperation, exchange, learning from each other, training new generations, etc. about technology and processes, implements and raw materials, market dynamics and government policies, etc. can be said to be part of management of knowledge by these people.

3. *Adivasi* communities have their methods of management of knowledge. Some of them may even have practical forms which can be called a *gyan panchayat*.

Areas like health, art, entertainment, etc. would have their own ways of management of knowledge in their specific domains. But when one talks about knowledge management none of these are on the table.

Knowledge management of the present was born to fulfil a need of large corporations. Large corporations have various departments who need to be strongly connected. Knowledge produced in different departments during the course of their activity needs to be available for efficient carrying out of activities elsewhere in the corporation, it could be overseas or it could be in a department which hardly ever comes into contact with it. For this, all knowledge internal to the corporation needs to be organized and stored online in specific desired ways. Apart from speedy access to desired destinations in general, there need to be installed methods which take into account things like context, purpose, etc. Need points should be efficiently connectable to where the source of needed knowledge is. Now this is a tall order. But knowledge management is a tall order. However, if it was restricted to only intra-corporation situations it would not be of great interest to us or to the world in general. It has spilled over. In tune with the proliferation of the knowledge terminology the use of the phrase 'knowledge management' is proliferating too. Wherever you have a knowledge activity, whether it is knowledge production, knowledge bank, knowledge platform, knowledge collaboration, knowledge partnership, knowledge distribution or anything else, you will also have knowledge management there. Though, it may also be true that use of the phrase 'knowledge management' at different places may not have the same meaning. A friend in the domain tells me that knowledge management may have been given fifty definitions by now. But what is undeniable is its spreading presence with the assumption of a command position wherever it goes. So let us try to investigate the situation a little deeper.

The worldwide web (www) has created a new world, the virtual world. Activities in the virtual world have ever been on the increase. From search, retrieval and access to dialogue co-operation, fighting, working together, even love-making is there in the virtual world. There are virtual communities and there are virtual experiments. The domain experts and the internet addicts can tell us much more about what all is possible in the virtual domain and how powerful it is for shaping human minds, relations and destinies. Knowledge management in the larger sense is the theory and practice of this virtual world. It may come to pass that KM actually becomes the name of this new science or may be a new name would replace it. Nevertheless a new science is born, the science of the virtual world.

Is the virtual world a world of representations? Or is this world a world of information? Is this world a world of lightening connections or such connectivity is only an instrument of creation of this world? The question of representation and its relation with reality had already moved to the centre of philosophical discourse through debates on post-modernity. But in and through the virtual world it appears in a totally new incarnation. Qualitatively at a higher plane it strengthens the claim that representations are no mere reflections, images, creations or descriptions, but in some sense more real. One can even argue that science itself is a representation, that all ideas are representations and their acceptability depends on relations of power, utility, ethical and aesthetic considerations etc. and not on what 'truly' the reality is which in itself is anyway a historical construct. One can make a case that aesthetic and ethical norms are as much applicable to the virtual world as they are to the so-called real world. It may be a less or more moral world but it is not non-moral. It may be less or more beautiful in almost the same sense of beauty which we use in our day-to-day life. Seen from a slightly different angle the virtual world is a world of information. With this meaning of information, my photograph is a piece of information about me. Laws of physics are information about the physical world. The advantages and disadvantages of the essences of certain plants and flowers is information about the botanical world and the field of healthcare. An artisan's ideas on design are information for an artist engaged in computer-aided design. So, it seems that KM transforms knowledge into information and the world of knowledge finds its representation in a world of information which calls itself a world of knowledge.

Thus, KM is not a discipline of management, but it is a new kind of knowledge that places itself at the top, for it manages all types of knowledge. This is part of the process of the shaping of the virtual world. KM is both the rationale and the fruit of the virtual world which is tending to become the new location of epistemic power and also inching towards claiming to redefine society, humanity, nature. In one word, a new world, a new science and a new philosophy are born. It is just the beginning, so we too can take only a preliminary view of it. It is too close to allow high resolution.

Lately, there has been a move afoot to build a new frontier of technologies, called Converging Technologies, which would devote themselves chiefly to improve human performance. Science as the science of nature with the associated technologies made a claim in theory and proceeded in practice to improve the performance of nature. The result was disorganization of societies and their exploitation worldwide resulting into abject poverty and death for hundreds of millions. And now the manipulation of nature threatens life on the earth, courtesy nuclear technology and the Climate Change. Now the converging technologies, viz. information technology, bio-technology, nano-technology and cognitive science are attempted to be merged into one to proceed to improve human performance. The project, not without reason, compares itself with the take-off, of industries with the steam engine and fears death of hundreds of millions as the sacrifice in the process of attaining the 'lofty' deliverables. The four technologies mentioned have very different knowledge bases from one another and there is no concern for tying them together with a common epistemic framework. What holds them together then? KM. Knowledge management alone has both the width and the cutting edge to provide the required unity.

A huge and epoch-making conflict is underway in the world of knowledge for contention for the place of command and therefore, on what would hence forward order the world of knowledge. The direction of the shift from science to KM tends to break the hierarchies of the old house of knowledge. Arts, management, design and software activities fetch greater value and have high esteem in the public realm than scientific and industrial activity. But their moving up inevitably changes the concept of knowledge we have become so familiar with through the age of science. Are language and creativity superior knowledge habitats than the scientific experiment and the theories of nature? Are we mistaken in thinking that the world in the ultimate analysis consists of things and forces? Is building scientific theory a very limited exercise and has largely run its course of usefulness to humanity? Is the virtual world and its theory, KM, on a world historic mission?

It seems that, through KM, the new dispensation is engaged in a double game with respect to people's knowledge traditions, *lokavidya*. Through recognition of the knowledge in society with peasants, artisans, women and *adivasi* communities a large coalition of epistemic forces is built against the domineering position of science. But along with it KM provides the epistemic wherewithal for the exploitation of the same knowledge with the people in the interest of powers that be. It is the task of a new knowledge politics to produce that unity within the knowledge in society and its bearers to challenge any uncontested position for KM.

## 7.9 Exploitation of Knowledge

The basis of the Information Age lies in exploitation of knowledge. Interests of corporations, the structure of the market and government policies bring about exploitation of all forms of knowledge. Information and communication technology is the largest instrument in the service of such exploitation. Exploitation of knowledge now accompanies exploitation of labour to weave the basis of a new type of capitalism. This section tries to cover various forms that this exploitation assumes in the cases of university knowledge, science, arts, *lokavidya* and knowledge as software.

### *7.9.1 Exploitation of Lokavidya*

*Lokavidya,* albeit in a truncated form, is being collected in the virtual domain and made available for unrestricted use. Peasants, artisans, women and *adivasis* have all kinds of knowledge. Relating to nature such knowledge is related to diverse bio-processes, healthcare, cattle, plants, leaves, flowers, roots and much more. Knowledge of production of goods, their physical and chemical qualities is another area. Art forms constitute another world by themselves. All this is collected mostly through dialogues and stored in the computers. This is known as traditional knowledge and is mostly available as information on line. A lot of it may be available free on the internet but a sizeable part remains with the agencies to develop competitive products for the market. The freedom on the internet is something like freedom in the open market. In reality these places work highly disproportionately to the advantage of the larger parties. Many commodities, processes and methods of use often undergo cosmetic changes so that their patents can be obtained. Huge debates take place on traditional knowledge. Who owns it? How should patent laws apply in such cases? How important is it to maintain the original values through variety of transference? What is the relation of such values with that knowledge and its owners are some of the issues which have been important.

Many think that once the knowledge of peasants, artisans, women or of any specific community reaches the companies and corporations and they find competitive uses for it, then it is inevitable that such arrangements (laws, policies) would come into existence such that that knowledge would in a generation or two disappear from those who may have preserved it and renewed and shaped it through generations. There has been discussion on how indulgence by the companies endangers bio-diversity, how environment and ecology suffer irrevocably and how even human life may face extinction. However, there is little discussion on how this constitutes the exploitation of *lokavidya* and how exploitation of knowledge is fast evolving as a support base of the information age. Evolution of knowledge politics of the poor and the ordinary people requires that this situation be understood as exploitation of knowledge.

The world of art is another victim in the exploitation of *lokavidya*. Cultural production is shaping itself as an autonomous structure of production. Popular songs, their tunes, their lyrics, textile designs, use of colours, and even the *rangolis* made before innumerable houses every morning and much more that constitutes local and popular art forms and enterprise have invited the gaze of the investors. Everything that constitutes popular art, the specific tasks they perform, programmes they organize, their imagination and methods of exhibition, everything has a use value in the highly competitive market of entertainment that is developing. Whether you call it theft, piracy, imitation, fraud, enterprise, entrepreneurship or imaginativeness depends on your point of view. Thus new technologies and new lifestyles have carved out a competitive place for people's art and local art in the sphere of cultural production but this through an entirely exploitative process. Huge returns are reaped by the agencies with precious little flowing back to the original artist or the communities.

It is not that cultural production has value only for the entertainment market. For everything from designing a website to making utensils, textiles, wooden and leather products and things both of use and decoration *lokakala* (*lokavidya*) has assumed a new role. It is being seen as a major resource for a competitive place in the market. The specialists do get returns piece-wise or on jobs better than their neighbours. This is common for sari designers, for those who have an eye for healthy leather and for those who have high art in the making of handicrafts. These people do get an extra rupee compared to others in their community, but occupy a negligible corner in the account books of the company. The exploitation of *lokavidya* exhibits as much diversity as there is in the international market or in *lokavidya* itself.

The market is directly the place of exploitation of knowledge of production of peasants and artisans. Strictly speaking their knowledge is not traditional knowledge, but it is a judicious combination of certain traditions of knowledge with modern knowledge, latest techniques. They have both traditional and modern resources in a limited form. Modern technology often reaches them in the form of a package. Their characteristic understanding lies in an imaginative proportion of all the factors of production, different forms of knowledge included. Constraints of social relations including social security, their own beliefs and economic compulsions weave that domain where he or she must deliver on the terms of the market. It is this holistic understanding and capacity that enables a marginal farmer, a potter, a carpenter, a shoe-maker, a weaver, a sculptor, a ring-maker, a vessel-forger and artisans that make toys from plastic, wood or mud to survive with their families. And let us not forget that they also fail to survive because in the market they never get returns that are compatible with a minimal life. The conditions of exchange in the market shape the system of exploitation of *lokavidya.*

With the new technology new ways have come into existence for collecting information on the market and for connecting with the market. There is the propaganda that small peasants will gain through this phenomenon. The information on the prices will be obtainable from the internet or on the mobile and then the peasants will be able to decide where to sell etc. But it is not clear how small peasants can benefit from this. On the contrary one can argue that the new system will work to the advantage of the larger parties. Also if there are greater uncertainties as a result of globalization the brunt will inevitably be felt maximum at the lowest end.

The social and political activists need to understand that all this is not just a matter of market or technology but the point is that the entire system is a system of exploitation of *lokavidya.* What is being called a neo-liberal economy is configuring the market and the technology such that the knowledge of peasants and artisans could be exploited systematically and consistently. The struggle against such exploitation involves struggle for social and economic dignity of *lokavidya* and also building an alternative dynamic of *lokavidya.* The third Congress on Traditional Sciences and Technologies of India called the *Lokavidya Mahadhiveshan* held in Varanasi in 1998 had laid the foundations of such a struggle.

### *7.9.2 Exploitation of University Knowledge*

Steadily now the companies are taking over the control of

production and distribution of knowledge (research and education) at the university. The debate on higher education is a proof of this. Almost the entire debate is on the quality of higher education. The companies say that the graduates from the universities and the professional colleges are in very great measure unemployable because their knowledge, skills or capacities are far too limited. So, improvement of quality in higher education is a precondition for the progress of companies without which higher rates of growth are not achievable. The debate on reservations in higher education does not take a turn towards asking how larger and larger numbers from the disadvantaged strata of society can get higher education but gravitates towards the question of quality in higher education. The entire debate almost converges on how the companies can exploit the knowledge in the universities, that is press this knowledge into their service, even if it is being carried out in the name of employment, jobs or economic progress of the nation.

The absence of quality is said to be due to absence of good teachers. The reason given for the absence of good teachers is that the remuneration in the universities is much less compared to that in the companies. The professors in the university get more than Rs. 50,000 per month and are provided with lifelong economic security. Health and education facilities for the family also come with it. It is being said that this return needs to increase threefold to retain competence in the teaching staff. Then quality of education would improve, graduates would have higher competence, they will be eligible for jobs in the companies, companies shall compete globally and the nation would progress fast. This means the universities should command much greater resources and the only way this can happen is by substantially increasing fees. The fees in the private engineering colleges would need to increase at least threefold. The net result would be that the companies would progress and higher education will move outside the reach of even the middle classes.

Systems based on exploitation of university knowledge would always be such that very few people get into higher education and the educated individual is a product to be used by the companies. It makes all the difference whether knowledge is considered a resource for exploitation or is it considered a resource and an instrument for a just reconstruction of the individual and society. If knowledge is considered a subject of exploitation then the place of science, arts, philosophy and society will steadily become weaker and weaker and higher education will focus on management, engineering, medical, computer and communications, media, law and the like.

Earlier too the knowledge in the university steered clear of the human concern. Science shaped that idea of knowledge in which human values had no place in it. This facilitated the process of turning knowledge into a subject of exploitation. Values of science too, like the criteria of experiment and search of truth were completely marginalized. Now principles of utility are applicable to knowledge and this principle in capitalism takes the form of the principle of exploitation.

The places of advanced research in science in the world talk about technology now. Information technology, nano-technology and bio-technology sweep the frontline knowledge discourse. The point of view of exploitation of knowledge has turned science and arts into technology, technique and skill. It has turned spiritualism into an instrument of curing psychological ailments and philosophy would soon stoop to write apologies for the new state of knowledge. Knowledge can free itself from such exploitation if its relation with capital is snapped. That means higher education would be cheap and production and distribution of knowledge in the institutions would have references other than mere economics. This means a radical change both in the content and form of knowledge. A genuine respectable and doable way available is to link the universities to *lokavidya*. Since the dynamics of *lokavidya* have a holistic human context the universal and abstract knowledge in the university would also rediscover its interface with enlightened human concerns. This would break the division between science and arts and knowledge activity will again become a cultural activity.

### *7.9.3 Exploitation of Software Knowledge*

What is software? Is it a language? Is it a machine? Or is it knowledge? Slowly the world of computers and communications has gravitated towards the last meaning. They call them knowledge products which fuel a knowledge economy. Actually the meaning of software may be as elusive as the meaning of language or knowledge. Mostly people do not discuss these meanings. Software are packages which perform in a certain way, deliver certain results, so for most people it is what there is on a Compact Disc (CD). Scientific activity, entertainment, music, art, banking, accounting, marketing, industrial controls, name any activity and there is a software with the help of which you carry out these activities on or by using a computer. Then there is browsing on the net, e-mail and connectivity software. All these software are ' knowledge' and activity using software is knowledge activity.

The world of software has ushered in a new era of patents. World trade and IT are the two chief propellers of the new era of patents. Certain basic and very large software make the desktop computer's working possible. These are very heavily patented. They are generally based on what is called a 'source code'. The source code is the patented private property of the companies who make them. Non-availability of the source code make it impossible to make even the smallest of improvements in the software that is based on that source code. This proves a great restriction to growth of knowledge and multiplication of software for different specific activities. This restriction and the laws governing it are set to give birth to completely unjust control on knowledge and its exploitation by the large companies. Opposition to this has a worldwide spread and calls itself Free and Open Source Software (FOSS) Movement. It is so specialized that we would need a FOSS activist to explain the details. However, the essential point is that the requirement of exploitation of knowledge hinders multiplication and growth of knowledge, which has in the field of software given birth to such a movement.

The FOSS activism should definitely be seen as part of a knowledge movement which frees the dynamics of knowledge from control by vested interests. How software and computers, in spite of, at the moment, being in the hands of a minority, can be carriers of knowledge and knowledge activity which is friendly to the great majority of people is the question that a people's knowledge activist will have to have an answer for.

## 7.10 Politics and Resistance

The preceding discussion on the social logic of knowledge, namely its variety, locations, production, organization, privatization, control, management and exploitation, in the context of the new technologies and ordinary life strongly suggests that it should be a significant factor in the politics of the day. But this is not the case. Although it is imperative to think in new ways politically since the inauguration of the Information Age since 1990, it has not been happening. The very idea of modern politics belongs mainly to the industrial age, though the beginnings can be traced back to the Enlightenment, Science, bourgeois commerce or the Renaissance. There is no particular reason to think that this idea of politics should continue to be meaningful and functional in the present age too. The excessive weight of centuries of practice seems to be the main cause. Politics derived its meaning from struggles in Europe, struggles against aristocracy, struggles against bourgeoisie, struggles of masses of people, workers and also struggles by powers that be to shape the institution of rule called the modern state. Ideas of equity, representation, equality, liberty and brotherhood underline the lofty goals that politics was supposed to enable men and women to achieve. Ideas of democracy and socialism swept land after land starting with Europe with a promise and a dream which appeared like a self-evident great goal for organization of human societies. Not untouched by these ideas the liberation struggles in the countries of the then Third World produced their own varieties of political conceptions. The high cases in Asia were the ones in India, China and Iran. Gandhi turned people's knowledge, ideas of justice and ways of thinking into a genuine source of strength through a fresh articulation of a conceptual apparatus at once immensely meaningful to the people and devastating for the British Empire. Mao Zedong produced a variety of socialism unthinkable in the European context to mobilize the great masses of the peasantry to defeat the Kuomintang and to lead the Chinese Revolution to success. Khomeini re-invigorated a variety of Islam to defeat the regime of the Shah by mobilizing the whole people of the nation as one, against the oppressive regime and the supporting imperialists, in particular America. This ideological sweep and variety seems to have been co-opted by now. This is not to suggest that followers of these ideologies are not engaged in struggles for justice. Huge struggles are going on across the world organized by Maoist leadership in spite of China making a historic adjustment with world capitalism. Iran continues to refuse being subdued by America, but the spread of Islamic militancy reflects a serious ideological narrowing. Gandhian ideas continue to be used for a radical take on issues of climate change, energy and poverty but there are no movements worth mention. However these streams of thinking have not reconstituted themselves to produce a political imagination for contention with the new forms of exploitation and property relations that the so-called Information Revolution has engendered.

The new dispensation known by different names like Information Age, Knowledge-based Society, Globalization, Neo-liberal Economy, Cognitive Capitalism, etc. occupies almost the entire public space. The absence of any politics of challenge is as much responsible for this state of affairs as the new media which is largely hand-in-glove with the new Empire. It will do well for us to take a look at the very large spread of resistances taking place all over the world. The following is a bird's eye view of the same.

a. Anti-Globalization Movement
   - (i) World Trade Organization (WTO) faces opposition all over the world. Organizations of workers and peasants are at the vanguard.
   - (ii) Opposition to Globalization often shapes as opposition to America in concrete cases and also generally.
   - (iii) The Left in Latin America is emerging with greater power with an anti-America focus.
   - (iv) World Social Forum (WSF) is a new platform for secular mobilization all over the world. It mops up to

a great extent the anti-Globalization Movement.

b. Anti-War Movement

(i) The American wars in Afganistan and Iraq are opposed by people on a very large scale.

(ii) The Anti-globalization movement in large part overlaps with the anti-war movement.

c. Islamic Militancy :

(i) This is primarily anti-America.

(ii) It is centred in West Asia.

(iii) It is an ideological movement.

(iv) It mobilizes Muslims all over the world.

d. Movements of peasants and *adivasis*:

(i) Farmers' movement against adverse terms of trade and against forcible acquisition of land for private industry and infrastructure projects.

(ii) Movement of *adivasis*, landless and very small peasants for land and forests under Maoist leadership.

e. Movement Against Displacement: The following are outstanding types of displacement which face opposition by the displaced. The civil society organizations have come forward but political parties stay aloof.

(i) Reorganization of the market is throwing out small shops, hawkers, etc.

(ii) Reorganization of the city habitat, transport, infrastructure is uprooting the settlements of workers, artisans and those earning their livelihood on the pavement.

(iii) River projects and land lease to corporations are displacing peasants and *adivasi* communities.

f. Resistance to social discrimination: Discrimination based on gender, caste, race, religion and education continues and also faces resistance from the discriminated. Such resistance is mostly local but sometimes organized on the political level.

g. Movement for Control Over Natural Resources:

(i) Resistances to acquisition of land by government and corporations.

(ii) Movement for control of forests and mountains by

the local populations.

(iii) Opposition to extensive use of water by multinational corporations.

h. Free and Open Source Software Movement :

(i) Movement against ownership of the source code and against copyrights.

(ii) Building and popularizing free and open operating systems.

i. Movement against Patenting of Indigenous Knowledge by Multinationals.

(i) Movement for community rights on indigenous and traditional knowledge

(ii) Legal contests by civil society organizations

Worthy as all these resistances are, understanding the sources of power of the new dispensation seems to elude them. To the extent they fail to understand the changes taking place in the epistemic world, they fail to see the source of real power of the new ruling classes, the new state in the making, the new empire. The new war machine, the new market, the financial powers and the global spread of media, all owe their power and intransigence to the emerging configuration in the world of knowledge in which Knowledge Management from the virtual domain is arrogating to itself the entire command. This is the ideological fountainhead of the new dispensation. Without standing up to this, one can only produce variants of the new oppressive order in the making. Let us not forget that it is science that made the greatest movements of the industrial age bend backwards to adjust with dispensations not commensurate with their goals.

It is our contention that a radical look at Gandhi can be the source of new ideas we are looking for, for Gandhi is the founder of a knowledge politics which provided us with the ideas of a radical critique of science and a political understanding to validate the variety of traditions of knowledge that inhere ordinary life and find support from ordinary life.

### 7.11 Towards a Knowledge Politics

Imperialism pushes people's initiatives and therefore their

sources of strength outside the public domain. A political imagination for the emancipation of the poor and the oppressed from the state they are in involves reconstitution of these strengths and initiatives so that they can assert in the public sphere for an equitable place in society. In the world of industries where industrial production was the high point of human civilization, village industries constituted that source of strength of the people which needed reorganization for people to be able to assert for their due place in society. This reconstruction of village industries was possible only through a reorientation of the public domain, through a public nurturing of values which could facilitate such reconstruction, by creating an atmosphere which welcomed the initiatives of bringing back into the public domain what was pushed out by imperialism, the new class interests, lifestyles and the requirements of domination. *Swadeshi*, non-cooperation, civil disobedience, etc. promoted such values. In one word *Satyagraha* led that package of ideas and practice which shook the public domain and enriched it with new values such that there was created space in it for reception of people's initiatives based on their strengths, village industries and the charkha (the hand-operated spinning wheel) in this case.

Is there not a strong parallel with *lokavidya* in the age of information? It is the same people, peasants, artisans, women, the communities in the remote areas and hawkers and small shopkeepers, whose strengths and initiatives one is talking about. A strength that expresses itself as village industries then, expresses itself as *lokavidya* now. Productive activity no more provides the refuge or a new starting point, for globalization has constructed those trade routes which reach out to the remotest economic activities to extract exploitative revenue for those leading the show. The need now is first to assert for an equitable place in the world of knowledge, to devise new forms of *satyagraha* to change the public discourse so that such assertion has a level of acceptance.

Just as steam engine and then electrical power had changed the world of production as never before, similarly or may be in a more enhanced form, computers and communications (internet) have changed the world of knowledge as never before.

And with new forms of knowledge, have come new classes with their interests, new lifestyles, and new forms of domination. Knowledge *Satyagraha* is that neo-Gandhian idea which promises to enrich the public realm with values that can make it receptive towards *lokavidya,* the primary source of strength and initiative of the people. Along with knowledge *satyagraha,* a process needs to be initiated which attempts to organize the people based on their knowledge. This is to activate *lokavidya* to come out from private forms and ruptured states to provide the basis of a knowledge politics. There is need to initiate a process of *Lokavidya Panchayat* with such an objective. Let us therefore look at these two concepts, *knowledge satyagraha* and *lokavidya panchayat* for what they are worth.

### *7.11.1 Knowledge Satyagraha*

*Knowledge Satyagaraha* is to cleanse the world of knowledge. It stands for a reorganization of the social logic of knowledge on the bases of equity and human concerns. It is the chief method to oppose hierarchies, privatization and restrictive use policies in connection with knowledge and knowledge activity. It intends to rediscover the principle of legitimization in the knowledge activity of the people (*lokavidya*), so that knowledge that destroys nature, knowledge that leads to exploitation of man by man and knowledge that creates a supra-nature, supra-human realm, be it through religion or through a virtual dispensation, can be refused the status of knowledge. All such 'knowledge' is *asuri* or *mayavi.* To be able to do all this requires that certain types of practices be adopted. The following is a list for consideration.

- To oppose the global knowledge strategies emanating from America and Western Europe. These are presently pressing in the reform of our higher education system through building of apex institutes of higher education. They relate to both the content of education and its organization. It is going to lead to an expansion in our country of bodies of knowledge and ways of thinking that destroy both nature and the human mind. It is already leading to severe hierarchy in the world of higher education. There may be in all some 50 institutions whose graduates would be worthy of any attention by the corporations and the international systems. The existing universities by and large would be out of this. To compete in this process would be wholly disastrous. The very large community of higher educated needs to reflect on the nature of knowledge, the content of higher education and the tasks before the universities. The requirement is to come out boldly in support of *lokavidya*, the knowledge in society. This support has epistemic, economic, social, cultural and political aspects.

- To recognize knowledge in society, knowledge with peasants and artisans and many other types of service providers as genuine knowledge. This needs to reflect in our philosophical writings and public stands.
- To support improvement of the economic value of *lokavidya*, at a minimum buy *lokavidya* products and argue in the public domain for this.
- To oppose restrictions on peasants and artisans in the use of their knowledge for their life purposes. Develop policies for this.
- To oppose the expropriation of *lokavidya* by the corporations. Develop protection policies for this.
- To develop and construct social processes for the dignity of *lokavidya*. This could mainly be in the form of building overlaps between formal education at all levels and *lokavidya*.
- To oppose the scintistic and virtual orientation of education and come out openly in support of the university as a centre of wide ranging cultural activity. To conceive the university chiefly as a place of representation of knowledge in society which is mainly an artistic, cultural act and not as a science and technology imitation ground.
- To formulate these ideas in a language appropriate and meaningful for the political community.

These practices cannot be conceived in isolation from the very large majority of the youth which aspires to enter the precincts of higher education to better their lives. They are at best struggling for a second rate life in their own country. It is the task of the knowledge *satyagrahis* to explain to these people the real situation and the flux in the world of knowledge and equip them with a new imagination of a world in which all streams of knowledge will have equal respect and equal economic returns. The strength of these boys and girls lies in this that they come from families with a *lokavidya* background. The success of the knowledge *satyagraha* depends on how and to what extent it is able to create and popularize values of respect for *lokavidya* and build social spaces for friendly cooperation between *lokavidya* and university knowledge.

### 7.11.2 *Lokavidya Panchayat*

*Lokavidya Panchayat* is a knowledge organization of people possessing *lokavidya*. Knowledge with the people, knowledge that resides in ordinary life needs to be organized to eventually provide the basis of a knowledge politics and a political imagination that would serve to erect a promise for the emancipation of the poor and the oppressed from the new global, financial and virtual dispensation. If these processes are to imbibe a Gandhian spirit, then respect for the knowledge of the last man in the society and an emancipatory political engagement are necessary conditions. It is for *lokavidya panchayat* as a knowledge organization of the people to create a pro-people atmosphere in the world of knowledge. The objectives of such a *panchayat* can be

- (i) To liberate *lokavidya* from the limitations of the family, village and the community.
- (ii) To work towards the dignity of *lokavidya* in the public domain.
- (iii) To struggle against its exploitation in the market and through the truncated transference into the virtual domain.
- (iv) To create a value of equality among all knowledge traditions and of fraternal relations between them.
- (v) To create a knowledge movement in society to deliver people's knowledge from political powerlessness,

> economic exploitation, cultural irrelevance, philosophical marginalization and social indignity.

Peasants, artisans, women, the variety of service providers and *adivasis* need to come together to form such *panchayat*s to do all that is necessary in pursuance of these objectives.

It is absolutely important that this *panchayat* founds an idea of knowledge organization distinct from the university. If *lokavidya* is not organized, people with such knowledge will never have any say in the realm of public affairs. It is the place from where the larger society will tell the right from the wrong on the basis of its own knowledge and through a democratic process and such judgements will not be based on isolated expert and scholarly opinions. A campaign needs to be unleashed to build such *panchayat*s to break the monopolistic stranglehold of the American and West European knowledge kings on the world of knowledge and by consequence open the world of politics for a new imagination.

# 8

# Invention, Innovation, and Freedom*

*Avinash Jha*

## 8.1 'Necessity is the Mother of Invention'

Yearning for freedom in a situation, which seems closed we come up with inventions. When we are up against a problem or a dilemma and all available solutions are either unacceptable or unworkable, the necessity of finding a new solution often inspires an invention. Freedom is not a condition of invention. Freedom is rather a consequence of invention.

Is this the reason that a large number of technological developments of the post Second World War era are rooted in the inventions made during that war in the industrial world? Maybe it is because of this intrinsic quality of inventions, that they embody a yearning for freedom, that any invention however evil ends they might have been invented for, there is a possibility of their being used for other ends. Even the desire of an elite of a country to conceive of a possible nuclear war and work for a communication system that would survive such war, their desire for that relative degree of freedom in the case of a nuclear showdown between two superpowers and their allies, equipped with vast arsenals of what are now selectively called weapons of mass destruction, desire of this elite for such freedom can lead to the invention of the Internet. We can use Internet technology for a variety of ends. But such a thing may not be possible for all inventions. I doubt whether the invention

* Originally written for the bulletin *Virtuality and Knowledge in Society*, published for a workshop in the World Social Forum, Karachi 2006.

of the nuclear bomb can be used for any end other than war, unless in an unlikely situation when an asteroid is hurtling towards the earth and we send a missile with a nuclear warhead to explode and scatter it. But if nuclear bombs were to be used for this purpose, they would be administered by astronomers and engineers through a transparent mechanism.

Necessity in human affairs materializes in a situation where options begin to close one by one. It is not only the force of circumstances and nature, but also desires and aspirations, and norms and values, which lead to necessity. Most of the time we manage with the acquired knowledge and learning to perform tasks that we need to do. Not all of it is a mechanical process since applying knowledge in new situations is itself a cognitive activity.

An invention may have limited applicability, or it may turn out to be broadly applicable. Sometimes, its applicability may be discovered after a time, or in a different place. A school or a sect may grow around an invention, which may spawn a new body of knowledge, or a new body of non-knowledge (*avidya*). The necessity which occasions an invention may be mundane or not so mundane, risky or not so risky. Fixing a running tap is also a necessity, and so could be escaping from prison for someone.

Does it mean that we do not invent in joy? Is it only under the yoke of dark necessity and in order to escape from it that we invent? When we hear 'the yoke of dark necessity', it is a particular tradition, or complex of traditions, that is speaking to us. There is a particular charge, a particular definition, or a particular comprehension of life that speaks through these words. It is a comprehension which views nature and society as constituting a menacing world in which the human essence can only be saved by a miracle or a by a knowledge which takes apart the world and reconstitutes it in the human image.

The necessity that we speak of results from the fact that we are born into a structure of commitments, into a web of relationships, that we have not chosen. Freedom in the context of natural and moral necessities does not result from escaping these but by discovering and constructing these relations through work in the world and work upon ourselves. Knowledge, luck, help from others and great inventions (social, technological, others) are aid to us in this task. Most of us experience moments of invention in our lives and these are driven by the desire of freedom in particular situations.

## 8.2 Innovations as the Sphere of Applications of Invention

Innovation is based on established inventions. We innovate when we produce variations in the process of applying an invention in different contexts for different purposes. We play around with invention, we try changing it in different ways, reverse-engineer it, and so on.

Take electronic mailing lists as a neat innovation to carry out dialogue among many. Of course, it could also be used merely as a reporting mechanism. It is based on other inventions. Invention of the letter-form (I mean the letters that we write, post and reply to) that was translated into e-mail communication upon invention of the Internet. Mailing list combines this with the idea of a public meeting, consultation or debate.

We need not absolutize the distinction between invention and innovation. Because innovations are, in the ultimate analysis, minor inventions. But these minor inventions are made when the background is already ripe for such inventions. Sooner or later, someone or the other, is going to stumble upon it. These inventions have virtually arrived before they are actually made.

Discoveries (or inventions) of science also result from a necessity that is generated conceptually or experimentally during scientific practice. What is the role of rigour that is demanded in scientific work? The path of scientific research is so narrow that only those solutions that meet the most rigorous criteria are allowed play. The narrower the path, the more possibilities of new discoveries and inventions. Once a major breakthrough is made, it occasions a flurry of efforts to apply it in a multiplicity of contexts. This results in various innovations.

In the industrial economy, scientific discoveries led to inventions, which were then made into innovative products by the business.

## 8.3 Innovations and the Dynamic of Global Knowledge Economy

We have moved to a post-industrial economy in the Internet

age. The Internet referred to here is not the Internet infrastructure but that realm of virtuality—the connected world. War, finance, knowledge, media are all reconstituted in this world and they are meshed together.

In the global knowledge economy of the Internet age, inventions are drawn from a wider pool. Inventions are gathered from various institutions, life situations, culture at large. Then the process of innovation begins—of converting them into products, and then into brands. The global economy seems to be based on appropriation of inventions combined with the dynamic of innovations. Inventions of the public sphere are taken and the power of capital and organization are put into it to produce innovations. There is a competition in innovations. By public sphere is simply meant the sphere outside the control of big capital. We can also call it the independent sector.

When this process is reversed, when innovations of the virtual sector are taken by the independent sector and further innovations are produced—like the thriving grey market of media products in India and several other countries, the so-called copy culture—it is called 'piracy'. Intellectual property regime is to protect the innovations by the big capital and to contain and kill the innovative culture of the independent sector.

This is obvious from the fact that the same big capital is not keen to apply intellectual property ownership to the inventions of natural knowledge traditions in many parts of the world. The appropriation of this knowledge has been termed 'biopiracy' in a counter move. This is often termed the question of traditional knowledge, or TK, in the intellectual property debates. The main obstruction in providing intellectual ownership rights for this kind of knowledge and inventions is supposed to be the fact that this knowledge does not belong to individuals, but to communities. Corporations are treated as legal personalities, i.e. as individuals in some sense, in the matters of property, but it has proved difficult to treat communities as individuals.

## 8.4 Knowledge Systems of the People

We have noted above the two different directions inventions flow towards innovations in the current global society and the role the IPR regime plays in facilitating the one and criminalizing the other.

Even earlier, with each new wave of technology coming, for whatever geopolitical and national compulsions, a kind of knowledge and variety of skills developed to assimilate it, to adapt it and to innovate upon it.

Farmers in India did not use the tools of modern agriculture in the way prescribed by the accredited experts. They developed their own ways in conditions where the odds were against them and the degree of freedom was quite restricted. The use of pepsicola as pesticide has been cited as a recent example of farmers' innovation. But I am sure this is only the most dramatic one. Unlike the grey market of media products these innovations in agriculture were not in the form of products with their markets. They were producing food in a system where both market forces and state were not favourable to them, because they were producing food for the national population and not just for themselves.

Despite the onset of modern agriculture, a great deal of indigenous seed economy, seed science, and seed sociality continued to thrive and modern seeds were part of this complex. This knowledge of modern seeds and their use could be very different from the conclusions of agricultural experts. Intellectual property regime intervenes here to stop the exchange and production of seeds that is taking place and restructure the seed sector.

Similarly many other knowledge traditions of non-modern origins are surviving. We are all familiar with medical knowledge traditions, much beyond the few well-known systems like *Ayurveda, Siddha* and *Unani*. In fact, there are a myriad knowledge traditions of different kinds undergoing change, development, transformations and producing hybrid traditions. These myriad knowledge systems that have survived in different forms did not do so because of any advocacy to save traditional knowledge, or because of the recognition they were accorded. As a matter of fact, the normative framework of modern science, which was the dominant knowledge system of the last two centuries, had little place for these knowledge systems, if any.

These knowledge systems survived because the people, whose knowledge systems these were, survived. With the slow crumbling of the authority of science to institute knowledge organization in the society, there is a greater recognition now for these knowledge systems. But what framework of knowledge is being constituted now in the age of the Internet? Have we escaped the devil only to find a precipice on the other side? Maybe the answer lies in exploring how the regime of knowledge is being reconstituted in the virtual world. What would be a regime of knowledge where people's knowledge can have full play in shaping life in society?

# 9

# Jaipur Lectures on the Knowledge Society

*Sunil Sahsrabudhey*

These lectures were part of a Technology-Philosophy course. The theme of the lectures was the present transition that the society is undergoing from an Industrial era to an Information era. The tables below neatly sum up this transition for an overview and reinforce the idea that this book attempts to communicate, namely that the world has moved on in a very big way and to understand this movement we need to gather our ideas and see the changing reality somewhere around a knowledge focus.

In what follows there may be some repetition of what may have been said elsewhere in this book, but the tables and the explanations that follow put so much together at one place that we have decided to present them here.

**Table I: Changes in the Areas of Economics, Politics, Technology, Culture and Philosophy from Industrial to Information Age**

| | Industrial Society | Knowledge Society |
|---|---|---|
| **Economics** | Labour is organized | Information is organized |
| | Built through colonization | Built through globalization |
| | Large units of production | Small and distributed units |
| | Sectors of profit: Manufacturing industry, material products, | Sectors of profit : Knowledge enterprises: software, connectivity |

| | | |
|---|---|---|
| | commodities | (mobile, internet), media, entertainment, education, healthcare, genetic modification. Knowledge products, commodities |
| | Material resources | Knowledge resource also *lokavidya*, the knowledge in society |
| | National control | Command of corporations |
| | Controls on movement across national boundaries.<br>Regulation by national governments | Easier movement of capital, goods, finance, natural resources, people, security, values and other human dimensions across national borders.<br>Towards regulation by WTO |
| **Politics** (post-World War II) | National state | Transnational state |
| | Welfare agenda | Only market criteria (for education, healthcare everything) |
| | Increasing participation | Lower participation |
| | Ideological politics | Absence of ideologies |
| | Industrial imperialism | New empire |
| **Technology** | Power-based industry<br>Organization of energy at high speeds | Small energy processes<br>Organization of information at high speeds |
| | High rate and scale of production | High rate and scale of handling knowledge |
| | Mechanical, electrical, civil, chemical, metallurgical and textile are the main areas | Converging technologies: Info, Nano, Bio technologies and Cognitive Science |
| | Enhancement of natural processes, construction | Improvement of human performance |

| | | |
|---|---|---|
| | of artificial processes and products | |
| **Culture** | National cultures in Western command | Sweep by media and entertainment guided by global lifestyles (music, games, cinema) |
| | Suppression of local culture | Explosion in local culture facilitated by the new media |
| | Scientific paradigm in art appreciation, criticism | Autonomy of art, no more a tailist position |
| **Philosophy** | Concept of knowledge and reality closely tied to science. | A new concept of knowledge is in the making. The shift from content to organization and production to communication has taken the world of thought by storm. The world of things and forces is being replaced by a world of representation, structure and meaning. |

**Table II: Changes in the World of Knowledge from Industrial to Information Age**

| **Knowledge** | **Industrial Society** | **Knowledge-based Society** |
|---|---|---|
| **Command** | Science, production of knowledge | Knowledge management, organization of knowledge |
| **Place** | University | Internet, virtual realm |
| **Legitimacy criterion** | Scientific method | Organizability by IT |
| **Hierarchy** | Strong order from high to low: physical sciences, life sciences, social sciences, art, languages, etc. | Knowledge management at the top and all others relative equals. |
| **Other knowledge systems** | No recognition as such, incorporation with scientific remodeling | Recognition of *lokavidya* |

| | | |
|---|---|---|
| **New sciences** | ——— | Information science, science of knowledge management, cognitive science |
| **Paradigm** | Only physical scientific paradigm | Emergence of new paradigms in science, acceptance of alternate paradigms |
| **Technology** | Power-based industrial technologies | Info, nano, and biotechnologies |
| **Commercial importance** | Science and technology | Media, art, design and language |
| **Controls** | National | Financial and corporate |
| **Knowledge movements** | Movement for village in dustries and local consumption, for preservation of bio-diversity, clean environment and ecological balance and forbio and solar energy. | Movement for rights on traditional knowledge, for control of natural resources by local communities, *Lokavidya Jan Andolan* and the Free and Open Source Software(FOSS)movement. |

The paragraphs below explain in brief each row of this table:

**Command**

Knowledge Management (KM) and organization and communication of knowledge is valued higher than the content and production of knowledge. Knowledge thus assumes new meaning. KM and work on computers themselves become the highest forms of knowledge activity, fetching more in the market and commanding higher social status. KM essentially connects the sources of knowledge to the locations where it is needed. It is not management of knowledge which has been there all along. KM is an activity in the virtual domain which makes it possible to collect all information that can be put on the computer and weaves a network of access. It involves a theory of knowledge which is neutral to production of knowledge and deals only with organization and communication of knowledge. In the information age thus KM assumes the command of all knowledge in the sense that it sets standards, criteria and direction of exploration in the world of knowledge. Contrast this with science which assumed the command with the claim that it is the only legitimate knowledge.

In industrial society science set the standards and governed the direction of exploration and production of knowledge. Production of knowledge in accordance with science was the most important type of knowledge activity. However in the information age this has been changing, KM assuming the position of pre-eminence.

**Place**

The importance of physical location is disappearing. Knowledge activity can take place anywhere on a computer/internet. University is the chief place of knowledge activity in the industrial age. Even now it is the case so far as physical space and location is concerned. It commanded respect and awe and it was the most prized product of that era. But all this has been changing with internet creating a new world of knowledge activity, power play and finance. This is the virtual world which seems to have something corresponding to everything that is there in the real world. There are virtual community, virtual society, virtual forest, virtual art gallery, virtual experiment, virtual conference and so on. It is from this virtual world that KM commands. The activity, development, interaction, formulation, transaction, creation, innovation, invention, discovery, collaboration, partnership, criticism, etc. in the virtual world have taken the lead and tend to give direction to human activity everywhere, finance, science, art, entertainment name any.

**Legitimacy**

The criteria of legitimate knowledge have changed. It does not matter now how knowledge is produced, who produced it and where. All that matters is its organizability by the ICTs.

Science so far has been the storehouse of the criteria of legitimacy in the world of knowledge. With its methods it was declared both the supreme form of knowledge and the only legitimate source of knowledge. It was declared value-free and culture-independent; these characteristics tending to assume the status of criteria of legitimacy, universality and even absoluteness. With the development of knowledge society there is a questioning of the absoluteness of science. The characteristic of value-freeness and culture-independence do not enjoy the same status now. Scientific method is no more of central importance and production of knowledge is not the chief concern. Instead, organizability by the new technology seems to occupy the central place in the cluster of criteria of legitimacy. ICTs are methods of organization and communication of knowledge.

**Hierarchy**

This changes the social value associated with different forms and locations of knowledge. A kind of equalization takes place among most activities which were strongly unequal earlier. Only computer/internet activity is special. Every human activity is a knowledge activity. Scientific research, production of new knowledge, teaching, design, explanation, comprehension, creative arts, management, writing software, collection, organization and dissemination of information, religion, spiritual enterprise, artisanry, farming, collecting food in forests, hunting, bringing up children, healthcare, organizing communities, name any human activity and you will find that it is a knowledge activity. Other than may be those which are performed purely on instruction like in rituals or by a worker on the assembly line, purely mechanically, human activity in general is knowledge activity. The age of science, as we know, weaves a pattern in this world of human activities from a standpoint of knowledge known as the scientific point of view. It had developed wide ranging criteria and methods to allocate any of these activities their 'rightful' place in the world of knowledge. These involved the ideas of experiment, testing, verification, reproduction, analytical content, systematic organization, universal applicability, value-independence, etc. This cluster of ideas constituted the general basis for producing a structure in the world of knowledge. Farming, food gathering, local healthcare, etc. would not be called knowledge activity at all but a simple application of knowledge which may have been handed down through generations. The arts were strictly distinguished from the sciences and placed lower down in the order. Writing for newspapers, making films or collecting information for reporting would hardly be considered knowledge activity. Computing would be a service and so would writing programs be. Economics, market or public finance were all tuned to this understanding. Is not all this changing in a big way? Science no more seems to order the world of knowledge.

This breakdown of hierarchy ordered by science has led partly to greater equality among various forms of knowledge activity. Concepts of validity and legitimacy are merging with concepts like what is valid and useful depends on who is using it, for what purpose, etc. But KM occupies a special space as the theory and practice of organization and management of all knowledge and with it assumes a place distinctly above others.

## Other Knowledge Systems

Traditional knowledge and practices assume a new respect in society. Other ways of thinking and doing, the variety of traditions of knowledge, were virtually relegated to the dump house by science. The world of industry required that the markets be available all over the world and raw materials be accessible anywhere in the world. Other ways of thinking and doing were seen as nothing but hurdles and therefore had to be decimated both in theory and practice. Indian astronomy, traditions of healthcare, metallurgy, architecture and a host of other traditions of knowledge were simply de-recognized as knowledge and labelled community practices. If and when any recognition was extended it was only based on a possible scientific explanation.

The information age comes with a whiff of fresh air in this respect. Knowledge in society, *lokavidya*, is getting new recognition. This can be seen in (i) the activity known as natural resource management mainly dealing with agriculture, animal husbandry, water management and forestry, (ii) healthcare, where massive campaigns are on for collecting the knowledge with the people and (iii) design, where people's knowledge and activity in specific areas like textiles, woodwork or metal work, is a serious input in developing market competitive products. But it is not only these areas and such recognition has extended to a variety of knowledge activity in society. However this also entails a certain emaciation or atrophy of knowledge in society. They are now seen as places of genuine knowledge activity only to the extent and in the manner they relate to virtual domain.

### New Sciences

A new concept of science is born with the appearance of sciences not reducible to physical science. The world of knowledge in the industrial society had no place for anything that was not reducible to science. However now there are areas of knowledge activity that are products of scientific development and yet are not reducible to science. One may not be too sure at the moment whether cognitive science belongs to such a category but information science may be a closer candidate. This includes both the science of organization and the science of connectivity, software and knowledge management respectively.

### Paradigm

There is a change in thinking about what constitutes a sound explanation of the happenings in the world. The structure of understanding has been, in the last two centuries, governed by the paradigm of science, in particular physics. Religion, art and even philosophy have been too eager to call themselves scientific. There have been attempts to show how even theory building in antiquity also conformed at least in a primitive manner to the scientific paradigm. This situation is changing in two ways now.

Even within science, new types of explanations are coming up. For example, there are increasing attempts to see the processes at cellular level primarily as processes of information organization and communication which are assisted, or are given shape to, by chemical and physical processes, whereas the earlier thinking is that chemical and physical processes are the primary phenomena with an information consequence.

Acceptance of *lokavidya* entails acceptance of other paradigms of knowledge. They are often holistic, non-reductionist and include relations with other objects as well as uses in the list of primitives, if there are any such primitives.

## Technology

The association of technology with 'large and big' is no more there. This would have its consequences for the idea of progress. Power, that is work done per unit time, that is rate of organization of energy, is central to modern industry. Mechanical, thermal, chemical, electrical and nuclear power have respectively provided the basis of both technological and scientific advances. The situation is different now. The converging technologies, namely Bio, Nano, Info technologies and Cognitive science, generally have small power needs and target changes in the biological world, plants, animals and human beings. Even in theory nature and truth are not among lead values.

## Commercial Importance

This greatly alters the direction of application of human genius, now more towards the soft world, human tests and relationships. It changes the way we look at the world. In the industrial society science and technology have decisive commercial interfaces. Funding is related with this and with national needs, defence, etc. Now we find standing side by side with S&T in commercial importance, media, art, language and design. Not just the world is changing but also the world of knowledge and knowledge-based activity. If science and technology could assume great commercial importance in a world in which agriculture and the crafts constituted the most widespread economic activity, why cannot media, art, design, language, software and knowledge management assume greater commercial importance than anything else in a world in which production of knowledge in the campuses and on sites of production constitutes the most widespread forms of knowledge activity? Not that it is desirable but it is surely possible. What matters is how the world of knowledge is ordered and what values govern the emerging lifestyles.

## Controls

The ideas of nationalism and patriotism now take a back seat. In the industrial age the controls are national. It is mainly through the national policy that the direction and development of science was influenced. There were industrial interests but that had to work through a national policy. The situation is considerably different now. National policy is now being decided rather squarely in favour of financial and corporate interests whose influence in the sphere of control of knowledge activity has been ever increasing. The wedding of globalization, internet and the new empire found its first fall out in privatization, liberalization, enormous control by financial institutions and an overnight take off of the information economy (first company Netscape in 1995 and see their population in just over a decade). Campuses in Europe and also at other places are replete with struggles against the corporatization of the university, against the control of the university by financial mechanisms.

**Knowledge Movement**

Now the movements of the common people claim that they know what to do with society and nature. This alters the concept of leadership in society. Gandhian movement for village industries and local consumption is a movement also for an alternative in the world of knowledge. The work and discourse on bio and solar energy is in the same strain and demand for preservation of bio diversity also stresses the need for live and diverse locations of human knowledge and activity. The movement against climate change in the name of Rights of Mother Earth and Rights of Nature is the latest in such a chain. But these movements do not see themselves explicitly as knowledge movements, although one can put up a fairly convincing argument that they are so. These same movements spill over into movements for control of natural resources by the localities, to be used by them as they may according to their knowledge and need. All these need to be seen as knowledge movements now for them to be able to chart an effective future course.

Further in the information age there are explicit knowledge movements. Rights of communities on traditional knowledge are at the centre of many struggles against patents. Campaign for the dignity of *lokavidya* is another. This is evolving into

*Lokavidya Jan Andolan*, an explicit knowledge movement of the bearers of *lokavidya*, namely peasants, artisans, *adivasis*, and the women of their households. The student movement in Europe today is an explicit knowledge movement identifying the present university as the hub of cognitive capitalism.

The movement for Free and Open Source Software (FOSS) is an example from the virtual world. FOSS is a movement against ownership of the source code and against copyright. It also builds and popularizes free and open operating systems. Linux for example. This raises, in very specific ways, the issues related to knowledge commons and those related to freedom, control, regulation, access and use with respect to knowledge.

# II

# *Lokavidya*: Epistemics and Politics

# 10

# *Lokavidya* Approach to the Women's Movement: Women's Knowledge Holds the Key*

*Chitra Sahasrabudhey*

## 10.1 Introduction

In India's Independence Movement women had participated in large numbers bringing into the public domain certain real and concrete forms of women's strengths and capacities. This had led to expectations that women would earn the right to a dignified life through large-scale active role of ordinary women in the social reconstruction of India through independence. But the number of women in public life went on decreasing after independence. In the economic sector the gates of their entry started closing down. The development model followed by India gave an opportunity to only a very small number of women and it took away whatever was possessed by the remaining very large majority of women. Some women (about one in ten thousand) became successful doctors, administrators, leaders, professors, engineers, pilots and writers. There was so much propaganda and noise made around this that it eclipsed the immense pain of the crores of women resulting from the steady disorganization of their lives. The Modern Women's Movement of the 1970s and 80s, once again gave expression to the very strong resentment against oppression of women. But

---

* This is an English translation of the Hindi original published in the book *Lokavidya Vichar* (2001) which puts together essays by activists engaged in the *lokavidya* movement.

the basis of the feminist idea attempted to be shaped by this movement was completely different from the values and ideas of women who were active during the Independence Movement.

This difference comes out clearly in all the aspects—social, economic, political. However, the social mainstream today reflects only the effects of the modern women's movement. The so-called 'progressive' literature, poetry, drama and other art forms create only such women's roles or situations related to women which are under the influence of this feminism. The depiction of the progressive woman has its basis in this feminism. The last two decades of the 20th century have witnessed much writing on the theoretical aspects of this feminism. The causes of the spread of this movement are not so much in the express ideas of this movement but more in the domineering status of Western nations and the enslaved like status of the Indian society. This is because this feminism hardly relates to the experience and thought of the Indian women, but has been derived from the processes in the West. This movement from its beginning till the end, had its reach limited to the large cities and even there only among the educated. These women are under the influence of thoughts and developments in Western nations and see them as the ideal reference for progress. This movement has attracted only women who have found a place in modern systems of industry, education, services, administration, etc. and it is these women's problems that have been raised by the movement. Art, literature, media and general propaganda generally gave full support to this movement because all these are in the service of that small segment of society which has benefited from the modern development policy.

The limitations in the spread of the modern women's movement stem from the limitations of its ideology. It is true that this movement brought into public debate the helplessness of modern women but it failed to provide any imagination of a just system. The issues put forward by this feminism hardly provide the basis for justice to all segments of the women's world or for developing just relationships with other segments of society. These are serious limitations and they make this feminism unnatural and inconsistent.

In this article we will discuss these limitations of feminism in some detail and proceed to identify women's knowledge and local market as the source of ideas which provide the real basis for women's interests and could possibly remove these limitations. The article proposes to conceptualize the basic ideas which may give the direction to the women's movement in the interest of the great majority of women. It has been attempted, therefore, to give shape to an idea of women's knowledge and argue that the strength and power of women is based in this women's knowledge. Women's knowledge includes their skill, art, knowledge, values, experience and their way of thinking, their genius. Women's knowledge does not refer only to knowledge of women but functions as that mirror which hopes to bring into the public domain those strengths, dispositions and capacities of the very large number of ordinary women which are either not recognized or strictly under-recognized in the conceptual apparatus of modern knowledge. Since these strengths and capacities span large areas and multiple dimensions, therefore they provide the concrete basis for increasing the participation in society of the majority of women. Women's knowledge is an important part of knowledge in society, namely *lokavidya* and therefore, it provides the criteria for estimating the degree of participation in society by the most disadvantaged, be they individuals, communities or larger segments and through this it also helps identify the direction in which such participation is increased. Therefore, the organization of women's strengths based on women's knowledge takes us towards imagining and shaping an alternative economic-social-political system which opens the doors of participation for very large numbers who have been, like women, kept out of the social mainstream, shaped by modern systems. The idea of the local market provides the basis for women's power and women's knowledge to assume just forms.

We shall carry out this discussion in four parts. The first part contains a discussion of issues raised by the modern women's movement and the sense in which they suffer serious limitations. The second part contains the discussions of how women's interest lies in the social expression of their strengths, that is their knowledge, point of view and values. The third part discusses the role of the local market in effectively shaping women's strength and also in the reconstruction of a just social order. The last part is about campaigns and programmes.

## 10.2 The Limitations of the Modern Women's Movement

The modern women's movement has mainly established the following ideas:

(a) women's independence
(b) man-woman equality
(c) patriarchy.

These three concepts are born out of the modern development in Europe. The fact that they are born in Western society cannot be the reason for any bias against them, however doubts do arise when one sees that they continue to serve the philosophy of life promoted by imperialism.

The development of the imperialist philosophy of life is based fundamentally in a conceptual apparatus whose main constituents are 'reason' and 'freedom' which have shaped publicly as Western science and politics. Before the Second World War, women in the West tried to obtain their rights guided by these concepts. After initial successes the limitations of the democratic system started becoming clear. It became clear how limited were the results of voting rights. At the same time the workers' movement brought into existence communism as a powerful alternative. The social and economic causes of exploitation in Western society were understood on the basis of socialist principles. This gave a new direction to the women's movement there. Marxist principles helped to identify the various dimensions of women's exploitation. These argument-forms gave birth to a concept of patriarchy. Such understanding led to a strong women's movement in Europe and America and as a result many nations of the West shaped new laws and systems in society. However, the ill-effects of these reforms started being apparent during the movement itself. For example, the divorce laws in America appeared to lead to situations where women would be helpless. It was by the demand of the movement that new divorce laws came into existence and it was then considered to be emancipatory for women. But such a reform led to increase in the social and economic inequality between men and women. Similar results were observed in the social, economic and political spheres including the sphere of the family. By 1980 this women's movement in the West started losing its steam and the women theorists there started revisiting the ideology of the movement. In the next 10 years this rethinking led some women theorists to feel that it was necessary to challenge 'reason' and 'freedom' which constituted the base of the Enligtenment values. It appears in clear relief in the writings of Kate Soper and Judith Evan that the women's movement cannot serve the women's cause justly without challenging/denying the Enlightenment ideas of Equality, Liberty and Fraternity, which are supposed to be based on 'reason'. It appears necessary that the special relation of women with nature be given the status of a basic principle and bring down the 'reason' based thinking from its unchallenged status. But to destabilize the status of 'reason' amounts to challenging Western science and to be sure the women theorists of this period attempted a serious critique of Western science from a value-laden perspective. Thinkers like Ruth Blayer, Barbara Rothman, Zina Koria, Rita Arditi, Evelyn Fox Keller and Sandra Harding charged Western science for its exploitation embodied character and seriously questioned its claims of search for truth and neutrality and also intentions inherent in its methods and fundamental principles.

Like science, the imperialist politics sitting on the concept of freedom too became the centre of criticism. The highly unequal and exploitative relationship between the developed nations and the poor nations of the world gave substance to this criticism. The first phase of the Western women's movement coincided with the period in which communism challenged imperialism and sowed the seeds of new hope in the oppressed people of the world. It was the time when a new atmosphere developed in favour of principles of 'justice' and 'social reconstruction'. The women's movement too came under its influence, but it chose 'reason' in the principles of communism and gave less importance to the moral aspect. As a result, the narrow and reactionary idea of 'patriarchy' was born. It seems that whenever the ideas of emancipation of the oppressed fail to accommodate the moral aspects in accordance with place and time, then 'reason' has no riders and the movements tend also to serve reactionary ends. The women thinkers of the West are now averse to value neutrality and feel the necessity of value-laden formulations in all branches of knowledge, but being part of an imperialist state and society in itself becomes an obstacle in developing value-laden thinking. The biggest question before them is how to overcome this limitation of the ideas of the women's movement.

Places like India where values have been integral to knowledge can become fertile grounds to overcome the limitations of the modern women's movement. In the modern women's movement in India which spanned the period 1976 to 1988, the question of value relatedness of the basic conceptual apparatus never became a matter of debate. The debate was limited to what could be called the Indian edition of the conceptual apparatus of the West. Further, this debate was limited to the small number which benefited from the policies and values of the modern state and who looked forward to a place in the same. We shall try here to specifically recognize the limitations inherent in these concepts and attempt to find directions of work which would help incorporate a value base.

### *10.2.1 Women's Independence*

The modern women's movement insists on the independent existence of women. What is the meaning of women's independence? In the traditional values and beliefs of the Western societies, the genesis of various elements is supposed to be for the use of man. The woman is also born for man. Such beliefs led to the woman becoming an object in the commodifying changes after the Industrial Revolution. It is to challenge this situation that in the later half of the 20$^{th}$ century, there arose this women's movement which formulated the idea of women's independence. It was said that women have their own lives and they should be independent in shaping them. They are not meant for men. That is a woman is not just a commodity to be had by man, she is also a human being who has independent desires and ambitions and she should have full rights to work for them. The movement made special efforts to prove that women had the capacities to think, take initiatives and take decisions.

This idea of women's independence was also propagated in India by the modern women's movement without ever thinking about the difference in conditions. Thus, two distinct limitations of the idea of women's independence came to the fore in these conditions: the first was in the basic idea of independence and the other due to the hollowness resulting from not paying attention to the different reality and historicity of Indian society.

The idea of independence shaped in the West is not just unnatural but also not consistent. It is very weakly related to the idea of justice or may be this relation is not there at all, whereas the meaning of progress or being civilized in human societies lies in constant increase in justice in life. The world makes progress when in the variety of its constituent elements the aspect of justice becomes stronger. The just aspects become stronger when every atom of the universe is embodied with consciousness and activity (just participation) according to the laws of universe. No two elements are completely independent of each other and that such independence causes injustice to grow and deprive the elements of their activity. Human beings are constituents of this universe and if different segments of human societies tend to become independent of one another it leads to increase in injustice in society creating hurdles in the activity of different segments. So the question of women's independence needs to be strongly related with the idea of justice. The question of independence for women to fulfil their desire or ambition is not separable from the question of establishment of justice in society. Because of imperialism more and more injustice is being heaped on women and in helpless situations the call for independence is both attractive and an effective medium to express one's anger and resentment, but it neither provides the real basis for women's lives, nor the basis for establishing justice in society.

Contrary to the traditional beliefs in the West, woman has been conceived as an active power in our society. In her form of constantly active nature, woman is not a thing to be used but she has been seen as a caring mother. She has been believed to be the master of all those powers which are the sources and strengths of creating the new, every day. That is woman has been seen as an active doer. So there is no question of such a woman being enslaved by others. She is neither made as an object to be used by man, nor can the meaning of her life be limited. Not just this, but the consciousness of the responsibility of creating and caring for the society leads her to see her own life-roles as part of establishment of justice in larger society. Religious and historical stories create such an image of the Indian womanhood. However, this is also true that this image has been maligned today. The spread of imperialism has dislodged such fundamental values (like women in the role of a doer and creator) of our society and constantly limited women's activity. One after another different aspects and areas of women's activity have been taken away from them, for example, variety of domestic industries, textiles, agricultural work, healthcare and feeding the family have been stolen from them, making them inactive, helpless and weak. In such a society how can the meaning of women's independence be limited to ideas of fulfilling individual desires and ambitions? So the idea of women's independence can be partly freed of its limitations by incorporating into it with some strength the elements of justice, the moral values. This can happen only by returning to women those areas and aspects of their work from which they have been displaced. Perhaps this value-laden independence requires naming afresh with a new word which refers clearly to the idea of constantly increasing the just participation of women and other segments of society.

### *10.2.2 Man-Woman Equality*

The idea of equality has been attractive for the oppressed classes. The women's movement developed the idea of man-woman equality and raised the demand of rights equal to those possessed by men. This idea also led to many distorted practical forms in Western nations. Here we will discuss how it was adopted by the women's movement in India. The movement put forth the thesis that the difference in capacities of men and women is mainly due to social conditions and that women can do all those tasks equal to men which demand hard labour or knowledge. So, why should women accept superiority of men in any areas—knowledge, strength, abilities and so on? Following such a lead, in the areas of general employment and also education a demand of equal opportunity and equal pay was raised. At first sight such a concept of equality appears just, however, now when the movement has become weak one can see the consequences which clearly underline the theoretical and practical limitations of this idea.

The present concept of equality has come from the West, so there is difficulty in understanding its essential meaning. However, in the last 100 years it has come to mean becoming like the dominant. There is no demand of any kind which relates to the dominant also being just. The meaning of the concept of man-woman equality also similarly strengthens the tendency of being like a man. In this way for women the nature of men became the ideal and internalizing his characteristics was seen as moving towards equality. Arguments were produced in favour of giving up one's womanhood to achieve such equality. Such an idea of equality provides no basis for justice, nor is it any kind of source of resistance to injustice. One may note that whenever the idea of equality has been asserted, new forms of exploitation of the weak have born. The idea of man-woman equality has also led to such results. In America the slogan of women's independence promoted women to live away from their families and the slogan of man-woman equality led them to do all such jobs in which it was easy to exploite both their labour and their bodies. What took place was womanization of poverty. In our country too the results are against the ordinary women in a big way. Women were made available as very cheap labour. All the talk of equal labour value became meaningless. The demand of equality in the roles of men and women in no way has led to increasing capacities to fight against exploitation but on the contrary it leads to convenience for a small number and strengthening this system of exploitation. Therefore, the idea of equality can transcend its limitations only if it is conceived as part of a challenge to the system of exploitation.

Just participation for various segments of society is a necessary precondition for the idea of equality to be meaningful. In this way the demand for equality between men and women and accordingly change in women's social role is not important, what is important is that their roles be autonomous and just.

### 10.2.3 Patriarchy

Where is the root cause of oppression of women today? Feminism sees it in patriarchy. According to patriarchy all social institutions like family, community, state, caste and religion are under men's control, their dictat. It is patriarchy that creates the basis of women's exploitation—social, economic, bodily and psychological. Women can free themselves from this exploitation by displacing men from their positions of control of the social institutions. We do not know how precisely this idea of patriarchy is applicable in Western societies but we do know that the Indian society has not developed under the compulsions of patriarchy. Highly centralized power was never a regular phenomenon here. The idea of men and women having autonomous and complementary powers seems to be the popular form here. Away from such understanding, here too, feminism introduced the idea of patriarchy, which depicted man as exploiting and ruling over women and family as an institution that kept women enslaved. It was not even mentioned that a large source of women's exploitation in the families leading ordinary lives was in the centralized state. As a result instead of directing women's resistance towards widespread exploitation it was turned into the family, engaging women in breaking their close relations leaving the oppressive system of exploitation untouched.

Another weakness in mobilizing women against so-called patriarchy is that there is no insistence either on justice or on putting an end to the system of exploitation. On the contrary, the tendency of behaving just as men do now, after displacing them from their positions, gains currency. It is true that a very large number of women are victims of oppressive behaviour by men today, but the reasons for this are not in so-called patriarchy. The idea of struggle against the so-called patriarchy has no capacity to give justice to women, on the contrary it plays an important role in disturbing women's just struggles. Patriarchy is produced in 'individual' centred societies. So keeping it in the centre in our society does not lead to serving any individual interest but works towards separating her or him from the society itself. The modern women's movement first made a list of close relations who exploit women. This includes mother, father, mother-in-law, father-in-law, brother, husband, brother-in-law, boys, friends, colleagues, neighbours, etc. To oppose patriarchy meant being in a constant struggle against all these. It also provided the context for women to move away from their traditional activity, so there was nothing wrong in acquiring men's places even if it meant giving up one's womanhood. And this almost concludes the argument that patriarchy is a baseless concept. If to assert their identity, women were required to give up their womanhood, then this surely was the greatest defeat of women.

It is not being said that the issues raised by the modern women's movement are not there in real life or that they do not deserve consideration or that our traditions have no fault lines. What is important is what kind of society the issues of the movement take us towards and whether for the large majority of women one sees the possibility of a safe and happy future. It is in this context that the theoretical limitations of the modern women's movement have been viewed.

The most reactionary result of the modern women's movement in our country is that it made women look in directions other than imperialist exploitation. The entire period suffers from imperialist American invasions of the countries of the Third World. It is during this period that in the newly independent countries imperialism made its roots firmer through democracies and development. They needed cheap labour which was provided by what followed the modern women's movement, which at the same time proved cosy for the lifestyle of well-to-do and modern women. The great misfortune is that women blinded by the shine and twinkle of modern development, saw this process as one which will make the poor and illiterate women self-dependent. This amply illustrates the limited reach as well as the theoretical limitations of the modern women's movement.

Today if the women's movement wishes to move in the direction of justice for women then it must come out of the influence of the philosophy of life now being shaped and guided by imperialism. History is witness that knowledge and philosophy that constitute the basis of exploitative arrangements of things and men/women cannot also become the guiding light of the emancipatory struggle of the oppressed peoples. The large example that we are all aware of are those of the movement for *swaraj* in the leadership of Mahatma Gandhi, the communist movements in Europe and Asia in the leadership of working classes and social movements of oppressed classes (devotional and knowledge-based) of medieval India. What we learn from these movements is that it is not enough to move away from the dominant thinking and give shape to struggles through women specific and one's own view of life but the basic thought and conceptual framework of the women's movement must itself embody the ideas of justice that need to pervade the broader society and the universe as whole. The concept of women's knowledge is part of such a philosophy of life.

## 10.3 Women's Knowledge—The Basis of Women's Strength

### *10.3.1 Women's Knowledge*

Women's betterment lies in increasing their dignified participation in society and attaining those forms of activity which preserve and lead to autonomy. Such autonomy or autonomous identity may be both obtainable and sustainable based on capacities specific to women. The cosmos has created women and men as two separate entities whose roles are different but not independent from each other. In accepting different roles lies also the acceptance of autonomy. A corollary is that the two are equipped with different types of basic strengths/powers/ability. These basic abilities can be based only in their own experience and knowledge. These experiences exhibit great variety which results in the variety of forms and types of activity and knowledge. Therefore, equality between men and women cannot be conceived or had by acquiring each other's strengths but it is possible by having them both contribute based on their experience and knowledge in making and remaking of life and society. In other words, equality between men and women lies in both getting full opportunity to use their strengths and fulfil their roles. This can be the basis of equality among different segments of society as it appears also close to the laws of nature. When the dynamics and systems of society produce hurdles in the creation of such opportunities, then different segments of society find their activity constrained. Those segments whose activities suffer are also subjected to exploitation.

The dynamics of the present society are constantly stealing the opportunities of women's activity. Areas of which women are considered specialists are being taken away from them under the modern dispensation. The modern dispensation completely negates women's knowledge, experiences and capacities. As a result women's activity (just participation) is in decline, which in turn has led to increased exploitation of women. Women's strength, women's outlook, women's knowledge and women's just participation are all embodied one into the other and women stand exploited through an active inactivation of women's strength. Let me explain this.

In independent India development meant Westernization and mechanization. Crores of women engaged in agriculture and industry suffered because of this. The disorganization of domestic industry turned them unemployed and the mechanization/modernization of agriculture made them leave the fields. The new industry was large, employed fewer people and was located only in some cities. Women have no place in them as workplaces and when the product of this industry reaches out to distant places, it destroys domestic industry. It is also important to know that modern industry is located outside the house, so everybody including women are forced to work there on alien conditions. This is a major obstacle to autonomous identities, existence and roles. Hybrid seeds, chemical fertilizers, insecticides, pesticides and the use of machines in various agricultural operations constitute modern agriculture which displaces women from agricultural work in a very big way. Women who are seen today in industry or agriculture are just working against a pittance, which is the smallest and negligible part of the wealth created in the process. Thus, this too acts only to violate her autonomy. Further, modern education is the condition of entry into the modern systems. So only a very small number of women can avail themselves of this opportunity, because education is expensive and places a heavy demand on time. Further the new and alien systems of administration and the complexity and aggression in the market has made women's activity in public places extremely difficult and unnatural. From where will they have confidence to move about freely in such places? The obtaining of rations, fuel, water and similar simple daily needs requires one to dialogue and connect with the local administration, from the methods of which she is as deprived as never before. Women have great knowledge of healthcare, bringing up children, organizing food for the family, food processing and storage of grains and satisfying the clothing needs of the family, in one word domestic management in its entirety at low costs and in a sustainable way. But the modern dispensation refuses to recognize any of this and they are thought fit only for training in all this by people who have never done any of this. This has led to a sweeping loss of self-confidence in women turning them dependent in making decisions even for small matters relating to daily life. The mechanization and Westernization has led to spread of Western values which have created an atmosphere of easy economic-social-psychological and bodily oppression of women. As a result, rape, dowry deaths, eve-teasing and unsafe existence in general has become a matter of everyday life. Since they have lost their work, they are seen as a load on society, ignorant and foolish. All this has de-activated their strengths, knowledge and capacities.

Betterment of women's condition depends upon regaining of respect for their strengths, that is in the re-legitimization of women's knowledge. For this, production, administration, services, everywhere women's knowledge needs to be incorporated in a just way. Only then can just participation of women increase at the desired speed. The large-scale participation of women in the Gandhian movement was possible only because women's knowledge and point of view had found an inclusion in the leading values. It is important that increase in women's activity (participation, justice) requires proper criteria for selection of relevant forms of women's knowledge. These forms of women's knowledge will make a great contribution in designing alternate policies and systems in all spheres of life—social, economic, political, administrative, religious, etc. So it is necessary that just forms of women's knowledge be recognized, criteria for such recognition be properly understood.

### *10.3.2 Just Forms of Women's Knowledge*

Those forms of women's knowledge which are with most women and without which ordinary life cannot be regulated can be said to be just forms. These forms may exhibit great variety depending on time, place, context, etc. The following are some ways to identify them:

1. Just forms of women's knowledge should provide concrete opportunities for the participation of a very large number of women including the most disadvantaged.
2. It should be clear that these forms are located in the context of justice in the larger society. That is those forms of women's knowledge would be just which facilitate the establishment of justice in society and nature.
3. Selection of these forms of women's knowledge requires understanding the difference between suffering and exploitation. Suffering is a necessary part of the life of the living being, which can be reduced by individual efforts, but exploitation is not inevitable and the path of liberation from it needs to be attained through social consciousness, organization and activity. Emancipation from exploitation would lead also to freedom from suffering but the converse is not only not true but entails a selfish and unjust process.
4. Forms of knowledge which strengthen autonomy of women shall be deemed just forms. This means that every process and tendency that turns a woman into a worker, working for wages, must be opposed.
5. Autonomous existence has its basis in living together and as a fraternity. This means that those forms of women's knowledge alone will be just which develop autonomy for women and in the process shape systems which will neither tolerate exploitation

(injustice) nor become instruments of exploitation (injustice).

How is one to identify the just forms of women's knowledge with the help of these points? To answer this question it is necessary to take a look at the conditions of ordinary life today and its regulation.

The key lies in identifying those forms of women's knowledge which promote the role of the majority of ordinary women in regulations of society. Food and clothing are primary human needs and any society needs them constantly. All women possess variety of knowledge and skills related to these two areas, for example, in the area of food materials women possess the knowledge of all the processes starting from production to feeding which includes a reasonable knowledge of agriculture, storage of produce, cleaning, grinding and cooking a variety of things finally served on the plate. This also applies to cloth and clothing. Women know how to handle cotton or wool starting from its production to cleaning, spinning, dyeing, weaving, knitting, printing, sewing, embroidery and everything else. If these two sectors are returned to women, unlimited possibilities of increasing their activity become real. Textiles and food are the two areas in which women still excel, they are capable of doing whatever may be the social need. Other than these the variety of daily needs, decoration materials, toys, home made healthcare facilities can become available by allowing women's knowledge to be active in these areas. Such participation will increase their capacities to take part actively in many more areas. Textiles and food constitute a rather large part of the economy, which are in constant need and in these areas nutrition, quality, required supply and people's interests can all be served by decentralized production which can be based on women's knowledge.

Even today things fulfilling the basic needs of life have the most widespread market. And in their production is the basis of the livelihoods of tens of millions. Textiles and food materials constitute the lion's share of this market. Capitalist and imperialist powers have right from the beginning attempted to wrest control of these sectors. Women were displaced in a very big way from the sector of production of cloth when it was organized through big industry. Such an imperialist move met with determined resistance which finds expression in the movement led by Mahatma Gandhi. However, imperialism has transformed itself by the end of the 20th century. Now through globalization it proposes to reorganize in a new way—the production of life needs. This reorganization is shaping women's exploitation by new methods. Now production is being transferred from large industry to household enterprise. Such production is achieved by the use of small machines and simple techniques based on the labour of the whole household - women, men and children. That is labour of the household is now becoming the basis of production. Imperialism now controls production on the strength of finance capital and distant markets managed by the information technology. This leads to an astonishing rise in its power. In India for forty years since independence women suffered all round displacement and now globalization presses her directly into the service of imperialism. The multinational companies have launched aggressive campaigns to control food processing with its market and production of cloth and its market. Therefore, the movement for reorganization of the production and market of textiles and food materials on the basis of women's knowledge can become the mainstay of emancipating women from the vicious web of exploitation and erecting a promising challenge to globalization.

So, agriculture and industry need to change to allow a greater role and use of women's knowledge. It should always be remembered that working on others' terms in alien and remote locations, be it in agriculture, industry or others' offices and houses, makes the exploitation of women's labour and bodies very easy and as if inevitable. Women's power and control may have broken down considerably even within the family today, however, it is only in domestic situations, in the household that she exercises some control, autonomy and authority, this being the place where there is maximum occasion to put to good and productive use her knowledge. The division of responsibility between men and women needs to be redone from a fresh end, a division that facilitates complementarity and living together with cooperation. This will release that strength in women which promotes mutual cooperation with autonomy between various segments of society and inaugurate social formations that are in continuity with such traditions in our society.

### *10.3.3 Hurdles in the Dignity of Women's Knowledge*

There are three main hurdles in the dignity of just forms of women's knowledge. These are market, politics and modern science. How do we try to overcome these hurdles?

#### (a) Market

Systems of modern market are a major obstacle in women's knowledge gaining dignity in the public domain. Markets in remote areas are selling company-made articles coming from distant places. So, local production done in the family is unable to sell itself. The reason for this is not in quality or some other intrinsic power in these distant articles. The main reason is in the support they receive from the state. The state gives the company land, electricity, raw materials and other things at nominal rates. Research institutes funded by the government also do work whose results are finally used by companies. Transport and propaganda media are all available to take their products and their voices to distant places. Enterprises based on very small capital in the cities are being demolished in the name of beautification and encroachment. In the resulting market gap the companies swiftly step in. Across society and economy men and women are being turned into wage labour. Family-based enterprises both in agriculture and in industry are steadily losing any autonomy they had and the controllers of the new market have become their masters. These conditions are extremely aggressive and alien to our tradition from the people's point of view. Spread of forced wage labour in any form is directly opposed to autonomy. People will keep working in their houses but no decision relating to either the production line or marketing their products will be upto them. This is the new form of assembly line. The market of things you make keeps expanding and you become more and more just a cog. The main question is how to reorganize the market such that production by the family finds a just place in the economy.

We need a system of the market which promotes family industry and grain production in agriculture. This requires that such families and communities control raw materials, technology and exchange in the market. In other words, if local resources are controlled by the local society the knowledge of the artisan, peasant and woman has scope for free play. Autonomy is not imaginable without such free play for the knowledge of the people. Local markets, therefore, need to be so reconstructed which reinstate the artisans and women as knowledgeable persons. These markets will have to give preference to the sale of local produce. Such a local market presupposes the concept of a self-reliant local society. Things from outside come only when it is necessary. This is a strong condition for women's knowledge to gain respect and thereby become the source of dignified life for women. Such local markets will also be the major means of cooperation between different segments of society and a basis for cooperation and healthy living together of men and women. This reduces the possibility of exploitation by distant outside powers. In fact women are a central and leading figures in such reorganization of the market.

### *(b) Politics*

Politics today is not people-oriented but it serves imperialism. No party whether national or local functions without adjustment with imperialism. Participation through such politics only amounts to strengthening the exploitative power. Politics today stands with falsehood, crime and corruption only leading to division in society. The demand of the times is to give shape to those public forms which can stand up to this politics. There was a time when such questions were raised as what is the duty of a woman whose husband brings home earnings obtained by illegitimate means. Whether she should succumb to the authority of her husband to manage the household with that money or refuse to cooperate with her husband? It was this question that had transformed itself in India's Freedom Struggle into the question whether people should cooperate with the British Raj? The women adopted under Gandhi's leadership a course of non-cooperation compelling their men to follow suit.

This very question has come up again in the context of present-day politics. But the times have changed and standing up to this politics may demand pursuing a more difficult path.

The challenge to this politics lies in the strength of non-political organizations built by the people in the local society. These local organizations need to have multiple objectives and their strength will be based in their ability to shoulder the responsibility to regulate the society at the local level. Women's knowledge is a major pillar of systems which can keep this local power just. Women have a major role to play in building such non-political organizations, in actualizing their effective forms and in finding practical and just solutions to problems of local society. Non-political movements of such non-political organizations could possibly give shape to self-rule of local societies. This provides the promising context today for the women's movement.

### (c) Modern Science

Modern science and the system of modern education established in accordance with it is the greatest obstacle in the spread and establishment of values inherent to the idea of women's knowledge. Modern science has insulted and refused to recognize as knowledge *lokavidya*, as well as wide ranging capacities of women. However, the great majority of the population of India lives on the basis of *lokavidya* and the knowledge available with ordinary women, so much so that life without such knowledge is inconceivable. Not only this, the lives of those also who swear by science depends in great part on *lokavidya.*

There are great obstacles in reaching out to modern science. It is very far from women. Globalization has made education private and very expensive which has made this distance even greater. In this way on the one hand the doors of modern education and science are closing fast on women and on the other the same modern systems of knowledge do not recognize women's knowledge as knowledge at all. This is a major source of loss of dignity for women in society. The question of respect for one's knowledge is directly connected to justice and respect in society.

Globalization promises to reorganize society as a knowledge-based society. This certainly does not exhibit any intention of making knowledge the basis of people's power, on the contrary it tends to exploit *lokavidya* for the process of capital formation. Said in straight words, globalization sets the processes of displacing people from the positions of controls of this knowledge and bringing this knowledge under the control of big capital. This is the process of collecting and storing people's knowledge, assisted by the information technology. Poor communities, weaker sections of society, backward areas, artisan and peasant populations and their women have great knowledge of nature and a great variety of processes. This knowledge is being taken away from them by giving practically nothing in return and the governments are assisting these processes. Women are a special target. Now by the side of people's labour stands their knowledge too as the chief source of prosperity and power of the imperialist system. These are new conditions in which women have to find their way. The chief question before the women's movement is how should ordinary women stay away from the deception and fraudulent imperialist networks and press one's own knowledge in the service of developing strengths worthy of taking the initiative under the present conditions.

### *10.3.4 Campaign for the Dignity of Women's Knowledge*

This is a campaign for organizing just forms of women's strength, mainly through re-legitimization and respect for women's knowledge. Women's knowledge is an important part of *lokavidya* which is present everywhere and equally provides the basis for the struggle against imperialist power and tendencies. The campaign aims at using women's knowledge to initiate reorganization of society such that it gradually inactivates the greedy and exploitative imperialist system. For more than five years now, the campaign has organized sustained dialogue with ordinary women in towns and villages. It has held women's camps to explain the promise that their knowledge still holds for their future. It has organized local markets and conferences and carried out publications to draw common women into this campaign. The campaign sees a close and friendly relation with the struggles of peasants and artisans. It sees itself as contributing to the theoretical and practical preparations for the dignity of *lokavidya* in society and for seeking justice for the larger society. The following are its programmes:

(i) To develop new ideals of man-woman unity from the *lokavidya* standpoint in the systems of production based on the exploitation of family labour and knowledge and on this basis organize struggles to seek justice.

(ii) To organize camps on Dignity of Women's Knowledge and through these camps take to women and others the idea of women's knowledge/*lokavidya* to develop unity in the local society to strengthen them.

(iii) To organize small and spread out constructive work initiatives to revive in ordinary women the awareness of their strength inherent in women's knowledge. Also to organize women to take the initiative in regulating society at the local level.

(iv) To survey local markets on food materials and textiles, to prepare a concrete basis for the dignity of *lokavidya* through constructive programmes in these two areas.

(v) To identify the policies and laws that promote the conditions of unpaid labour and very cheap labour for women and start a public debate on these issues.

(vi) To prepare women to intervene actively in the local systems of healthcare, education and public security and facilities and shape programmes to reorganize them in the interest of the people.

(vii) To campaign for market protection to products made by women in the local market. During this campaign organize public debate to popularize the idea of reorganization of markets in the interest of people and find ways to take further steps. For example:

- If the sectors of textiles and food materials are to be controlled by women, how are we to go about it?
- If a definite part of food and clothing needs of a

village or a town is to be fulfilled by the women of the same village or town, then what methods need to be adopted?

- When the things that women of a village or town make or can make are brought from outside, what are the results, whose interests it serves and who suffers?
- Why is it necessary to provide the local producers organizing production in their houses, raw materials at cheap rates and on priority?
- How can we include the view of local producers and the local society in general in formulating rules for testing quality, registration and import-export in family-based production?

(viii) Different segments of the local society suffer imperialist exploitation in different ways. But the women are subject to exploitation by all these ways together. So women literally experience the suffering of others and this enables them to take the initiative in organizing resistance to exploitation of local societies. This campaign for the Dignity of Women's Knowledge attempts to voice and organize such concerns.

# 11

# A *Lokavidya* Perspective on Today's Social Movements*

*Sunil Sahasrabudhey*

The 20th century saw the movement of science, modern Western science, to an absolute undisputed apex position in the world of knowledge. It became the reference for the legitimacy, correctness, rationality of all other streams of knowledge, methods of inquiry and human attitudes and beliefs. From ordinary everyday beliefs and practices to theoretical and spiritual enterprise in the religious world, all had to be scientific, that is true to science. People's movements, political process, educational enterprise, economic activity, everything had to swear in the name of science; had to be scientific. Science assumed the status of an all pervasive value, being both a source of enlightenment and wealth. Products of 18th century Europe the Enlightenment and the Wealth of Nations assumed through the 20th century a status not known to any predecessor in the history of humanity. No wonder the 20th century started appearing to many as an absolute climax. There was talk of end of ideology and end of politics, signifying that thought and change had run their course and the world was now the playground of a single player, science including technology. Nations of the Third World becoming independent from the colonial rule after the Second World War, one after another, adopted the path of economic development, education and

* Paper presented at a national seminar on Science, Technology and Nation: In search of a Moral Fulcrum, February 24-26, 2011 at the University of Hyderabad.

social reconstruction squarely based on science. In the footsteps of the West they paid tribute to science for having delivered them from darkness and want.

But is there not a limit to the enjoyment of success and rule in a world which changes irrespective of the theories that men build? Three things were major misfits: virtue, poverty and nature. Science right from the day of its birth has allied with the market, bourgeois enterprise in particular and even theoretically refuses anything to do with virtue. It claims that it is the engine for eradication of poverty, but through the centuries it has ruled, there has been no indication of progress in such a direction. Undoubtedly the riches have grown but so has poverty. That 'natural science' has all along been against nature, no more requires proof. Whereas it is debatable whether science has produced greater understanding of and control over nature, it is beyond doubt that it has destroyed nature, climate change being the very visible, unmistakable tip of the iceberg.

By the time the 20$^{th}$ century drew to a close, science started losing its absolute grip on the world of knowledge and the rational argument. With globalization, changing political dispensation of the world and the advances in computer and communication technologies, the received theories, practically about everything, have started taking a beating. Science during this time has relied more and more on the 'technology' argument. Information-technology, bio-technology and nano-technology constitute the new frontiers. And they have brought back the moral question into the discourse of science. The issue of what kind of moral and social sanctions these new technologies should have is a serious point in the debate spread this time across the world. The intensifying debate on the question of climate change brings back the issue of the relationship of science with nature at the centre of public concern. And the continued poverty and oppression of the people mainly in the poor parts of the world has given rise to popular movements that often do not derive ideological or organizational continuity from the people's movements of the industrial age. Thus, development policy, including science policy now must take into account these situations of flux on the science front. They cannot any more take the uncritical positions that were so prevalent during the 20th century. The moral question, issues related to man's relationship with nature and the continued pressure of poverty-ridden human existence must all significantly contribute to reconsideration of policy frames, but how is it to be done, when the theory house of yesteryears is in shambles? Direct experience and perception then must come to our rescue. It may do well to look into the various movements of people, directly or indirectly addressing these issues in the present-day circumstances and then see where such an argument leads us to.

These movements discussed below are (i) indigenous people's movement in South America, (ii) international farmers movement , via Campesina, (iii) the farmers' movement of India, (iv) the *adivasi* movement in India, (v) the struggles led by the National Alliance of People's Movements in India, (vi) Student Movement in the West and (vii) the Islamic Movement.

## 11.1 Indigenous People's Movement in South America

Through the 1990s a new kind of indigenous people's movement grew in South America. Often struggles of the new type were connected with destruction of nature in the Amazon valley. Struggles of the indigenous people of Peru against the destruction of rain forests and for their way of life received worldwide attention after a showdown with the state in June, 2009. An idea of Mother Earth slowly took shape in the meetings of these people across the continent which finally presented itself before the world in Cochabamba, Bolivia during April 19-22, 2010 at the World People's Conference on Climate Change and the Rights of Mother Earth. The Conference called by Evo Morales, the President of Bolivia, who is himself from an indigenous people's community was organized to challenge the outcomes of the Copenhagen Climate Change Convention sponsored by the United Nations during December 2009. This conference of the civil society and governments in Bolivia was attended by 30,000 participants from over 100 countries. There was a strong presence in the conference of NGOs and people's movements. It has been argued that among others certain areas of South America are likely to be worst victims of the destruction that climate change is leading to and this may be a matter of just 30 years or so from now. Through this conference Bolivia put together the grievances of the indigenous people in a novel way and with force on the world stage.

*Rights of the Mother Earth* creates around itself an entirely different set of arguments to contest the UN-sponsored positions on climate change which favour unashamedly the rich countries and the corporate business. The debate at the conference, the speakers and the ensuing declaration, contest the major assumptions of modern civilization. Was Gandhi not doing the same while arguing against the industrialism of the West? This conference has taken the struggle of *adivasis* and peasants the world over to the next stage, they are no more asking for better terms in the given world, they are pressing for an idea and reality which makes for another world. The World Social Forum (WSF), since 2000, has given a slogan to the anti-globalization movement in the world, namely 'Another World is Possible'. The Rights of Mother Earth Conference has taken the much desired actual step in this direction. The Bolivian government under Evo Morales' leadership pressed this position further in Cancun, Mexico, where a follow-up of Copenhagen took place in early December 2010. They objected single-handedly both to the arbitrary and one-sided procedures and content of the final resolutions which they said favoured the rich and the business world and were completely against the indigenous people.

## 11.2 International Farmers' Movement - Via Campesina

Via Campesina has been noticed now by a much wider world, for it organized a 10,000 strong procession and demonstration in Cancun on December 7, 2010, during the United Nations Climate Change Conference. It is an international peasants' organization which includes the landless rural workers, rural women, *adivasis* and rural youth. It stands for cultural plurality and autonomy and is not connected with any political parties or corporate economic enterprise. It got to a start in 1993 in Belgium where the first conference gave it its bye-laws, structure, etc., with the second international conference in Mexico 1996, the third in Bangalore in 2000, fourth in Brazil in 2004 and the fifth in Mozambique in 2008. It is a place of unity for peasant organizations across the world. Amongst its chief objectives are included, social justice and gender parity in economic relations, preservation of ground water and natural resources, sustainable agricultural production and food sovereignty with the rider that all this be based in small and middle producers.

Via Campesina believes that peasants do agriculture based on generations of experience in local cultural and productive traditions, using local resources. If their production is mainly for domestic use and the local market then they have the capacity to feed everybody with appropriate quantities and quality of food. The present-day agriculture is industrialized and everything there is determined by the big market and the big capital. As a result there is exploitation of workers and peasants and economic and political concentration takes place. It is desired that production, processing, distribution and use be woven in a decentralized form which is controlled by the people and the communities and not by the multinational companies.

The right of determination of agriculture and food policy is Food Sovereignty, specifically it means organization of production and use of food with the priority of the needs of local use and local communities. It includes saving the domestic market from cheap imports of agricultural produce and safeguarding the national and community rights for protection and regulation of agriculture and cattle wealth production. It insists that both peasants and the landless must be provided land, water, seeds, other productive resources and the public services which are their need.

Food Sovereignty is a new idiom created by this movement. It has the capacity to affect a paradigm shift in the debate on sustainability and the well-being of the rural communities. It not only reorders the priorities, but such a change in the idiom of the movement opens ways of reconceptualizing the world order such that land and those on the land constitute the first consideration. Discussing via Campesina and Food Sovereignty one cannot help but be reminded of the Gandhian position on the desired world order.

### 11.3 India's Farmers' Movement

India witnessed a huge farmers' movement in the 1980s. Mainly spread across the states of Tamil Nadu, Karnataka, Maharashtra,

Gujarat, Haryana, Punjab and Uttar Pradesh the movement mobilized tens of millions of peasants. The main issues were prices for agricultural produce, debts of peasants and supply and rates of electricity. Of course, mobilization on local issues like those related to water, seeds, fertilizers, administrative highhandedness and corruption did make its contribution to the movement. The Bharat-India formulation is a contribution of this movement to the Indian political scene. The basic thesis was and is that the causes of poverty of the Indian villages lie outside rural India. The movement was largely peaceful and is responsible for bringing into existence new forms of struggle mainly *'rail roko'* and *'rasta roko'*. Most of the state level farmers' organizations that led the movement declared that they were non-political, but most of them took to the path of elections after they became weak and as a consequence lost their remaining strength. The movement has survived chiefly in Uttar Pradesh and commands some activity in the neighbouring states of Punjab, Haryana, Madhya Pradesh and Bihar. Chaudhary Mahendra Singh Tikait is the undisputed leader for over 20 years now. (He was alive when this article was written, but has died since, in May 2011.)

This movement provided a break from the movements in the rural areas led by communists, socialists or sarvodaya workers, who in one way or another accepted the canons of industrial society and gave primacy to inequality and contradictions within the rural society. The farmers' movement both by practice and ideology focused on exploitation and deprivation caused from outside and maintained a primacy of peasant interest which produced a naive but robust connection straight with Gandhi which was acknowledged as such by the leadership in different states. Today the movement is grappling with forced land acquisition and severely unequal distribution of national resources, electricity in particular. The movement has taken a stand against WTO and against GM seeds. It is connected with Via Campesina internationally and allies with *adivasi* movements within the country. Although the movement today does not command the same striking power as it did in the 1980s, it is the only mass movement in the present and distinguishes itself by claiming primacy of land and peasant for any processes of change.

The middle classes, the intellectuals, the so-called progressives, never supported the movement, on the contrary, debunked it as being in the interest of the rich peasantry. The movement claims that there is no such thing as rich peasantry. In fact there are no rich people in the countryside and those who may be said to be rich by rural standards are so not because of income from the land but because of income from other sources. The idea of primacy of land and peasant is alien to the educated world which is the reason why in spite of the great sympathy we see for Gandhi these days across classes there is no sympathy for his economic ideas or for his love for the village.

This movement provides space, both by its ideological formulations and insistence on the primacy of land and peasant, for the idea that those outside the world of the educated today namely, peasants, *adivasis*, artisans, women and very small business people have their own knowledge, *lokavidya,* by which they live and by which they would like to rebuild this world to become equal and honourable citizens.

## 11.4 *Adivasi* Movement in India

*Adivasis* in India today are in open revolt against the Indian State, the cause being their complete displacement from where they live, to grab land for corporate enterprise mainly related to the mineral wealth. In the 1980s the movement was centred in Jharkhand on the question of identity and statehood. Today the epicentre is in Chhattisgarh and the movement is openly against the state oppression. Led by the Communist Party of India (Maoist), this movement is spread mainly in the states of Chhattisgarh, Jharkhand, West Bengal, Bihar and Orissa. It has noticeable presence in Maharashtra and Andhra Pradesh. The movement is in the form of a people's war. In fact the movement was built by the organization called People's War Group starting in the early 1980s from Andhra Pradesh. The Indian state has launched a war level military initiative called Green Hunt to exterminate the movement.

The Maoist Party derives its heritage from the Naxalbari peasant revolt of 1967, which soon split the Communist Party of India (Marxist) to give birth to a new party CPI (Marxist-

Leninist) in 1969. The new activism that came into existence as a result of the Naxalbari event came to be known as Naxalism. More than 40 years have elapsed and the movement has gone through its highs and lows, moving from one region to another, organizationally through various splits and unity moves and now rests unequivocally in the leadership of the CPI (Maoist). If you leave out the gut level opposition and the extreme rightist take most people would be inclined to think that the outcome of this war in central India is not predictable. What is a matter of intense debate among the concerned intellectuals is the ideological and political stand of the Maoist Party. The party is banned and there is no easy way to lay your hands on the party literature.

So, the debate is highly speculative and dominated by preconceived notions based on one's understanding of the communist movement in the world, which has a long history. But both the traps need to be consciously avoided. No major advance in the communist movement has been predictable. In the expansion from the working class in Europe to the worker-peasant alliance in Russia and then to the four-class alliance with the peasantry as the main force in China, the movement of ideas could not have been anticipated. The commitment to the peasant base in China led to the cultural revolution for which even broad contours of a Marxist theory were not available. Now in India the communist movement has its main base among the *adivasis*. Commitment to this social base can surely be expected to produce ideas of change which cannot be anticipated. The central issue of the movement involves saving land and settlements of *adivasis*. There are reports from leading journalists and writers and scholars like Arundhati Roy, Gautam Navalakha and Nandini Sundar which give an indication of the kind of reconstruction the Maoist Party is attempting in areas it controls. This generally includes community involvement in water and land management, educational reform, settlement of disputes, etc. They have given the *Gondi* language its first books used also for education of children. Both in reconstruction and militant struggle women, young women in particular, are involved in a very big way.

How do we then make an assessment of the contribution

that this movement could be making to the politics of change, to the building of another world? It is best perhaps to stay with the demands of the movement and not go by the theories propounded during the industrial age. The biggest demand of the movement is that those on the land, manly *adivasis* in those areas, ought not to be displaced and two, they must get their rightful share in the national resources (this often comes in the name of development). This is no different from the demands of the farmers' movement and necessarily makes one subscribe to the idea of land first, the village first, the farmer first, and the *adivasi* first. All planning then needs to respect this priority.

### 11.5 *Jal, Jangal aur Zameen* (Water, Forest and Land) Movement

A movement that started to save the life, land and settlements threatened by the Sardar Sarovar Dam in 1984 later grew into one of the largest catchments of social activists known by the name of National Alliance of People's Movement (NAPM). Medha Patkar, its undisputed leader, started working among the *adivasis* in the mid-1980s in the region where Maharashtra, Gujarat and Madhya Pradesh meet and founded Narmada Bachao Andolan. Then in the mid-1990s a number of social movements of different backgrounds came together to found NAPM. Its first struggle was against ENRON Thermal Power Project in Maharashtra. Since then, it has struggled constantly against the assault on people's rights on the natural resources, namely; water, forest and land. In recent years the struggle has been mainly against forced land acquisitions for SEZs, huge power projects and other corporate enterprises. The movement against land acquisition found its latest expression in a week long dharna in Delhi in the fourth week of October 2010. Thousands participated representing a variety of struggle oriented organizations and NGOs from several states of India. It is a federal organization with broadly social democratic ideals. The stress on people's control of natural resources gives it, its characteristic outlook which is constantly in a tensed dialectic with the stated ideals of the movement as peace, democracy and justice. Right from the days of Narmada Bachao Andolan (NBA), it has attracted young men and women of educated background to struggle and argue against this mode of development which displaces *adivasi* and peasant populations from their natural locations, disorganizes their life completely and turns them into cheap labour, often migrant. Different organizations attached to NAPM may have different political and ideological stands, but together they have provided a huge non-party political space where *adivasis*, peasants, social activists and concerned intellectuals can work together to build alternative strategies of development based on people's initiatives.

### 11.6 Student Movement in the West

Globalization of economies and the information revolution leading to new forms of management has led to corporatization of education. This has meant more formal curricula, tighter schedules, higher fees, restricted entry to universities and apex institutions, closing down of social science and humanities departments and an unprecedented enhancement of the importance of management, law and engineering studies. In Europe this 'educational reform' is known as the Bologna Process started in 2000 by a meeting of education ministers of European countries in Bologna, Italy. By about 2006 a noticeable unrest of students in various European universities started. There is student unrest in America and England and also in certain South American universities and some East Asian universities. Ostensibly the movement is against severe cuts in public spending on higher education. The movement of course is struggle oriented in Europe involving considerable mobilization in Athens, Zagreb, Rome, Paris, Amsterdam, Vienna, Bonn and many more cities. In March 2010, there was a huge congregation in Vienna and in mid-February 2011 about one hundred student organizations from Europe, England, America and Canada are slated to meet in Paris. (This meeting took place on 14$^{th}$ February and the result was formation of a Knowledge Liberation Front.)

There are two strands to this movement. One of course which opposes the cut in public spending and asks for student debt relief and in general opposes the tightening of entry, higher fees and closure of cultural spaces leading to onedimensionalization of the university to suit the production of graduates as a cog in the corporate machine. The second aspect of the movement dwells on the possible and desired reconstruction of the university as cultural spaces of self-organization of education. This is an interesting debate discussing a variety of ideas and initiatives spread, for example, in the names of autonomous global university, solidarity university, virtual university, open university, the informational university, social university, democratic university, unbounded university, street university, commoniversity, multiversity and a university of the people, for the people, etc.

During this process a certain variety of European left has organized itself as Edu-Factory Collective through an online interactive dialogue. They denote the present period by the name Cognitive Capitalism. They say that a transition has taken place from industrial capitalism to cognitive capitalism and that the chief site of struggle has shifted from the factory to the university. They are very particular about clarifying that this thought welcomes no nostalgia, no going back to the university of the earlier times but new thoughts and new ideas need to take shape to build a new university and that this process of building a new university has to be independent of the dictates of capital and control by corporations and therefore, a process concomitant with a process of social change that liberates society from the rule of capital.

These are times of change and new ideas. Their ideas of reorganization of universities revolve around concepts of living knowledge, self-organization and autonomy. They say that the corporate university teaches dead knowledge. A new university needs to be global in nature in the sense that networked relationships and mutual learning needs to be a part of it. One wonders how a student movement of this type can connect itself to *adivasi* and peasant movements across the world. Can the student movement of Europe eventually give a call for Europe to go back to its villages?

### 11.7 The Islamic Movement

There is a huge movement across the world mobilizing Muslims in the name of Islam to challenge America and the Western ways and re-establish the Islamic State and the Islamic way of life. After the bombing of the towers of the World Trade Centre in New York on 11 September, 2002, the world powers gave Islamic militancy the name of terrorism. The Islamic movement is militant almost everywhere though it may be led by different organizations. In recent history these struggles date back to the Arab-Israel conflict of 1970, the rise of the Palestinian Liberation Organization (PLO) during the 1970s and the Iranian Revolution of 1979. The Muslim Brotherhood of Egypt of course dates back to the early 20$^{th}$ century. The latest organization of international standing is Al-Qaeda, originating in Saudi Arabia.

Apparently to counter Islamic militancy America attacked Iraq and Afghanistan and now has a huge military presence in these and adjoining states like Pakistan. The Islamic movement commands huge support among the Muslims of the world. They want reorganization of the world on the Islamic concepts of justice and brotherhood, they are opposed to Western ways and America's domination. Huge churning has taken place among Muslim intellectuals and however Westernized the majority of them appear wedded to Islam, albeit of the Islam of their interpretation. The Islamic world-view among other things, subscribes to a concept of knowledge and being which is at severe odds with the so-called modern scientific outlook and the values of the modern West. What is significant is that, a fair share of modern Muslim intellectuals are sympathetic to such a world-view. If the world is moving towards a multi-polar arrangement, then they too have a chance.

### 11.8 The Knowledge Issue

Consideration of these movements clearly shows that the question of science and science policy must transform itself into a question of knowledge and the state policy on knowledge which would include the issue of science. Since the information reality and discourse also favours the knowledge idiom, the transition ought to be smooth. The questions that we had identified in the beginning were focused on morality, nature and poverty. All these have been addressed in their own ways by the movements discussed above with the possible exception of the student movement in Europe which nevertheless addresses the question of knowledge directly. The Islamic movement has a distinct civilizational approach where knowledge is inconceivable without virtue. The *adivasi* and peasant movements whether against displacement or for control of natural resources or centred on threats of climate change, all argue for a world in which the land, the peasant and the surrounding nature (forests) occupy the central place and life is to be generated and regenerated here with the initiative of these people, based on the knowledge they possess and in the framework of local cultural traditions. Priority of such considerations leads to a new language of discourse for social transformation. Rights of Mother Earth, food sovereignty, cognitive capitalism, the Bharat-India divide are some such idioms which have already found currency. Add to this *lokavidya* and we are much closer to a Gandhian way of thinking.

The question of human knowledge needs to be addressed in its entirety. No movements discussed above appear to subscribe to science as the basis of human knowledge, on the contrary some explicitly and some implicitly hold science responsible as an integral part of the Western ways which have brought most people of the world to the present miserable state. However, it seems that the idea of knowledge will have to be confronted directly and fundamentally in so many words to steer clear of digressions and misconceptions for a realistic imagination of another world and a strategy of struggle for the same. The idea of *lokavidya*, that is knowledge in society, knowledge with the people, knowledge outside the present-day university, seems to possess that quality which can show us the essential unity among the movements discussed above. Does this lead us to a concept of people's knowledge movement, *Lokavidya Jan Andolan*?

# 12

# *Agaria-Vidya*: A Link in the Philosophy of Emancipation*

*Sunil Sahasrabudhey*

This article attempts a social-philosophical analysis of the ferrous science tradition of the *agaria adivasis*, mostly living in Central India. The central concern is to investigate the kind of social and epistemic standards and values demanded by such a knowledge system and by the knowledge tradition extant among various components of the *swadeshi samaj* which are completely different from modern science. An attempt is also made to see how such traditions of knowledge can become sources of strengths for the society and how they can play their role in helping the people-oriented philosophies to assume social power.

## 12.1 The *Agaria*

The *agarias* of Chhattisgarh have preserved the ferrous technology tradition of this civilization. These people who make pure iron by smelting the ordinary iron ore in very small furnaces located in their house-premises and are the preservers of such high art and science are just about the poorest in this country and untouchable in the larger society whose part they are. It is difficult to find a more telling example of how this great source of strength in society has been kept in a state of choice-less, powerless existence.

---

* This is an English translation of the Hindi original published in the book *Lokavidya Vichar* (2001) which puts together essays by activists engaged in the *lokavidya* movement.

We had an opportunity to meet the *agaria* in 1990. Then we were investigating the idea of living traditions as a starting point for opening pathways of thought and action which may lead to a society free of exploitation. The concept of non-political power was already born in the context of the farmers' movement, further, attempts were live for realizing as its basis, at least in theory, those forms of knowledge and social power which were independent of modern science and the modern state and had the capacity to challenge these instruments of rule by man over man. It is at such a time that PPST (Patriotic and People-oriented Science and Technology Foundation) got a project for work on the live ferrous tradition. This project brought forth a variety of interesting points about this industrial tradition and later the context of the First Congress on Traditional Sciences and Technologies of India held at the Indian Institute of Technology, Bombay in 1993 provided an opportunity to organize this work from Varanasi.

The Indian steel industry has a long history. Archaeometallurgy is a well defined subject in the universities. Steel making has touched rather high points in this land. The Damascus Swords were made from Indian steel. It is this tradition which we see living among the *agaria.* Far from the cities, towns and the roads, deep into the forest and mountain ranges where the agents of the government find it too troublesome to go, there are villages in the district of *Sarguja* in Chhattisgarh, where in a number of houses one can find the red glow in the small furnaces; iron-smelting goes on here. The furnace is just about a yard in height and may be a foot and a half the measure of its outer diameter. The cylindrical contraption is somewhat wider at the base and narrow at the top with a vertical hole in the centre whose diameter is about 8-10 inches. It is made of earth mixed with a little rice husk, the central hole is from where the iron ore and the charcoal are charged from above. The ore is usually found near the mountains and the rivers. The charcoal is made by partially burning the picked up twigs and branches of trees in the forest. The furnace has two horizontal holes at the bottom at about 100 degrees from each other meeting the vertical hole at the lowest end. One of these holes is for the slag to flow out and the other is used for supplying air to the high temperature zone using a bamboo with a longitudinal hole and a leather contraption for bellows. After a process of about 3 hours the *agaria* engineer opens the air supply hole and pulls out a red iron bloom of about 3-4 kilogram weight by a long pair of tongs. The iron bloom is then squeezed by heavy hammering. This is almost 100 per cent pure wrought iron, malleable, ductile, etc. It is not pig iron, the carbon content is somewhere around 0.03 per cent. This simple looking process in fact seems to be woven by a balanced coordination of some of the very fine processes. Attempts to replicate in the university campuses are yet to deliver. The *agaria* seems to be a great master. You may change the charcoal, the source of the ore, the place or climate and the *agraia* engineer takes one or two experiments to settle on the new combination of different factors to deliver the *sponge* again. If you see him through the entire exercise you will be surprised to find that each time he does an errorless job of smelting without use of any machine, without me*asuri*ng the rate of supply of air, the temperature, the rate of charge of ore and charcoal from above and without looking at the watch even once.

The details available in books tell us that this wrought iron was taken in small pieces and fired for 48 hours in small crucibles mixed with some organic matter, to produce high carbon steel known as wootz. Making of wootz is considered the highest point of this tradition of ferrous technology. There must be *agaria* workmen even now who know how to make *wootz,* who may even be doing it. What appears to an educated eye just a technique or a living practice is in fact an activity which is integral to the history, geography, belief system, culture and economy of the society of the *agaria* and it is perhaps in this unity that it finds the basis of survival in spite of the very heavy odds.

The studies on the *agaria* tell us that iron has a central role in the life of the individual and the community. Iron has a critical and important ritualistic role in every significant event from birth through marriage, etc. to death. Their mythology and the actual real life economic activities all have iron at their centre. An understanding of such a context is necessary to understand the relation between knowledge and society. We would like our investigation to address questions like what is the form of such knowledge, what can be its role in the social dynamic, whether it can become a source of strength for the *agaria* community and/or for the larger society, does it entail ontological possibilities not admitted in modern science, does *adivasi-vidya* constitute a just and emancipative form of knowledge and does the *lokavidya* point of view provide sufficient basis to address these questions? However, before we get on to these questions it may be useful to have a look at the relationship that the *agaria* has with the larger society and the modern state.

The chief sources of livelihood of the *agarias* are agriculture, repairs and maintenance of agricultural implements, wage labour, smelting and fabrication of iron implements, livestock (goats, pigs, hens, etc.) and collection of forest produce including hunting of small animals, etc. The total income is so small that no aspect of life is even passably well attended. They live in clusters of houses ranging from 2-3 to 10-12 at a place on the outskirts of villages. Most villages, which includes both *adivasis* and non-*adivasis*, treat them as untouchable. The experts among them, do get some recognition in the local society and these specialists too ordinarily do not work for wages on others' premises. Their activity of iron smelting may be shown as violating the Minerals Act and the Forest Act which gives space to the local forest guard and the policemen to scare them and obtain small favours. After independence the government organized campaigns to stop local iron smelting. In these campaigns the *agaria* have suffered also from police action, imprisonment, etc. The *agaria* are so poor and weak that all this scares them. When we went out into the open in search of these furnaces, the stock reply we got was that all this had ended long ago. Those who were themselves operating the furnaces, also gave this reply. Because of untouchability, they are unable to derive any strength from the larger *adivasi* society too. Those from the modern world presume that even if smelting furnaces are being worked at some places they are bound to die out soon, it being only a matter of time. Archaeologists, metallurgists and professors of universities look at the whole process as some living remnant of a great tradition but fail to acknowledge the scientific status of such experts and do not give them a status higher than that of a skilled worker. These people think that they know more about iron making than the *agaria*, perhaps because they can write about it but the *agaria* cannot. Even such political leaders who have no vested interest are also guided by the standpoint of the University Science. Social activists working for the transformation of society with the intervention of modern technologies also do not see the knowledge of the *agaria* as a source of strength in society, but only as a remnant of a once valued tradition which is bound to die out with the passage of time. Thus here too there is no hope. It is only the standpoint of *lokavidya* inspired by Gandhi's philosophy which provides the starting point for such analysis and investigation which may break fresh ground for infusion of a new dynamic in society.

## 12.2 Form of Knowledge

Professors in the Universities are not prepared to grant it the status of knowledge. Since this is the value of the ruling classes and has widespread existence in society, the knowledge of the *agaria* does not get the respect it deserves. The *lokavidya* standpoint recognizes the systematic falsehood present in such a view and with its help one may attempt to uncover the reality of the knowledge of the *agaria*. This section tries to underline the possible salient features of such an attempt.

Structure of a system of knowledge can be understood through the ingrained values, the body of knowledge and ontological commitments. This understanding is the result of combining the *lokavidya* standpoint with philosophical analyses of modern sciences and it is presented here not as some ultimate truth or understanding but as an analytical tool necessary for theoretical activity today.

### *12.2.1 Value*

An *agaria* family (two brothers, Ram Saputtar and Ram Sundar and their children) from village Pendari, Wardruffnagar, Sarguja, Chhattisgarh (then Madhya Pradesh) performed a successful demonstration of their iron smelting method in

*Swadeshi Vigyan Karyashala* organized in October 1993 at the Gandhian Institute of Studies, Varanasi. Thousands of people saw two furnaces operated for three days. This was the first demonstration ever of the *swadeshi* iron smelting in any modern institution of learning. The chief expert Sri Ram Sunder sacrificed a cock before starting the work wearing a brand new *dhoti*. He was not ready to compromise on these preconditions. Since a cock was sacrificed in an institution running in the name of Gandhi, it gave rise to considerable debate before and after the event.

During our *lokavidya* work we have met all kinds of experts who are not ready to separate their faith and values from the knowledge system they master. Social historians have often seen it as superstition. If at all a rationale is granted it is only as fulfilling a need in his social security. The *lokavidya* standpoint argues that these methods of understanding the specialization and custom in larger society are extremely weak and are nothing but an ugly and false expression of the so-called secular values of modern science.

Knowledge is always value-laden. Social values which provide the concrete context of the development of any stream of knowledge are also its internal values. Any spontaneous, self-propelling and autonomous activity must have the same external and internal values. Just as human beings are in a constant state of interaction with their environment and cannot be conceived as independent of their environment (in fact the basic elements of the two are perhaps fundamentally not distinguishable) similarly knowledge systems are not separable from the values they embody and are embedded in and if we do this we draw only a false picture of the knowledge system. It is this picture, which gives birth to the dream of completely transforming knowledge into machine.

The *agaria* himself does not see his smelting capacity as separable from his society, traditions, faith and values. If we completely disregard the *agaria*'s view of his *own* knowledge while forming a view on *his* knowledge then we are bound to depart away from truth and the error would be greatly compounded if we think that his view of his knowledge is incorrect. Don't we all accept that the *agaria* is neither a machine nor a remnant but a living human being?

### 12.2.2 *Body of Knowledge*

Autonomous streams of knowledge have autonomous view points on the question of knowledge. Who knows through what theoretical categories are understood the ore and its purity, charcoal from the wood of different trees, ceramic properties of furnaces, quality of product, process temperature, rate of operation of bellows, etc.? The *agaria* ought to know how he does it. There is no reason to believe that categories and objects of knowledge assumed and prescribed by modern science should be acceptable in other knowledge systems too.

Everybody knows that the theoretical categories of modern medical science are completely different from those in *ayurveda.* Just as results of pathological tests do not make sense to a *vaidya,* similarly doctors of modern medicine do not understand the language of *Vayu-pitta-cuf.* The situation is similar perhaps between a professor of metallurgy and the *agaria.*

Another question of great importance is about the relation between technical knowledge and society. If somebody says that the *agaria* is doing iron smelting for 2-3 millennia and during this period this community has developed a special relationship with iron, this relation being part of the *agaria's* knowledge of iron works and that any group or community or even individual cannot develop this understanding in a few years, then how are we to respond to this? Will this understanding be considered sufficiently human or as one limiting human capacity and activity to racial specificity? Or will this understanding open new broad ways for just human activity through an understanding of racial autonomy and dynamic? The answer to these questions is related to whether a body of knowledge has some simple and absolute existence or whether it takes shape according to different societies and streams of knowledge prevalent among them.

### 12.2.3 *Logic*

The logic of the knowledge of the *agaria* is certainly different. We have seen Ram Sundar at the smelting operations. We do not know how he decided on the size and relative amount of the ore and the charcoal. However, with the change of source and therefore, type and quality of these materials he successfully affected the change in relative amounts and whatever else was necessary to complete the process. It took about three hours. His younger brothers and nephews worked on the bellows and he just watched from a distance the smoke, colour of the flame, the rate of coming out of slag and perhaps many other things and kept deciding from time to time whether pumping of air was to be increased or decreased, whether further charcoal was to be added, how much more and with what particle size the ore had to be added, etc. Sri Ram Sundar and his team successfully performed again in December 1993 at IIT Mumbai during the First Congress of Traditional Sciences & Technologies of India. In the city of Mumbai it was difficult to find charcoal. From the neighbourhood one could obtain only low quality charcoal. This did put the *agarias* into difficulties, however, Ram Sundar was able to change the various parameters to successfully demonstrate the smelting operation. All that is needed to be done starting from the raw materials to the end product, the standards that need to be followed and the rational arguments that the artisan uses for experimentation, improvement and change are connected with one another by innumerable linkages. The dynamic of the network of these linkages is what may be called the logic of knowledge. Just as human beings cannot be replaced by machines, similarly the logic of knowledge cannot be entirely replaced by mathematics and the language of computers.

When Deshabandhu Chittaranjan Das first met Gandhi he came back and told his friends that he (Gandhiji) believed in magic and not in logic. *Agaria's* iron smelting seems to be such a magic. In this sense science too believes in magic but in black magic, the magic of Gandhi and the *agaria* is white.

We do not know how much the logic of one knowledge system can be comprehended from the standpoint of the logic of some other knowledge system. However, it is perhaps reasonable to assume that questions related to such comprehension are not static but dynamic. The main source of confusion in the discussion on logic of knowledge lies in the claim of modern science that its logic is context-free and value-free and eventually free even from any relation with truth. A discursive exercise in the sphere of logic of the knowledge of *agaria* may help us in liberating ourselves from the compelling epistemic and 'logical' circumstances that modern science creates.

### *12.2.4 Ontology*

The foregoing discussion on value, knowledge and logic may now be of some help in defining the ontological questions. If the present reality and forms of power are born together with value-free absolute knowledge and its independent-of-everything logic, then can the knowledge streams like those of the *agaria* bring forth that basic reality and forms of power in which there is no provision for the rule of man over man? The ontology of *lokavidya* does not allow conceptualizing hierarchy of basic entities and as a result also does not allow social hierarchy. The reality of these ideas may come home if we look at the social structure and public institutions of non-political societies. The knowledge of the *agaria* lends credibility to the claim of *lokavidya* that with social dignity it can bring before everybody thoughts of such social organization and social power which have been precluded from debate by modern science and modern education. This is the thought of non-political power which is based on the autonomy and equality of different knowledge streams in society.

## 12.3 The Social Dynamic

What is the role of the *agaria,* his knowledge or of our studies into the knowledge of the *agaria* from the point of view of mobilizing the forces of justice against exploitation for infusing a new dynamic in the society? There are several levels on which this question can be understood. For example first, how and what role can the knowledge of the *agaria* play in transforming his present condition of existence? Second, what is the value of these things in the campaigns of the *swadeshi samaj* against imperialism? Third, what is the role of this technology in the context of the National Industrial Policy? And fourth, how can the debate on the knowledge of the *agaria* help in elevating philosophy to a position of social force? Now with the help of these questions we will try to understand the problem of infusing a new dynamic in society.

### 12.3.1 The Agaria Community

The *agaria* community knows that it is the master of a very special system of knowledge. In this he sees both the source of his dignity and identity. In spite of untouchability he sees in his knowledge a source of his strength. But he does not know how in reality he can convert it into actual strength. During our investigations we raised this idea to the status of a principle that the knowledge of the *agaria* must primarily serve to strengthen his social organization and enhance his strengths in the larger society. For this three factors were given special importance: one, organizational development of his social (community) *panchayat*, two, development of the local market for the products of his activity and three, a process of cultural regeneration based on his own system of beliefs.

An *agaria panchayat* was called on 30-31 May 1993 at village Chichlikh, in Nagwan block of district Sonbhadra of Uttar Pradesh. The second *panchayat* was held in village Pendari, Wardruffnagar, district Sarguja (Chhattisgarh), on April 10, 1994. Both the *panchayats* were attended by about 200 *agarias* coming from villages in a circle of about 30-kilometre radius. These *panchayats* primarily discussed how their command of iron processes can play a role in the improvement of their economic condition. The sources of income of the better-off in the *agaria* community too are now based in agriculture or service. Those doing iron smelting live deep in the interior, they are very poor and have no influence even within the community. Therefore, the community values agriculture and education more that anything else but they also attach value to iron works from the point of view of identity, dignity and lasting interest.

The iron products that they make fetch a good price in the market but owing to fear of the local police and the forest office they have to keep the activity at a low level. What is needed for them is permission from the government for local iron smelting.

Cultural regeneration is necessary for revival of self-confidence. This is possible and desirable only through their *panchayat*. We were unable to link the process of *panchayat* called by us to the process of their traditional *panchayat*, so starting points for a process of cultural regeneration could not be found.

### *12.3.2 Swadeshi Samaj*

This work among the *agaria* has significant lessons for the entire *swadeshi samaj*. It is a part of the defining characteristics of the *swadeshi samaj* that it is the master of knowledge that belongs to this land, whose standards he himself decides and all the high experts are within itself. This study of the *agaria* community strengthens our belief that the basis of artisan-organization must be in his own knowledge and expertise. Only when this happens can he develop the strength to challenge the modern industrial system and proceed to give shape to a system of *swadeshi* industries.

This study of the iron-works of the *agaria* introduces us to that dynamic of the artisan with whose praise glow the pages of history. It is a source of astonishing power and possibilities. It is this dynamic, which has the capacity to recreate the world afresh. The dynamic of the artisan and *lokavidya* cannot be comprehended independent of one another. It is this dynamic, which has the capacity to mobilize peasants, women and the whole of the *adivasi samaj* for unity with the artisan.

### *12.3.3 National Society*

Friends doing metallurgy tell us that the kind of iron made by *agarias* is imported at very high prices. So if the iron-works of the *agarias* are promoted it may be possible to save on foreign exchange, reduce external dependence and affect economic relief to the *agarias*. Other than this the *agaria* specialists may be identified for experimentation to make wootz which is special high-carbon beautiful steel. To be able to do this will be a major step from the metallurgical point of view. Further it will greatly help in restoring self-respect and the public image of *swadeshi vidya*. One does not find forces in the ruling configurations who may wish to do this, therefore, these tasks will have to be taken up by social campaigns.

## 12.4 Philosophy: A Social Force

As globalization is progressing, we find that whereas the

capitalists, traders and political leaders are becoming more and more aggressive, those individuals and organizations who challenge them appear weaker by the day. In the last 50 years the knowledge of *swadeshi samaj* was neither considered a source of thought nor of any strength. However, the discussion above under "form of knowledge" and "social dynamic" brings to light such points which can become the basis for the *agaria*'s knowledge to act as the starting point for a philosophical campaign. Such a philosophical campaign will be able to stand up against the false weight and glitter of wealth, market and the modern sciences. Today an anti-human, anti-social false and poverty-stricken system is coming into existence in the name of knowledge-based society. To erect the challenge to this, such a new ideological movement is needed which is based on the struggle of peasants and artisans and in their living traditions of knowledge. It is this philosophical campaign to which the *agaria-vidya* can contribute fundamentally from many angles and in many ways. Any people-oriented philosophy which is in the interest of the people has to be based in *lokavidya. Agaria-vidya* is such a part of *lokavidya* that it may even get listed in "believe-it-or-not."

# 13

# Knowledge and Politics: The Dialectics of Change*

*Sunil Sahasrabudhey*

The knowledge terminology now with inroads into almost every sphere has come to stay. It is underlining the beginnings of the emergence of a radically new reality. There are people and I am among them, who think that the changes being witnessed are going to be more sweeping than our imagination permits us to think today. Should we take the help of our leaders of the 20th century to break some fresh ground? The line of thinking suggested below is one such attempt.

## 13.1 A Polity Has a Knowledge Basis

Science is a historical event which is not there for all time to come and not also any inevitable result of some underlying logic of progress in human knowledge through history. A neutral scientist and a Western hawk should both agree to this now because of the new flux caused by computer and communication sciences and technologies (called the new sciences) and the change in life brought about by the internet. Others did not need an argument even before. With the breakdown of 'absoluteness' of science in the realm of knowledge and society, freer and more varied relationships are conceivable between knowledge and society. Starting with the social basis of real

---

* Article in the bulletin *Virtuality and Knowledge in Society: Dialogue on Knowledge in Society II*, published for the Vidya Ashram Workshop in the World Social Forum, Karachi, Pakistan, March 2006.

politics one can show that there is always a knowledge basis of the structure and evolution of a polity.

The structures of polity we are all familiar with are those that have come into existence in the last 200 years, i.e. Post-Industrial Revolution. These are capitalist structures with their imperial variants and later socialist structures in some places. This is also the period of institutionalization of science with the claim that it is the only legitimate body of knowledge, the scientific method acclaimed as the only legitimate and reliable method of seeking and producing knowledge. So every real structure—of society which is social formation, of polity which is the State, of religion which is their organization, of education which is the school, of knowledge which is the university, of industry and others and of small or big institutions—had to have its essential structure conform to the structure of science in some strong sense, perhaps be isomorphic with it to be 'legitimate' in the modern world and therefore viable at all. Everything that did not so conform was desecrated. Even philosophies were not spared. Buddhism, Hinduism or Islam in their abstract forms had to be 'scientific' to be acceptable in the public domain.

Under such widespread domination local and remote politics based on knowledge other than science, having values other than capitalist or socialist values and having structures other than the modern hierarchical structures, turned inward, became inactive or even obsolete so far as the public realm was concerned. In the public realm they were seen as defeated polities, the Mughals, the Marathas, regional polities and tribal confederacies, etc. These polities had their own knowledge bases. These were the streams of knowledge that governed people's relation with nature, among themselves and with oneself. These knowledge streams governed people's economic and religious activities, they governed their political activity, in fact provided the ultimate conceptual bases of governance and self-governance. The polities were defeated but not these streams of knowledge which developed their own defences by turning inward and private, in the process incurring huge losses but avoiding death, thus moving from a path of progress through invention and discovery to a path of artisanal innovation circumscribed by the stringent survival needs. But nothing lasts for ever, so with the domination of science and the polity of the 20th century. Perhaps it is time now for people to reassert for politics based on their own streams of knowledge.

## 13.2 Traditions of Knowledge

Let this not be confused with traditional knowledge. 'Traditional knowledge' has been interpreted in a variety of ways including or excluding all or part of scriptural knowledge and skills and practices of the people acquired outside the formal educational system. It mainly refers to a body of knowledge, whereas 'traditions of knowledge' see knowledge as a process, activity, values, organization, its relationship with the society including a host of other dynamic elements. Traditions of knowledge are like a double helix interconnected through active exchanges of traditions of organized knowledge and *lokavidya* traditions. We shall call it the double tradition, for there is a tendency to see one or the other as the sole repository depending on the view point one possesses.

Traditions of organized knowledge of a great many places are no more living. For example, *Sankhya* or *Mimansa* traditions are not living traditions. Scriptures are often the places from where such organized knowledge needs to be dug out. Aspects of such traditions can be said to have survived through absorption in what may be called religious thought and practices of monastic orders. Another place where these traditions find a transformed and modern expression are the departments of ancient learnings and philosophies in the universities. There is of course a third place where perhaps the greater part of such traditions finds a living expression, this is the *lokavidya* tradition.

Modern science is the biggest tradition of organized knowledge today. Its ubiquitous presence through the modern state, technology and the educational system has led to its penetration of other traditions of knowledge. This penetration is sometimes through the use of technology, sometimes by direct presence of ideas and otherwise generally by a structural and paradigmatic adaptation.

*Lokavidya* traditions are traditions of knowledge in society, not in the university and not in the research institutions or laboratories. People who have not been to the university organize their lives on the basis of their own resources of knowledge. This is one resource which cannot be simply taken away from them by the fiat of an act passed by the parliament or by a government order. Human beings are epistemic beings, *lokavidya* being that fundamental characterizer which gives them an intrinsic human identity. *Lokavidya* is not traditional knowledge, it itself constitutes composite traditions of knowledge. It is by nature a living tradition. Leave alone being stagnant, *lokavidya* is not static even for a day, even for a moment. Assimilation, incorporation , rejection, improvement, innovation and so on keeps occurring all the time, the criteria being the criteria of truth and acceptability in ordinary life. Ordinary people of most countries, peasants, artisans, workers, women, tribals, small shopkeepers and many others engaged in subsistence or somewhat better economic activity are those who live by *lokavidya* and enrich it every day. *Lokavidya* has a presence in various traditions of organized knowledge. Life in the monasteries is not without it. The university scorns at *lokavidya* but technological (industrial) practices keep deriving advantage from the fact that workers come from definite *lokavidya* backgrounds and are adept at using the *lokavidya* reasoning and criteria.

Traditions of knowledge can also be called streams of knowledge. This has an advantage of freeing us from the disputed and debatable use of 'tradition'. In substance it makes no difference and favours freshness and open destinies. Every stream of knowledge is understood or known by a body of knowledge and information, its values, the ethical world enmeshed with it and not separable from it, a concept of cosmos (rule, power, existence, etc.) and its mode of abstraction, structure, sound argument type, mould of explanation, etc. Now this is not to construct any definition of how to recognize or identify a stream of knowledge. It is only to capture some major ways of interacting with, observing, understanding a stream of knowledge, for some such ways would be needed to see relationships between streams of knowledge and structures of polity.

## 13.3 Politics and *Lokavidya*

Knowledge in society expresses itself in many ways. It may also not be entirely correct to see it in terms of the double tradition, namely a double helical stream of organized knowledge and *lokavidya*. The epistemic reality is far too divergent in form, content, essences, styles, usefulness, aesthetics, ethics and so on to lend itself to some so-called 'correct' interpretation. The double tradition is that robust phenomenon which we encounter in the erstwhile colonies, by and large the Third World. *Lokavidya* traditions, unlike Europe, are live in this part of the world.

In the field of ideas the greatest obstacle to the development of the state and political society in these areas are the ideas of public life and politics based on *lokavidya*. The repeated defeat of the indigenous forces involved their failure to understand the modern state and politics. Even today peasants, artisans, women and tribals in general do not understand the nature of modern politics which is based on a knowledge tradition alien to them. Politics based on *lokavidya* is generally the politics of self-governance. It is in as much opposition to modern politics as is *lokavidya* to modern science. In practice, the politics based on *lokavidya* takes the form of local dissent, mostly unsustainable in a world of extreme centralization of all power. However, there have been occasions where very large movements which challenge the edifice of the modern world based on science and capital took recourse to a knowledge basis which had equal respect, if not more, for *lokavidya*.

## 13.4 Emancipatory Dialectic in the Industrial Age

Radical mass leaders in Asia in the 20th century across the full ideological spectrum show a keen awareness of the double knowledge tradition. Their practice reveals this awareness and a new consciousness thereof. Theoretical propositions they put forward exhibit, as if, a new unity of and within the double tradition pointing towards new politics. The cases in sight are those of Mahatma Gandhi, Chairman Mao and Ayatollah Khomeini.

Like the popular leaders of very high stature down the

human history these leaders too exhibit naive (and not so naive) dialectic between their positions based on some kind of direct and immediate perception of reality and their allegiance to an (their) organized knowledge tradition. To the extent this dialectic is naive these direct perceptions are more like sound saintly truths and in senses in which this naiveté breaks down or in the sense in which the dialectic is self-conscious and strategic they tend to inaugurate a theoretical standpoint.

Gandhi's allegiance to orthodox philosophy in Indian tradition and its constant reference to and preference for people's ways of doing things as opposed to scriptural directions shows this play, dilemma or dialectic that is being suggested above. His pan-moral approach is seen by political societies as a moral approach. However, people perhaps do not have a strict analytical, 'moral' category. Gandhi himself does not have such a theoretical 'moral' category. To intervene so strongly in the public domain without strictly dichotomizing fact and value requires an essential synthesis of the double tradition discussed above. His allegiance to *Geeta* (*Vedanta*) on the one hand and on the other his philosophy of *Swadeshi* and *Swaraj* amount to first an acknowledgement of the double tradition and then an attempt at a new synthesis. It is such a synthesis on a grand scale that lays the basis of a totally different polity which is not by any reckoning a variant of the state and politics emanating from the West. Gandhi's vision has the sweep of a civilizational mission in which for everything that there is, there is another way of doing it. For this not to be utopian it needs to be understood as squarely placed on also what there is then. What exists as a basis in the double knowledge tradition and the complex web of human activity owing allegiance to one or the other or mostly in practice to both streams of the knowledge tradition. It is the synthesis of the two streams that lifts the base reality to the level of political promise.

In the case of Mao Tse-tung his successes and failures underline his awareness of this dialectic. Success in leading the Chinese Revolution to eventual victory in 1949 and failure embodied by the withdrawal of the Cultural Revolution in the early 1970s. It is interesting to note that through the 1920s, 30s and 40s, Mao uses the Marxist terminology, but the international communist movement constantly sees him and the path of the Chinese Communist Party under his leadership as a deviant one. In the early 1960s during the Great Leap Forward he promotes a programme characterized by 'steel in the backyard' and 'let a hundred flowers bloom'. This is a path divergent from the very strictly laid out Western 'scientific' path. Then there is the attack on 'capitalist roaders', a term nowhere to be found in the Marxist lexicon. While inaugurating and pursuing the Cultural Revolution he ceases to use the Marxist lexicon, for the activity unleashed just cannot be understood through the received Marxian concepts. Add to this the fact that right from the beginning he uses examples from Chinese history as sources of wisdom for social and political action. The Chinese Revolution puts workers and peasants in power but when the Cultural Revolution tries to put workers and peasants in the university it fails.

The Chinese Revolution leads to a polity, which is a variant of the State in Europe. The leadership changes but the basis in science remains. So, for the one rooted in people's tradition one more revolution is needed to develop a stable pro-people polity. This is the Cultural Revolution which is lost for words in the European knowledge tradition. So the leader of the Cultural Revolution ought to have a deep consciousness of the relation between traditions of knowledge and structures of polity, which gives us a lesson or two in our present context.

Ayatollah Khomeini was the leader of the Islamic Revolution in the late 1970s and early 1980s in Iran which dethroned the Shah (king) and pushed out the American forces. He spoke against the West and put both the Soviet Union and the United States of America in the same box as the accused. He spoke against democratic polity because it was Western and insisted that following the West, the way we have, leads to completely incapacitating alienation, emasculation and emaciation. He spoke in the name of Islam. The revolution attempted to install such a polity and set of values in Iranian society which would not be just a variation of the State in Europe and which would be based on Islamic tradition, whose cornerstone was justice.

There are Islamic states in other countries which are stooges of the American state, so calling oneself Islamic proves nothing in the present-day world. The only way to be 'genuine' is through accepting the criteria of ordinary life and popular tradition. Iran stood out in the 1980s in its war with Iraq by virtue of the popular mobilization. It is close to 30 years now that it has been in steady opposition to America, economics, diplomacy, media attack and threat of actual war notwithstanding. It is just to suggest here that the Iranian political dispensation needs to be seen or investigated as possibly eventually based on traditions of knowledge that weave a synthesis of the Book with popular traditions.

Traditions of knowledge other than modern science are difficult to understand with the approach of the 'educated'. We need a political eye for an epistemic comprehension. Just as structures of polity have their knowledge bases, understanding radically different knowledge bases requires a political imagination which recognizes people and their lives as the only starting point and destiny at the same time.

## 13.5 The New Dialectic

Creation of the network society and the virtual domain have opened radically new spaces for defining the relationship within the double knowledge tradition, perhaps even for producing a new unity. How do we define our continuities and the way forward now in the new condition from where a Gandhi, Mao or Khomeini might be said to have left us? How do we transcend the political dichotomies of the bygone era, namely left-right, communal-secular, democratic-dictatorial, subsistence-productive, East-West, South-North, Third World-First World, etc.?

Let us start with the turbulence in the knowledge domain. Science is giving way to knowledge management to occupy the place of command in the realm of knowledge. Scientific method is no more the inviolable, supreme and unique method of acquiring knowledge. It no more constitutes the legitimacy criterion for knowledge. The new world respects 'organization' of knowledge more than anything else. Organizability by the Information & Communication Technologies (ICTs) now occupies the place of legitimacy criterion. Nothing that is not organizable by the ICTs can be legitimate knowledge. But then this tends to legitimize various traditions of knowledge which were not even legitimate candidates to be tested against the legitimacy criterion of the scientific-industrial era. But this legitimization comes with an undoing price. *Lokavidya*, for the Information Age, is legitimate knowledge only in so far as and to the extent it serves the network society. So various traditions of knowledge expressed in a great variety of bodies of information, skills, techniques and practices divested from the values and ways of thinking, modes of abstraction of the people involved become a new resource pressed into the service of the network society. High as it may appear this price has come with an equal boon. Let the legitimization of other knowledge systems not be undervalued for it fulfils a necessary and robust condition for developing the politics of emancipation and recreation of a society which will not be based on capital, technology and management as we know them.

Legitimizing traditions of knowledge not built on an internal hierarchy necessarily legitimizes also the possibility of a new polity not based on hierarchy. Today the idea and reality of the nation is ceasing to be the most suited instrument of the State and the network society is attempting to build trans-national instrumentalities. The other end, the people's end has been pushed into an amorphous state. That is organizations and representations of the oppressed are no more political. Breakdown of unionization, sell out of national political processes and the spread of NGOs all underline this. The place of recreation of emancipatory politics therefore lies where local and popular knowledge traditions make sense to the people and where a Gandhi, a Mao or a Khomeini, depending upon where you are, make great sense. People's movements, local markets and education are the places where traditions of knowledge of the locality need to assert themselves to pave the way for a new synthesis of the double tradition which alone may provide the basis of radical politics in this new age.

# 14

# Knowledge in Society and the Knowledge Society: Opening the Debate for a New Millennium*

*Ananya Vajpeyi*

## 14.1

The larger project of which this review is a part seeks to develop a fresh theory of knowledge in contemporary Indian society. A full or even partial theoretical articulation of such a theory will not be attempted here. My point of entry into the discourse on knowledge, to the extent that it has been articulated at all in India today, is Sunil Sahasrabudhey's small but important recent volume, *Gandhi's Challenge to Modern Science* (The Other India Press, Goa: 2002, p. 90). The author positions his work as perhaps the first significant commentary on, as well as further development of, Gandhi's *Hind Swaraj* (1909), in the 21st century.[1] *Hind Swaraj* is itself a highly compressed book; Sahasrabudhey retains this *sutra*-like quality in his commentarial text. It is clear that an elaborate exposition of Gandhi's politics before and after *Hind Swaraj* must be read back into it in order to unpack its terse formulations. In a similar fashion, an understanding of the People's Science, the Alternative Science, the Appropriate Technology, the Green and the Peace movements in India and elsewhere in the world from the late 1970s to the mid-90s is necessary for a proper reading

* Originally written for the bulletin *A Dialogue on Knowledge in Society*, published for a workshop in the World Social Forum, Mumbai 2004.

of *Gandhi's Challenge....*[2] Unfortunately it is not possible to undertake such exercises in the limited scope of this article.

**14.2**

From the rich array of materials compacted within *Hind Swaraj*, Sahasrabudhey is most concerned with Gandhi's critiques of "civilization" and of the "machine." Sahasrabudhey calls Gandhi "a philosopher of the future," and the Mahatma's vision about the way science and technology would impact our lives in a capitalist world is indeed astounding (*GCMS*: 12). Not only his prescience, but the power of his metaphors is also striking:

> A man, whilst he is dreaming, believes in his dream; he is undeceived only when he is awakened from his sleep. A man labouring under the bane of civilization is like a dreaming man. (...). But there is no end to the victims destroyed in the fire of civilization. Its deadly effect is that people come under its scorching flames believing it to be all good. (*Hind Swaraj*: 35, 43).

Gandhi's critique of "civilization" has everything to do with the role of science—what Sahasrabudhey insists we call "modern science"—in the present time. That so much tragedy underlies scientific advances in modernity is a surprise only to those who, like Gandhi's sleeping man, dream the dream of civilization. In Sahasrabudhey's redaction of Gandhi, modern science is not a moral science. This is because rationality, in the West, is falsely construed as being value-free.

> Science is the victor. Its drawing room is full of shields, medals and cups. And while it reigns, who can ask how they were won? (...). Science – and often even technology – stands exonerated of all disasters and antihuman consequences. These are clubbed under the label of 'misuse' of science and technology and the entire blame is shifted over to users, planners and politicians. Is it not paradoxical that one side in the balance sheet of science is entirely vacant? (...). If science is credited with good consequences, it ought to be blamed for its bad consequences. It is here precisely that the question of the relation of science with morality arises. (...). [Values] according to Gandhi must be internal to science. It is not enough that it is done by moral men and women, which itself is a tall order, but science itself should be moral.
>
> For moral science, pure reason must give way to a concept of human reason. (...). [And] if pure reason is to be replaced by human

> reason then scientific temper has to be replaced by humanist temper. (*GCMS*: 1, 27, 33).

In a series of arguments about the ontology, the epistemology, the logic, and the ethics of dominant knowledge systems originating in the West—arguments I will not reproduce here—Sahasrabudhey establishes that modern science rests on four fallacies. First (as already mentioned) is the position that reason is amoral. Second is the idea that the scientific society promotes the freedom of the individual. Third is the notion that the social life of human beings carries on in some plane that is not the plane of their natural life, or that society and nature can continue to function indefinitely at odds with one another. And fourth (following from two and three) is the most fallacious of all statements, that the enterprise of modern science is divorced from the project of social control. The power that these four propositions have exercised in the last two centuries is at least in part responsible for the world we inhabit today: a world of nuclear accidents and indestructible industrial waste, of starving workers and suicidal peasants, of innumerable camps and millions of refugees, of Western prosperity and misery for the rest of the planet. According to Sahasrabudhey, it was Gandhi alone who, among the great thinkers in the 20th century, foresaw such ghastly end-results from the big and small experiments of modern science in its vast laboratory, humanity itself.

**14.3**

"What comes to pass resists debate," writes Sahasrabudhey, in his characteristically aphoristic way, "So with the machine" (*GCMS*: 41). He substitutes the machine with technology and vice versa throughout his book, evidently to invoke Marx at some points and Gandhi at others. The paired and interchangeable terms, "machine" and "technology," allow Sahasrabudhey to bring into his analysis several key Marxian categories without wandering too far from the Gandhian core of his argument: capital, state, alienation, useful work, human activity, labour, man-as-maker, and even art. Power, especially, is treated in its scientific and its social meanings, since it relates to technology in *both* its senses. In one direction it extends to the problem of energy; in the other, it encompasses the state and its apparatuses, including, eventually, weaponry and war.[3]

"Power", says Sahasrabudhey in another phrase at once memorable and true, "is the blood of the modern machine" (*GCMS*: 52). Hobbes, Heidegger and Foucault, all hover above his reading of *Hind Swaraj*. But they flutter about the text without bearing away the reader on their wings into the skies of European political philosophy, in a way that might have made it difficult for her to then engage with the down-to-earth concepts invented by Gandhi for India. The purpose of Sahasrabudhey's brief but dense work is precisely to challenge that which pervades our post-industrial—and now even post-globalization—world, and therefore is resistant to debate, i.e. technology. "The machine organizes men, materials, energy and information on a scale unknown before and at an ever-increasing speed. So does it disorganize societies and destroy their knowledge bases elsewhere on a colossal scale with equal speed" (*GCMS*: 45-6). We may construe this as Sahasrabudhey's gloss on Gandhi's polemic against the railways, summed up in his objection to *speed* as the most desirable end for modern societies obsessed with technology: "But evil has wings" (*Hind Swaraj*: 48). Sahasrabudhey, too, objects:

> Technology ought to be the technique of doing things, not undoing them. Only in this way can it be part of the extension of truth, an instrument of man's labour for emancipation. (...). [Instead, it] has produced wealth and glitter for a few, and poverty, darkness, and 'noise' for the rest. Underlying both creation and destruction, organization and disorganization, lies a common characteristic of modern technology: violence. Modern technology is violent for all. (*GCMS*: 17, 46).

Gandhi's principle of non-violence (*ahimsa*) is central to the construction of his challenge to modern science. "Non-violence" is a flat translation of *ahimsa*, a word more or less available in all the modern Indian languages, not just Gandhi's Gujarati. In the Sanskrit, two roots *han-* and *himsa-* yield two different nouns, *hatya* and *ahimsa, Hatya*, straightforwardly, is "murder," killing without legal sanction. *Himsa*, on the other hand, has a more general sense of "violence," including an entire range of meanings from "injury" to "killing," and connoting verbal, bodily as well as psychological harm. If we go into its etymological antecedents, it also has a residual desiderative, preserved fleetingly in the form, but mostly lost in the usage, as "desire to harm." We may carry this subtler sense of *himsa* into its opposite, *ahimsa*, to translate it as "absence of the desire to harm." Such an nuanced meaning, perhaps first occurring in pre-modern Jain and Buddhist thought, brings us closer to what Gandhi intended by *ahimsa* than the more opaque "non-violence"[4]. It is on the back of *ahimsa* that Sahasrabudhey is able to put on the table a constellation of related Gandhian ideas: *Satyagraha*, *Swadeshi*, and *Swaraj*. Unfortunately, this is not the place to go into each one of these categories in detail, and because they will be left unanalysed, no ready—and potentially inadequate or even misleading—translations for them are provided. Suffice to say that violence is to technology what Gandhi's *ahimsa* is to a new category that Sahasrabudhey introduces in his book, and that is *lokavidya*.[5]

What is *lokavidya*? It is more than likely that many readers would jump to making literal translations, and come up with something like "knowledge (*vidya*) of the people (*loka*)" or "arts (in the sense of "skills") of the people." But Sahasrabudhey is intent on keeping that which is moral inseparably tied to his notion of *vidya*, morality for him, as an avowed Gandhian, being as firmly wedded to *vidya* as it is divorced from modern science. Knowledge as *vidya* is by definition humane, whereas modern science is rational. *Lokavidya*, then, cannot be taken away from a people. It is lost forever if a people is eliminated from the face of the earth. It is never derivative; it is always already *owned* by a people, in the sense of *being made its own* by that people. *Lokavidya* is not only what a people knows, not only a people's "fund of knowledge" (Sanskrit *jñåna-bhandåra*/Hindi *gyån-bhandår*). It is related somehow to a people's experience, to their perception of that which is. I am conscious that none of the foregoing statements constitutes an exhaustive definition of *lokavidya*. But together these statements characterize *lokavidya* in a manner that begins to make the concept emerge from the obscurity of its mere translation into cognitive relief for the reader.

**14.4**

In Parts I to III of this essay, I have, no doubt very quickly and inadequately, tried to present everything in the root-text *Hind Swaraj* and in its commentary *GCMS*, that would allow us to use, in however make-shift a way, the term *lokavidya*. The questions to be raised now are as follows: Can we posit *lokavidya* to be the same as "indigenous knowledge"? If so, then what is indigenous knowledge? If not, then how are the two different? What are the political entailments of trying to equate the two, regardless of whether or not they are in fact the same? Moreover, what is the future of *lokavidya* and of indigenous knowledge, either as identical or as distinct categories, in the new knowledge society—a society that is genealogically related to industrial society via the persistent and ever-more powerful machine?

"Indigenous knowledge" is what increasingly appears in activist as well as academic talk in contemporary India under the name of "non-modern"/"traditional"/"folk" knowledge. Under the sway of right-wing ideologies that we witness in our public sphere and in our intellectual life nowadays, "indigenous knowledge" enjoys a certain degree of attention from all kinds of quarters and gets many more champions than might be good for it. It would be interesting, in a different context, to flesh out the relationship of this "indigenous knowledge" to other categories that have been available in anthropological discourse for a while now, most notably "practice" and "craft". But the far more pressing, indeed, non-deferable task, is to understand both *lokavidya* and indigenous knowledge with respect to (i) ownership; and (ii) economic activity.

First of all, who owns *lokavidya*? Who owns indigenous knowledge? Whose property is *lokavidya*? Whose property is indigenous knowledge? Does it even make sense to speak of ownership when discussing one or both of these categories? If we do not want to cast the debate in terms of ownership, then how are we to engage with the whole discourse on intellectual property and the patent régime that currently preoccupies those who are concerned with scientific knowledge proper? Without clarity on ownership and proprietary claims, how do we position either indigenous knowledge or *lokavidya* vis-à-vis individuals, communities, corporations, and states (in which we can count both nation-states and the global state)? Secondly, does either indigenous knowledge or *lokavidya* generate wealth? Does it result in a surplus? Does either one provide employment? Is either one really a form of life rather than a source of livelihood? In Marxist terminology, what is the relationship of each of these terms to means of production and to relations of production? These questions beg answers, which can only come from a systematic theory of knowledge in society that works for more than just modern science, i.e. a theory that works for indigenous knowledge and for *lokavidya*, whatever the particularities of these entities turn out to be in a full-fledged descriptive account.

There is much in Gandhi's thought that is provocative for a social theorist like Sahasrabudhey. He toys with Gandhi's spinning wheel (*charkha*). He flirts with social groups that the late D.R. Nagaraj (1944-1998) used to call the "technological communities" of South Asia, like the *agariyas*, who traditionally manufactured high-quality iron and steel using non-industrial processes that remain poorly understood and, curiously, difficult if not impossible to replicate under laboratory conditions. But ultimately Sahasrabudhey's intellectual effort is to transcend the fetish object, whether it be the machine or its product. He seeks to get beyond a definition of knowledge that rests purely on the content of knowledge. He attempts, albeit with only partial success, to characterize *lokavidya* such that its meaning encompasses a phenomenology, an epistemology, an ontology, a logic, a morality, an ethics, a politics, a history, a value-system, and a method. He seeks to define a way of knowing that is necessarily associated with a way of being. Whatever its other features turn out to be, the most important thing to note about *lokavidya* is that it is grounded in the principle of *ahimsa*. It is one weapon with which to challenge—and who knows, maybe even ultimately defeat—what Gandhi called the "monster" of civilization (*Hind Swaraj*: 42).

## 14.5

The trouble with all indigenist theories, whether they be theories in linguistics, in literary criticism, in historiography, in the study of religions, in epistemology, or in any other discipline, is that they tend to valorize whatever is indigenous to a given non-Western culture because it is indigenous.[6] So-called "civilizational" critiques of Western knowledge also have the same tendency, to accord greater legitimacy to the knowledges that have their genealogy in the knowledge systems of non-Western civilizations simply because of the accident of their birth, as it were.[7] The nature of the truth claims made on behalf of indigenous knowledge and civilizational knowledge can vary from:

(i) "It's better because it's ours", to
(ii) "It's better because it works better for us", to
(iii) "It's better because it has been dominated, marginalized, and almost rendered extinct, first by Western imperialism and colonialism, and currently the neo-colonial enterprise, and now it's time to set the record straight", to
(iv) "Let all knowledges coexist in peace, there's no such thing as truth anyway, or at any rate, our way of reaching for—and eventually falling short of—the truth is no better or worse than anyone else's way".

Through these statements I am trying to trace a cline, in a rough-and-ready fashion, from:

(i) crude nativism, to
(ii) cultural relativism, to
(iii) a position whose name I do not know, but which is premised on some notion of the need for a historical balancing-out of large scale cultural and civilizational inequalities. This position makes a call for what might be described as social justice for hitherto-oppressed knowledges. The last statement,
(iv) is simply the bottom-line of post-modernism, albeit presented as a caricature of itself.

The test that must determine the strength of *lokavidya* as a robust—that is to say, as a defensible—category, a category we can work with without simplistically valorizing that which is supposedly ours over that which is allegedly not ours, is perhaps its relationship to violence.[8] Gandhi does *not* become germane to the discussion on *lokavidya* because he experimented with various concepts that incorporate, through the prefix "*swa-*"

(literally: "own", or "of the self") the sense of a knowledge or a practice being owned by, and proper to, Indic peoples—*swadeshi* and *swaraj*, for example. Gandhi is relevant here because of his humane and ultimately universalist insistence on *ahimsa* (non-violence). If modern science and technology produce and sustain violence (*himsa*: harm, as well the desire to harm) in communities and their natural habitats, is *lokavidya* any less harmful? We could be revivalists, glorifying the past. We could be utopians, imagining a glorious hereafter. Both revivalists and utopians have a dangerous inclination to recruit an as-yet fuzzy and ill-defined entity like *lokavidya* to their respective constructivist agendas. But we have to actually assess *lokavidya*'s once and future record in history, in terms of its relationship to violence, its proven failures already and its potential for doing harm in times to come. Only then can we decide if this is to be our chosen weapon with which to wage war on inequality and oppression in human societies.

## REFERENCES

1. Anthony J. Parel (ed.), *M.K. Gandhi, Hind Swaraj and Other Writings*. Cambridge University Press (1997). Henceforth this text will be referred to as Hind Swaraj. Originally published in 1909.
2. Sunil Sahasrabudhey, *Gandhi's Challenge to Modern Science*. Goa: The Other India Press (2002). Henceforth this text will be referred to as GCMS.
3. The author doesn't make a note of this, but power is inscribed at the dead centre of our national flag, in the Asokan motif of the dhamma-cakra, the wheel of dharma that turns and turns incessantly in the firmament of the political life of human beings.
4. I am grateful to Professors George Cardona and Madhav Deshpande for permitting me these semantic manoeuvres within the strict limits set by Sanskrit grammar, of which they are both masters.
5. The history of the word/concept of "lokavidya" is a complicated one, and by his own admission it is not quite accurate to name Sahasrabudhey as its single author. Since the early 1970s, a mutating group of activists and intellectuals, originating from IIT-Kanpur, and operating in Kanpur, Jhansi, Varanasi, and Nagpur, first produced a journal called *Mazdoor Kisan Niti*, then another journal called *Autonomy*, and finally a journal that still

continues to be published, called *Lokavidya Samvad*. The size and nature of the collective, and its relationship with the alternative science and technology movements on the one hand, and the farmer and trade union movements on the other, have varied greatly over the last three decades and across different parts of India. It is probably fair to characterize Sahasrabudhey as a key actor in this discourse and its associated political activity, but to credit him with the invention of the very idea of *lokavidya* would be, by his own lights, excessive.

6. I thank Sudhir Chella Rajan for alerting me to the discomfort that many in the left feel with indigenism, even when it purports to be critical.
7. See Meera Nanda, Postmodernism, Hindu Nationalism and 'Vedic Science'. *Frontline* (January 2, 2004):78-82.
8. I am indebted to Dilip Simeon for this very simple, but, it seems to me, key, insight into the centrality of violence as a criterion by which to predict the politics that, even if it is not dictated by, might eventually become entailed by, a given theoretical position on what constitutes valid knowledge.

# 15

# Traditional Knowledge – or 'Nature's' Knowledge?*

*K.B. Jinan*

I have been living with rural and tribal communities for the last 20 years now. I did not go to them with intentions of 'developing' them or educating them. I went to them to recover my own cultural roots which I had lost in the process of getting educated. I went to learn from them. For having escaped 'education' and 'development' they are still original and authentic and are holding on to the culture and world view which sustained them for centuries.

This unique stand point gives me a different picture of the rural tribal communities as being wise and evolved and it is only by learning from them that we can learn to lead sustainable life. Of course, understanding the traditional knowledge has been a very difficult task for me as my framework or categories for understanding itself is Western. So in the process of de-colonizing and recovering my authenticity I have been able to get glimpses of the traditional knowledge process. This has been like the peeling of the onion. I am getting to know more and more as I continue my de-colonization process.

In the process of rediscovering myself, I had to remake and redefine new meanings of several words and concepts the colonizer had instilled in me. I realized that the biggest tragedy of the people of this country was they are being colonized, culturally uprooted and spiritually alienated by the process

---

* Originally written for the bulletin *A Dialogue on Knowledge in Society*, published for a workshop in the World Social Forum, Mumbai 2004.

called schooling and the more we spend time in the educational institutions the more dangerous it is, and the more elitist the institution, the more uprooted and colonized one becomes. We are taught the Western notion of knowledge, Western world view and even the Western sense of beauty. *If one's sense of beauty is conditioned, then what is left of that person?* I have been exploring the relation between conditioning and creativity, and asking what role does culture play in all this? What sparks spontaneity? What is sense of beauty? Is it an intellectual process? What is intuition? What does it mean to be original, authentic...?

Here I look at four issues in the context of traditional knowledge: An experiment in initiating creativity in a traditional potters' community, notion of waste in traditional communities, children in traditional communities, natural learning process or traditional knowledge.

## 15.1 An Experiment in Initiating Creativity

A fundamental premise of the training interventions at Aruvacode is the cultural, aesthetic and creative superiority of the trainees, compared to the 'developed' mainstream of Indian society. Thus the basic attempt at the training programme is to help the individuals regain their wisdom and confidence which lies embedded within their own communities and culture.

During the first training conducted in 1993, it was very difficult to convince the women about their abilities. The hangover of my NID days did not help matters either. But subsequent training programmes showed marked improvements. And the latest of my interventions at initiating creativity among the village children proved beyond doubt that the trainers' interventions, if at all, in natural learning processes need to be restricted to erecting a fence against outside influences that corrupt the genuine aesthetic sensibility and sense of perfection of the craftspeople. Through the series of efforts at recovering creativity, the realization also dawned that what is actually happening in the name of teaching and training of rural and artisan communities is the corruption of their sense of knowing.

Initially when training methods were introduced with a group of women, we began with drawing straight lines, circles, etc. in free hand and moved on to exploring clay and making objects giving free vent to their imagination. We then sat together and started improvising on the designs to make them functional. In 1995 again there was a formal 6 months' 'training' programme. This time most of the trainees were of the younger lot—13, 14, 15 year olds. While the method was the same—freehand drawing, colours, clay work, etc. my confidence about minimalist interventions had indeed grown and I deliberately kept myself away from the scene as far as possible. Their creations were simply superb. Several new designs emerged and an entire product range—coiled tiles was the result of the exercise.

The third training programme which began during the KRPLLD (Kerala Research Programme on Local Level Development) project was a major turning point. During this project I re-assessed my understanding of the indigenous/traditional process of transmitting skills more closely. As coincidence would have it, I came across during the period a potter girl in Mana Madurai scooping out in perfect circle the opening of a smokeless choola. I realized the futility of importing to the artisan milieu, training methods—drawing of lines, shapes, etc.—that suited urban, alienated people.

Well after 8 months of conducting the programme to develop a methodology for training artisans' children I had to re-look at many of the assumptions I had made regarding the craft, traditional learning process, etc. Suffice it is to say that the Do Nothing natural farming philosophy of Fukuoka would find ready application here.

### 15.2 Notion of Waste

Waste is a modern concept. Notion of waste is non-existent in traditional cultures. They are always used till it disappears or disintegrates. Often all their technologies made use of bio-degrading materials. Most crafts have evolved from utilizing "waste". I remember reading a *sloka* on the use of materials in one of the books on traditional architecture. It said that it has taken millions of years for a rock to evolve. That was the reason why traditional cultures used rock, only to build temples which for them symbolized permanence, continuity of culture and sanctity. Even the palaces were made of mud.

Traditions have always responded creatively to challenges thrown up by time. To give an example, after the earthquake of the 19th century in Kutch the traditional way of building changed to round-shaped houses to counter the effects of the earthquakes on buildings. The testimony to their genius is in the fact of their survival in the recent earthquake that brought down every other type of buildings. How did this knowledge happen? In traditional cultures the very act of living is learning they are constantly observing their surroundings making use of whatever comes in their way. The worldview of the traditional cultures did not allow them to waste and sustainability was part and parcel of their lifestyle.

It is worthwhile to look at how traditional societies have responded to the waste generated by the result of modern knowledge. Plastic in various grades and forms. All around the countryside one can see interesting reuse of plastic. The potters in my village use plastic to burnish their wares. In the farm one can see the carry bags hung to keep the birds away. Owing to the wind the bag flutters and keeps the birds away. Plastc buckets are reused by sticking with another piece. I have seen the milk packets turned in to *chattayi* for sitting on the ground. There are several types of chattayis depending on the type of plastic. My mother uses it to plant seeds. This is seen all over. The reuse the modernity's waste is seen all over the traditional communities all over the world. The modernity creates the waste and the tradition clears it.

## 15.3 Children in Traditional Communities

Children in natural learning cultures are like any other newborn animal. The nature has its ways to make them grow and all the skills of an adult world are introduced in the games, toys children make. The way they explore the world of senses is by interaction with nature and the world of nature through the senses. Senses are a two-way tool—to know the outside and the inside.

### *15.3.1 Toys*

Children from sustainable cultures make their own toys. Toys need not be anything in particular but anything that catches the interest of the child. The toy is most often incomplete without the toy maker. Most of these toys are made from materials found around the place. Children's world in the traditional communities are always populated and mixed with the adult's world unlike the modern culture where every category is fragmented and compartmentalized.

Children, adult, men, women are all strictly segregated and compartmentalized and so are learning, play and work. Children are usually left somewhat free to explore nature in the surrounding areas. Most children in Aruvacode know the sounds of the birds, their behaviour, etc. Their ears are very alert to the sounds of nature. They are familiar with all the berries and the leaves that can be eaten and which are not edible. As regards smell children are always after flowers and are also familiar with smells of various leaves. Sight is the most powerful sense. Children go for hunting or for catching birds or even dragon flies they need to observe with total attention. They are watching all the time. Most of the games children play are for developing the senses.

### *15.3.2 Natural Learning Process*

While I was in the process of developing exercises and activities to help children learn pottery, I was intrigued by the way with which the master potters arrive at a form. I wondered how the things they make could be so beautiful. I was keen to know what at first guides them to arrive at a particular form and then a perfect proportion. Mulling over it for several days I realized that there is a biological assistance that guides our sense of beauty. People undefiled by modern ways are far more open and receptive to this biological guidance. This insight opened up a completely new dimension in my search to understand the traditional and indigenous knowledge systems.

In fact, delving somewhat further into the biological aspect of knowledge, I soon realized that all the games children play in the villages is a kind of a response to their individual biological needs. Children in natural learning cultures are similar to any newborn living being and nature has its own precious pace to make them grow.

Senses therefore play a very important role in the process of learning and are a sort of a reciprocal device that helps creation establish communion with the inner self. In the traditional societies every situation was a learning situation. It was a rhythm followed from birth to death. If we consider knowledge to be a biological response to sustain life, then the present level of estrangement between man and nature is unimaginable. How could knowledge and destruction go hand in hand to the extent that the very survival of the earth now edges on the brink of cessation? Knowledge, devoid of the biological content fostered the grounds for depredation. As I closely observe the primal ways of the indigenous people I find every connective tissue an extension of nature. Their dwellings, their artifacts all seem sprouted from the earth. Inspiringly concordant—like the bird, the branch, the nest, the twigs. It is imperative that we re-institute the traditional knowledge systems and restore the earth its pristine beauty.

The more I reflect upon, the more I see the diametrically opposite direction in which education has led us from nature. 'Western' no longer confines to the West. The ripples of Western knowledge have far-reaching consequences. Their world view or the lack of it has proved catastrophic to the entire humankind.

In a particular region with specific climatic, geographic and ecological conditions a particular life form emerges and survives. Similarly knowledge must evolve naturally without any external thrust of shammed theories and counter theories. The fundamental difference, in the evolution of knowledge systems in the modern and traditional cultures is about revering nature in its totality. Indigenous cultures have for generations honoured nature's sanctity and their quest for knowledge was armoured with tools of intuition, sensitivity and creativity which bestowed a sense of un-intrusive and peaceful existence to every pulsating entity.

## 15.4 Traditional Knowledge and Modern Knowledge

Modern education has shifted the centre of knowledge from nature to human, from collective to ego, from heart to intellect/mind, from intuition to reason, from experience to information, from holistic to compartmental. The effects of the modern education on the individual are compartmentalization, alienation, intellectualization, conceptualization, etc. The larger and more dangerous effects of modern education on the planet are that we have destroyed its ecosystems, finished non-renewable wealth, made extinct many animals, plants, etc. In traditional cultures the very act of living is learning they are constantly observing their surroundings making use of what ever comes in their way. Words like heritage conservation, sustainability, holistic, waste, documentation, boredom, alienation are all modernity's creation.

These are not the issues of intuitive cultures at all. The fundamental difference between indigenous cultures and the Western culture is that the indigenous cultures use intuition as a framework for creating, transmitting and sustaining knowledge and the West uses reason. Through the present educational system this shift is being brought about thus cutting us off from our roots in a very fundamental way. So, recovering indigenous culture lies in recovering our intuitive abilities consciously.

Only from this state of being can we begin to address our problems and to search for solutions.

Otherwise we will continue to plunder, the reason-dominated human beings have been doing for the past 600 years. The present destruction of the eco systems is a direct result of the domination of reason over intuition, conscious over sub conscious, individual over collective, self over self-less, materialism over spiritual, of anthropocentrism over nature centrism and so-called scientific (Western) knowledge over wisdom knowledge.

Recovering indigenous culture does not lie in getting back the artifacts from the Western museums or doing all kinds of researches and documentation or sending our children to the present-day schools. There is no true knowledge in the schools. It also destroys intuition, our very tool for acquiring 'life sustaining wisdom knowledge'. In fact recovering indigenous culture might even mean doing away with the present school system, the present institutions/museums, documentation, etc.

Our main obstacle will be how to get rid of the ghost of reason and intellectuality from our being.

# 16

# Re-legitimization of Knowledge in Society*

*B. Krishnarajulu*

## 16.1 Knowledge in Society: *Lokavidya*

A society is characterized, in the main, by its knowledge-base and the degrees of freedom that this knowledge-base allows that society to enjoy. The functions and functioning of society are governed by this knowledge-base as are its existence and sustainability. The knowledge-base is dynamic and is continuously expanding and changing; with the society changing concomitantly.

Traditional India was based in the local knowledge system (*lokavidya*), that had developed over the centuries preceeding British rule and had formed the connerstone of life and society —its organization, its governance, its development and its outlook on life—in short, what could be called the 'culture' of pre-British Indian society.

Occupations in the traditional society were caste-based, that is, each caste/sub-caste (*jati*) was, in the main, characterized by its work-role in societal activities. People seldom chose occupations/avocations outside the caste-defined one.

> It is extremely difficult to learn the arts of the Indians for the same caste, from father to son, exercises the same trade and the

* Paper presented at a conference on "The Emerging Organization of Knowledge and the Future of Universities," December 2008, 32nd Indian Social Sciences Congress, Jamia Millia Islamia, New Delhi.

> punishment of being excluded the caste on doing anything injurious to its interests is so dreadful that it is often impossible to find an inducement to make them communicate anything. They, in general, care nothing for money if they have enough to buy their food—and little is sufficient for that purpose.[1]

Training/ education and learning were within the ambit of the family and community, and children learnt through work. Since each caste contributed to the overall upkeep and progress of society—and due respect was paid in special ways to each specific activity—there was no social pressure for switching occupations or for 'moving' up a 'hierarchical' social order. The caste system provided, in the main, the social (organizational) base of *lokavidya*.

British rule in India brought in a new knowledge system with new occupations, new modes of governance, new modes and methods of education and a new way of life—a new culture. All this was in conflict with *lokavidya*; and resulted in a lot of social tension. Significantly the initial protests against some aspects of British rule were rooted in *lokavidya* and marked by civil disobedience—a precursor to Gandhi's *satyagraha*.

British rule brought in new institutions of governance, education, healthcare, engineering, technology, etc . The new institutions of education and the methods of instruction/ training were designed to serve, in the first instance, the needs of the institutions of governance and control; and later to consolidate revenue through organized collection (of imposed taxes and raw materials) and supply and production of capital goods, commodities and services.These new institutions did not take cognisance of the existing education, skills, training that were characteristic of the various castes (*jatis)* that traditional society was comprised of; with the result that *lokavidya* was disregarded either on purpose or through ignorance of its importance.

The departure of the British, however, did not herald a significant shift from the modes of governance, education, healthcare and occupational preferences introduced and legitimized by British rule. A vast section of the population, however, continued to live by a community identity and pursue and practise their caste (*jati*)-based occupations; they never having been 'incorporated' into the centralized-colonial enterprise OR having opted to stay with *lokavidya*. The process of urbanization/westernization continues with vigour and, today, but for agriculture and a few artisanal occupations (weaving, carpentry, goldsmithy, metal-working, etc) and tribal societies; the traditional sector and way of life (culture of pre-British India) has been doomed to obsolesence. Yet, as mentioned, a large fraction of the populace (the peasants, artisans, tribal people, etc.) base their lives and occupations on *lokavidya* and live on the fringes of modern society as the disinherited (*Bahishkrit Samaj*).

## 16.2 The Delegitimization of *Lokavidya*

The first observations of *lokavidya* by the Europeans were marked by awe—they had encountered a truly advanced society with a knowledge-base that encompassed every facet of the then known aspects of knowledge—agriculture, science, mathematics, astronomy, healthcare, conflict resolution, education and training, etc. The debunking and delegitimization of *lokavidya* began when the need to establish British rule became imperative. This is best expressed by the words of Lord Macaulay, who while addressing Parliament on February 2, 1835 said:

> I have travelled across the length and breadth of India and I have not seen one person who is a beggar, who is a thief such wealth I have seen in this country, such high moral values, people of such calibre, that I do not think we would ever conquer this country, unless we break the very backbone of this nation, which is her spiritual and cultural heritage, and, therefore, I propose that we replace her old and ancient education system, her culture, for if the Indians think that all that foreign and English is good and greater than their own, they will lose their self-esteem, their native culture and they will become what we want them, a truly dominated nation.

[About two decades before this both William Wilberforce and John Stuart Mill had derisively written off Indian society and *lokavidya* with a view, probably, of wantonly showing Indian society in a poor light].

The new institutions and opportunities for employment,

backed by the imperial power, served to break the established caste-based training and occupational systems of the traditional sector. The field was 'open' to competition and such of those castes that could acquire the 'new literacy' and skills were absorbed in the new occupations. The upper castes were, by a sizable majority, able to acquire new 'qualifications' and skills amenable to occupations in the modern sector. In the bureaucracy and education they dominated as no one else could —as writers, pleaders, dubashis, teachers in schools, as doctors and scientific workers. With time, education in the modern sector acquired a premium and the traditional system of public education, where a majority of students belonged to the non-Brahmin castes, slowly withered away (see Dharampal, *The Beautiful Tree*). The traditional castes (and occupations) also slowly morphed (weavers were employed in textile mills, farmers and agricultural workers as gardeners, lower order Sudras and outcastes as sanitation workers, etc.) and the education/training structure came under great strain and was in disarray.

The process of 'replacement', that Macaulay talked about, was multi-pronged and education was one of the more important of its aspects. Healthcare was another while industrialization, with the often forcible destruction of the local cottage industries, was the Trojan horse against the established systems of traditional education and training . All these aspects were characterized by explicit delocalization—children were made to travel long distances to get to school, traders were encouraged to patronise and develop urban marketplaces. The banks mobilized financial resources away from the traditional (localized) moneylenders.Wholesale trade in food, essential commodities and raw materials were channellised for export while imported finished products were dumped into the urban markets.Occupations in the modern sector were made lucarative and those of the traditional sector became moribund.

> ...a phenomenon began to operate amongst non-agricultural occupation groups... especially amongst the skilled craftsmen. From a state of self-employment... they were reduced to an employee status, or of contractual labour ; as happened on a vast scale amongst the weavers of India... in time all this had a

> deteriorating impact on their know-how, tools and technologies.If any group cohesiveness still remained amongst these occupation groups, this continued more at the level of kinship and ritual rather than of techniques or craftsmanship...such a state in time split Indian society asunder and all older norms and relationships having got eroded, even the subjugated India in time became two nations, the one of the few ... who made peace with the alien system and the other of the predominantly weak and poor who from year to year got reduced to ever increasing indignity, pauperization and loss of confidence in themselves.... Initially, the craftsmen, especially those engaged in the making of cloth, in the mining and manufacture of metals, and those engaged in construction, stone work, etc. were through fiscal and other devices reduced to a state of penury and homelessness.... this turned most of the technological and industrial innovators, designers and craftsmen into mere labourers....the craftsmen and their families had enjoyed a citizenship status in the villages as well as the small towns...most of them had rights to house sites, back gardens...and received a substantial proportion of the agricultural produce at the time of harvest.Similarly, many of them received incomes in various shapes from those engaged in commerce, banking and trade....As the localities began to deteriorate and crumble....most of the craftsmen became impoversished.[2]

The new education system was based on the British Public School concept and every child had, in principle, access to general education covering all areas of study/training. People with this general education, were prefered for employment in 'government service'. Technical education meant, among other things, that every traditional activity was, in effect, packaged as an acquirable skill; acquired in the sense that the 'study' of the pertinent packaged knowledge conferred the right to practise that skill. The most glaring example being medicine/healthcare. Practitioners of traditional medicine were 'unlicensed' in spite of their knowledge-base in the discipline. Artisans—bricklayers, metal workers, blacksmiths, weavers, leather workers, etc., whose skills were based in their inherited knowledge-bases; were sought to be disinherited and marginalized. Because, these 'skills' were offered as packaged knowledge modules for a price to anyone who wished to acquire such skills. Unlike traditional skills, which were largely determined by birth (caste/*jati*), the new skills could be acquired by anyone who had access to the institutions providing these 'recognized qualifications'.

As the 'modern' knowledge-base expanded, the space available to *lokavidya* got restricted—by disuse and through constricted or limited dissemination. This process was (and continues to be) marked by the gradual but steady "withering away " of traditional society. Modern life stepped into the space "vacated" by traditional society and often appeared as "new found" knowledge with new "standards". Lifestyles were sought to be altered to meet the requirements of this knowledge-base. *Lokavidya* was slowly but surely being made redundant. The de-legitimization of *lokavidya*; through hegemonistic assimilation/supplantation is a very visible process even today. The proponents of modernization, however, proclaim enthusiastically, the dawn of a "seamless" knowledge society in a "global village".

*Lokavidya* is based on non-anagonistic division of labour, inherent mutual interdependence and a role-based identity. In the (rural) society, in which it was and is dominant, there were no inherent knowledge conflicts, hierarchy or exploitation. [This system,however, came under pressure (and often succumbed) every time the society was in conflict with (or threat from) 'invaders' and their knowledge systems.] The de-legitimization of *lokavidya* and the social order (and system) that supported it, began with the direct or indirect thrusting of Western knowledge systems and lifestyles (culture) on the populace. What remains today and sustains the rural populace survives, albeit in a fractured form, in the ambit of the traditional social order; namely, the caste system and a community identity. The caste system has also become almost redundant in the process of the delegitimization of *lokavidya*.

### 16.3 Re-legitimization of *Lokavidya*: The Imperative

Society needs to be organized in such a manner that all necessary occupations are adequately and automatically apportioned the requisite trained manpower from the given population. As the population grows and occupational expansion and diversification takes place, the trained manpower requirements would necessarily have to be met. Traditional society apparently provided a framework for such development

> ...in the Indian social balance, traditionally, persons from all sections of society appear to have been able to receive an optimum schooling which, amongst others, had enabled them to participate openly and appropriately and with dignity not only in the social and cultural life of of their locality but, if they wished, ensured participation at the more extended levels.

The social division that grew out of and on this occupation-cum-caste organization never caused debilitating conflicts or heartburn; except, maybe, in the case of the outcastes (*Dalits*). This role-based identity was an inclusive one and every caste provided the requisite training and occupational role for the individual in society. There was no need for everyone to seek to become (formally) literate. Or for anyone to acquire training in an out-of-caste occupation or avocation. *Lokavidya* provided the framework wherein every child was trained and groomed by the community in the occupation and way of life. This holistic, self-sustaining societal framework based on *lokavidya*, ensured the stability and uniform growth of society.

The modern sector had ,what might be considered in retrospect, a 'plus' point. It 'freed' the castes, especially the outcastes (*Dalits*) and the middle castes from the 'bondage' of hereditary occupations. The education system also provided a platform for members of these castes to acquire knowledge and training in various hitherto 'forbidden' avocations and seek occupations based on this education and training. It however, broke the mutual bond of accommodation (respect) between the various castes and their occupations. A strong cultural linkage (*lokaniti)* snapped and was replaced by a wholly imported (imposed) relationship based on purely materialistic interdependance; this new culture continuously sought guidance from the authors of modernity, i.e. the West and the degree of modernization and Westernization were unmistakably the benchmarks of the new society . In spite of these 'liberating' aspects of Westernization, a vast majority of Indian people continue to live by a self-perpetuating caste/ community identity; superimposed, in the case of urban Indians, on a neo-liberal, non-hereditary identity of 'self-made' individuality. This section is forced, for its survival and growth, to take a cue on all aspects of life and living from the West; while the majority continue to live, albeit in self-deprecating poverty, on *lokavidya.*

The social order, which serves as the foundation of modern western thought (namely Science), is democracy; based on individual freedom, rights and obligations. It does not recognize or promote community identities, so much so that most modern day democratic constitutions talk only of individuals and their rights and duties. In countries like India( which, incidentally, is the largest democracy) the basic identity, however, is still a community/caste-based identity

> Indian society from ancient times had been organized on the basis of communities rather than of individuals. It is not that the individual in India had no separate or private existence, in fact, in the sphere of the spirit the individual had been supreme from time immemorial, however, in the social sphere the individual had socially been an integral part of units larger than himself... firstly as a member of a family, then family being part of a larger kinship group integrated into a caste or sub-caste and these achieving varying local and wider integration amongst themselves. Simultaneously, the family or kinship group have been constituents of geographical entities such as hamlet, village, small town or sections of great cities.[3]

This dichotomy has led to confusion and conflict of interest. We see the phenomenon of a growing number of purely caste/ community-based political parties and movements springing up all over the country—all in the name of democracy! The entire backward class movement has transformed itself into a fight for community space within the polity!

The concept of development has gone much beyond mundane ideas such as GDP, per capita income, per capita energy consumption, etc. In fact many fall-outs of 20th century development, such as environmental degradation, global warming, pollution, decreasing forest area, decreasing species, etc are now seen as anathema to development and could, in fact, become markers for 'retrograde' development! As a corollary to this development, conflicts have arisen over the control and sharing of resources—both material and human.

These conflicts have time and again led to wars, some localized and some worldwide. Both development and the conflicts that have arisen have their roots in various ideologies that mandate this path (of development) and (broadly) those opposed to it. It is now increasingly being felt that development that is inclusive and in harmony with nature in a holistic way is true development; very much in line with Gandhiji's concept of development. This path of development was, ostensibly, what obtained in pre-British India and its conception(rooted in *lokavidya*) was an integral part of the culture of pre-British India. If the majority of the populace needs to be included in such a development process as contributing, dignified partners; it is imperative that their knowledge-base, viz. *lokavidya*, be relegitimized and recast in today's context.

In the realm of formal higher education too, we see a clear process of de-skilling of society. The caste, socio-economic and cultural background of the students is not taken into account when syllabi are framed nor do these influence teaching methodolgy. All students are put through a general proficiency course at lower levels and, at higher levels, there is an extensive imitation of the courses and syllabi obtaining in the West. So that the students, who pass through this system, if found employable, are wholly dependent on the society(modelled after the West) and its market to provide them gainful employment. It is this debunking of *lokavidya* and the inherent skills of (traditional) society that has led to a complete de-skilling of generations of students. Clearly the form and format of education at the school and University level needs a thorough relook and reappraisal.

> ...the past century's unthinking transplanting of European Sciences and Technologies in India have mainly resulted in retarding and blunting of indigenous innovation and creativity.[4]
>
> The present educational system modelled on the Western pattern has neither produced the right type of manpower nor improved the educaion of the masses. Neglect of traditional technologies and local skills has undermined the local confidence and affected the ability of technologists to tackle grass-root problems.[5]

## 16.4 Re-legitimization of *Lokavidya:* The Future

The imposition of alien norms over several generations... subverted the norms by which the society had for centuries past governed itself and treated one another with regard and courtesy...any real solution of this and allied phenomena can therefore arise when the resources of India are shared in such a manner that all sections (of society) begin to feel that they have a role in the running of their society, and also in the integrity and prosperity of the country....[6]

The way forward is, not surprisingly, by 'looking back'. *Lokavidya,* through its foundation in an inclusive social order, could provide the basis for a new development paradigm with a concomitant reorganization of human society. This may be based on a assertion-negation-transcendence 'algorithm' . *Lokavidya* and the caste system being the assertion, modern knowledge systems and their individualistic hierarchy-based social order providing the negation. We look for a transcending knowledge system based in a social order that is non-hierarchical and non-exploitative and which provides a new identity. The basis for this transcendence would come from the inclusivity and mutual acculturation of role-based social organization that was the hallmark of the social milieu in which *lokavidya* grew and developed. The expression of this quest finds an echo, for example, in the anti-consumerism, pro-environment and green movements. All these movements are opposed to a (non-sustainable) energy intensive path of development and they are all votaries of inclusive social order—what is good for the community and environment is good, everything else is less than good or even bad.

The new identity would be a role/knowledge-based identity. People would not be bound to any hereditary occupation or identity.There would be no inherent hierarchy. Social organization and interaction would then be based on the classical principle of 'from each according to his ability/training to each according to his need'.

What is to be done? The foremost step is to understand this phenomenon and provide a simple schema by which ordinary people can understand it. The resolution of conflicts that are and will increasingly arise will have to be left to mankind, especially those of the traditional Third World societies, to resolve. However, we may set out some guidelines on the knowledge issue; guidelines that help in formulating an understanding of this phenomenon and coping with it (in the first instance) and then, maybe, laying the foundation for an alternate paradigm for the growth and dissemination of knowledge in society.

### 16.5 Knowledge

In this era, when everything that is marketable is packaged as a commodity and put into the market; we need to come to a consensus upon the following aspects of knowledge:

a. *Knowledge is the basis of life of mankind*

How does mankind survive? What keeps this species from becomming extinct? What provides this species the ability to adapt and change and/or meet new environmental conditions? What helps this species predict future possibilities and plan for future contingencies? Knowledge is the basis for its existence.

b. *Knowledge is societal inheritance*

Society has always inherited only knowledge. All material inheritance has a finite lifetime, after which it decays or falls into ruin. Knowledge, on the other hand, grows from generation to generation. Knowledge is never lost, only updated or extended. The body of knowledge grows from generation to generation and from age to age. It is this body of knowledge that human society inherits.

c. *Knowledge is not an industry*

Knowledge (creation/utilisation) is an innate human activity—akin to digestion, reproduction, etc.—and cannot form the basis of directed collective activity whose aim is the efficient increase in quantity/volumes. From this view, it cannot serve as the basis of (or as ) industry.

d. *Knowledge is not for profit making*

Knowledge, being societal in nature, cannot form the basis of exploitation of man by man.Lack of knowledge may result in loss of life and property. Keeping people in the dark wilfully so that it leads to loss and misery, is exploitation in its crassest form. Any attempt to hold back or prevent access to knowledge is therefore criminal. Profit-making through knowledge is exploitation.

e. Knowledge is not private property and should not become the instrument of exploitation. Exploitation of knowledge is a crime against humanity. Knowledge, by its very definition, cannot be confined to the domain of the individual. The very process of knowledge generation (information validation and acceptance) is a social process. Any information/cogitative conclusion that cannot be shared, falls out of the realm of true knowledge. Hence knowledge cannot be private property nor should it be patented(for exploitation).

f. Every form/aspect of knowledge is inherently equal to other forms/aspects. If we believe in the inherent equality of man in society then knowledge, that springs from and sustains different forms of social activity, must also reflect this equality. Moreover, if we accept that knowledge formation is a consensual social activity, this inherent equality is mandatory.

g. Education should be such as to remove societal inequality. Education, seen as a process of transmission of knowledge and its upgradation, cannot and should not promote any practice that militates against this equality. In fact, it should assist in recognition of any incipient inequality and outline the path to its mitigation or obliteration.

h. Knowledge is for the development of individuals and society. Thus, knowledge is the basis of life and development. The enlightenment of individuals is based on free access to the growing body of knowledge and its constructive deployment leads to the development of society.

When we critically examine *lokavidya* we see that it scores quite well on the above points; so it could serve as a pointer to the new knowledge paradigm. This added to the fact that, on ground, *lokavidya* is the basis of life and the motive force for a very vast section of mankind (local *lokavidyas* of almost all Third-World countries of the Orient/East play a similar role in their societies) makes it imperative to take directives on reorganization from *lokavidya* if only to keep a vast multitude of people integrated into the new development paradigm. A view echoed in this quotation:

> ...the basic workforce of Indian industry largely come from earlier industrial occupations and *jatis*, which had practised similar pursuits traditionally and historically..and would be of great value to India if they were to become the backbone of a regenerated and flourishing Indian industry..... Bringing back the thus far ignorned indigenous Indian professional industrial skills into public life, should be able to provide a new life and direction to Indian industry and expand the base as well as the production of Indian industry.[7]

### 14.6 Education

The role of educational institutions—as much as their structure —needs an overhaul. We now find that the student-products of our institutions are neither fit nor willing to take up their family/community avocation on the one hand and are, in general, seen as misfits(unemployable) in modern industry and commerce. They need special coaching schools to sharpen and shape their technical, communication and soft skills. Already, we see some key players in the modern industrial sector (IT for example) setting up their own 'finishing schools'; where specialized, intensive training in a particular technical area is imparted along with a rigid soft-skills training programme mixed with an 'appealing' emphasis on (social) values. [which translates to personality development along with skill-set enhancement in a corporate environment for the globalized man]. The 'worthy' through-puts of these schools are deemed fit for whole-time employment. It is interesting to note that these finishing schools and other similar advanced training institutions (as opposed to the general University) such as the Business Schools, the Administrative Academies and Staff Colleges are really, in their form, modern-day analogues of the traditional *Gurukuls*.

The *Gurukuls* and *Acharya-kuls* were traditional centres of learning and training. They were of varied form but, in general, localised geographically and built around an *Acharya*—a fountainhead of specialized knowledge. Most of these *kuls* were supported by the local *panchayat/samudhayam* (or sometimes the dominant religious authority). Only those of the live-in students who were deemed fit to receive expert knowledge progressed in these institutions and in turn became innovators, planners or *Gurus* themselves. Needless to add these *kuls* were predominantly caste-based and most (average) students became practitioners of the taught skills in society. In any event, the system used all the manpower so generated and the practitioners themselves were able to lead a dignified life.These structures supported and sustained the growth and development of *lokavidya* .

The University system, introduced after the 1857 revolt, formalized a system of education and training that was considered legitimate by the Empire. That system is now under strain and decay and seems unable to meet the growing needs of industry and commerce. The Universities have practically become redundant and have made way (in many ways) to the coaching institutions on the one hand and the finishing schools on the other. The finishing schools are becoming predominant and have taken over the lead role in the higher education scenario and, interestingly, we find that the form of the finishing schools and industry-specific institutions, is similar to the traditional institutions of learning/training, namely the *Gurukuls*. Leading experts (practitioners) in various fields of manufacture, service, marketing, human resource development, etc. form the core of these institutions (akin to the *Gurus* in the *Gurukuls*) and student-trainees are, invariably, full-time resident members of these institutions. The filtering process at admission is aimed at getting only the 'really worthy' students into the institution. The training is rigorous and students adapt to the training programme seriously. Needless to add, students who pass out of such institutions command a key position in the job market as managers, planners and decision-makers. Students from these institutions now constitute the new 'ruling class' in society—the bureaucrats, the managers, the information technologists, the investment bankers, the marketing strategists, the media controllers, etc.; they control and direct the destiny of the nation as also the lives of the vast population of the *Bahishkrit Samaj*. Be that as it may, the fact that the form of these modern-day institutions of 'higher learning' hark back to the institutions that were the life-blood of *lokavidya;* provides the direction, which desirable changes in the modes and methods of higher education, ought to take.

The way forward would be to recreate modern-day *Gurukuls*, based on latent skills, in a contemporary context. Skill upgradation would take place in these institutions by providing knowledge inputs, in relevant areas, based on modern science and technology; to the inherent(though moribund) skills.

> The solution lies in the reversal of the process which brought about our present problems (and) if one held to the belief that cultures and civilizations can renew themselves only through ways which have their source in their own psyche and the concepts which shape their society(then) one has to fall back on indigenous resources.[8]

The question of concomitant social reorganization also needs to be tackled and a workable concept of social organization arrived at, that could provide a basis for truly cooperative complementary human endeavour.

In conclusion, it is imperative that *lokavidya* in all its dimensions be put on centre stage, with special emphasis on those aspects that will provide guiding principles for knowledge dissemination and education in a new socio-economic paradigm.

## REFERENCES

1. Dharampal, *Indian Science and Technology in the 18th Century*, SIDH, (2007), p. 253.
2. Dharampal, *Rediscovering India*, SIDH, (2007), pp. 36, 45,186-87.
3. Ibid., pp. 29-30.
4. Dharampal, *Indian Science and Technology in the 18th Century*, SIDH, (2007), p. 35.
5. Y. Nayudamma, former DG, CSIR and VC, JNU.
6. Dharampal, *Rediscovering India*, SIDH, (2007), p. 28.
7. Ibid., pp. 188-89.
8. Ibid., pp. 13, 103.

# 17

# Infinity of Web, Reality of *Lokavidya* and Coming of Global Gods*

*K.K. Surendran*

Passages in the Rigveda suggest that the gods were first witnessed by the human beings who realized the expanding vastness of the human mind. That is also perhaps the beginning of the crystallization of *lokavidya*, the encoding of the dialogue of man with nature, including his own self. Are we witnessing the beginning of *lokavidya* discovering new gods, now global in scope and so strange and unfamiliar? For, to dream, to see the gods in the newborn is the creed of *lokavidya*. In this essay we are trying to picture a dialogue among those witnessing the rise of the new star for deliverance of humanity by attempting to listen to the following analogies:

1. Knowledge Dialogue and Human Mental Reflection.
2. Logico-mathematical Universe and Knowledge on the World Wide Web.
3. The Human Neocortex and the Networked World Wide Web.
4. *Lokavidya* and the Emotional Brain.

## 17.1 Knowledge Dialogue in Society and Internal Dialogue of a Being

We are attempting the similarity of what we understand by Knowledge Dialogue in society and the internal dialogue of the

* Article in the bulletin *Virtuality and Knowledge in Society: Dialogue on Knowledge in Society II*, published for Vidya Ashram Workshop in the World Social Forum, Karachi, Pakistan, March 2006.

human mind, mental reflection. What one would like to insist is that this dialogue fundamentally characterizes the reality of society and the human being. That is to say, we attempt to draw a parallel between the internal dialogue of the human being and the knowledge dialogue in society and assert that as the only path open to society to discover the true goal and achieve it. We find that the key roles in this royal path have a time element associated with it. Roughly, science <-> society's dialogue with nature (future), politics <-> society's dialogue with itself (present) and philosophy<->society's dialogue with its spirits (past).

They are in some sense related to their way of being aware of the time element in some fundamental way. They do not refer to the mass of things in the classification of activities, but aspects of its being which seems to be a reflection of the awareness of time. In this way we would like to elevate the activities of human society to a level from where we may be able to comprehend Knowledge Dialogue at least to the level required to effect that difficult conceptual leap. For there is a sense in which at the end of it we are likely to prescribe Knowledge Dialogue as the remedy for all ills of society, just as the yoga practitioner, who has taken the difficult conceptual leap regarding the internal dialogue, seems to prescribe yoga as the cure of all ills of the individual. (We will not dwell on the importance of 'yoga' terminology for practising internal dialogue, but it may prove to be an important analogy in discovering the 'now' aspect of Knowledge Dialogue, politics).

Politics is characterized by a conception of history, an active interpretation of it and in so far as the *lokavidya* standpoint is a statement of the history in the context of the seemingly unstoppable growth of science and technology in the modern era, its understanding is crucial to any human steering of the destiny of mankind. And for the same reason, it appears that an enlightened understanding of time is a primary prerequisite. For, just as the reductionist science and technology seems necessarily inherently violent, in that it lives by supplying the instruments of war in the hands of the clever manipulators, not unlike the royal blacksmith's science and technology supplying the sharpest swords.

So, then, the characterization of *lokavidya* as beyond organization and algorithmic description, qualities so amenable to virtualization and synthesis, captures this transcendent nature of human societies. But, that is also its weakness! For, there is already in anyone's comprehension of *lokavidya*, an organization of that knowledge, however rudimentary, which if followed and pursued carefully (experimentation, e.g. as in *Prayog parivar*) seems to lead to organized knowledge. And perhaps it is this fact which is exploited in the virtualization process faced by *lokavidya*. Here it appears that much of the activity taking place in the virtual domain is akin to the unstoppable internal dialog of this mind. Also, much of the organized and seemingly directed representation of reality there (by governments, corporates, research centres and conferences etc.)—the stuff of everyday life of networked society—is akin to the bodily functions driven by the senses.

At the risk of gross oversimplification, we state the goal as elaboration of the dictum: Aim of Knowledge Dialogue is to develop the intuition of society regarding the reality of the forces apparently at work in guiding its fate. In discovering the intuition we are inquiring into the possibility of drawing a parallel between the seemingly infinite virtual universe of knowledge opened up by Information Communication Technologies and the seemingly endless universe thrown open by the mathematical modelling of physical reality.

We have the following ascending chain:

1) Thought itself is fundamentally synthetic and is presented analytically only in so far as it is organized to carry on life.
2) There is already some organization and rudimentary virtualization of any category at the level of thought itself.
3) Human language is the reflection of this process. It is synthetic in origin, words are organized wholes held by inductive logic, as opposed to grammar constructed by deductive logic to conform to some requirement of consistency and relationships.
4) *Lokavidya* is the organized reduction of the transcendent human life and is the only form of

knowledge which embeds time.

5) This bestows the quality of Divinity (absolutely outside the domain of human manipulation and control) to ancestral life, to dialogues of ancestors.
6) Knowledge dialogue is that process by which *lokavidya* expands, as if by engaging time in conversation.
7) Thus *lokavidya* is the accumulated output of Dialogue of Knowledge-in-Society.

So, there is an embedding of history in *lokavidya*.

## 17.2 Logico-mathematical Universe and Knowledge on the World Wide Web

While reflecting on the mathematical modelling of physical reality we see a different kind of embedding in science which seems to believe that understanding of 'things' can be reduced to 'other things' in a single ended manner. Briefly it is? → Society → Living Organisms → Molecules → Atoms → Elementary Particles – Energy – ?.

It is generally understood that that this reduction has been 'achieved' by the success of the description in terms of the primitives, but in reality it is the possibility of a technology to reverse the reduction that is its basis. In other words, science has been preoccupied with the ways to effect the the reduction up and down the scale – that is technology. ?→ Energy Realm → Coherent State of Elementary Particles → Coherent State of Stable Atoms and Molecules → Coherent State of Biomolecules and Genetic Code → Coherent State of Evolved Organisms and Species →?

From this view point, scientific understanding is the understanding of history. History falls into correspondence with knowledge—public objective knowledge. Thus the understanding of the structure of matter is the description of the history of matter, how solids crystallized, liquids cooled to form crystals, liquids cooled off from gas, gas from molecules, molecules from atoms and atoms from particles. The description of the physical properties in terms of fundamental laws is the tracing of the history of the formation of matter—the evolution of it. Scientific explanation amounts to historical explanation, not in the sense of objective universal history of objects, but in terms of the embedding of the coherent states in the next higher coherent state and that evolution is historical. So also scientific explanation of living organisms in terms of cells, cells in terms of nucleic acids and proteins in the tracing of the evolution of life. Scientific understanding of life is but the history of life.

It may thus be argued that the limitless expansion of the logical-mathematical thought/literature compared to the limited and often meagre examples of physical reality fuelling it. This is borne out by the state of every flourishing branch of mathematics (and mathematical sciences) today. Their history is the story of this limitless expansion and its virtuality is self-evident. They have at their base one or two (may be a few) elements of physical reality (with simple, easy to model logical connections!)— a flow, a motion, a behaviour, .... For example, we may look at the genesis of non-Euclidean geometry and the endless possibilities of constructing imaginary numbers or infinitesimals and infinities to appreciate the expansion of this virtual edifice and which elements of physical reality have managed to connect to it and when.

Everything else that takes place in science is the construction of machines, technology to reverse the embedding by construction. The 'understanding' of the structure of matter, living and non-living coupled with an incomplete understanding of time, bestows in the Western society an apparent invincibility to create (machines) and destroy (life and societies) an infinite variety. And it is this power which is at the base of the Knowledge Management-subjugation of other knowledge systems. That is, here power directly enters as a characteristic of knowledge—awesome power!

The exponential expansion of the virtual universe of the web apparently provides limitless possibilities for any individual, community, any entity whatsoever, which is connected to it. However this freedom appears to be similar to the limitless possibilities for knowledge on any object of physical reality provided that it is 'connected to the mind'. And, this similarity though qualitative may also turn out to be quantitative in some appropriate sense of measure. However, the mind is not 'open' to acquiring the knowledge from the infinite resources, busy as it is with its immediate functions, defined by an axis of relevance as it were, seemingly fixed by the major forces at work, often struggling against them. And most of all, except a measure-zero set of objective reality, fall by the wayside, unable to make the connection.

Thus it appears that it may be useful to describe the condition of *lokavidya* by saying : Knowledge-in-Society has lost power, in terms of a characteristic—'*power*'. This quantity, if we agree that it is a quantifiable entity, may help us to understand the process of virtualization better.... Is it something like temperature of physical systems? That power of knowledge in some suitable sense runs engines of change in society? That brings us to the analogy of networking aspect of WWW with the structure of the rational edifice of the human brain, the neocortex.

## 17.3 The Human Neocortex and the World Wide Web

Thus we are led to the next analogy: similarity of the knowledge technology of the web to the neocortex (the so-called seat of rational logico-mathematical thought). Apparently the most striking feature of the neocortex is that its very existence is a delayed rationalization of anything 'connecting' to it to be consistent with the action 'which apparently follows' giving it the sense of 'causality' and the resulting idea of power of 'creation'. Something similar happens in the virtual universe of the web masquerading as the 'source', putting out a 'causal' chain for action and apparently displays awesome creative power, while everything originated in *lokavidya* long before. The similarity in hardware connectivity is qualitative, but may be even quantitative.

One of the important characteristics of the virtual universe is that one may 'connect' to it from anywhere and it appears to be the 'same'. This feature is almost identical to that of conscious thought or neocortex thought starting with the connection of any 'piece of physical reality' as it were. That is, given some axis of relevance or focus, the domain of convergence of knowledge is in a sense independent of the starting point. In the virtual universe this is enabled by the logico-mathematical modelling and the generic entities residing there. Thus we are led to the next analogy by our understanding of the emotional brain and autonomous systems as the source of action.

### 17.4 *Lokavidya* and the Emotional brain

So, while there is a parallel between the the virtual knowledge universe of the web supported by infinite possibility of logico-mathematical models and neocortex, the knowledge technologies preceding it may be compared to the emotional brain. The brain stem or the old brain, often considered (in a limited sense may be) the seat of the emotional being, has to struggle to connect to the rational edifice of the neocortex. The problem of information overloading, discussed widely in the context of WWW, is analogous to the rational brain getting lost with the problem of completeness, while the emotional brain is struggling to 'connect' to it regarding its 'feelings'. The struggle of *lokavidya* to 'connect' to the web is similar. In the struggles of *lokavidya* we see the image of struggles of the 'emotional human mind' engaging in 'creative','meaningful' and 'harmonious' actions. And yet, nothing seems to be above this connection! If there is a realm escaping this connection, it is the mind of a different being, yet to arrive.

From this perspective, it is inconceivable how we may argue in favour of an exclusive category/status for *lokavidya* in relation to either its connectivity to the web or consequences of that connectivity. Instead, it appears that *lokavidya* with its immortal encoding of time and history and connections of the human interface to nature, becomes the true experimental basis for the evolution of the language and culture of the new mind in the making. The new struggles may well be in establishing the right connection to this mind. *Lokavidya* is experienced in precisely doing this, in shaping the mind of communities of living men and women, only that now the community is global!

### 17.5 Summing Up

The Knowledge Dialogue we are involved in is analogous to the process of conscious reflection of the human mind, beyond the 'real'—'virtual' duality and inherently goes beyond materialist interpretation of (knowledge) society as hitherto understood . It is to be the visible face of the inner voice of the mind in the making, and not merely some part of the incessant internal dialogue of the Internet. Should not the guiding principle be one of building the higher mind of society in the image of the higher mind of human beings? If it is so and what we see is indeed the beginning of a primitive mind of global humanity, then may be, by our own understanding of our history, there must come into being new primitive (tribal, pagan, ...) deities, the beginnings of real-gods for the entire humanity!

# 18

# *Lokavidya* and Ordinary Life*

*Sunil Sahasrabudhey*

Unconditional knowledge and unconditional life is *lokavidya* and ordinary life. *Lokavidya* is the knowledge with the people which changes with their experience, needs, change of ethical and aesthetic contexts and so on. It incorporates their way of thinking, principles of organization, mode of abstraction, etc. It is made up of a body of information, practices, techniques, expertise and what have you. There is nothing in *lokavidya* which is not changeable. It grows with ordinary life, gels with it and never dies, because ordinary life never dies. Ordinary life is life without condition. It assumes no science, no technology, no religion, no methods of organization and communication of knowledge, it assumes nothing. It is not true, austere or moral life, for there is falsehood, extravaganza and immorality in ordinary life. But it has the criteria of truth, morality, justice, wisdom, etc. in it.

*Lokavidya* constitutes the epistemic strength of the people. It is constituted of those traditions of knowledge which refuse to die and produce ever new modes of subsistence, innovation and growth under oppression, marginalization or distortion by alien intervention. Ironically, they die out if the bearers of these traditions become expansionist, colonizers and oppressors. This

---

* Note in the bullet in *Radical Politics and the Knowledge Question: Dialogue on Knowledge in Society IV*, published by Vidya Ashram for distribution in the World Social Forum, Nairobi, Kenya, January 2007.

is a kind of socio-epistemic law. So *lokavidya* is an inexhaustible source of strength of the people. The chief value associated with *lokavidya* is that of ordinary life. Not austere life, not simple life, just ordinary life. From the twin concepts of *lokavidya* and ordinary life we can proceed to develop concepts which would enable us to build emancipatory resistance both in the epistemic realm and the realm of physical activity.

The new ruling classes are emerging and organizing themselves with 'knowledge' at the centre of theory and practice, 'knowledge management' being the most prized (and priced ) theoretical as well as practical activity. This makes the 'digital divide' a radical 'knowledge divide', for the other side consists mainly of knowledge in society, *lokavidya,* which is expected increasingly to assimilate science and religious knowledge into it as it engages itself in a struggle across the digital divide.

The life on the Internet is leading to fantastic imageries for human life, imageries which were never part of human imagination, even fiction, what with virtual experiment, cyber sex and the like. This is life without contact with the world of things, men, women, other objects. So it also produces hankering for ordinary life which is just human and natural and does not assume any technology.

We do not assume that one or other form of knowledge can not contribute to development of emancipatory politics, for we think that knowledge cannot essentially be limited. Every concept, piece of information and even method of inference of a type of knowledge may be limited (say by its historical roots, cultural or regional genesis and application or by embodying elements of some specific cosmology, etc.), but knowledge per se is not limited in any of its locations. So what is proposed is a dialogue between all locations of knowledge. *Lokavidya* and ordinary life constitute our normative framework for this dialogue between various streams of knowledge, locations of knowledge. Since *lokavidya* and ordinary life are not just primary expressions of people's knowledge and life but also constitute the primary sources of strength of the people, therefore the normative framework of *lokavidya* and ordinary life radically favours political formations for emancipation of the people from the digital divide.

The *lokavidya* standpoint is the people's standpoint in the Age of Information. To say that so many respectable and genuine traditions of knowledge exist is not to say that some or all of them have answers to people's problems and a sufficiently wide basis for reconstructing the world differently. To say that *lokavidya* and ordinary life reinforce, enliven, protect and move each other is not to say that they are complete unto themselves and the ideology they may spin out has recipes for reconstruction of another world. It is only to say that they constitute our starting point, constant reference and also the ultimate criteria. The *lokavidya* standpoint is the standpoint of truth and justice in the Age of Information. It enables us to fight against falsehood imposed upon the world in the name of a future global and connected world, courtesy Globalization and Knowledge Management. It enables our struggles to last out because it enables us to think differently. What is common between Islamic resisters, Gandhians, Marxists and innumerable local traditions and formations in their resistance and campaign against American expansion? It is their commitment to the interest of the people and to justice. This commitment is rooted in the respective traditions of thought and knowledge. The *lokavidya* standpoint is the standpoint of respect to these traditions of knowledge and many more. People's struggles alone will transform these traditions into new contemporary versions able to challenge the basis of the present society and hold a promise for a realizable different world.

# 19

# The Promise of *Lokavidya*

*Vijay Kundaji*

Could *lokavidya* approaches provide answers to our troubled, incomplete and flawed relationship with, and understanding of, our world?

The 'modern' understanding of the world around us appears exposed or at least incomplete and flawed in many ways. Survival-threatening environmental degradation, loss of natural resources, poor understanding of the value of the natural world, worsening social and economic inequity perpetrated by the modern economic and political order, pervasive violence and the increasing fragmentation of our consciousness all seem to be somehow inextricably linked to our ways of life which are built on a certain understanding of the world and our relationship to it.

## 19.1 Knowledge Legitimacy

Acceptable and legitimate knowledge, we have been instructed and have come to believe, is only produced in certain crucibles —such as the modern 'university system' or within scientific establishments—in a certain way, using particular methods, within a certain kind of organization, requiring access to certain levels of resources, from within certain professional communities, and so on. All other knowledge is debunked using a variety of terms and descriptors, well-known to everyone; terms such as 'not being reason based', subjective, experiential, empirical, non-verifiable, prone to hijacking, non-scientific, unsophisticated, uneducated, etc. All these are supposed to suggest that such knowledge is fraudulent, inferior and deficient.

**Note:** There is a new emerging dimension to knowledge, in the age of the internet, that is currently the subject of much articulation and debate, in *lokavidya* circles and beyond. This is the dimension of knowledge as represented digitally and shared and collaborated upon over networks. In some ways this is seen as a new representation of knowledge—and perhaps new knowledge itself. However, this piece will not refer to this aspect of knowledge (which would render knowledge that this note refers to as 'modern' out of date!) other than to bring up the example of the wikipedia phenomenon as a possible manifestation of a limited *lokavidya* event in the age of the internet.

Even in non-modern societies, knowledge seems/seemed to have been an attribute in determining position in the social hierarchy. Yet, knowledge of ordinary life often placed those in possession of it lowest down in the social hierarchy. So, clearly, some kinds of knowledge (knowledge of scripture, doctrine, custom, astrology, etc.) are/were legitimized to a greater degree. The age of reason did not emancipate people or knowledge from this arbitrariness. Another knowledge elite (of the modern university system and knowledge establishment) replaced the old one. Those who were on top of the old knowledge pyramid merely leapt to the top of the *new* knowledge pyramid. This is especially true, today, about societies, such as, say, India, in which modernity appears to have been grafted upon a traditional base.

Knowledge generated or derived through means and methods other than those recognized in modern systems of education and training is what has kept, and continues to keep, vast numbers in our society functioning, creative and productive despite oppressive social and economic inequities, lack of 'access' and opportunity, and despite the dysfunctional nature of our modern institutions, and their manifestations. Yet modern school and college education imposes a complete blindness to the recognition and acknowledgement of such knowledge and its enduring, resilient and possibly unique qualities.

## 19.2 Is There an Alternate, 'More Naturally Attuned', View of the World?

If our current predicament lies in the inherent nature of modern knowledge, and its structure, rather than on imperfections of its application, then—is there an alternate view of the world that might result in more sustainable, creative, integrated ways of life? Might this be the question which will provide a stage entry for *lokavidya* in our times?

## 19.3 The Promise of *Lokavidya* and Some Open Questions

Several questions beset the idea of *lokavidya* and may need further explication and debate before it can be formulated robustly at a philosophical level. Yet, to most people who have lived in societies with large populations that have not entirely 'modernized' their ways of life and learning, it is apparent that there is a totally alternative system of (and approach to) producing, propagating and applying knowledge to life, art, community and in the pursuit of happiness.

Without calling for a return to any imagined idyllic, simpler, traditional, pre-industrial way of life, the *lokavidya* world may be centred around an alternative basis for knowledge and the organization of society.

*Lokavidya* may have no 'historical' element to it. It is not as if there was a point in our distant human or civilizational past when we lived immersed and amidst a state of *lokavidya* and it is not as if it disappeared at the stroke of the onset of the industrial age. As commentators on *lokavidya* have pointed out —it morphs and adapts in all times and at all places. Despite its informal status and non-acknowledgement, resulting in a kind of 'invisibility', is has existed all along and may even coexist in a modern industrial environment.

As an example, many of India's mechanics, (the many thousands who run small repair shops and self-styled businesses across the length and breadth of the country and these days may even have found their way into formal employment) may in some ways be a product of the *lokavidya* world. They have never been 'formally' trained (in fact their modes of learning and imparting training would themselves be an interesting area for more study) and some may be from traditional artisanal communities who have worked with machines and mechanical systems. Today, they may be found applying their entirely experientially learned, non-formally-trained knowledge to modern machines and on modern production lines. In contemporary Western societies most mechanics and technicians are both literate and, to varying extents, formally trained. They resort to technical manuals, drawings and training courses to learn their skills and perform their analysis and tasks. Many *lokavidya* mechanics may be semi or illiterate, may have no familiarity with the use of drawings, tables and charts and yet may be fully productive and creative with modern machines and mechanical systems. This may well have been the situation that existed in Europe at the dawn of the industrial age—where mechanics were artisans who were perhaps illiterate and certainly not from or 'of' the 'university'. Their specific *vidya* and their application perhaps of *lokavidya* might well have been the source of all the innovation that followed, before it was trapped and captured within the philosophical construction of 'scientific' or 'technical' knowledge.

In fact, might formal *vidya* (if we may use this term to refer to the forms of modern 'legitimized' knowledge) and *lokavidya* be two sides of the same coin—one the 'captured' and 'privileged' side of the other more liberated and free form entity? Is this duality also perhaps at the root of other opposing attributes of one and the other?

## 19.4 *Lokavidya* and Work

Modern modes of work and production result in the well known (and much documented), alienation of workers and labour; in the yearning modern desire and need for a separation of 'work' and 'life' (sometimes even a return to 'life' through a full break from 'work'). The politics of modern work resulting in the division and stratification of labour, ultra specialization, a sense of loss of ownership, a lack of control, absence of the 'big picture', the fragmentation of the supply and production chain (witness globally dispersed sources of raw materials, processing, parts, sub-assemblies, the separation of design and prototyping from production, separation of even production and testing), and so on, based on modern economic models, clearly has much to do with this. A *lokavidya* world might promise a more integrated continuum of work, life and labour.

### 19.5 *Lokavidya* Education?

Can *lokavidya* be propagated in a formal way through a 'system' of education? Is *lokavidya's* central advantage the fact that it is democratically produced in a highly nebulous, decentralized way? Is there any meaningful instruction possible inside a classroom and outside the domain of ordinary life? Will this work against *lokavidya's* incorporation into a 'system' of education? Indeed, if so—can there be any notion of 'protection' for *lokavidya*, at all? Perhaps *lokavidya* is an open source and therein lies its strength and equity?

### 19.6 *Lokavidya* Economics

Could *lokavidya* result in a new economics, one that would, for example, assign 'real' costs to products and services? We all accept that modern economics is full of counter-intuitive ideas —things such as economy of scale and the globalization of production and distribution—many of which result in well-known absurdities such as products that are manufactured in diverse global locations and transported to distant markets being 'cheaper' than locally produced ones; or, the cost of mass produced meat and meat products, being cheaper than vegetable products or those from small-scale enterprises. It is also a fact that in societies that are behind on the 'modernization' curve some of the product cost relationships are inverted with respect to those in the integrated world—and are often attributed to production inefficiency, never to real or hidden costs.

### 19.7 *Lokavidya* and Violence

Is there something in the basis of *lokavidya*, that might result in solutions, technologies and institutions that are inherently less violent and more equitable and compassionate? Linkages have been made between *lokavidya* and Gandhian approaches to knowledge and possibly a Gandhian science. Could deeply recyclable and renewable technologies, for example, have emerged via *lokavidya*? If even the central focus parameter of a technological solution is changed just slightly—we all know that new and very different products may result—an example being the internal combustion engine that has been designed for power rather than efficiency. Could a fundamental shift towards *lokavidya* result in more radical changes in our world?

# III

# Economics of *Lokavidya*

# 20

# Local Market: A Fundamental Basis to Challenge Globalization*

*Sunil Sahasrabudhey*

The idea of "Local Market" is an integral part of the ideology for creation of a society free from exploitation. When the produce manufactured in home-based units and in the countless small units will necessarily sell locally, then there can be no doubt about the general happiness and prosperity inhabiting the life in rural and local areas (*anchal*). This is not a new idea. Gandhiji shaped the idea of *Khadi*, village industries and localized consumption to fight imperialism. That very same idea, in the form of the "local market" today, provides the basis for a decisive fight against globalization, which is nothing but the newly emerging form of imperialism. New areas of struggle need to be devised in the face of great changes taking place in organization of production, capital, technology and structure of markets. Focus of economic debates has shifted from modes of production to forms of market. In this, the free market and foreign trade policies are the main subjects of debate. The idea of public-welfare-through-state-intervention is disappearing and in its place the idea of "economic might is right" is being propagated. In this process, the market is getting so reconstituted that the pavement hawkers who work with limited capital are getting ruined, and the real income of the farmers and

---

* Translated from Hindi by Dr. Naresh Sharma, who teaches economics in the University of Hyderabad. The original was published in *Lokavidya Samvad*, a periodical started in 1998 during the preparation of Lokavidya Mahadhiveshan in Varanasi.

artisans is continuously declining. The main task of the state intervention is to hasten these processes to completion through new policies and police repression. There appears to be wider political consensus on this, and one does not perceive any signs of protest within the political process. There have been sporadic protests against this process by organizations of farmers, artisans and *adivasis*. The "local market" is an idea that provides the basis for an organized and long-term struggle against this.

The ideas of *lokavidya, anchal* and *swadeshi-samaj* along with "local market" are taking shape as an ideological basis of a struggle for creating an exploitation-free society. The social and political developments of the last one hundred years have brought the dreams of Gandhi and Marx to a common meeting ground, obliterating the differences. This can be understood through an analysis of the changes occurring in different constituent parts of the economic system and the critical role of the "local market" in the process of fundamental social change can also be understood through such an analysis. This is the subject matter of the present article.

## 20.1 Globalization

To understand the changes taking place in the economic system of our society and the world, we shall organize our discussion under six heads. These are: capital, unit of production, market, technology, resources and producer classes.

### *20.1.1 Capital*

Finance capital is becoming the dominant form of capital today. There can be several forms of capital in a society at any given time. The most important among these are: industrial capital (means of production, machines) and finance capital. The industrial capital alone ruled after the Industrial Revolution in Europe. Owners of this capital were called capitalists. Karl Marx saw the basis of exploitation in the private ownership of this capital and hence emancipation from exploitation was seen in the socialization (social ownership of) capital through revolution. Under capitalism, this capital first becomes monopoly capital and subsequently transforms into finance capital. Finance capital spread extensively in Europe after World

War I. This is indicated by development of banks and financial institutions. The newly liberated countries of the Third World adopted industrialization based on the Western technology after World War II. This provided a new lease of life to the industrial capital.

However, that era seems to be coming to an end after fifty years and even in countries like India, we can see undisputed ascendancy of the finance capital over industrial capital. All industries—from gigantic corporations to tiny household units—depend on debt capital from banks and financial institutions. It does not mean that the private capital is any less important today. The finance capital exists in both forms: private and public. Capital has its own dynamics, its own laws of motion. If its movement is impeded by state ownership, then it moves into other private or public forms and if the private ownership stultifies it, then it would tend to transform itself into other public forms, or the society will create forms and arrangements other than private and public categories to accommodate capital.

In any case, the transformation of industrial capital into finance capital has opened up the economic system to far-reaching changes in all its aspects. The power of the capitalist has multiplied manifold in the sense that he is no more bound to any one form of capital and at the same time he has also freed himself from being seen as the enemy of labour. At the same time, since now the capital has found its most abstract and generalized form, it stands in uniform relation to all components of the exploited classes. As a result, all sections, groups, components of the exploited classes can now, more easily, perceive the sameness (of their condition), and hence a wider, all encompassing unity of the exploited classes becomes a definite possibility. The basis for this unity is no more to capture any particular forms of capital but to annihilate capital and its motions forever. The "local market" is an important component of the concrete programme towards the above goal.

### *20.1.2 Organization of Production: Unit of Production*

Unprecedented changes occurring in the organization of production has left the political and economic understanding developed over the past one hundred and fifty years in a state of shock. The large and heavy industry is no more the ideal. Production organized in smaller units is becoming the model. This is in accordance with the necessary requirements of capitalism and the laws of motion of capital. Taking the textile industry in India as an example, the textile units of Mumbai never reopened after the lockout of 1980, following the strike. Textile production shifted to household-based power looms. Instead of running the textile mills, the capitalist found it more profitable to get the various components of work, such as weaving, dyeing, printing, etc. done by artisans located separately and then simply stamping its brand name on the product. Thus, he was freed from all responsibilities of a mill-owner, such as regular pay, bonus, arrangements for housing, health, children's education, insurance, work safety norms, etc. At the same time his profit swelled. Considering just the pay, we see that a worker in weaving would have been paid Rs. 5,000 per month in the mill, he now earns no more than Rs. 2,000-2,500 per month while weaving on his power loom. In other words, the income of the erstwhile mill worker has been reduced by half. The market price of cloth has not come down. So where did the money go? The obvious answer is that it is pocketed by the capitalist.

This change is more clearly seen in the case of the textile industry. However, it may not be so obvious in other fields of industrial activity. In the engineering industry, manufacturing of parts is carried out in numerous small units in a big way. All big industries want ancillaries to be organized as many small units. The machines, component parts and equipment used in these small and tiny units are owned by the households in whose premises these units are located. Thus, the power of the capitalist is not based on the ownership of physical capital (machines) since the capitalist is simply not its owner. The power of the capitalist flows from his control of finance capital. This allows him to bring all the constituent units of a particular industry into a coherent whole.

Big industry was the ideal in the era of the steam engine. For that form of energy and technology, the large industry was the most profitable form. The big industry was presented as such an ideal in countries like India after independence, so much so that it became a synonym for economic development. Big industry has remained an ideal for a fairly long period. Many principles were propounded in this model including economies of scale, efficiency, principles of management, dignity of labor etc. Now, the whole world is coming down crashing. All the structures since the Industrial Revolution of Europe and all social and economic theories in their support or in opposition to them will crash eventually. Thus, requirements born out of the motion of capital are also giving birth to that historic opportunity when it may be possible to annihilate capital itself—lock, stock and barrel. Now, when the basis of exploitation does not lie in the ownership of the means of production, it is imperative that the followers of Karl Marx turn to those recesses of his philosophy which provide the fundamental explanation of the relation between man and capital. They will have to find the basis for struggle in the coming decades on the two legs of the fundamental understanding of the relation of man and capital and the dream of a classless society. They, too, will need to turn to the "local market".

Establishment of the organization of production in small units as a model implies that those modes of management and market are taking shape, which facilitate the transfer of value from these small production units to the capitalists. New telecom technologies including telephones, cellular phones, E-mail, Internet, computer and television are providing the means of new controls. In this scenario, supporting households and tiny industries pose no opposition to this new form of imperialism. In this first round, what is produced in small units and what is produced in big industry will be decided by the international economic power, as per its needs. There will be limits and pressures, arising out of the nature of technology and political forces, in actually carrying through these designs, but let there be no mistake regarding the direction of change. This change neither implies any movement towards small capital nor does it mean any type of political or economic decentralization.

The capitalist will continue to hold all the controls, the concentration of capital will increase and power of the state will increase accordingly. In all this, a section, representing the politics of big capital, will vociferously talk of promoting household industry, *swadeshi* and the artisans. This way it will try to establish itself in the continuity of Gandhi since *khadi* and village industries occupy a central place in Gandhi's schema. It is necessary to understand that *khadi* and village industries provided the political basis for challenging imperialism in Gandhi's time. However, the world economic order is undergoing fundamental changes. Hence, unless we add local market to *swadeshi* and home-based industry, the new capitalist politics in fact gets support from the politics of *swadeshi* and home-based industry. Now, when Gandhi's legacy and continuity with his thought is being claimed through false propaganda, it becomes necessary for the faithful followers of Gandhi to understand these new changes, bring about necessary changes in themselves for attaining their objectives, and for this, they must accord the same pride of place to the local market in their economic philosophy as given to village industries and home-based industries.

Whereas this change in favour of production being organized in small units serves the interests of the capitalist class, at the same time it also fulfils an important condition for social change from the Gandhian perspective. It is helping in accomplishing the great task of changing the material conditions of production of those who will change society. It is becoming the state policy itself to close down the large factories and promote organization of production in small units. Now the main change required is in the institutions of finance and in the organization of life dictated by consumption. It is not difficult to see that the 'local market' will occupy the central place in both these changes.

### *20.1.3 Market*

"Market" is the most talked about entity in discussions about changes taking place in the name of globalization. Three sources have been identified as responsible for the unestimable wealth of Europe and America: one, appropriation of the labour of the worker; two, development of science and technology; and three, unequal exchange in the market. When the appropriation of labour takes place not in Europe or America but in the countries of the Third World, then this appropriated value gets transferred to Europe and America through unequal exchange. New technology opens up new ways of creating value, but the value thus created also finds its ways to the coffers of a small number of capitalists or reaches a few centres of the world, again, only through the unequal exchange in the market. In this way, it is the market or the expansion of trade that alone prepares the foundation for the concentration of unlimited wealth. The unprecedented prosperity of Europe and America after the Second World War is seen to be based on such expansion of trade with the Third World countries. Now, once again attempts are being made to expand the markets to qualitatively new levels in the name of globalization.

When any commodity sells far away from its place of production, then returns realized by the two parties to such an exchange are in proportion to their power in society. Hence, exchanges over long distance (which, in other words, are also exchanges outside the control of the actual producers) always favour the elite and powerful. This is what trade is about. All the rest is nothing more than shopkeeping.[1] Today, an effort is on to absorb all the shopkeeping into trade. That is why we often witness no expansion of market materially (i.e. total volume of exchange of commodities may hardly change) and yet inexorable expansion of trade is going on all the time. Just to cite one stark example, witness the lucrative prospects in retail business dangled before large business houses including the multinationals by market research agencies and the management experts. In this process much of productive activity, which was hitherto outside the world market system, will be absorbed into it. Handicraft fairs are doing this today. Commodities produced with family labour and skills and with the help of very little capital, that used to be available in the neighbourhood shops, will be absorbed in the system of trade. What cannot be absorbed under trade, will be produced no more. Thus, expansion of trade aims at incorporating all production under trade, irrespective of the structure of ownership or mode of production and finish off all that which cannot be incorporated under trade. In other words, people will live at their sufferance or not live at all.

Trade is the biggest enemy of man. It is the expressed form of finance capital. The root cause of the local society—farmers and artisans, women and *adivasis*—not having control over their own lives is located in trade. Trade is also responsible for erosion of *swadeshi* and human creativity, for all pervasive alienation and for loss of human values in the life of human beings (both the producer and the purveyor of trade). Trade takes the man away from his human triumphs and tribulations leaving him in the clutches of abstract, blind, demonic forces. The ultimate basis for colonialism, imperialism, capitalism, exploitation of labour, exploitation of *vidya* (people's knowledge, skill, faculty to separate right from wrong, values, etc.) and usurpation of the entitlements (rights) of the ordinary man is to be found in trade. Trade has altered the relationship of man with himself. In this world created by trade, the man has become a stranger to his own feelings and experiences. In other words, the relation between knowledge and sensitivity has been ruptured. Hence, man does not know what is in his own interest, what is it that he wants, because when he peeps within, he finds someone else sitting there, to whom he relates only through trade. Thus, when he thinks about himself, actually he is thinking of the man sitting in there and hence he thinks in the interests of trade. His own experiences (perceptions) are lost to perceptions centred in trade. This is the same old story of the chicken and egg: is this alienation of the man a result of trade or is trade born out of the man losing his soul? The entire edifice of the economic system today is built on the foundation of trade and this has distorted, deformed and perverted the nature of man, and so are capital, market, profit, interest, wealth and state built the same way. Therefore, annihilation of trade is a necessary condition for reconstruction of a society in the interests of man. And the idea of the local market provides the foundation for a sustained and decisive struggle against trade.

### 20.1.4 Technology

Developments in telecommunications and biotechnology have been termed technological revolution. These technologies have specially attracted attention in the context of environmental destruction caused by modern industry. Telecommunications is not a technology of production. However, this often escapes perception owing to its almost all pervasive spread and its effectiveness in collection, dissemination and organization of information and in general management.

Biotechnology is a technology of production which has brought about new biological processes, entities and new methods of production. Biotechnology avoids damages to soil, food and environment caused by chemical fertilizers. The debate on impact of biotechnology on ecology and hence the nature and extent of the adverse consequences of biotechnology on the interests and very existence of man, is still at a nascent stage. Many ethical issues have also acquired importance in this context. From an economic perspective, the important thing to note is that there is nothing to indicate that either of the two technologies—telecommunications and biotechnology—will serve the interests of the ordinary man. Both technologies are highly cost and capital intensive. At most, these may cause a shift in the balance of power within the ruling classes. These technologies have accelerated the process of economic concentration further and have facilitated expansion in areas of production across different social classes and geographical areas while retaining financial and managerial control.

Further, an important change at the level of ideas has occurred in the field of technology. Traditional technologies of various societies have attracted attention. Twenty years ago, no one was willing to hear about traditional science and technology, while today there seems to be a great race to collect traditional knowledge regarding various processes and methods of production. This is because traditional sciences and technologies can possibly provide great expansion to trade, if they can bring about effective methods of production—and these may be in any areas such as: agriculture, industry, health, architecture, construction, metal work and metallurgy, textiles, dyeing, etc. This is the attraction of traditional science and technology. However, in the process, the traditional systems of knowledge of non-Western societies become relevant in new contexts. This creates the conditions where it is possible to bring the nature of knowledge into public debate. This opens up the possibilities for challenging modern science as the sole claimant of true and valid knowledge. World imperialism, surely, can not be happy with it.

On the other hand, the fact of the matter is that the knowledge of traditional technologies and processes of nature, and the talent, skill and expertise required for them is available with those communities, which are rejected today. If their skill, talent, expertise and knowledge is to be retrieved from the abyss of rejection and humiliation, and if these are to be incorporated into a new progressive economic system, then it is not possible to prevent their knowledge and capabilities being accorded the status of theory. The movement for enthronement of *lokavidya* (*Lokavidya Pratishtha Abhiyan*) is a movement in that direction.

The local market is the natural habitat of *lokavidya* and also the arena to challenge the monopoly of modern science as the only claimant to knowledge. Whereas, opening up of avenues for traditional technologies is bringing new forms of slavery for the communities in whom such *lokavidya* (and its one component usable by the world market and trade, namely, traditional technology) inheres, at the same time the very processes, needed to create these new modes of slavery, must traverse those pathways from where these societies, communities and classes will be able to raise a formidable challenge to the world imperialism. Together with *lokavidya*, the local market is both the idea and the location for giving shape to this challenge.

### *20.1.5 Resources*

Technological developments also enlarge the scope of resources. Just as the steam engine converted coal into an important resource, in the same way the development of new processes and technologies facilitates in incorporating more and more natural resources into the ever expanding list of raw materials. Biotechnology and traditional sciences and technologies have enormously expanded the list of material resources. Biodiversity, plants, trees, shrubs, roots, shoots, herbs, all sorts of flora and fauna have all become raw materials. These resources are in vital use by a great majority of people, quite unlike coal, petroleum or bauxite, which were either of no use or of very little use to man before the development of modern technology.

An important characteristic feature of imperialism is that it engenders trade in raw materials. Before the Industrial Revolution of Europe, all trade was in consumption goods, whether for everyday needs, or for ornamental and conspicuous consumption or in goods of occasional use. But modern technology has been based on trade in raw materials from the beginning. Hence, now even biodiversity is becoming an object of trade. These are those local resources which are extensively used by the people. Villagers and *adivasis* very extensively use bio resources in their everyday life. These include all aspects of life such as food, fodder, fuel, health, manufacture by artisans, agriculture and so on, all of which use bio resources in a big way. Now under the direction and control of biotechnology and finance capital, the traditional technology will turn all these natural resources into raw materials and this will give rise to large-scale trade in these resources. As a consequence the local people will be progressively deprived of the use of nature around them.

There are already movements for protecting community rights in biological wealth. The issue here is the same as that of tribal rights to the forests. In this connection, two important questions must be considered: (1) Can this struggle for these rights be fought within the context of law and social rights? Or on the other hand (2) will it be necessary to resort to the idea of an alternative economic organization and how such an organization can be created? Even if it was possible to win a legal-social struggle, the only consequence will be that the form and mode of trade in local bio-resources will change but it will not stop such trade. It is perhaps only the local market which can be the basis of that new local economic organization which can wage a decisive battle against trade in bio resources and win it.

### *20.1.6 Producer Classes*

It is to be expected that changes occurring in capital, organization of production, market, technology and resources would lead to far-reaching changes in the real condition of the producing people and in their social and economic organization. It was around industrial labour alone that productive activity was conceived in the idea of pure capitalism. Something akin to this in the form of the proletariat did come into existence during a stage in Western capitalism but nothing similar happened in the countries of the Third World. In a country like India, farmers by and large continued to remain farmers. The first stage of capitalist development after independence brought about the abolition of *zamindari* and other intermediaries and thus brought the farmer in direct relation to capital. Owners of small plots and land came to form a new farmer class and for the past 20-25 years, their movement has been known as the New Farmers' Movement.

This was a period of development of big industry. In all this, the master of traditional knowledge and skills, the artisan, who organized his production in family units, was progressively ruined. However, just as India, though impoverished and emaciated by plunder by the British, could not be finished, likewise, though the artisan has been ruined, impoverished and famished through the colonial period and subsequent development of big industry, yet the artisan communities could not be finished. Neither any plunderer, nor capital can grasp and measure up to the depths of the knowledge, talent and values that got their sustenance from those very artisans who have sustained the great traditions of this country. That knowledge and talent has survived in its fragmented form to provide the foundation for reconstruction of the *Karigar samaj* (the class of artisans). The changes now occurring in the organization of production and other economic aspects are transforming the *Karigar samaj* into a social class.

Now, since trade has been rendered possible in any commodity—however produced and wherever produced, the market has reached every town, village, hamlet or habitation—however near or remote. Therefore, the economic status of all artisans is the same, irrespective of method or place of production. Since the finance capital makes no basic distinction between one kind of technology or other, hence there is no fundamental difference between an artisan practising his traditional crafts or a skilled worker using modern technology.

Now, when bio-resources have been brought on par with physical resources, the productive activity and the life of the *adivasi*, the woman and the farmer, is in no fundamental sense different from that of an artisan. Consequently, the working class that can challenge capitalism is now taking shape as *Karigar samaj*. This *karigar samaj* has its own tradition, its own history, its own *vidya* and also its own regional and local sense and perception. These define its *swadharma*. This *karigar samaj* is there on the front against globalization and its *swadharma* forms the foundation of reconstruction of a new society. Local market has an effective role in both: one, to forge a unity in struggle against globalization, and two, in giving a concrete local, rooted, expression to the *swadharma* of the *karigar samaj*.

### 20.2 The Idea of Local Market

Local market is a great calling of this age. This is perhaps the only way for the producer classes to reclaim their life. In modern life, market is the place of social interaction associated with economic aspects of our life. In the field of knowledge (*vidya)*, the school or university is the corresponding place where people come face to face with each other or with their ancestors, where they establish their relations with the generations to come, and where they give a form to their interactions. In religion, temples, mosques or churches are not the places for man to establish a relation with God. No public places are required for man to relate to God. Rituals associated with such public places are to facilitate people to relate to other people. Thus, there are always public norms to facilitate relations among people in different aspects of life. These legislations or norms are not eternal and quite often, with the passage of time, they are unable to fulfil their objectives in a just manner. And then, change in them becomes necessary. We know that schools, temples and markets of today do not provide avenues for interactions based on justice, respectively in the areas of knowledge (*vidya*), religion (*dharma*) and economy. Perhaps this was the reason why Gandhiji came forward with ideas of basic education, prayer meetings, village industries and rural markets. Just as the values and practice of basic education (*buniyadi taaleem*) are entirely different from that of modern education, and just as prayer meetings (*prarthana sabhas*) tried to promote those beliefs and practices which had become alien to temples, in the same way the idea of 'consumption near the place of production' brings forth the idea of the local market which is fundamentally different from the market as it exists today, both in terms of its basis and purpose.

Neighbourhood shops located in various nooks and corners of towns, villages and *mohalla*s provide all the necessary articles of daily use. Neighbourhood artisans and *mistris* provide myriad repair services in addition to manufacturing a variety of big and small articles of use. Women within their households bring their knowledge of health and local medicines to look after health and sicknesses of people—from babies to adults—and where they are unable to do so, there are people in local societies who are competent and knowledgeable in various aspects of healthcare and medical care. Thus, the needs of daily life are fulfilled through mutual cooperation and local exchange. This is a picture of a self-dependent society which leaves very little scope for exploitation and injustice. The fulcrum of the economy of this society is the local market. Local market may take various forms according to place and time but truth, non-violence and justice in a society are directly proportional to the share of the local market in the economy.

Nature of trade is totally different from that of the local market. Traders bring their goods from far off places and sell their goods very widely in distant places. We all know the global market today. Even within a country raw material and finished goods are transported over long distances. With the onset of globalization, all sorts of concessions are being given to promote foreign trade, and for big business within a country in the name of free market. Goods from distant places dominate in all markets—small or big. The *karigar* is forced to migrate hundreds and even thousands of miles in search of work as a labourer. A section among the farmers too is keen to sell its produce in the international market. This expansion in trade has resulted in unprecedented growth in exploitation, injustice, crime, poverty, unemployment, immorality and vulgarity. To rise in struggle against this state of affairs, to build up *lokashakti* (people's power), to enthrone *lokavidya* (people's knowledge), and to establish *lokaniti* (people's values), it is imperative to properly understand the opposing roles and natures of trade and the local market, and to understand the role of the local market for establishment of the rule of truth and justice in society. Therefore, an attempt is made below to present a comparative study of roles of trade and the local market.

### *20.2.1 Basis of Exchange*

It is at the very foundation of trade that goods are transported over long distances before exchange. In trade, everything including labour, capital, goods of use, resources obtained from nature, etc. travel over long distances before they are transacted. Goods of one society sell in another society. Therefore, the partners in exchange normally hold very different social and economic values and norms, as a result of which a pure economic logic comes into being and questions of justice become secondary. Since the objective of trade is maximization of profit, use of force becomes integral to such exchange. In medieval and colonial era, force was openly employed in defence of trade, which has been given a constitutional basis under the capitalist state. Such coercion is effected by governments with the help of police and army in the name of law and order. In direct contrast, exchange in the local market is premised on shared social and economic values. Since, people living in the same locality are connected to one another through innumerable social, economic, cultural and familial links, hence force or coercion is not needed to resolve opposing interests. Even today it can be observed that the small shopkeeper often gives concessions while selling to the poor in their society.

### *20.2.2 Exploitation or Convenience*

All, other than the capitalist class, are exploited through trade. This is one of the principles of trade that the exchange will be more unequal as it takes place further away from the place where goods are produced or obtained. In other words, the powerful partner corners the lion's share in such exchange. Look at prices of any of the goods available in the market today. Prices are increased excessively for any of the goods—from tooth powder and soap to rice, wheat, clothes and other goods. The farmer or the *karigar* gets no part of these high prices. Indeed they are compelled to sell their produce at the lowest possible prices. All the profit is skimmed by big business and the traders. The expansion of trade to the farthest corners of society in the name of free market and globalization, as is being aggressively pushed today, will further deepen and widen this exploitative system. In contrast to this exploitative character of trade, the very objective of the local market is benefit of the local society. The local market does not purport to create new needs, desires or attractions for new things but basically to satisfy the needs of the people. Nobody produces all things required for life in a society. Institutions of exchange are required in any society. The local market is that institution. This market composed of small shops makes most of goods and services needed by people available to them at fair prices.

### *20.2.3 Monopoly versus Availability*

As the trade expands and the market is filled with goods brought from distant places, variety of available goods shrinks. On the one hand, there is much greater variety in availability of goods that are expensive and glittering, as can be seen at the upper end of the market for any of the goods like soaps, oils, dental care goods, food stuff, sweets, textiles, ready-made clothes, utensils, housing, etc. On the other hand, not even half the variety is available in any of these categories of goods for the common people. The rich and prosperous argue that there is a great increase in variety with expansion of international and domestic trade. However, all these goods are beyond the reach of at least 80 per cent of people and there is hardly any choice of the goods available within their reach. An important aspect of the local market is that this will give opportunities to *all* to find goods of their choice.

### *20.2.4 Glitter or Quality*

Whenever the question of local market for the local produce is raised, the prosperous raise the question of quality. Whether it is the question of foodstuff or textiles or metals or plastic products, they don't tire in claiming that packaged goods facilitated by large-scale trade are of high quality and that the locally produced goods are not standardized, are of uncertain quality and therefore cannot be trusted. But then, what can one say, if we lose our sense of aesthetics and taste, and if we start considering everything that glitters, that makes a big show of itself as synonym for high quality? Implementation of standards in a society, from the point of view of quality, is the task of the consumers. It is a task, which can neither be entrusted to any government agencies, nor to any organizations or laboratories created by and part and parcel of the institutions of trade. Today attractive packaging and glitter have become synonymous with quality. It is necessary to challenge such manifestations for the health of any society. Hence, the market must be so organized that the local consumer alone has the right to judge the quality. This is exactly the case with the local market.

### 20.2.5 Competition or Complementarity

The very basis of the idea of a free market lies in the idea of competition, which does not respect any bounds or limits or decorum. This is nothing but the principle of "economic might is right". Companies engage in a fight to finish with one another; traders dream of finishing their rivals and also act accordingly. It is claimed that competition provides the basis for production of best quality goods at the lowest possible price. But this claim is as empty as the claim that the free market ensures equality of opportunity for all. Neither does it provide equality of opportunity for all, nor does it ensure quality in the goods, nor does it make a greater variety available to all consumers, and nor are the goods available at the cheapest possible price through competition. If anything is true then it is this that it facilitates emergence of monopoly in the name of competition, and renders the market itself a puppet in the hands of traders through false advertising. In direct contrast to this free market, the basis of the local market lies not in competition but in complementarity. A self-dependent society is characterized by a dynamic and active local market. This is that place of economic exchange where everyone comes into contact with economic complementarities with respect to his own economic activities. Whereas the philosophy behind trade today treats every individual as complete in oneself and in competition with all other such complete selves, the concept of the local market is based on a philosophy, which treats man, family, community, village, etc. as autonomous and mutually complementary units. Therefore, the local market provides a broad-based foundation for re-establishment of sentiments and feelings of cooperation in the society.

### 20.2.6 Crime versus Sociability

There is a very close relationship between trade and crime. That world of crime, which could not be created in the long history of highway robberies, stealing and property disputes, came into being in a very short time in the age of today's trade. The underworlds of Mumbai and Delhi are a part of the world of trade. Under their protection and also independently, there has been incredible growth in crime in all small or big towns and cities. This happens in the urban centres because they are the centres of trade and the markets are located there. No one can stop the unrestrained competition from transforming into crime. It is not that trade or traders necessarily use criminals, but that, at the highest level, there is, in principle, very little difference between trade and crime. This becomes abundantly clear if we make no distinction between economic crimes and other crimes. Falsehood, deception, treachery, duplicity, fraud, swindle, forgery, dacoity, murder are all linked to each other and any one of them engenders the others. The world of trade is the haven to them all. The constitution of the local market liberates the society from this trade and hence to a large measure also from these crimes. There is no place for unrestrained activities in the local market and its institutions keep everyone so linked to all the others that causing harm to any one leads to harm being done to all. This breaks the backbone of crime. This arrangement that makes for the commonality of interests and suffering, strengthens the economic basis for experiencing sufferings of the others in the society. Therefore, the principle of complementarity as incorporated in the notion of the local market engenders the feeling of sympathy and empathy for one another. The basis for sociability lies in this very feeling and no society can exist without this disposition. Anyone, who is moved by the suffering of the others, cannot commit any crime.

The above discussion on 'trade' in a comparative framework shows how the notion of the local market, in today's context, carries a message of a non-exploitative society. However, it still remains to identity those forms of struggle, which can provide a firm basis to challenge globalization and to establish how the local market occupies a central place in these struggles to challenge globalization.

## 20.3 The Challenge

With new modes of exploitation emerging on account of the market today the distinctions between different producing social classes of those living on their own labour and skills are getting erased. Globalization is pushing the farmer, the labourer, the *adivasi*, the woman and the *karigar* all into an identical economic state. A farmer generally owns a small piece of land and a *karigar* typically has machines, equipment and tools sufficient for home-based industry. Both of them depend on credit and carry out their production with family-based labour, skills, knowledge of material and the natural world, and managerial capabilities. People drawn from their own families and classes only sell the commodities produced by them, but they do not realize even a small fraction of profit generated in this whole process.

Let us take an example, to understand this. There was this big edible oil (mustard oil) scandal in 1998. It was said that a dangerous disease is spreading because of adulterated edible oil. Some big companies marketing packaged edible oil were accused of adulteration and they even accepted this. The government took it "very seriously" and talked of bringing legislation to strictly regulate production and marketing of edible oil and suggested a ban on the sale of unpackaged oil. Police repression was let loose on all small shops selling loose edible oil in the following weeks and then things slowly became as before. Sale of loose oil resumed as also all types of packaged oils were back in the market. None of the political parties raised a voice of protest against the government. This indicates that there is a political consensus—under whatever compulsions or pressures—on the ban of sale of loose oil and that only packaged oil be allowed in the market. This is a decision of enormous proportions that will impact millions of people and business worth billions of rupees will change hands. Inevitably, there will arise great opposition against this accompanied by hopelessness, destruction and ruin. Consequently the government will take steps to minimize the damage. The proposal to ban the sale of loose oil in the market has already been mooted and now they will lie in wait for opportunities to take legislative action.

Tomorrow you may hear a farmer proclaim: "Look here. This land is mine. It is I who took the decision to grow mustard on that; and I purchased the seed. My family members and I have toiled hard to produce this mustard. My brother has a shop in the neighbouring town and he has installed an oil press there. He extracts oil from my mustard in his oil press. However, he is not allowed to directly sell the mustard oil thus produced. A van comes every third day and takes away all this oil. This very same oil returns in that very same van after being packaged. And then my brother sells this packaged oil in his shop. Now, be so kind as to explain to me: what sort of economic system is this where the owner of oil company packaging the oil has many buildings in the city, his children go to the most expensive schools, and they adorn themselves in the most expensive clothes, whereas I am increasingly sinking in debt, my children can't go to school or college, and I can't even provide proper medical care to my family members?"

The same story will be repeated for the toiling *karigar*. He will own the shed and the necessary tools, he will provide all the necessary labour from within his family, and even the articles of use that he will manufacture from myriad materials such as wood, clay, iron and other metals, glass, cotton, yarn, plastics, etc. also will be owned by him. However he will have no control over avenues of marketing any of these. He will suffer loss in every act of sale or purchase.

The concept of the local market belongs to that system of transactions in goods where this cannot happen. Oil packaging companies will not be able to mop up all the profit in oil business and the traders and institutions of finance will not be able to corner all the profit from the work of the *karigar*. The only way to do that is for the local society to seize control of the local markets and reconstruct these markets after banishing trade from them. Gaining control of the local markets by local society and reconstruction of local markets is the chief form of erecting the decisive challenge to globalization.

India is a country of villages, towns and other numerous small cities. Go to any of its habitations, you will find most people engaged in farming, handicrafts and home-based industries. Farmers cultivating their own small holdings and the home-based *karigar*s are representative workers of agriculture and industry. From among these and connected to them are small shop owners who, today, are themselves in the grip of men of trade. These people together with their families constitute a local society. Government servants, skilled workers of big industries, and school, college or university teachers neither profess the interests of this local society nor do they work to further these interests. Interests of the farmer and the *karigar* are so much alike in this era of globalization that their unity seems to provide the natural foundation for the unity of the local society. This unity of the local society is a necessary precondition to build up a challenge to globalization and to capture the local markets for their reconstruction. Only a society constituted of autonomous local units has the potential to liberate from exploitation in society and provide justice and dignity to its people. The local market is a defining characteristic feature of the autonomous local society.

In any society, people from different walks of life, classes, communities, occupations feel compelled to come together in movements and agitate in support of their demands, because they suffer various infirmities. Some examples of such movements include: movements of tenant-cultivators and sharecroppers for ownership of land; farmers' movements for remunerative prices for the agricultural produce; movements of industrial and agricultural labour for improvement in their working conditions and for raising their wages; agitations of the urban middle classes against high prices; students' movements for educational reforms and employment; women's movements for dignity, security and social recognition in society; 'save the forest' movements of *adivasis*; anti-dam movements of the displaced communities; and movements for social justice of the backward castes, etc. This country has witnessed all these movements. Demands raised by each of these movements were just. Even so, if we look deeply—with utmost sincerity and sympathy—into these movements, we will find that, by themselves, none of them pose a serious challenge to the imperialistic exploitation or to the economic system dominated by the capitalists and the men of trade. And, it will also be revealed that these movements will actually complement and strengthen any such challenge (to imperialistic exploitation, etc.), once it is posed.

There were four streams of challenge to imperialism during the national movement for independence. The first stream consisted of the movement for national independence per se; the second, the stream of Gandhi's *swaraj* based on *khadi* and village industries; the third stream was that of the communist movement; and the Islamic movement constituted the fourth stream. The challenge to imperialism, then, derived its strength to the extent of the reality of accordance between all these four streams. The national independence and Islam are now no longer relevant for posing a challenge to imperialism in this country. It is the concept of the local market that must be seen as the new basis for realizing the dreams of Gandhi and Marx today. The challenge which the idea of the local market can pose to imperialism of today, namely globalization, is capable of revitalizing every section of society in a just struggle and also of drawing strength from every such section.

The demand of women today for reserving the areas of food and textile production for them under localized arrangements is in continuity with the *khadi* and village industry movement of the erstwhile period and it is further a part of the process of control and reconstruction of the local market by the local society. The local market can become the mainstream of the women's movement in the context of farmer-*karigar* unity. This will also find natural support from movements of opposition to multinational companies. Boycott of their goods is the wider manifestation of the opposition to multinational corporations. This opposition can be further expanded and deepened by opposing the goods of everyday use coming from distant places. It then becomes a part of the local market movement. Today all markets are flooded with goods from outside their localities.

Local production of all sorts of goods has stopped over the past three-four decades. Once goods coming from distant places are boycotted, then it won't take more than a few weeks or a few months before local production of all such goods is resumed. Indeed, the idea of the local market is a harbinger of widespread prosperity, activeness, and creativity for the poor people.

It is pertinent to focus on another important development in this context, because it may provide important starting points for the local market movement. We are referring to the currently ongoing operation, by the civil administration, of forcibly uprooting the small and tiny shops, kiosks, hawkers, etc. from pavements, roadsides, and *mohalla*s of urban areas. This is a very large operation of devastation being carried out throughout the country. It is just possible that this is happening in other countries of the Third World as well. All the aspects of this development including the constitutional aspects, the human rights angle, urban planning, means of livelihood, displacement and the aspects pertaining to the market, are important. Here we shall comment briefly only on the aspect relating to the market. The first obvious point is that all the business that has been carried on so far on the pavements will be transferred to the permanent shops. This involves huge amounts. If 20,000 tiny shops and hawkers, in a small city, doing business worth no more than Rs. 200 are demolished, then in the aggregate it means finishing off a business of about Rs. 150 crores. When this business is transferred to the big shops, it becomes worth Rs. 200-250 crores. Further, its impact on the movement of money, investment and other related aspects of trade will serve and promote the interests of only the rich classes and the trade. Those, who are thus ruined, will join the ranks of the 'labour with cheap skills'.

The second significant aspect is that this "market on footpaths" is that the market within the urban market, which by and large does not know how to follow the laws of trade. Since the pavement sellers are in close contact with people of their localities and themselves experience all the trials and tribulations of a poor man, they first and foremost relate themselves with the world of the worker and the *karigar* rather than with the world of trade. Consequently, there remains a local market in operation within the urban market.

Rural markets, weekly markets, fairs, etc. are, in many ways, the traditional forms of the local market, but there are limitations in conceptualizing physical forms of the local market. The nature and characteristic features of the local market can be better understood in contrast with trade, as we have earlier attempted in this article. Hence, this operation of uprooting and ruination that is being carried out in urban areas, is, in many ways, aimed at destroying that form and quality of market, which can possibly challenge trade.

This operation of devastation has been carried out with strong police force in attendance in all places and any protest has been swiftly repressed. It is significant—as well as natural—that the government squads have faced opposition at every place and they had often to withdraw. Until and unless these sellers and all *karigar* and working class localities are organized under a local market movement, this opposition will remain unorganized, scattered and isolated. This operation of uprooting is the glaringly visible form of globalization that is knocking at the door of every poor man. The local market movement is the answer to the operation of converting every poor man into a cog in a machine, which is sometimes put to some use, and left to rot at other times. The challenge thus erected will have the capacity to turn the tables on globalization.

## REFERENCES

1. Two important and inter-related characteristics of trade as specifically conceptualized here are: (1) it is over quite long distances, implying necessarily a separation of consumption from production and (2) its fairly wide (and large) area of operation. Defined in this fashion, trade can be entirely within a country and does not necessarily mean "foreign trade". Of course exchange across national borders is an outstanding example of all the characteristics of trade being discussed here. Trade will be used in this sense throughout this article.

# 21

# *Karigar Samaj*: The Liberator of Enslaved Societies*

*Chitra Sahasrabudhey*

## 21.1 Introduction

The modern mode of imperialism is globalization. We are being inexorably drawn into its web. If we are unable to beat the trap today it is because the producer classes (farmers, artisans, *adivasis*, and women) of our society have been divested of their autonomous creative powers, metamorphosing them into mere labourers. This metamorphosis forms the basis of subjugation of the entire society. If we want to liberate ourselves from the crisis, and rebuild a social life full of human creativity then we have to initiate actively a movement to restore autonomous creativity of producing classes. If one ponders on the meaning of this creativity and on the question of who will be at the vanguard of this struggle, the nascent and hidden potential of the *karigar samaj* emerges with clarity. The task of organizing this power and of founding the principles of justice and fraternity inherent in it as the fundamental principles of social life is today the task of reinstalling *satya* (truth) and *dharma*.

It seems that every social era witnesses a blurring of the divide between truth and falsehood, just as it witnesses efforts to redraw the line. These efforts are always full of challenge and demand a level of sacrifice and tolerance that is capable of nurturing human creativity in a just social milieu. All this

---

* Translated from Hindi by Dr. Girish Sahasrabudhey. The original was published in the book *Lokavidya Vichar* (2001).

doesn't at all mean that falsehood is a power invincible. Quite the opposite. It means that truth cannot be obliterated from the face of the earth. Perhaps falsehood is like the dust, which has to be shaken off every now and then. A constant dusting off of falsehood defines *dharma*. Understood in this way, *dharma* is dynamic, to be defined anew as falsehood dons new attire at every turn of social life. It is the task of *dharma* to be able to pierce these outer coverings and explore the true nature of things. Or else, the dust will collect, its layers hiding injustice and suppression of creativity. To tolerate this injustice, or to be indifferent towards it, is the true nature of subjugation.

Liberation from subjugation in any era demands a correct identification of the specific form of injustice and falsehood characterizing that era as well as of social forces and the basis of their power to challenge that injustice and falsehood. The efforts and the struggles which shape this power hold the true potential to resurrect human creativity in society and show it the path of truth. Such efforts and struggles are the preeminent need of the day. This article is a modest step in search of them.

Where do the roots of injustice and falsehood lie today? Imperialism strives to control productive forces and enhance profits. Today its mode of operation is control of world markets through the process of globalization. The most sweeping forms of injustice and untruth can be seen today in the production process sought to be established under the garb of globalization. We see in them the basis of the process of metamorphosis of the artisan into the labourer. Here we will try to understand this phenomenon.

The *lokavidya* standpoint provides us with an understanding of the artisan, his produce, the production process and the movement and consumption of this produce. It is an understanding, which promotes a just and fraternal relationship between man and man and between man and nature. It contains the seeds of theory of the struggle for liberation from the new forms of subjugation implied by unjust globalization. A large part of this article is devoted to a clarification of this thesis.

The past has witnessed differentiated exploitative processes and mechanisms in different sections of the dispossessed. There has been an inevitable width to, and variety in, the forms of struggle against exploitation. But, the spread of forces of globalization and their uncontrolled urge for greater hegemony have laid the basis for a coming together of these struggles. This emerging unity promises to be of an altogether novel type, the glimpses of which can be seen from a *lokavidya* viewpoint. The last part of this article is devoted to a discussion of this unity.

## 21.2 Basis of the Industrial System

We have been witnessing a transformation of historic dimensions in the industrial system of our country for the last two decades. The process of founding big industries, which was started by the British, continued with renewed vigour after independence. Then the tide ebbed as many large industries closed down. That did not mean a change of attitude of the state towards capitalists or a decrease in the power of the latter. It only indicated their new needs and signalled the birth of a new industrial system forced by those needs. Forces of imperialism are championing these changes. We are on the threshold of new forms of injustice, exploitation and anarchy. It is our historical duty to identify the possible consequences of the emerging system and to seek ways to liberate ourselves of them.

The new industrial system is based on exploitation of family labour. It operates through the market. We will discuss here the main features of this system.

### *21.2.1 Family Labour*

Production has come to be highly decentralized. The site of production has shifted from large factories to the small houses and huts in towns and villages. Here the whole family works for wages of one man.

For three decades we had a system in which the organization of production was two-tier: large factories in the organized sector and small-scale factories in the unorganized sector. The unorganized sector comprised two distinct modes—small-scale family-based industry, and industry based on family labour. The former was the dominant mode. The movement today, under the influence of globalization and the emerging industrial system, is towards family-labour as the dominant mode.

Under the new system capitalists exercise tight control in the market of raw material and finished products. Production is organized through a supply of raw material to sites of production spread out in houses and huts. A battery of middlemen and contractors operates at several levels. In many cases these levels are so numerous that the producer knows nothing about the master. Wage and quality controls are exercised by middlemen. This arrangement has spread quickly in textiles, hosiery, readymade clothes, electrical devices, small machines and leather works. Of late, iron-work, clay-work, carpentry and stone-work has also been brought within the ambit of this system. We are witnessing a transformation of villages, *mohallas* and towns into large factories, a transformation, which has no precedent.

The fulcrum on which the system rests is procurement of labour of a whole family for wages of a single individual. Women and children of the family make major contributions to the production process. This is an industry based on family-labour. Quite often the family fulfils its needs on the basis of loans and thereafter its members work as bonded labourers. The head of this producer family becomes a puppet in the hands of the master, quite often toiling to fetch raw material from and deliver finished produce to the middleman. It is he who needs work, not the middleman. In many ways he toils for no return.

### *21.2.2 Managerial Costs*

In the new system, there has been a drastic reduction in the managerial costs incurred by captains of industry. In addition they exercise great control on labour costs. This has led to huge increases in the profits.

The capitalist is now free of the headaches of strikes, off days and the like, apart from divesting himself, as he has, of all responsibility towards the welfare of the labourers, bonus and compensations for accidents are things of the past. He is not responsible for the education or health of family members of the worker. Nor is he called upon to provide housing to workers' families.

The procurement of means of labour and the task of training

for quality production are no longer concerns of the capitalist. Just as these are a bother of the labourer, so also is the maintenance of the machinery and steady supply of electricity and water. In this manner, almost the entire cost of managing sustained production has been transferred to producers.

Perhaps the most devastating power that the capitalist exercises today is that of keeping wages to the minimum. He is free to transfer work to a neighbouring village or *mohalla* if the families in some village become more demanding. This has the added advantage of sowing seeds of discord between brothers of a trade, which in turn fuels the unjust system he heads. The system has posited the most terrifying bargaining power in the hands of the captains of the industry, the degree of which is perhaps unequalled in the past. The producer is pushed into the quagmire of indebtedness with all the more certainty and becomes a bonded labourer.

### *21.2.3 Exploitation of Lokavidya*

The new system has created sweeping opportunities for profiteering on the basis of the knowledge and skills—i.e. on the basis of *lokavidya*—of producers. This was impossible in the dying system of production done to a plan within factories. In it the producer gives everything he has—his knowledge, skills, his aesthetic sense, his tradition, his safety, his labour—in return for nothing. He is also called upon to experiment, discover and invent. He gets neither a return nor the credit for all this.

Globalization is deepening this condition. It strives to profit out of the smallest productive and distributive activity in the remotest corners of the world. As it does so, the technique and technology of production will not be its concern. It will no longer be necessary to derogate local technologies and the beliefs tied to them as 'unscientific'. Nor will there be any hurdle in calling these 'scientific' as long as the profits flow to the mainland of globalization. A blood-sucking phase of the process is in the offing. It remains a major question as to how this phenomenal task of siphoning profits from production units and markets, spread wide over the globe, will be organized and accomplished. The emerging technologies will be an important tool in accomplishment of this task. In the new system, the local population will be distanced from produce of the region to a far greater degree. Quality goods will be available in plenty for elite consumption, whereas, large sections of the people will buy second-rate produce. The global system will find stranger and stranger principles and structures to justify these changes. Some of these—like decentralization, opposition to mechanization, regional prestige, etc.—may even be borrowed from the 20th century era of spread industrialization and opposition to imperial expansion. In the offing are large-scale changes in systems of knowledge, education, production, services, trade and governance, which have emerged and taken shape in the last 150-200 years. The basis of such changes, envisaged and effected within the ambit of globalization, will be exploitation of *lokavidya*. We are already witnessing them in education, trade, healthcare and production of consumer goods.

### *21.2.4 The Spread of Market-Liberalization*

Today the worker is not tied down to a single master. He toils not in a single factory, nor for one capitalist. Surely, he is robbed of the value of his labour just as before. But the robber is an abstract mechanism known as the market. The market holds the power to dispossess him of the fruits of his *vidya*, his skills, his labour and his tradition. It works to devalue all his creative and productive capacities, as much as is possible. At the same time, it also forces him to pay dearly for what he needs for his own consumption for renewal of his capacities. The global system creates a market where the worker is exploited in both his incarnations—as the seller of his productive powers and as the buyer of his needs. Such an exploitative market is necessarily a distant market. Trade at a distance is a necessary requirement for endowing the market with demonic character to perpetuate looting farmers and artisans in far corners of the globe. The policy of liberalization is the policy of expansion of such a market. The tool par excellence for control of such markets is finance capital.

### *21.2.5 The Role of the State*

The new industrial system establishes itself with the full support and connivance of the state. The role of the state lies in enacting and enforcing laws. It owns all the resources of the nation. Oceans, rivers, lakes, mountains, forests, minerals and land are all under the control of the state. The state commands the policy of their use, and the legal system governing it. Who is allowed such use and for what purpose, largely determines the character of the state. Globalization progresses by enactment of laws which make partisan use of resources by a chosen, few possible. Which goods are produced where, where does the raw material come from, where is the produce sold are questions of state law. Anyone who dares transgress the legal boundaries in this regard is liable to be punished. What use is made of waters in the river in the village, what is sown in the fields are not to be determined by local initiative and need. Incidence of such initiative on natural resources is a crime against the state. The boundaries of social use of *lokavidya* are subject to law of the state. That means that any public activity based on people's initiative is open to legal ban.

The state under globalization will wield unlimited power on a scale never imagined earlier, quite independent of the degree of political stability of the government in power at any time.

### *21.2.6 The Effect on Civil Society*

The new industrial system has already produced deep cleavages in the society. The disorganization in political, administrative and educational spheres is just as apparent as that in economy. This is the process of reorganization of the society in service of globalization. Such reorganization is led by the primacy of finance capital over industrial capital and emergence of the market as the determinant of all economic activity. Foisting of policies of economic liberalization and global markets serves the same reorganization. The new industrial system puts all the tools at its command in service of the transformation taking place. The transformation requires and demands a new value system. It is only proper to take note of the emerging values.

**Acceptance of Slavery:** The market governed industrial system produces acceptance of slavery as a value. The new value seeks the satisfaction of the urge to live by labour in secure employment acquired through employment schemes or development programmes of the government or in private industry. Such security of employment, be it riddled with injustice and inhuman work conditions and atmosphere, is equated with poverty removal and self-reliance. Such slavish employment pervades all sections of society. Slavery becomes just and commands wide acceptance in political, social, economic, administrative, educational, cultural and institutionalized religious spheres of life. The basis for disruption of the moral fabric of society must be seen in this condition. Corruption and lumpen culture are mere symbols of this state of affairs. Rooted in the same condition is distortion of values of pride, duty and *dharma*.

**Deceit and Hypocrisy:** The emerging system has produced new forms of deceit and hypocrisy, a bane in any era. These new forms have been forced by the need to expand markets and productive activity. It is necessary to mention at least some of these.

Efforts to glorify traditional forms of arts and sciences, rituals and practices and create a hallowed incarnation of Indian culture constitute the greatest deception and hypocrisy. Such efforts are accompanied with active support for systems based on exploitation of communities and people who alone can be considered to be the carriers and owners of these traditional knowledge systems, systems designed precisely to earn profit out of labour of these peoples. These are the people engaged in productive activities in various regions. They have an attachment to their land and culture, the like of which is conspicuously absent in modern industrial labourers. The sentiment is exploited, at times unknowingly by those who are part of such production centres and by intellectuals, to create a myth of social prestige to traditional arts. The reality of course is one of exploitation of *lokavidya* in service of the market system. The equation between expansion of exports and foreign exchange reserves and progress of the whole nation is another such form of hypocrisy. The prestige, which was once attached, and is still attached, to consumption of imported goods is now bestowed on to export-related production and trade. The new-found champions of *swadeshi* are equally enthusiastic propagandists of such export. A partial and anti-people reinterpretation of *swadeshi* is the hallmark of the hypocrisy. (The decades following independence witnessed spread of heavy industry and the equation of such spread with national progress. Modern Western science and technology acquired a sacred halo. The deception in making export the testing ground of national progress is bound to glorify the policies of trade liberalization. The success of finance and insurance needs the deception. Large sections of society must be made to believe that these are painless ways of converting their savings into capital which will earn them unheard of profits.

## 21.3 The *Lokavidya* Standpoint

The *lokavidya* standpoint is the thought of a comprehensive challenge to globalization. It is the standpoint which expresses itself through the worldview of producer classes and in their routine life-activity and life-organization. In other words it is the product of the natural epistemic processes in the life of producer classes, a life governed by wisdom and discernment. It is the inexhaustible storehouse of living traditions, tested routinely and continuously. It cannot therefore be circumscribed within any school of thought, any ism, science or religion. The *lokavidya* standpoint is the inspiration of and for humanity, which creates conditions and basis for challenge to inhuman systems. Here we will try to examine human activity in the context of present conditions and in the light of the *lokavidya* standpoint.

### *21.3.1 The Meaning of Productive Activity*

Till about two centuries ago our society felt no need to differentiate articles of use from articles of art. There was no dichotomy between utility and aesthetic value. This is what we must read in the observation that art pervaded all aspects of life. The windows and doors, the verandah, the walls—every part of a house had art written into it. The altar on the well, the household oil mill, the kitchen stone, the wooden tools, the earthenware, the metal ware, the sleeping cot, the swing, the diwan, the trunks—all bore works of art on them. Jewellery and designs on clothes displayed an artistic beauty and variety, which it is impossible to describe in words. Toys, the articles of worship, icons of gods displayed art in its highest forms. Not a single facet of ordinary life was without a stroke of art. Art existed not for an elite but as part of ordinary life. It is this condition which posits into artistic creation the meaning of life, its philosophy and wisdom. It is this condition that guards it from hedonism. It is this condition in which social organization and dynamic of productive activity add new dimensions to cooperative human activity.

As industry was by and large domestic, and consumption by and large local, art, technology and economy could command a firm and distributed support. So also could industry command innovation routinely, and expertise of various types could be nourished. Such industry was naturally inclined to respect rules of nature in regard to its artistic, technological as well as economic aspects. The systems of value, faith and public activity it produced, also carried such respect. Thus it turns out that in societies, where such conditions prevailed, art, technique, economics and society existed in a value-driven dynamic state. The notion that in ordinary life one beholds truth by devotion to productive activity to create necessities of life, defined a strong current in society. This notion provides a serious philosophical basis to the meaning of productive activity. It is the basis to understand the fundamental values associated with the meaning and purpose of life, organization of social life and the unity of humanity—a basis at once simple and pure. In our society it was the tradition of saints which popularized this understanding of the productive activity of man. Armed with this understanding parasitic life and accumulation of wealth could be denounced as sinful. The persuasion of fraternity and *ahimsa* belonged to the producer sections of society. One may say art defined the body, to which the structure was provided by technique, and the circulation of blood and control by the mind of producer. The social institutions, which stood in a positive relationship with the productive activity, infused life into this body. The producer experiences, like a saint or an ascetic, deeply meditative phases and evinces, through his activity, a deep grasp of matters of knowledge, science, technology, art, value, *dharma* and society. His mind finds expression in the product of his labour and traditions of consumption of that product. The producer is neither the slave nor the machine. He is the creator of society, its mentor and the source of its dynamics.

Modernization, mechanization and Westernization cleared the way for capitalism and later imperialism, forces which destroyed productive activity per se. Aesthetics was divorced from utility. The basis of art was severed from that of science. Not only did they lose their common and compatible roots, they also acquired a neutrality towards social value. Art became hedonistic and science acquired the character of a tool of exploitation of nature, and of man, by man. The unity of aesthetics, utility and justice was destroyed. An inevitable fallout of this process was a transformation in the ways of looking at the productive activity and its social paradigm.

Manufacture of consumer articles in factories by machines transformed the productive activity into a robotic, mindless occupation, and the producer into a labourer. Labour became a contemptible and lowly activity and the labourer was driven out of the mainstream of society. Industry witnessed a differentiation between handicraft and consumer industry. The machine worker became a wage labourer and the craftsman faced extinction of his knowledge and loss of livelihood. Their ranks included artisans, farmers, *adivasis* and women. Their extradition from the social centre-stage led to the banishment of justice, fraternity, simplicity and *purushartha*. Hoarding, parasitism, rowdyism and decadence gained prestige. Competition to accumulate the luxuries of life, to increase intensity of productive activity and competition to extract more work in return for less remuneration became the fulcrum of social systems.

Such a society subjugated producer sections and enslaved productive activity in service of other sections of society. The producer became subject to doles and handouts and his life activity the basis of luxury of the parasitic sections of society. This was the time when Gandhiji forged his challenge to capitalism and imperialism. It was the challenge of a saint, a challenge rooted on the conception of unity of truth, value and aesthetics in a society guided by a consonance and harmony between labour, knowledge and creativity as the basis of productive activity. It was a challenge to the demon in society.

We live today in a new phase of imperialism-globalization. Productive activity stands degraded today to a level never reached earlier. The very existence of the producer as a human being is threatened. Mechanization and industrialization could affect only a small section of society. Globalization breaks these limitations. It makes it conceivable to extract surpluses from production in any nook or corner of the globe. It makes the specific form of productive activity irrelevant. This means that any and every creative activity of man is a potential and conceivable source for imperialist siphon, and, therefore, a vulnerable target. Imperialism is ready to regard beauty and ugliness, utility and lack of it, compassion and cruelty, love and hatred with the same calm and extract profits out of good and bad deeds alike. Given such a cataclysm, it is no wonder that human activity per se faces obliteration and banishment from the view of life being forcefully propagated today.

Is it possible that productive activity will once again define human creativity and become the foundation for truth and justice in society? Will it again create those ideals and conceptions which can effectively challenge globalization? To be able to answer such questions, it is necessary to examine the creative activity of the artisan, his knowledge, its meaning, the relationships it defines and its diversity.

### *21.3.2 Artisan and His Vidya*

The term artisan (*karigar*) has been used for someone who produces the necessities of life. It has come to refer to one who possesses skills. The term worker came onto popular discourse with the establishment of modern industry. All those directly connected with production in such industry became workers. A worker may be skilled or unskilled. But both are workers, and worker is a slave, at most a wage-earner slave. The titles of artisan and a worker for a producer are not a mere matter of words. They indicate the status of the producer and his social-economic condition.

An artisan is the person who is accomplished in the art of production of some type. As such he is the repository of knowledge of every material input and process and their internal and external relationships. He meditates about the social, economic and environmental facets of these elements of production as he develops and rejuvenates his activity. He is able to conceive of the totality of his activity as part of another totality. This is the specific character of his activity. It endows his knowledge with the requirement of a just relationship with nature and society. All the transformations in his natural and social environment, large and small, the entire dynamic and unfolding process around him—all find their place in the continuity and flow of his productive activity. He responds to all this, and thus expands the horizons and the meaning of justice.

The basis of this character of the productive activity of the artisan is in his autonomous existence. It is an existence the essence of which is creation of a relationship of mutual prosperity between the artisan and the means of his activity—a relationship like that between mother and child. The specific nature of the artisan's autonomous existence is defined by this relationship and it endows him with a definite view of using, preserving and enhancing the means of his productive activity. The concrete form of this view is *karigar vidya*—artisan's knowledge.

Thus the artisan is the lord of his own activity, be he a farmer, a producer of articles or a provider of some social service. He cannot sustain his activity in servitude. Exploitation of his art, his thought, his knowledge, his labour, his dedication, his devotion or his tradition, without his participation and concurrence, is possible only within an unjust system of state. Any such attempt forces him into enslavement and breaks the condition of his expertise, his autonomous existence and destroys the basis of his relationship with nature. Such devastation is the beginning of a chain of processes characterized by injustice. This means that any process which harms the creative and autonomous existence of the artisan poisons the entire human society. Thus all those organizational and institutional forms, which help to enslave the artisan, divest him of his creativity and destroy the condition for basic thought and creation in general. The societies which allow this to happen ultimately lose their ability to exist autonomously.

Thus, the relative strength of artisans and workers in a society determines the level of justice within it. A system of production which denies to the producer control over means of production as well as any say in the movement, price, consumption and export of his produce and which regards his knowledge with contempt, transforms artisans into workers. Any one of these conditions suffices to increase the ranks of workers in the society. In our society today, all the three obtain. The first condition for building a just society is to build systems which can liberate workers and make them into artisans. The need is for efforts to identify such systems and structures and to begin the process of their creation.

### *21.3.3 The Dynamic of Karigar Samaj*

That the rule of the British meant massive loot of the farmer and the artisan, is a matter of broad agreement. Agriculture was devastated and industry dismantled. The result was a huge army of those without a trade. This meant enslavement of *karigar samaj*. The process forced large numbers to work for a pittance in British-founded industries. The dishonour of becoming workers was the second dimension of the calamity.

The first half of the last century witnessed two parallel phenomena of reorganization of these workers. One of these was the coming together of workers against exploitation in big industry supported and aided by the state. These working sections formed a small portion of the population. The experience of developments, which led to two world wars, had taught them that they were lifeless cogs in the wheel of uninterrupted large-scale production. They, therefore, championed the cause of an industrial system in the interests of the working sections. The second phenomenon was organization, under the leadership of Gandhiji, of those large sections outside the ambit of large-scale industry, which were uprooted from means of their life by British policies and rule. The aim and effort was creation of an industrial and social system based on *khadi* and *gramodyog*, which will allow the worker to earn with honour and to establish himself as an artisan. These two parallel phenomena threw up conceptions of alternative systems, which were at variance with each other.

Although it is conceivable to argue about their relative positions and historical importance, the fact is that neither of these conceptions survived actively in the post-independence era. After independence, all thought of building any alternative industrial system was shunned.

Independent India adapted the capitalist industrial structure erected by the British. This meant equating social progress with ever expanding production. Such a conception ignored the enslavement of the worker in big industry as well as the devastation caused by the sale of produce of this industry all over the country. This great deception of large sections of the population was given out to be a necessity. This necessity implied that the efforts of mobilization of all resources in service of big industry be recognized as national service par excellence. Programmes for erection of big dams and canals, for spread of cash-crop cultivation, for establishment of a banking network and for building of a transport infrastructure were taken up in due course. All these efforts serviced the policy of expansion of the modern industrial structure of big factories and mass production, which no one could question. Modernization of industry and agriculture, with the aim of increase in productivity, was taken up in a big way. The system of subsidies and soft policies was put in place. Large, modern research and development organizations with their army of scientific experts were established. Legal and fiscal measures to ensure supply of raw material to feed the system were implemented. The inevitable consequence was increase in levels of production and capitalist profits. Some of the profits and spoils were shared by the political, bureaucratic and scientific elite. A tiny portion was also shared with the workers in the big industry. This portion, however small, was still huge compared to the earnings of those from among whom these workers came into the fold of big industry.

The initial decades of independent India thus went through a phase in which many industries were established and government projects started. This increased the employment in the industrial sector and many from the unemployed could earn their living. Those among them, who were employed on a regular basis, organized to obtain a greater share of profits and facilities. Workers' struggle took shape. The struggle, however, failed in bringing about any transformation in structure of industry or organization of society. Quite the contrary. The struggle fell into the trap of supporting the capitalist industrial system. The strength of workers' unions waned. At the same time, the numbers of those who were victims of increased production within modern industry swelled. These people were unorganized. By the turn of the last quarter of the 20th century the industrial system had brought the whole country once again into a situation in which very large sections of the populations were uprooted from their systems of sustenance and ready to offer their labour cheaply.

The international situation had changed rapidly during this time. The imperialist forces were finding it increasingly difficult to continue their control of economy on old foundations. Depression seemed imminent. The challenges to imperialism which had developed early in the century had spent themselves. Imperialism could reorganize itself. There was breathing space available. The reorganization came in the form of liberalization and globalization. Imperialism got a new lease of life. New opportunities and mechanisms to buy off the capitalist sections of poor countries were created. Once again imperialism emerged as an all powerful organism with new myths of its own. Capitalist classes in countries like India fell into line proclaiming the inevitability of globalization. These classes find themselves compelled to adapt and enact many anti-people measures in service of the imperialist formations.

### *21.3.4 Social Justice: Primacy of Lokavidya*

The struggles of industrial workers in the post-independence era raised the question of social justice. Injustice, however, has acquired new forms in the emerging situation. Today, struggles for social prestige for *lokavidya* based on identification of its nascent potential hold the key to an effective challenge to imperialism.

Those who produce the innumerable necessities of life have not acquired their knowledge in universities. They renew their knowledge every day. Collation of expertise of different types and intelligent working of materials and processes are part of their productive activity. In spite of modern science and technology, their spread and domination, in spite of the devastation of their communities, their knowledge still holds the power of creation. It is this that ensures supply of many daily needs to a large section of society. And yet they are held in contempt, their knowledge derogated and neglected. A struggle to reinstall the prestige of this knowledge and ensure to it an honourable place in the order of the society is the basis for struggle for social justice.

The *karigar samaj* is identified today in terms of the backward and scheduled castes. Many of them lost their traditional means of livelihood and work in various professions. However, existence of their caste organizations continues. Although these organizations have faced a progressive erosion of their base, at times the *karigar samaj* has mobilized under their leadership against exploitation. This mobilization is often based on the belief that entry into modern systems will create conditions in which they can expect justice and status. Demand for reservations in educational institutions, salaried jobs, democratic institutions, administrative infrastructure and political positions thus became their main agenda. The modern system, however, is strongly limited as far as the number of people it can absorb goes. The agenda could not have been met. *Karigar samaj* can come into the mainstream of society only on the basis of what it already has, only if the struggle for recognition of its knowledge succeeds. Only such struggle can even conceive of the transformation in production, trade, education and market, which will make social justice a reality.

*Karigar samaj* fulfilled the needs of the society in the past when the modern knowledge systems were not there. It can do the same even if experts of this knowledge have no role to play in future. Its knowledge holds the potential and power to fulfil its role against all odds. The character of this knowledge is a unity in the act of the intellect and the act of the hand. It encompasses knowledge, concept, skill and value within its fold. The character of modern knowledge is just the opposite—to differentiate theory from practice, principle from its application. As a consequence champions of modern knowledge see mere labour in the work of the *karigar*, and the *karigar* only as a labourer. They hold this work—and the worldview and the knowledge interwoven into it—in contempt. This is an obstacle in the path of social justice.

The question of status and prestige of *lokavidya* poses a challenge to the absolute and unique position of modern Western science. It generates the hope for a reorganization of various dimensions of the society, which will accord a just and honourable participation for each section of society and a harmony to the relation between nature and society. The knowledge systems of different sections of the *karigar samaj* can exist only in mutual benefit and for mutual good. The thread of justice runs strong within them. Thus it is that social justice is inconceivable without honour and prestige to them.

The essence of this status and honour is in control of resources, their maintenance, regeneration and distribution by those who possess the knowledge and the skills to work these resources. It is in a reasonable state say in allied areas like market, finance, import and export. The *karigar* must be recognized as the expert that he is. The foundation of this status and honour is in social structures which function to nurture and grow productive processes rooted in knowledge with the *karigar samaj*.

In the present society the producer possesses the knowledge, and others the right to profit by it. Minute details of river and ocean waters, its fauna and flora are known to the fisherman but the university professor of hydrology holds the right to knowledgeability and the right to a fat salary. The knowledge of the potter is no less than that of the ceramic engineer, nor that of the weaver any less than that of the textile engineer. But it is not valued more than his meagre wages. This is the injustice which pervades society. The *karigar samaj* must break it in order to establish a position of honour for itself.

### *21.3.5 The Expanse of Karigar Samaj*

The genesis of *karigar samaj* is in that specific type and character of its knowledge, which conceives unity within its own ranks and within communities which cooperate with it. The *karigar samaj* thus encompasses within itself all those who relate to agriculture, forests, rivers, oceans and services. All those who so relate, possess a common worldview—the standpoint of *lokavidya*. It is armed with this view that they fulfil the needs of the society. Imperialism fears and abhors this and, as such, dispossesses them. So it is that we may formulate some idea of the expanse of *karigar samaj* from the identity of those who are dispossessed and from the character of their deprivation.

In our country we have a very large number of people who can work with iron, wood, clay, stone, plastics, cotton, yarn, silk, cloth, leather and eatables. Those who work as agricultural labourers, or do manual jobs, like plying a rickshaw and carrying heavy loads, hold skills and knowledge of this type. They are all artisans turned labourers. Those who collect utilities of life from the waters and forests also belong to *karigar samaj*. Farmers with small holdings have been forced to take up work in industries and have joined the ranks of this *samaj*. Most women are producer artisans in their own right. Many of them have been forced into wage labour. Small shop-owners, who organize their trade on the strength and abilities of their family members, are allies of *karigar samaj*. Sections of youth thrown out of the education system must also be considered as allies. Thus very large sections of the local society belong to *karigar samaj*.

Most of these people are forced to lead a very hard life in spite of the fact that they work 8-12 hours a day. They are denied a proper status in society. The conditions into which these people are forced by the ruling system are also the cause of a developing unity within them.

The strength of *karigar samaj* is in its numbers and in its knowledge, which makes it capable of shaping a just industrial social system. Through its struggle for honour, which is its due, it can pose a challenge to the unjust imperialist social order. Its demand for a proper return for its labour is the demand for control of the market and its reorganization in the interests of the local community. Its demand for honour is the demand for control of local resources. In the ultimate analysis it is the demand for an autonomous social life under the leadership of *karigar samaj*. Both these demands pose an effective challenge to the existing system. For initiatives in this direction to germinate into a far-reaching struggle for a just society, unity of local society is the first condition.

### 21.3.6 *The Meaning and the Role of Local Society*

The basis of local society is the universe of human sensitivity, which regulates the activity of man. Those who stand in a direct give and take relationship share their perceptions. The relation of give and take could be economic, social or emotional and, just like between men, may exist between any two things, living or non-living, in nature. It is the nature of this relation to transform the act of perceiving pain of others and the urge to be of assistance into a value-duty. The relationship of shared perceptions and sensitivities is space and time bound. Outside the boundaries its intensity wanes. These boundaries define the local society. This is the space of man's routine life and activity. It is the unitary totality within the larger society, which is the cornerstone of social justice in its multifarious dimensions.

The present society is built on ruins of the local society. Its life-blood is opposition to each and every condition which favours unity of the local society. The very basis of its existence, politics, administration and structures of production is in a complete and total denial of human sensitivity. Not surprisingly, its success has made different sections of society insensitive towards each other. Unfortunately the disease afflicts even sections of the exploited. The market and modern education have played a pivotal role in the destruction of human sensitivity.

Only such social action can engender sensitivity in the internal and external relationships of the local society as is aimed at creation of those social structures and institutions. ruled, organized and guided by the local society, which establish the primacy of *karigar samaj* in productive activities. Struggles for a system of production based on household industry, for control of local resources and markets by local society led by *karigar samaj* and for prestige and honour of *lokavidya* constitute such action. They are the struggle for liberation from imperialist enslavement in its phase of globalization.

### 21.4 *Karigar Samaj*: Sculptor of the New Era

The basis of life is in the knowledge of *karigar samaj*. The thread of justice runs strong and uninterrupted in this knowledge and world view. Thus he is the potential creator, the sculptor of the future society. Organized this potential poses a challenge to globalization. To understand the nature of this challenge and the society it promises it is necessary to understand the welfare dimension of the production system. This understanding is the *lokavidya* standpoint. In the fast changing world, organization and struggles, shaped by the *lokavidya* standpoint, will force states to work in the interests of the people at large.

### *21.4.1 Welfare Production System*

The depth and expanse of the industrial system of production based on exploitation of family labour and the transformation this has brought about in social relations and modes of governance need extended and serious study. Such study will look at the various forms of contract labour at all stages in production and delivery of raw materials, the work being done by the producers, their skills, their cultural tradition and so on. It will help identify the basis of a welfare system of production, which forces no one into wage-labour and which is built around a profession for all.

Several towns in the Ganges valley today serve as good examples of the modern industrial system. The same is true, possibly to a greater extent, of cities and towns in Punjab, Haryana, Maharashtra, Gujarat and Tamil Nadu. The industry based on water and forest resources is structured similarly. A city like Varanasi, the industry in which is thought popularly to be traditional, is actually a good example of how traditional industry can be transformed and put entirely into service of the capitalist system. Discussions with the workers in these industries throw light on what may the essential features of a welfare production system be.

The population of Varanasi is around a million, most of which is in the industrial production sector. The silk sari industry is the major industry. Many activities like yarn making, design, polishing, printing, jari making, which support the silk sari industry, are organized as independent industries. Weaving and its ancillary industry like tool making and repairing are organized independently. Carpet making and handicrafts in clay, wood and stone are other major industries. Many are employed in metal-based industries like making pumps, metal nets, fans, scissors and electroplating. Workers in industries like ready-made garments and hosiery, leather works, zardozi and plastic industries are numerous. The *nishad* and rajak communities on the banks of Ganges are water-based industries. The farmer in the rural areas of the district produces grain, fruits and vegetables. Many of them are small landholders. Many families are engaged in necklace and bidi industries. About three quarters of the population are producers. They produce goods worth crores of rupees every day, much of which goes to fill the coffers of the state and into pockets of the traders. Much of the produce is not for local consumption. However, increase in export levels has done nothing to change deprivation of the local population. Mainly three points emerge out of discussions with these people.

**Cost of Production:** The fixation of returns to labour in all industries is unjust. The producer plays no part in it. He sells his labour and skills cheap and, as a consumer, buys necessities at a high price. Price fixation is the reserve of those not engaged in production—traders and the government. The principle of this fixation is to tie the producer up to the industry, not his welfare. A welfare production system must devolve the control of remuneration levels on to the producer.

**Capital:** There is a scarcity of capital available to the producers. This forces them to become wage-workers. The producers of capital are deprived of capital. This means that if the wealth generated within a locality is correctly estimated and a part of it is available to makers of that locality then there would be no dearth of capital for the producers there. The basis of capital scarcity is the loot of wealth, generated locally, by the governments and the traders. The meagre returns are at times further diminished due to the insurance premia paid to finance and insurance agencies. Such insurance payments are even praised by the elite in society as schemes for welfare of the producer. A true welfare production system must divert capital flows in the interests of local society.

**Raw Material:** Resources are controlled by the state. Through its partisan policy the state passes them on to big trade and industry. Minerals and forest products are even reserved for use by the big industry. Restrictions are enacted and enforced on their use by local producers. Several such legislations have been recently added to the law book in the name of environment, human rights, hygiene and beautification of cities. The *dhobis* of Varanasi cannot make use of the Ganges and pond waters, the *nishads* are not allowed to fish and potters are denied clay from the ponds. Terrorization of weavers in the name of prevention of child labour, removal of hawkers from the pavements in the name of beautification of the cities, banning of the sale of tea, *lassi, pakaudi, chat*, sugar-cane juice and so on by hawkers in the name of healthcare are all examples of such legislation. The essence of such policy and action is severance of the relation between nature and the producer and the consequence is alienation of the producer from his own environment and in his own locality. Moreover, someone—not necessarily standing in any positive relation whatsoever with the local society and its land, waters and forests—can claim a right to use of these resources. Anyone, possibly a rank outsider, can lord over the wealth of the locality.

A welfare production system is inconceivable without control of preservation, distribution and use of local resources by local producers.

**Market:** The market is under the control of big traders. The state policy is in their interest. Infrastructure supports their activity. No wonder that the local producer is unable to sell his product. He finds that he must sell through big companies and traders, if at all. The market mechanism in existence today plays a pivotal role in transformation of the producer into wage labourer.

Local needs are to be fulfilled by the local producer. A welfare production system will have to adapt this principle. Markets will have to be reserved for the local producer. Distant trade must be restricted by definite controls and within definite boundaries. Only such markets can give justice to the producer, transform him into a *karigar* and give him true recognition. Only then will the society and the producer exist in a mutually beneficial and healthy relationship.

**Civil Rights:** The state, which fills its coffers with revenue earned from his produce, denies the producer elementary civil rights. The total disorganization and anarchy in systems of drinking water and electricity supplies and of sewer lines, hygiene and roads in residential localities of producer classes is tantamount to their de-recognition as citizens. Hospitals and schools for their children are in a shambles. The look and feel of artisan colonies and residential areas reminds one of description of workers' localities in 18th century European cities.

A welfare production system must attend to such disorganization of civil amenities and systems.

### *21.4.2 A Path for Liberation from Slavery*

The slavery implicit in the post-independence systems of production expresses itself in everything. The present polity is the machine which renews and sustains this slavery. The programmes of development and social reform glorify it. The thinking of the intelligentsia is a meek reflection of it. The potential to expose this slavery for what it is, and fight it lies in a process, which promises to progressively transform family labour into family industry. Only such a process can liberate the producer and, therefore, the larger society. Such a process can be started, such a path traversed, it seems, only with the initiative of the *karigar samaj*, forced today into family labour.

In nature, values, habits, tendencies and characteristics of *karigar samaj* differ totally from workers in factory-based industries. In the factory system, the worker contributed only his labour and served merely as a lifeless cog in the machine. The *karigar* contributes his all—labour, expertise, skill, knowledge, technique, a creative and progressive grasp of the process, tools and other means, tradition and a readiness to take risks. They have their own criteria of quality of the produce and the ability to produce goods according to those criteria. For them, mere marketability of mass-produced articles as the criterion of quality is a vulgarity they have been forced to bow down to. That, given availability of capital, raw material and markets, they can build their own independent industry cannot be doubted. This trinity, however, is not at the command, as everyone knows, of potential, ability and expertise of individuals and communities. It is under the command of state power. The control exercised on capital, raw material and markets by the big traders and capitalists and owners of finance capital is based on state support. If this support is exercised in the interests of *karigar samaj* then family labour will progressively give way to family-based industry. That, control of raw materials should reside only with those who put in their labour, knowledge and skills in working it, is only just. The credit for the quality of produce on the market should also devolve only on to the producer. The unjust system of today allows neither. Those without ability exercise monopoly control of capital and raw material apart from freely claiming the credit for produce that is not their own.

A system of production in which control is exercised in the interest of the producer opens the path of liberation from exploitation of all types and lays the foundation of an autonomous, proud and healthy society. Such a system will routinely fight slavery, hypocrisy and deception of any type. It will have wage labour only as an exception. It seems that only family-based industry holds the promise of a welfare production system.

Establishment of such a system of production will mean a total reorganization of local knowledge, resources and local markets. The criterion and principle of such reorganization will have to be autonomy and self-sufficiency of local society.

Activists agitating for preservation of environment, those opposed to globalization, and those opposed to the capitalist system, supporters of the people-oriented dimensions within cultural traditions, champions of re-installation of values have all always desired such a production system. They must renew and strengthen their struggle. A reconsideration, on their part, of their positions and programmes in the new and changed condition and an appreciation of the potential nascent in *karigar samaj* is, however, called for.

### *21.4.3 Organization and Direction of Struggle*

India, with its abundance of natural resources and substantial proportion of a large population in possession of knowledge and skills of various types, is an important potential catch for the imperialist net. The shackles of slavery can only tighten if the imperialist design succeeds. As the process of transformation of the producer-artisan into labourer deepens and acquires newer dimensions, the process of emergence of *karigar samaj* takes shape on the world scale.

The character of this emerging *samaj* is different from working classes of the factory-based industry. It is closer to local society. The imperialist system lives on the loot of his labour, his knowledge, his art, his aesthetic ability—his everything. This loot and the chains of slavery it has created can be broken only with building of a production system inspired by *lokavidya*, which is a repository of natural justice. *Karigar samaj*, the lord of *lokavidya*, holds the potential to do so. The process of organization of *karigar samaj*, which begins with the objective of building of a just production system is also the process of liberation of the larger society from the clutches of globalization. There is no escape from the shackles of globalization without the liberation of the *karigar samaj*. The political, social and industry-specific organizations of producer-artisans transformed into labourers must recognize this. A process of organized opposition to exploitation of *karigar samaj* involving the larger society must also start. Thus the organization of *karigar samaj* will also shape that of the society. (As the chief mechanism of the loot of *karigar samaj* is imperialist markets, and as the chief source of wealth looted is *karigar vidya*, the pivot of organization of *karigar samaj* is transformation of the market and recognition, honour and prestige to *lokavidya*. Markets will have to be the battlefield, where the *karigar samaj* will mobilize for its recognition and prestige and where it will fight the battle against the loot of cost of creation and local resources. Thus it will start a process of unifying the local society. The battle will be fought from localities and regions where the local producers will sow the seeds of autonomous lokasatta. In the soil of fraternity within the *karigar samaj* these seeds will germinate into trees, which, like the trees in the forests, will live and grow together. It is only in the cool shade of these trees that man will once again conquer the demon within him and experience the harmonious music of nature, without which he has been distanced from humanity itself. Our saintly tradition will once again guide us on this path of reconstruction.

# 22

# Knowledge, Work, and Education*

*Amit Basole*

## 22.1 Introduction

India has recently enjoyed global prominence due to its high profile software sector and its service contribution to the global knowledge economy (such as call centres). The National Knowledge Commission has been set up as a "high-level advisory body to the Prime Minister of India with the objective of transforming India into a knowledge society."[1] In this paper I argue that historic transformations in the world of knowledge, which are reflected in the setting up of the Knowledge Commission, have opened the way for a new vision of education in India that is socially inclusive and responsive to India's needs. The majority of Indians who have thus far been shut out of the university system can find a place in it for themselves and their knowledge. In the process, not only can universities become more relevant to Indian society but the hegemony of modern science over the "commanding heights" of higher education can also be effectively challenged and space can be created for other types of knowledge which have always existed in Indian society.

But for this to occur the limited conception of "Knowledge" that haunts the current discourse on the Knowledge Society must be broadened. To some extent this movement has already

---

* Paper presented at a conference on "The Emerging Organization of Knowledge and the Future of Universities," December 2008, 32nd Indian Social Sciences Congress, Jamia Millia Islamia, New Delhi.

begun. A large international literature has emerged on concepts such as "indigenous knowledge," "traditional knowledge," "local knowledge," etc., making the case that the poor and the dispossessed, while they may lack access to tangible resources (such as land, water, and capital), have a rich store of intangible knowledge resources that they can use to sustain themselves under resource-poor conditions (Brokensha, Warren and Werner 1980, Warren, Slikkerveer and Brokensha 1995, Sillitoe, Bikker and Pottier 2002, Finger and Schuler, 2004, World Bank 2004 and Sillitoe 2006).

The idea that society is knowledge-abundant rather than knowledge-scarce may come as no surprise to over 80% of Indians who work in the informal economy and who have routinely relied on knowledge gained outside the formal network of universities and other modern institutions of knowledge production and distribution. Restoring respect for this *lokavidya* and ensuring that its holders benefit from their knowledge are important steps towards creating a poverty-free society (Sahasrabudhey and Sahasrabudhey, 2001). *Lokavidya* is a broader concept than "traditional and indigenous knowledge", and I will use the former in preference to the latter when referring to knowledge in society.

The communal nature of *lokavidya* makes it difficult to design effective property rights which might ensure that *lokavidya* producers get due rewards for their knowledge-activity. As *lokavidya* is archived in online databases, dangers of appropriation correspondingly increase and as a protective measure there is a strong push to commoditize this knowledge. A new hierarchy is emerging between knowledge that is organized or represented on the Internet and that which is not. I argue that there is an urgent need to widen the scope of the debate beyond protection or appropriation of "disembodied" forms of *lokavidya* (*lokavidya* as a pool of knowledge in society) to include support of the work processes that *embody* it and that create and sustain this knowledge.

In part, the *lokavidya* commons survives and thrives because of shallow production hierarchies, i.e. little separation between design and implementation, and because of the self-directed, autonomously creative nature of work that often characterizes small-scale and artisanal production. By contrast, deep hierarchies in large-scale industry have traditionally led to a separation of conception/design from execution/production destroying the producer's *lokavidya* in the process, reducing the artisan to a labourer and further exacerbating the traditional hierarchy between mental and manual labour (Braverman 1974).

Hierarchies of knowledge are thus intimately connected with hierarchies of labour: intellectual labour, manual labour, women's labor and so on. However this link between labour or work, and knowledge is largely missing from the writings on indigenous and traditional knowledge. Relatively little attention has been given to exactly how this knowledge is produced and transmitted, how innovation takes place and what can be done to support the work processes that generate this knowledge. Even less thought has been devoted to how the existing network of universities can be used to restore prestige to *lokavidya* and how inclusion of *lokavidya*-holders in the higher education system can achieve the dual goals of democratizing education and fighting poverty and oppression.

Hence, the debate over "indigenous and traditional knowledge" needs to be extended in two major ways. First, *work* needs to be put back into the discourse on knowledge. Knowledge is produced only in the concrete context of a labour process. And labour hierarchies are causally connected to knowledge hierarchies in ways that I will elaborate later. Second, proposals need to be put forward for transforming the traditional university and the education process itself, by restoring respect to knowledge in society, as opposed to knowledge in the university.

Before we go any further, it is important to clarify what type of knowledge we are talking about. The vast bulk of the literature on indigenous and traditional knowledge focuses on biodiversity, natural resource management and herbal medicines. Some attention is also paid to governance institutions, agronomy, and meteorological knowledge. Artisanal knowledge, i.e. dispersed knowledge used in small-scale industrial activity (such as knowledge related to manufacture of various articles of necessity and luxury—cloth, utensils, furniture, housing, decorative items, toys, soap, food items, small machinery and so on) is only just finding a place in this literature. Although I will focus on artisanal knowledge my argument is general enough to apply to other types of *lokavidya*.

*Lokavidya* holders are often deprived of material resources that are needed to apply their knowledge, as with exclusion of local communities from forests and fisheries commons, resulting in impoverishment. In the urban, industrial milieu, failure to recognize the value of *lokavidya* accompanies social exclusion of informal workers and transformation of artisans into labourers. A recent United Nations report estimates, for example, that over the last 30 years the number of artisans in India has declined by at least 30% as many skilled workers seek employment as casual wage labourers or in other more vulnerable informal jobs (quoted in Seth 1995).

## 22.2 The Knowledge Society and "Flattening" of Knowledge Hierarchies

Various terms such as "Post-industrial society," "Postmodern Age," "Information Age," "Knowledge Society," "Network Society," "Informational Capitalism," "Cognitive Capitalism" and so on, collectively point to a growing recognition that major economic, cultural, political, epistemic shifts have occurred in the later half of the 20$^{th}$ century (see Fuchs 2008, in particular Chapter 4 for a review of this literature).

The decade of the 1970s was witness to two major developments that set in motion the transition from the "Age of Industry" to the "Age of Knowledge." The first was the demise of the Keynesian Welfare State which stood for state-managed capitalism, repression of finance, large vertically integrated production with managerial hierarchies and capital-labour compact, and its replacement by the Neoliberal Regime powered by a belief in free-markets, emphasis on profitability at the expense of the interests of the working class, rise of finance capitalism and a transition from centralized, bureaucratic corporations to decentralized, flexible production on a global scale. The second development was a revolution in Information and Communication Technologies (ICTs) which made possible a type of globalization that allowed extraction of surplus value not only via a global trade in commodities but via the construction of value chains that globalized production itself. Just as, in the Industrial Age, agriculture was transformed according to the logic of Industry (mass production, capital intensive techniques, world markets), so also in the Age of Knowledge, Industry is being transformed according to the network logic of informational and knowledge flows.[2]

At the level of discourse and representation, just as the paradigm of "production" defined the Age of Industry in the first half of the 20th century, so the paradigm of "knowledge management" defines the Age of Knowledge in the second half. And as "Science" was the motive power behind massive increase in productive forces, "Internet" seems to be the driving force of reorganization in the world of knowledge (Sahasrabudhey 2008). In other words, Science, Industry and Production are *no longer the paradigms that define our times*. Their place has been taken by Knowledge and the Internet.

In the new knowledge society, which is said to be emerging in the industrialized countries, the majority of those employed are involved in provisioning of services, not in the production of tangible goods. "What counts is not raw muscle power, or energy, but information" (Bell 1973, p. 127).[3] Production of information, signals, symbols and images assumes new and greater importance. Knowledge is seen as the principal force of production and increasingly becomes a commodity to be bought and sold in the market. To quote from a recent UNESCO report "Towards Knowledge Societies," (Binte 2005)

> The Knowledge Economy is a particular knowledge-driven stage of capitalist development...succeeding a phase marked by the accumulation of physical capital....wealth created is being measured less on the output of work itself, measurable and quantifiable, and more and more on the general level of science and the progress of technology. (p. 46)

The Information or Knowledge-based economy is said to rely more on intangible assets such as human capital in the form of education, research and development, and an emphasis on income generated by knowledge products with the help of patents, copyrights, trademarks and so on.

Curiously, the discourse of the brave new world of

Knowledge is at the same time too ambitious and not ambitious enough. It is too ambitious because in its celebratory rhetoric it sometimes glosses over the fact that the North-South divide of the Age of Industry is reproduced and reinforced in Information Age as the "digital divide." One measure of this divide is that only about 11% of the world's population has access to the internet (though this number is rapidly growing) and 90% of those connected are from industrialized countries (North America-30%, Europe-30% and Asia-Pacific-30%) (Binte 2005).

It is not ambitious enough because the definition of what constitutes "Knowledge" remains severely constrained. Thus Binte (2005) cautions that in India even though the share of the service sector in GDP has risen to 50% "75% of the population still lives on agriculture and almost 40% is illiterate" (p. 46). In one fell-swoop, all farmers and millions of artisans, women and *adivasis* who may not be able to read and write, are dismissed from consideration as holders of knowledge or as participants of the "Knowledge Society." Even in the chapter on "Local and indigenous knowledge, linguistic diversity and knowledge societies" Binte notes,

> ...when we talk about knowledge societies, what kind of knowledge are we referring to? Are we referring just to scientific and technological knowledge, *mainly the preserve of the industrialized countries*? (p. 147, emphasis added)

Once again, the scientific and technical knowledge that is the preserve of farmers and artisans in countries such as India is completely dismissed in this view. Binte's assertion that scientific and technological knowledge is "mainly the preserve of the industrialized countries" was the commonly held view during the Industrial Age. Science was defined as the knowledge produced in universities and research institutes created in Europe in the 19th and 20th centuries. Science, thus narrowly defined, was the unquestioned hegemonic system of knowledge and a clear hierarchy was constructed between knowledge that was "scientific" and that which was not. Even Europe's own numerous artisanal traditions, which were themselves the progenitors of its scientific and technical revolution were no longer deemed scientific. Rather their "craft knowledge" was seen to be in need of being made scientific through formalization and rationalization. The story of how the link between artisans and science was broken and new hierarchies erected for labour and knowledge is very relevant for today's debates (see Braverman 1974 and Conner 2005 for historical accounts).

Significantly, despite *repeated failures* on part of philosophers of science in solving the "demarcation problem,"[4] there was a consensus of sorts that knowledge that was produced at loci other than modern universities, laboratories or modern industry, was either simply superstition or more charitably informal, rule-of-thumb knowledge in need for a scientific grounding to make it serious. Philosophical difficulties encountered in marking the boundary between science and non-science were deemed inconsequential, particularly by practising scientists and engineers because the spectacular success of science was self-evident and proof of the pudding was in eating it. In this atmosphere, Gandhi was one of the few modern thinkers who rejected this hierarchy during its heyday and refused to accord to science the place of privilege it claimed for itself (Sahasrabudhey 2002).

The hierarchy between scientific and non-scientific knowledge, that went nearly unquestioned in the first half of the 20th century, has since then come under attack. Several factors have come together to ensure this. As awareness of the social and ecological costs of large-scale industrialization and industrial agriculture has grown, as top-down and largely non-participatory models of economic development are questioned, more attention is being given in the Global Academy to what is often referred to as "traditional and indigenous knowledge." There is a growing interest in knowledge traditions and paradigms all across the world that were previously considered non-legitimate or non-scientific. An implicit, if not explicit intellectual link exists between this new literature and writings from the 1970s and 80s on "alternative science" and "appropriate technology."

Despite the limitations mentioned above, the discourse of the Knowledge Society has contributed to the flattening of hierarchies between scientific and non-scientific knowledge. In part because the language of science is now somewhat outdated and the language of Knowledge is ascendant, some room has been created for recognition of other knowledge systems. The rise to visibility of these systems is made more salient by the emergence of the Internet as a global medium for organizing and distributing knowledge, and by a global search for profits from any type of labour process, traditional or modern, based on any type of knowledge. Unlike traditional methods of knowledge distribution such as universities, scholarly journals, and books, the Internet functions in a far more decentralized and "un-policed" manner. The result has been that slowly, but surely, knowledge produced in modern institutions such as universities, laboratories, etc., is no longer being viewed as the sole paradigm of knowledge. Or to put it another way, universities and research laboratories, once the exclusive preserve of science, have begun to acknowledge and interact with other knowledge paradigms.

This is in evidence everywhere as alternative and holistic medicine enjoys a renaissance, peasant knowledge of agro-biodiversity finds new recognition in universities and agricultural colleges, and artisanal crafts enjoy new world markets. The terms indigenous knowledge, traditional knowledge, people's knowledge, local knowledge and so on are all attempts to define knowledge in society that is not produced within the paradigm of modern science but which has been lifted into global visibility, flattening the traditional knowledge hierarchies in the process.

## 22.3 *Lokavidya* and Intellectual Property Rights (IPRs)

We have seen so far that unlike during the Industrial Age, *lokavidya* has found recognition in the Knowledge Age. However, this recognition is contingent on economic value and economic exploitation. Finger and Schuler (2004) note:

To the extent that the international community has paid attention to knowledge in developing countries, it has focused on two issues:

- The defence of "traditional knowledge" against misappropriation by industrial country interests.
- The policing of "biopiracy" on the part of industrial country interests, that is, exploitation of the biodiversity that exists in developing countries to develop agricultural products,

healthcare products, and so forth, without proper compensation to the "traditional communities" that first discovered the usefulness of such genetic material.

The legal system of patents, copyrights, trademarks and intellectual property rights (IPR) regimes in general is key to ensuring that knowledge can be traded in the market as a commodity. However, commoditizing knowledge is difficult due to its non-rival nature.[5] Since knowledge grows rather than becoming scarce by distributing it, there has been significant resistance to making knowledge artificially scarce via private property rights and recent scholarship has explored the possibility of a Knowledge Commons (Hess and Ostrom 2007). The problems inherent in commoditizing knowledge are further compounded in the case of *lokavidya*. A key distinguishing feature between *lokavidya* and knowledge produced in the formal sector is that a given type of *lokavidya* is often "owned" and practised by a community of producers that has no legal status that might allow private property rights to be accorded to it. On the other hand, *lokavidya* is, by and large, subaltern knowledge, or knowledge possessed by the disadvantaged, marginalized sections of society. Hence, a vigorous debate has raged over the protection of *lokavidya* from appropriation and over the development of effective intellectual property rights. To this end traditional knowledge online databases are being created to make information on prior art more easily accessible to patent-granting agencies which in turn would prevent the granting of illegitimate patents.[6]

However some commentators have also noted that as *lokavidya* is archived in online databases, dangers of appropriation, rather than decreasing, may even increase since this knowledge is now more easily available. As a response, in addition to cataloguing and documentation, there is a strong push to develop IPRs specific to *lokavidya* as a protective measure. A new hierarchy is emerging between knowledge that is organized or represented on the Internet and that which is not. As representation on the Internet becomes the new legitimizing criterion for knowledge, the proponents of *lokavidya* find themselves caught between the *Scylla* and *Charybdis* of denial of knowledge-status on the one hand and appropriation on the other.

The double-edged nature of IPRs becomes obvious when the rhetoric surrounding the knowledge commons is examined. Note that "piracy" is the name given to sharing music, movies and other creative products electronically, in violation of copyright. In this instance the term is used to imply that those who assert the non-rival nature of knowledge by "freeing" it are thieves. In this case the corporate sector usually labels individuals and file-sharing communities "pirates." Conversely "biopiracy" (Shiva 1997) is a commonly used term that implies that corporations which bio-prospect genetic resources and traditional knowledge are engaging in thievery. This time the corporations finds themselves accused of the same crime of which they accuse FOSS proponents and other internet file-sharers. This is more than mere irony. Rather, it illustrates how IPRs can be used selectively for protection or appropriation as suits powerful commercial interests.

The issue of effective property rights has attracted immense attention largely because of its economic significance. According to a UN estimate developing countries lose US$5 billion annually in the form of unpaid royalties to multinational corporations that appropriate traditional knowledge (McLeod cited in Visser 2004).

Ten Kate and Laird (2004) note:

> Annual global markets for products in the healthcare, agriculture, horticulture, and biotechnology sectors derived from genetic resources lie between US$500 billion and US$800 billion...Direct links can still be made between many products on the market and knowledge systems dating back millennia. For example, of the approximately 120 pharmaceutical products derived from plants in 1985, 75 per cent were discovered through the study of their traditional medical use.

An incremental advance over *lokavidya* can thus generate windfall profits with the help of patenting regimes. And going further, in some instances *lokavidya* holders may even be denied the right to use their own knowledge under formal patent laws although thankfully this has occurred only in very few instances thus far.

The above scenario calls for some hard thinking on ways and means to protect *lokavidya* from such appropriation. However, *lokavidya* by its nature is dispersed and difficult to trace to a single source. How can it be patented or copyrighted? More fundamentally, should it be? What other ways exist besides modern IPR regimes to give *lokavidya* its due recognition and make sure *lokavidya*-holders are rewarded for their efforts? I would like to suggest here that while the debate over protection of *lokavidya* is important, it should not define the entirety of the conversation. Rather we should identify and support work processes that embody *lokavidya*.

The importance of this in-situ approach has been discussed in the literature on crop genetic diversity by Brush (2000). Brush points out that ex-situ preservation of seed varieties (products of *lokavidya*) in seed-banks can only be one part of the solution at best. The other part is to ensure that small farmers who actually produce this seed diversity are supported and rewarded for their efforts. Generalizing the argument beyond biodiversity, we may assert that the *lokavidya* commons survives and thrives because of shallow production hierarchies, i.e. little separation between design and implementation and the self-directed nature of work that often characterizes small-scale and artisanal production. By contrast, deep hierarchies in large-scale industry have traditionally led to a separation of conception/ design from execution/ production destroying the producer's *lokavidya* in the process, reducing the artisan to a labourer and further exacerbating the traditional hierarchy between mental and manual labour (Braverman 1974, Marglin 1990). A new hierarchy is created between the knowledge of the manager and designer on the one hand, and the knowledge of the worker, on the other.

In the remainder of the paper, I elaborate on two other dimensions: first, recognition and support of the concrete work practices that produce *lokavidya* and second, the need for building institutional mechanisms for *lokavidya* holders to inform knowledge production and transmission in formal institutions such as universities.

## 22.4 Work and Knowledge

Over 90% of India's working population, in its informal economy, fulfils its needs and the needs of society largely without reliance on formal education. The knowledge that these farmers, artisans, women, *adivasis*, and small retailers possess is found abundantly in society. However, it is not seen as knowledge. Low wages, harsh exploitation and unsafe working conditions often characterize this sector of the economy. Job security, unemployment insurance, health and retirement facilities are unheard of luxuries.[7] It is the main argument of this paper that restoring respect for *lokavidya*, ensuring that its holders benefit from their knowledge, and integrating it into the education system, are important steps towards changing these oppressive circumstances and creating a poverty-free society.

Post-colonial economic development in countries such as India was supposed to be a story of the gradual replacement of the "traditional economy" by the more productive modern, capitalist sector (see Lewis 1954 for one such influential model). The economy of artisans, women, small farmers, indigenous peoples, and small retail, which accounts for almost 90% of the working population, ("informal economy," ILO 1972) was destined for disappearance. In knowledge terms, this can be seen as a replacement of an economy based on *lokavidya* to one based on organized/ formal ("modern") knowledge. Classical development theory developed in the 1940s and 1950s was grounded in a model of *knowledge scarcity*. India and other developing countries were seen to be knowledge-poor and in need of first importing modern knowledge (embodied in imported technology and machinery) and then developing a programme for "import-substitution" and investing in its own modern knowledge production industry. Newly set up universities and research institutes, and the knowledge they produced were seen to be independent of the wealth of knowledge that existed among the people. This knowledge of the people was largely ignored if not denigrated.

But in India, the organized sector has so far failed to grow rapidly enough and even today formal manufacturing accounts for less than 25% of manufacturing employment (Saha et al.,

2004). The informal economy has not disappeared. By some measures it has even grown in size (Jhabvala et al., 2003, Government of India 2007, Harris-White and Sinha 2007). Even now, although economists have come to terms with the existence of this informal economy and its importance in supporting livelihoods, they typically overlook the large and dynamic pool of knowledge that is created and sustained within it. This knowledge not only helps to sustain hundreds of millions of livelihoods, but it also confers benefits to people outside the informal economy as evidenced by the data cited earlier on use of traditional remedies by the organized pharmaceutical industry or of seed varieties by the biotechnology industry.

*Lokavidya* is not simply "traditional knowledge." For example, knowledge possessed by communities of artisans who work with wood, clay, iron, plastic, and many other raw materials to produce articles of daily use, utensils, clothes, food items, toys, soaps, even small machine parts and repairing and servicing of larger machines, is dynamic and changes in accordance with raw material availability, market forces, technical progress and so on. This knowledge is both *traditional*, in the sense of tracing lineage to pre-colonial periods and *modern* since it has continued to adapt to newer circumstances (Gupta 2000, Haynes 1996, 2001). Furthermore it is dynamic as it constantly adapts to changing circumstances. *The lokavidya perspective recognizes that ordinary life is a centre of knowledge production* and not merely an "implementer" of knowledge generated elsewhere.

The concepts of traditional and indigenous knowledge have performed an important role in raising *lokavidya* into international visibility. However, to go beyond simple recognition and to provide an argument for the inclusion of *lokavidya* and *lokavidya*-holders in the coming transformation of the University in the new Knowledge Society, we need to clarify some analytical issues. Firstly, the terms traditional or indigenous, despite the author's intentions, conjure up a timeline along which societies possessing traditional knowledge are transformed into those possessing scientific knowledge. Further "traditional knowledge" generates a static picture that goes against the inherently dynamic character of knowledge.

Tradition is useless if it is not capable of changing in order to meet today's challenges. *Lokavidya*, in contrast with traditional knowledge, constantly evolves, adapts and changes. It does not seek to tie people to ways of knowing and doing of the past *for its own sake*. It does not romanticize the past or the future. *The sole criterion is the use and control (production and management) of the knowledge by the people in the course of their ordinary life.*

Work as opposed to alienated wage-labour is an integral component of ordinary life and is the foundation of knowledge. Through *lokavidya* we grasp the fundamental relation between knowledge and work. The classical economists such as Adam Smith and Karl Marx understood the importance of work in shaping human character and the development on the human psyche. Unfortunately modern economics has jettisoned this comprehensive view in exchange for a much reduced concept of work as a *necessary evil*, something that confers disutility but which must be done in order to earn a livelihood. It is easy to see why this is the case. In an advanced industrial capitalist economy, the predominant form of work is alienated wage labour. Not only that, most work has undergone a deep *technical* division of labour over the last hundred and fifty years.[8] Bureaucratic managerial hierarchies, rationalized supervision and control are the norm. Under such circumstances work quickly loses its broader meaning and becomes a routine chore.

By contrast artisanal production (whether in agriculture or industry), even under harshly exploitative conditions, often retains a more holistic meaning of work. This is particularly true if the labor process is self-directed and tied to the identity of the artisan. What consequence does this have for knowledge production? The nature of knowledge production in artisanal and small producer communities has not been investigated adequately. Could what has been called "peer production" in the context of the Free and Open Source Software (FOSS) Movement be a useful model for production of *lokavidya* as well?

Peer-production allows a more democratic production of knowledge within the knowledge community (however defined) rather than the one-way traffic between experts/managers and workers/implementers or consumers that we are used to in traditional hierarchical production. In other words, the *lokavidya* commons may survive and thrive because of *shallow production hierarchies*, i.e. little separation between design and implementation that exist in small-scale production. By contrast, deep hierarchies in large capitalist firms have traditionally led to a separation of conception from execution destroying the producer's *lokavidya* in the process, and reducing the artisan to a labourer. The organic link between farmers/artisans and science was broken during the 19th and 20th centuries partly due to professionalization of science and partly due to the rise of the factory system in place of the craft-based system of production. There exists an extensive literature on how the labour process, within which knowledge is both created and applied, is controlled in the industrial capitalist framework.

The father of "Scientific Management," F.W. Taylor, recognized clearly that his methods and techniques were as much about maximizing labour productivity, as about gaining control of the labour process by removing its self-directed nature and the *lokavidya*-basis of production. Taylor takes it as given that workers possess knowledge, detailed and intimate knowledge about their work. In his words

> ...the managers recognize frankly that the...workmen, included in the twenty or thirty trades, who are under them, possess this mass of traditional knowledge, a large part of which is not in the possession of management. (Taylor 1911/1998, p. 32)

Thus in a Taylorist enterprise,

> The managers assume...the burden of gathering together all the traditional knowledge which in the past has been possessed by workmen and then of classifying, tabulating, and reducing this knowledge to rules, laws and formulae... (p. 36)

This is the core principle that entails a *separation of conception from execution*. The producer is no longer capable of a self-directed labour process in which she retains a vision of the entire product and is "able to conceive of the totality of his activity as part of another totality." (Sahasrabudhey 2001) [9]

This has far-reaching consequences not only in the organization of labour and the deskilling of the artisan, but also in the way new knowledge is produced. Braverman (1974) puts it thus:

> As craftsmanship is destroyed or increasingly emptied of its traditional content, the remaining ties, already tenuous and weakened, between the working population and science are more or less completely broken. This connection was, in the past, made chiefly through the craftsman or artisan section of the working class... (p. 131)

The ancient relationship between artisanal production and the development of science and technology continued down to the immediate pre-industrial period in England, where such iconic figures of the Industrial Revolution as James Watt and George Stephenson were craftsmen-turned-inventors. Further the craftsmen were intimately tied to the scientific and technical knowledge of their time as embodied in the daily practices of their craft.[10] And even today in India, the multitude of artisans are possessors of scientific and technical knowledge relevant to their work.

The organic connection between production of articles of necessity and innovation, though far broken in the advanced industrial countries, having been substituted by a professional innovative class (R and D), still remains to some extent in India. As was noted before, artisans have not been completely replaced by the factory worker in the Indian case. Gandhi's insistence of craft-based production by the masses (as opposed to capital-intensive mass production) can be seen in this context as not only a response to mass unemployment, but rather an attempt to *preserve the link between the masses and science*. Patnaik (2000) recognizes Gandhi's fundamental grasp of this issue:

> For Gandhi and for Lohia, the mode of industrialization is a central and fundamental factor in carrying out civilizational change and this means making new inventions. Unfortunately, the culture of invention/research has changed completely. Now the invention of useful machines has become the provenance of the state or of big business. (p. 94, translated from Hindi)

While conditions may still permit the re-forging of a link between the producing classes and science, as Gandhi and Lohia wished for, the self-directed and autonomously creative nature of the artisanal production process is threatened in new ways under globalization. Loss of control over factor and product markets and insertion into extensive sub-contracting arrangements are widespread. To an extent lack of access to finance and lack of knowledge of markets has always bedevilled the artisan but today she finds herself embedded in extensive middlemen networks and global commodity chains. This produces a new variety of Taylorism that undermines control over design, not by constructing deep managerial hierarchies in a factory setting, but rather by ensuring coordination and control over dispersed and decentralized production processes via Information and Communications Technologies. For the employer, this "neo-Taylorism" reaps the advantages of reduced managerial and overhead costs while retaining control of the production process and achieving a fragmented labour process as well as dispersed, difficult to organize, labour. This increases exploitation of artisanal *lokavidya* and undermines conditions under which it can flourish. It is thus necessary to restore to the artisan her self-direction and control over the various aspects of production. The work of *Vidya Ashram* in this regard assumes a vital importance, not only as a popularizer of the *lokavidya* perspective, but also as an organizer of artisan labour with the specific demands of access to the market, access to raw materials, and control over finance (Sahasrabudhey 2001, Maurya 2001).

## 22.5 *Lokavidya* and the University

A farmer has never gone to agricultural college where an agricultural scientist works. Both have knowledge but the knowledge of both is valued differently by society and by the market. These two will never compete directly for the same job (can the farmer be a visiting professor at our hypothetical university?). The scientist produces knowledge in the form of scholarly publications. The farmer produces knowledge in the activity of growing his crop. The veracity of the scientist's knowledge is tested by peer-review and replication in the laboratory or field. The veracity of the farmer's knowledge is tested by nature's "review" and replication in life. In response to a mistake, the scientist retracts his research paper/finding, in response to a mistake a farmer may lose a significant proportion of his income and go into lifelong debt. Further the farmer's knowledge activity feeds us. Yet we value his knowledge less.

When we think about the characteristics of a new university appropriate to the Information/Knowledge Age, we should think about how it will incorporate different types of knowledge. As we have seen, in India, a very large part of knowledge production and transmission, particularly of the kind that is directly relevant to sustaining livelihoods, takes place outside the university. A university would be required to be conscious of the multiple locations of knowledge production in society, be they with farmers, artisans, women, indigenous peoples. Such a university would be founded on a holistic view of the relationship between work and knowledge and would consciously challenge the hierarchy between "intellectual" and "manual" labour. It will recognize that all work is "knowledge work."

Gandhi's much discussed concept of *Nai talim* was, of course, precisely one such attempt and it deserves to be reinterpreted and extended for contemporary times. *Nai talim* insisted on transcending the dichotomy between head and hand, between mental and manual labour that plagues education systems all over the world and in the process it merged the world of work with the world of knowledge. According to Gandhi the brain must be educated via the hand. Only then will knowledge production be consistent with the demands of social justice. We must also distinguish *Nai talim* from vocational education. Gandhi himself is clear on this distinction: "The core of my suggestion is that handicrafts are to be taught, not merely for productive works, but for developing the intellect of the pupils." (Gandhi 1962, p. 82)

Gandhi sees the purpose of *Nai talim* to be twofold. First, to relieve the toiling masses of relentless and poorly paid work, which is a result of the denigration of their knowledge and denial of access to resources; and second to make the existing schools and colleges relevant to the rest of society by producing individuals who are not derisive of manual work. It is heartening to note that the National Focus Group on "Work and Education" chaired by Prof. Anil Sadgopal as part of the National Curricular Framework 2005 has taken this issue on squarely:

The exclusionary character of the education system in India

is to a great extent founded on the artificially instituted dichotomy between work and knowledge (also reflected in the widening gap between school and society). Those who work with their hands and produce wealth are denied access to formal education while those who have access to formal education not only denigrate productive manual work but also lack the necessary skills for the same.[11]

The authors of the report contend "that the exclusionary character of Indian education can at least be partly challenged by utilizing the knowledge base of the vast productive sections of society as a powerful means to transform the education system." (p. iii)

This is precisely the goal of bringing *lokavidya* into the university curriculum. Although both *Nai talim* and the NCERT report are primarily concerned with reform of the basic education system, the argument applies with modifications to the higher education system as well. The works of *Vidya Ashram*, as well as my own arguments presented here, seek to establish that it is time the prevalent hierarchies of knowledge in society were challenged and dismantled. The universities can be allies in this process rather than being adversaries and can become relevant to the majority of Indians if this is achieved. In some ways, the international discourse on the Knowledge Society has made this task easier.

Unlike the present-day Indian University which is modelled on the 19th century European University, the "New University" will not be the supreme source of knowledge, nor even just another site of knowledge production, but rather a process of dialogue and cooperation among *multiple sites of knowledge production* (Basole 2008). It will value *lokavidya* and the labour involved in producing this knowledge on par with formal knowledge. Furthermore, it will view knowledge as a means of resistance and reconstruction (*sangharsh aur nirman*). The inclusion of artisanal *vidya* in the university engineering curricula does not only carry the promise of finding a place for these producers in the education system, thereby making it relevant to their needs, but it also carries the potential to change the epistemic assumptions regarding superior and inferior knowledge that is so deep-seated in our society.

A concrete proposal on restructuring the university is outside the scope of the present paper and forms the ongoing work of *Vidya Ashram* (see for for example *Vidya Ashram* 2008). At least two objections however can be foreseen straightaway. These are summarized well by the NCERT Report on Work and Education:

> In view of their historical experience, the deprived sections (especially, *dalits*, tribals, religious and linguistic minorities) would understandably tend to look upon such a proposal as yet another strategy to deny them access to 'certified' and 'valid' knowledge, and, therefore, to vertical mobility, a just share in the economic cake and equitable participation in political power. On the other hand, the elite consensus on the education system may counter by labeling this as a 'conspiracy' to freeze the nation in pre-modern times and prevent her from becoming 'an economic superpower by 2020', the ongoing debate on such myopic notions of India notwithstanding (Sadgopal et al., 2007, p. 64)

Undoubtedly other challenges will present themselves. However, *lokavidya*-proponents would be remiss in not availing of the historic opportunity created by the new fluxes in the world of knowledge that were discussed earlier.

## 22.6 Conclusion

In this paper I have argued that the emergence of the Knowledge Society has created a historic opportunity by raising into visibility the knowledge possessed by the ordinary working poor across the world. However much of this attention has taken the form of a debate over the importance of IPRs in protecting people's knowledge from appropriation, or of strong property rights for ensuring that the knowledge-holders benefit economically from their knowledge activity.

I have made a case that more attention should be focused on identifying and supporting the work processes that generate this knowledge. Artisans and other small producers across the world are struggling under the impact of neoliberal economic policy. While some have benefited from exposure to international markets, many more are suffering from destruction of the local market due to competition, shortage of finance or usurious finance, lack of access to raw materials due to enclosure of the commons and so on. The denial of knowledge-status to *lokavidya* typically translates into an inability of *lokavidya*-holders to gain access to resources on which to apply their knowledge.

This can be remedied, in part, by including *lokavidya* and *lokavidya*-holders in the University curriculum. This will achieve the dual objectives of making the higher education system relevant to the mainstream and restoring prestige to *lokavidya*. The challenge ahead is to make this theoretical vision a reality. The present conference is an important step in this regard.

Acknowledgements: I thank Sunil and Chitra Sahasrabudhey, Avinash Jha, Jim Boyce and Mohan Rao for valuable insights. Responsibility for errors is, of course, mine.

## 22.7 Bibliography

Basole, A., 2008. Eurocentrism, the University and Multiplicity of Knowledge Production Sites, in *The Global University: The New Market for Knowledge* (Italian), Rome: manifestolibri.

Basole, A., 2006. *Lokavidya* Goes Virtual? Indigenous Knowledge in the Gatesian Age. Proceedings of a workshop on *Dialogues on Knowledge in Society- Part 2*, World Social Forum, 2006, Karachi, Pakistan. Available at http://www.*vidyaashram*.org/karachi.html

Bell, D., 1973. *The Coming of Post-Industrial Society*, Basic Books, New York.

Binté, J. et al., 2005. *Towards Knowledge Societies*, UNESCO World Report (www.unesco.org)

Braverman, H. 1974. *Labor and Monopoly Capital: The Degradation of Work in the Twentieth Century*. Monthly Review Press, New York.

Breman, J., 1996. *Footloose Labor: Working in India's Informal Economy*. Cambridge University Press.

Brokensha, D., Warren, D.M., Werner O., 1980. *Indigenous Knowledge Systems and Development*. University Press of America.

Brush, S.B., 2000. *Genes in the Field: On-Farm Conservation of Crop Diversity*. Lewis Publishers, New York.

Chattopadhyaya, D., 1986. *History of Science and Technology in Ancient India: The Beginnings*. Firma KLM, Calcutta.

Conner, C.D., 2005. *A People's History of Science: Miners, Midwives and "Low Mechanics"*. Nation Books, New York.

De Neve, G., 2005. *The Everyday Politics of Labor: Working Lives in India's Informal Economy*. Social Science Press, New Delhi.

Farrington, B., 1947. *Head and Hand in Ancient Greece: Four Studies in the Social Relations of Thought*. Watts and Co., London.

Finger, J.M., Schuler, P., (eds.), 2004. *Poor People's Knowledge: Promoting Intellectual Property in Developing Countries*. World Bank and Oxford University Press.

Fuchs, C., 2008. *Internet and Society: Social Theory in the Information Age*, Routledge, New York.

Gandhi, M.K., 1962 *Village Swaraj*. Navjivan, Ahmedabad.

Gereffi, G. et al., 1994. 'Introduction: Global Commodity Chains' in *Commodity Chains and Global Capitalism*, Gereffi and Korzeniewicz eds., Greenwood Press, Connecticut.

Government of India, 2007. *Manual on Survey of Informal Employment and Informal Sector.*

Gupta, A., 2000. *Postcolonial Developments: Agriculture in the Making of Modern India*. Duke University Press, Durham.

Harris-White B., Sinha A., (eds), 2007. *Trade Liberalisation and India's Informal Economy*, Delhi: OUP.

Haynes, D., 1996. The Dynamics of Continuity in Indian Domestic Industry: Jari Manufacture in Surat, 1900-47 in Roy, T., (ed.), 1996. *Cloth and Commerce: Textiles in Colonial India*, Sage Publications, New Delhi.

Haynes, D., 2001. Artisan Cloth-Producers and the Emergence of Powerloom Manufacture in Western India 1920-1950. *Past and Present*, 172, pp. 170-198.

Hess, C., Ostrom E., 2007. *Understanding Knowledge as a Commons: From Theory to Practice*. MIT Press, Cambridge.

ILO, 1972. Employment, Incomes and Equity: A Strategy for Increasing Productive Employment in Kenya. International Labour Organization Report.

Jhabvala, R., Sudarshan R.M., Unni, J. 2003. *Informal Economy Centerstage: New Structures of Employment*. Sage Publications, New Delhi.

Lewis, W.A., 1954. Economic Development with Unlimited Supplies of Labour. *Manchester School of Economic and Social Studies*, 22(2), pp. 139

Marglin, S., 1990. Losing Touch: The Cultural Conditions of Worker Accommodation and Resistance, in Marglin, S. and Apffel-Marglin (eds.), *Dominating Knowledge*, Clarendon Press, Oxford.

Marx, K., 1867/1976. *Capital: A Critique of Political Economy*, Vol. 1. Penguin Publishers.

Maurya, L.P., 2001. Aritsanal Struggle and Organizing, in S. Sahasrabudhey and C. Sahasrabudhey (eds.), *Lokavidya Vichar*

(Hindi).

Sadgopal, Anil, et al., 2007. "Work and Education" National Focus Group Position Paper. NCERT.

Saha, Kar and Bhaskaran, 2004. *Measuring Informal Economy through Income and Expenditure Surveys*, Report of the Expert Group on Informal Sector Statistics (Delhi Group).

Sahasrabudhey, C., 1992. *Kashi ke Hastshilp Udyog* (The Handicraft Industries of Kashi) (Hindi).

Sahasrabudhey, C., 2001. *Karigar Samaj* (Artisanal Society), in Sahasrabudhey and Sashrabudhey (eds.), *Lokavidya Vichar* (Hindi). Vikalp, Varanasi.

Sahasrabudhey, S., 2002. *Gandhi's Challenge to Modern Science*. Other India Press, Goa.

Sahasrabudhey, S., 2008. Knowledge Flux and the Demand on Thought. Paper presented at the Indian Association for Cultivation of Sciences, Kolkata, April, 15, 2008.

Sahasrabudhey, S. and Sahasrabudhey, C. (eds.) 2001. *Lokavidya Vichar* (Hindi), Vikalp, Varanasi.

Seth, S., 1995. Towards a Volunteer Movement of Artisan Support, *Craft News*, 6:4.

Shiva, V., 1997. *Biopiracy: The Plunder of Nature and Knowledge*. South End Press

Sillitoe, P., (ed.), 2006. *Local Science versus Global Science: Approaches to Indigenous Knowledge in International Development*. Berghahn Books.

Sillitoe, P., Bicker A., and Pottier, J., 2002. *Participating in Development: Approaches to Indigenous Knowledge*. Routledge.

Taylor, 1911/1998. *The Principles of Scientific Management*. Dover, New York.

Ten Kate, K. and Laird, S.A. 2004. Bioprospecting Agreements and Benefit Sharing with Local Communities, in J. Michael Finger and Philip Schuler (eds.), *Poor People's Knowledge: Promoting Intellectual Property in Developing Countries*. World Bank and OUP.

Visser, C.J. 2004. Making Intellectual Property Laws Work for Traditional Knowledge, in J. Michael Finger and Philip Schuler (eds.), *Poor People's Knowledge: Promoting Intellectual Property in Developing Countries*. World Bank and OUP.

Warren, D.M., Slikkerveer, L.J., Brokensha, D. (eds.). *The Cultural Dimension of Development: Indigenous Knowledge Systems*. Intermediate Technology Publications, London.

World Bank (2004) *Indigenous Knowledge: Local Pathways to Global Development*. Knowledge and Learning Group, Africa Region.

## REFERENCES

1. http://www.knowledgecommission.gov.in/.
2. To take just two examples, by 1992, components of the Ford Escort car were being manufactured and assembled in fifteen different countries across three continents (Gereffi et al., 1994). Nike does not own any shoe factories at all, relying instead on short-term contracts from a diverse array of suppliers. Nike's contribution is not in the material production domain (say in centralized manufacturing practices) but in the intangible domain of ideas and symbols (i.e. marketing of the Nike logo or brand). These types of global production chains are made possible by the rapid advances in ICTs and in turn the imperatives of accumulation on a global scale fuel new innovation in ICTs.
3. Measured in terms of output, an information or knowledge society is one in which more than 50% of the Gross National Product (GNP) is accounted for by "knowledge sectors" such as Research and Development (R & D), Education, Information Technology, and certain types of services (such as Marketing, Management and Advertising).
4. The "demarcation problem" in the philosophy of science refers to the problem of developing adequate criteria for distinguishing science from non-science. The logical positivists of the Vienna Circle, and later more famously Sir Karl Popper, wrote extensively on this issue. Later philosophers of science, in part reacting to the failed attempts on the early 20th century, took a more pragmatic view of the problem and gave up the search for surefire formulas.
5. Non-rivalry means that the use of the commodity by one person does not preclude simultaneous use by another. Thus unlike a shirt or a computer, a design, a blueprint, a way of doing things, can be used by many people at once. This non-rival nature of Knowledge has been appreciated for centuries.
6. See Finger and Schuler (2005) for several approaches to the problem of developing IPRs for *lokavidya* and Basole (2006) for a discussion of virtual representations of *lokavidya*. Also, recently some experiments have been undertaken in creating a common property rights regime for traditional knowledge in Kerala (http://www.hindu.com/2008/06/28/stories/2008062856600100.htm).
7. See Breman (1996) and De Neve (2005) for two ethnographic accounts of informal labour.

8. As Marx (1867/1976) and Braverman (1974) describe, with the real as opposed to formal subsumption of the labour process to the needs of capital, there arose a new type of division of labour. Not the division associated with traditional crafts such as carpentry, medicine, metal-work and so on, but rather the parcellation of a complex job into simpler parts and the delegation of these simpler parts to different people, such that one person might perform only a very simple repetitive task all day. One powerful motivation for breaking down a complex task into simpler parts is that workers can be hired precisely according to the skill-levels required by the various parts. If instead all the parts were combined to be executed by one person, that person would have to possess the skills required to finish the most difficult of the jobs.
9. At this juncture one may object that the division of mental and manual labour and the hierarchy between the two is hardly a modern phenomenon. The Brahmin's knowledge has been considered superior to the chamar's for many thousands of years. The low status of the artisanal castes in general is ample testament of this fact. Philosophers and mathematicians were always distinct from artisans and manual workers. This view is only partly correct. Much evidence now exists from historians of science that the earliest philosophy and mathematics were the product of artisans, of manual workers, and grew in intimate connection with the solving of practical problems, rather than divorced from them. (e.g. Farrington 1947, Chattopadhyay 1986, Conner 2005).
10. Braverman (1974) notes that craft apprenticeship "commonly included training in mathematics, including algebra, geometry, and trigonometry, in the properties and provenance of the materials common to the craft, in the physical sciences and in mechanical drawing." (pp. 133) See Conner (2005) for such a peasant and artisan-driven "people's history of science."
11. The report continues: "The socio-economic, religio-cultural, gender and disability-related dimensions of this dichotomy have serious implications for education in India. Over a period of time and through systematic practice, such a notion of education has come to be embedded in the knowledge system, representing the dominant classes/castes/cultures/languages with patriarchy in each of these categories playing a decisive role. The education system has tended to 'certify' this form of knowledge as being the only 'valid' form. In the process, the knowledge inherent

among the vast productive forces along with the related values and skills has been excluded from the school curriculum. The legacy of colonial education was built upon precisely such a Brahminical concept of 'certified' or 'valid' knowledge that is alienated from productive work and its social ethos." Sadgopal et al. (2007), p. iii.

# 23

# *Lokavidya* Goes Virtual: Indigenous Knowledge in the Gatesian Age*

*Amit Basole*

## 23.1 *Lokavidya* and Indigenous Knowledge Systems: Introduction

> Virtuality seems to legitimize all traditions and locations of knowledge while elevating itself to a higher position from where all knowledge is sorted and organized. In the process it creates a new hierarchy in the sphere of knowledge. [Locations of knowledge] are now seen as places of genuine human activity only to the extent and in the manner they relate to virtuality. Can we propose a radical equality of all knowledge locations as the basis of a future democratic society which is also at peace with virtuality? (from http://www.indigen.org.in/wsf2006_poser.html)
>
> *Lokavidya* is what it is because it is not organizable through a paradigm acceptable to organized knowledge systems, both traditional and modern.
>
> - Sunil Sahasrabudhey
> (http://www.indigen.org.in/eforum/show.php?f=0&topic=20051211124655&u=10)

The above two quotations introduce the main preoccupation of this short essay, viz. how does the virtual domain relate to, appropriate or accommodate knowledge generated within the *lokavidya* paradigm? In the last few years we have seen a

* Originally written for the bulletin *Virtuality and Knowledge in Society*, published for a workshop in the World Social Forum, Karachi 2006.

substantial interest in "indigenous knowledge systems"[1] (IK systems) as evidenced by the increasing number of international NGOs and other agencies that have sprung to defend such knowledge from Western/transnational corporation exploitation and to classify and systematize it with the intention of "integrating it with modern science" and using it for "sustainable and participatory development". Is this efflorescence of interest in IK systems something to be celebrated by the proponents of *lokavidya*? Or is it yet another way in which people's knowledge is being systematized for maximum exploitation by the elites of the new Knowledge-based/virtual Economy? Are the knowledge formations or systems that have been labelled variously as indigenous, traditional, non-formal, tacit, people's knowledge, etc., the virtual domain manifestations of *lokavidya*? If so, does the "virtualization" transform them from *vidya* into *avidya*?[2] Can *lokavidya* exist *on its own terms* even as it is subsumed into the virtual domain? Or is it by its very nature non-organizable and therefore non-virtualizable? Such questions are of great interest and relevance to the *lokavidya* perspective.

I will not attempt to answer the questions posed above in any great detail here. Indeed I am not competent to do so. I will merely outline some current developments that relate to this issue and attempt a partial answer. At the outset let me say that I am not going to offer case studies from development projects that seek to apply indigenous knowledge to some social or environmental issue. There are many specific attempts that, for for example, apply Native American ecological knowledge to forest conservation in Canada or catalogue Indian indigenous knowledge of medicine in online databases, etc. I will not go into the details of such attempts but merely mention them as examples to make certain points. The notes at the end of the essay provide a list of websites and other references for those who are interested in further details.

But before I begin, a word about definitions. I am using the word *lokavidya* in the sense that has been developed in the last few years by Sahasrabudhey and others.[3] Briefly, *lokavidya* is the *vidya* (value-laden knowledge or wisdom) possessed by the farmers, artisans, women and tribal societies the world over (in both, the so-called First and Third Worlds). *Lokavidya* is inseparable from their world-view and value system and is a dynamic entity that grows and is continually tested and modified on the anvil of everyday experience. *Lokavidya* is contrasted with modern science and university-based organized knowledge and the latter is seen to be in conflict with *lokavidya* in particular with the rise of colonialism/imperialism and growth of the modern state, capitalist class society, etc. *Lokavidya* has also been conceptualized as inherently (or by definition) an unorganized form of knowledge in society. If this is taken to be true, then of course, no virtual (and therefore necessarily organized) representation of *lokavidya* can exist. However, here I am interested in examining the ways in which the virtual domain, in its increasingly all-encompassing reach, has approached and appropriated the domain of *lokavidya*.

In much of the literature available on the Internet a general distinction is usually made between indigenous knowledge (which is supposed to be location and/or culture specific, generated within communities and which forms the basis for survival and day-to-day activity, is predominantly rural, oral and not systematically documented), and formal knowledge (which is university or research laboratory-based, dependent on modern science, systematized, urban, etc). This distinction is quite similar to the one we have already set out in the previous paragraph, from the *lokavidya* perspective. I will not attempt to make this any more concrete at this point.

That there has been in recent years an ample acknowledgement of the existence of IK systems everywhere in the world is evident from even a cursory search on the World Wide Web. For example, a search on www.google.com using the term "indigenous and knowledge" retrieves approximately 16 million results (admittedly not all of direct relevance). Skimming even the first 100 or so of these, reveals websites dealing with issues of how IK systems relate to economic development, conservation of biodiversity, biopiracy and intellectual property rights, weather forecasting, forest management, globalization, health, etc. Moreover there are many attempts to link IK systems and modern science at the philosophical as well as the "application" level.

Does all this attention signify a celebration of *lokavidya*? We will attempt to answer this question in the next few pages. How the virtual domain relates to *lokavidya* can perhaps be broken further into two questions, viz. how is this relationship manifesting itself today and how in principle, they can be reconciled together. As for the first part, the main issues being debated today in the virtual domain (and those issues considered here), relate to economic development, ecology/ biodiversity and intellectual property rights. The second part of the question is briefly taken up at the end.

## 23.2 Sustainable Development or Sustainable Imperialism?

A "Best Practices on Indigenous Knowledge" report, issued in 1999 emphasizes the growing interest in IK systems and the role they can play in "truly participatory approaches to sustainable development".[4] The authors of the report comment that it is not a coincidence that governments in the developing world are adopting more IK-friendly attitudes just as the more orthodox development models have run their course and failed to deliver the promised goods. Can we expect this increased attention being given to IK, to play a positive role in the current struggle of the marginalized peoples (artisans, farmers, tribal minorities, women) against capitalist (post)modernity/ imperialism?[5] My answer is a qualified "no". It is possible to argue that the marriage of *lokavidya* with information and communication technologies, resulting in what is being called indigenous knowledge in this essay may protect some types of knowledge from being stolen in the form of international patents to pharmaceutical companies, etc. However it is also very likely that the systematization of such knowledge will make exploitation and theft much easier in these "newly discovered" domains of *lokavidya*. But I do not think that discussing the "gains and losses" from virtualization is the right terrain over which the debate should range.

To the extent that the larger sustainable development discourse[6] is itself unable to break free from the paradigm of "developmentalism", IK systems risk being appropriated in the service of Imperialism. Development ideology of the post-Second World War, "Fordist" regime of capitalist accumulation has been extensively critiqued since the 1970s (the decade which also saw the Fordist regime encounter its first serious crises) for being Eurocentric, imperialist, neo-colonial, stagist, non-participatory and elitist, top-down, etc. Concomitantly, the rise of environmentalism in the "advanced" industrial economies has made prominent the notion of *unsustainable development*. Thus the Johannesburg Declaration on Sustainable Development aims to confront the "indignity and indecency occasioned by poverty, environmental degradation and patterns of unsustainable development". It recognizes "that poverty eradication, changing consumption and production patterns and protecting and managing the natural resource base for economic and social development are overarching objectives of and essential requirements for sustainable development" and it reaffirms "the vital role of the indigenous peoples in sustainable development". Thus sustainable development is the new avatar of developmentalism for the 21st century or the "Gatesian" age and in addition to the more "appropriate" application of modern science, a greater reliance on traditional wisdom or indigenous knowledge is being claimed at the "right way to develop". John Madeley, a well-known science journalist, wrote in a 1993 editorial in the journal *International Agricultural Development* that "...indigenous knowledge is the largest single knowledge resource not yet mobilized in the development enterprise."[7] If one reads the "development enterprise" to mean imperialism ("globalization" in the rhetoric of today), then one can begin to understand the true imperative that is driving the current need to systematize and virtualize IK systems from everywhere on earth. If one subscribes to the view that modern science advances everywhere by destruction of *lokavidya*, then the appropriation of *lokavidya* into the virtual domain under the pretext of economic development is the next battle in this ongoing war. Suffocation by embrace would perhaps be the relevant analogy.

Of course, the proponents of IK systems are well aware of such critiques and there exists plenty of rhetoric on the World Wide Web, which proclaims the urgent need to ensure that IK is used in a participatory manner, giving due credit to the peoples that produce the knowledge. Participatory development

(PD) is (next perhaps only to sustainable development) the current buzz-word in the economic development discourse. One writer defines "participation" in this context as

> ...involvement by a local population and, at times, additional stakeholders in the creation, content and conduct of a programme or policy designed to change their lives. Built on a belief that citizens can be trusted to shape their own future, participatory development uses local decision-making and capacities to steer and define the nature of an intervention.[8]

The United States Agency for International Development (USAID) has extensive documentation on its website relating to participatory development initiatives all over the world.[9] A prominent feature of many such initiatives is the emphasis on practices based on local knowledge.

Words such as "participatory" and "sustainable" like the words "freedom" and "democracy" are chosen carefully for who could be against things like fuller participation and more democracy? However, as always, of more interest than the rhetoric is the larger structural and socio-economic context in which this participation occurs. Participation from local communities "affected" by development projects, even if the demands that the project meets have been made by members of the community themselves, stops short of a radical change to the order being pushed, in this case by the international NGOs, USAID, etc. The consequences of a community actually asserting its right to self-determination are still serious and examples from many parts of the world can be multiplied to make this case.

## 23.3 IKS and IPRs: Protecting and Systematizing Indigenous Knowledge

A large body of literature on the Internet deals with the issue of how indigenous knowledge systems should be reconciled with the currently prevailing intellectual property rights regimes (IPRs), e.g. TRIPS. The World Intellectual Property Organization (WIPO) has taken much interest in indigenous and traditional knowledge systems. The WIPO uses the term traditional knowledge

> to refer to tradition-based literary, artistic or scientific works; performances, inventions, scientific discoveries, designs, marks, names and symbols, undisclosed information and all other tradition-based innovations and creations resulting from intellectual activity in the industrial, scientific, literary or artistic fields.[10]

Concomitantly "bio-piracy" has become a concern with those who seek to protect IK from exploitation by (mostly Western, but not necessarily so) transnational corporations. In this context, the cases of neem, turmeric and basmati rice are too well-known to bear repetition here. One solution to bio-piracy which has been enthusiastically received by the virtual community is the construction of "Traditional Knowledge Digital Libraries" that "may be used as evidence of prior art to defeat a claim to a patent."[11] The WIPO terms this, "defensive protection of traditional knowledge."[12] Not surprisingly, the information and communication revolution has made the systematization of such knowledge much simpler and there are large-scale efforts underway, such as India-based Gene Campaign's project for the protection of indigenous knowledge of biodiversity. Another example is India's *Ayurveda* "digital library" which contains information on 35,000 formulations, all "in a format accessible by international patent offices to prevent the granting of inappropriate patents."[13] This and other similar libraries seek to catalogue, organize and virtualize IK systems in order to protect them. And of course, the very same virtualization and systematization process is being heralded as an efficient way to globalize local knowledge. Thus we read that,

> ...electronic communication will make information on indigenous knowledge more accessible and easier to disseminate. As the existing global network of indigenous knowledge resource centres becomes linked by a common electronic communications system, indigenous knowledge and technologies found to be effective in dealing with small-farm circumstances in an agro-ecozone in one part of the globe can be transferred for consideration to a centre in another part of the world where a similar agro-ecozone exists. Examples of this transfer of technology already exist. The use of vetiver grass for soil and water management and the use of neem tree seeds as a biopesticide are both technologies discovered by

> farmers in South Asia many generations ago. These technologies have now been adopted by small-scale farmers in many other parts of the world through networking mechanisms provided by the World Bank and other development agencies.[14]

However, systematizing IK into "virtual libraries" serves to divorce this knowledge from its site of production and from its own dynamics, which by definition is amongst the people, not amongst the "virtual elite". If the solution to this divorce or alienation is to bring the producers of *lokavidya* into the virtual fold (i.e. to bridge the so-called "digital divide"), the solution itself recalls to mind the age-old paternalist rhetoric (Marxist as well as imperialist) to "help the masses modernize or progress", simply updated for the Gatesian age. Not to mention the fact that extending the virtual elites' "consumption and production patterns" to the people at large may threaten the very basis of "sustainable development" that IK systems are supposed to promote.

The sheer gulf that yawns between the *lokavidya* perspective and the Western property rights regimes is (unknowingly) revealed by the way that the US government has justified the problems posed by these patents (such as those awarded to turmeric for its "newly discovered" healing properties):

> ...informal systems of knowledge often depend upon face-to-face communication, thereby limiting access to the information to persons in direct contact with one another. The public at large does not benefit from the knowledge nor can the knowledge be built upon. In addition, if information is not written down, that information is completely inaccessible to patent examiners everywhere as prior art when they are examining patent applications. It is possible, therefore, for a patent to be issued claiming as an invention technology that is known to a particular indigenous community. The fault lies not with the patent system, however, but with the inaccessibility of the knowledge involved beyond the indigenous community.[15]

## 23.4 Virtualization of *Lokavidya* and the Commodification of Knowledge

As seen so far, most of the development debate remains trapped in the "gains and losses from virtualization" paradigm and the participants seem largely unwilling or unable to recognize a fundamental contradiction that exists between indigenous and modern systems in the way knowledge (in the most abstract sense) is viewed. This is the contradiction of commodification. The issue of systematization or organization, which appears as a very prominent aspect of the difference between modern science and *lokavidya*, I think, arises from this contradiction. The modern need to organize every aspect of human knowledge is to be distinguished from the prevalence, since ancient times, of organized knowledge to do with, say the occurrence of eclipses or the schools of epistemology or medicine, etc. The main distinguishing feature is that with the capitalist drive for converting knowledge into a commodity, comes a strong impetus to systematize and organize. The organization of knowledge is no longer one activity amongst many in the knowledge sphere but it becomes the sole touchstone for estimating the validity of knowledge itself. Lack of formal organization is then equated with inefficiency (as was implied in the statement from the US patent office, quoted above) or even worse, unorganized (in the modern sense) forms of knowledge are simply rendered invisible, ripe for "rediscovery" at the opportune moment.

An analogy can be made to the way in which a large part of the economy of the "developing world" called the "informal sector" is rendered invisible to or un-analysable by modern economics (neo-classical or Marxist). This point relates to Sahasrabudhey's contention in the quote from the beginning of this essay, that "*lokavidya* is what it is because it is not organizable through a paradigm acceptable to organized knowledge systems, both traditional and modern." I read this remark, in the light of my arguments above, not as a blanket statement against the systematization of *lokavidya* as such, but as a contention that any such systematization occurring in the current neo-liberal imperialist and, more fundamentally, the (post)modernist order is bound to alienate the *vidya* from its producers. But of course this interpretation is open to debate.

Through a wider theoretical lens, one can see that imperialism in the age of the capitalist world-economy is another name for the expansion of social relations of production and exchange that are conducive to expansion of value.[16] It has been increasingly clear during the course of the 20th century that imperial domination need not take the form of a hegemonic relation between nation states. If we confine ourselves to the level of the nation state most countries are in fact nominally capitalist. But can it be said that the whole world is capitalist? Clearly this is not the case. Significant domains of human activity remain that have not yet been subsumed under capitalist social relations. The commodification of housework and caring labour (e.g. child care) is an example of capitalist expansion into newer domains. Particularly in societies where capitalism came via colonialism and imperial domination, the capitalist transformation of society is far from complete and such transformation forms an important part of the drive for accumulation today.

The ICT revolution makes much easier the next logical step in the process of capital accumulation, viz. the expansion of capitalist social relations into the domain of knowledge. After land, labour, and money, knowledge constitutes the fourth fictitious commodity (in Polanyi's sense). Indeed all the more fictitious since, unlike the first three it is not rival in nature. That is to say, the scarcity of knowledge must be created, where none need exist. The reorganization of society along the logic of the knowledge revolution makes possible such scarcity conditions, under the guise of *greater access* to knowledge and information. The greater access does exist, although only for those already privileged by their position in the modern economy. Those who were on the periphery earlier lose even what little they had before.[17] The exclusive possession of knowledge has long been a method of exploitation alongside ownership of capital (financial, industrial or agricultural). Just as capital needed to be brought into a domain where the abstract and inhuman "laws of the market" could be seen (falsely) to control it, so also the reorganization of society to bring knowledge into the purview of the market has become important for the expansion and continued domination of imperialism in the 21st century.

## 23.5 *Lokavidya* and Indigenous Knowledge Systems: Conclusion

All knowledge is real (material) and virtual at the same time. By this I mean that all knowledge collectively possessed by a society is instantiated in one of another kind of material base. The material base of the virtual society is still that age-old adversary: industrial capitalism. It is true that capitalism is nothing if not dynamic and today displays itself in evermore rapidly changing forms. However, the old logic, discussed by Marx, using such concepts as capital accumulation, value expansion and alienated labour still assumes great relevance today. As does the Gandhian critique of the machine as destroyer of civilization since, in the Gatesian age, knowledge itself is being defined in terms of organizability by machines.

I have tried to show here the ways in which knowledge that has been generated for centuries within the *lokavidya* paradigm is being virtualized under the name of indigenous knowledge and *in* the name of participatory and sustainable development, biodiversity conservation and protection of indigenous intellectual property rights. To put it bluntly and to provoke debate, this is the language of the new imperialism for the Gatesian Age. Thus IK is the "web-friendly" and appropriated (i.e. a domesticated) version of *lokavidya*. Some proponents of this virtualization process openly admit that "by vesting legally recognized ownership of knowledge in communities through IPRs it will raise the profile of that knowledge and encourage respect for it both inside and outside the knowledge holding communities."[18] With regard to this "taming of *lokavidya*" it is worth quoting Shields,

> The propositions of the knowledge-based economy (KBE) involve simplified notions of knowledge as information. Although this builds on the modernist bias against embodied skill, tacit knowledge and experience in favour of abstracted supervisory knowledge, it also adds a new degree of formalization. Knowledge that cannot be captured in the databases of Information Technology (IT) systems and information management or knowledge management software is screened out, often being explicitly referred to in the literature as 'tacit', begging the question of how these forms and knowledge processes are maintained.[19]

That said if one recognizes the existence and the importance of loci of knowledge that cannot be virtualized, what should be the attitude towards the juggernaut of virtualization?

The virtual domain is the creation of modern science. But it is also true that the virtual domain has displayed a logic/mode of operation and a reputation quite distinct from modern science. In particular this is evidenced by the mass exodus of youth from science/engineering fields to information technology and by the need shown by the World Summit on Information Society, in its proclamation of principles, to state that science has a central role in the development of the Information Society. The very need to announce what seems to be a truism indicates that in perception, if not in reality, the Information Society has an existence apart form modern science.

But ultimately the material roots of the virtual society lie too deeply in the soil of modern science for it to be uprooted without a great deal of force. In other words, for all the talk of the postmodern, postindustrial, virtual society of the 21st century, in many ways the political economy of production, distribution and exchange is still that of the 20th. This includes a firm foundation in the science, technology, the very epistemology of modernity.[20] It is true that the organization of production for instance has undergone rapid change and many small or family units now produce commodities where large industrial units might have done so before. But this very decentralization of production (so-called post-Fordist mode), which manifests itself in sweatshops and other small-producer arrangements, is associated with the increased emphasis on managing/governing the distributed world economy. This is one imperative behind the coming of the "Information Society."

*Lokavidya* is often characterized by inbuilt wisdom regarding the uncertainty and unpredictability of ecosystems. It also tends to possess the quality of non-violence (*ahimsa*), to be exercised in the *lokahita* (in the interest of all) and to be more genuinely democratic (i.e. in favour of *lokaniti* as opposed to *rajniti*). Hence *lokavidya* (meaning now, not just knowledge, but a particular epistemology and ontology, a worldview) can stand as a challenge to the virtual society and remains one of the only genuine hopes for a different future.

## REFERENCES

1. According to the Indigenous Knowledge pages, http://www.ik-pages.net/about-ik.html, the characteristics of indigenous knowledge are that it is generated within communities, is location and culture-specific, is the basis for decision-making and survival strategies, is not systematically documented, is dynamic and based on innovation, adaptation, and experimentation, is oral and rural in nature, and covers critical issues such as primary production, human and animal life, natural resources management.
2. I am using the terms vidya and avidya in the sense developed by Sunil Sahasrabudhey in his book *Gandhi's Challenge to Modern Science* (published by the Other India Press, Goa). Briefly, *vidya* which is constituted by technology, science and the arts, gives direction of truth to man's struggle and unity with nature, while *avidya* is the source of disruption and violence with nature.
3. For example, see essays in the book *Lokavidya Vichar* (Lokavidya Pratishtha Abhiyan, Varanasi) and also issues of the periodical *Lokavidya Samvad* (Vidya Ashram, Sarnath, Varanasi).
4. The report was issued by the Netherlands Organization for International Cooperation in Higher Education/Indigenous Knowledge (NUFFIC/IK-Unit) in cooperation with UNESCO's Management of Social Transformations Programme (MOST) and can be found here: http://www.unesco.org/most/bpikpub.htm. A periodical called *Indigenous Knowledge and Development Monitor* was also published by NUFFIC and has recently been taken over by a consortium of organizations including the International Institute of Rural Reconstruction (IIRR) of the Philippines.
5. For lack of a better term, I have used capitalist modernity/Imperialism to cover a wide variety of social phenomena, such as what is commonly called globalization, but also related issues such as intra-national struggles of tribals and other minorities against "developmental projects". Later on I deal with Imperialism in what may be termed a more technically Marxist sense.
6. For example, see the Johannesburg Declaration on Sustainable Development: http://www.un.org/esa/sustdev/documents/WSSD_POI_PD/English/POI_PD.htm
7. Quoted in http://www.ik-pages.net/ik-network.html
8. Jennings, Ray, Participatory Development as New Paradigm: The Transition of Development Professionalism, October 2000.

Conference on "Community-based Reintegration and Rehabilitation in Post-conflict Settings.

9. http://www.usaid.gov/about/part_devel/.
10. Traditional Knowledge and Intellectual Property, A Discussion Paper by Carlos M. Correa, p. 4.
11. http://www.scidev.net/News/index.cfm?fuseaction=readNews&itemid=1840&language=1. The website www.scidev.net has a comprehensive dossier on "Indigenous Knowledge" available at: http://www.scidev.net/dossiers/index.cfm?fuseaction=dossierItem&Dossier=7.
12. http://www.wipo.int/tk/en/tk/.
13. http://www.scidev.net/News/index.cfm?fuseaction=readNews&itemid=1840&language=1.
14. http://www.ik-pages.net/ik-network.html.
15. US General Declaration to the First Meeting of the WIPO Committee, May 1, 2001.
16. In this part of the discussion I am of course following in the footsteps of Lenin, Rosa Luxemburg and many other Marxist critics of Imperialism.
17. I would like to clarify that my intention is not to deny what little improvement there has been in the material life of the middle and lower-middle classes all over the world owing to the transformations created by the Information Revolution. However, in this as in all previous such social transformations one must insistently ask, "at what cost?" and "who benefits, who pays?"
18. Quote from The Crucible Group Report cited in *Traditional Knowledge and Intellectual Property*, A Discussion Paper by Carlos M. Correa, p. 7.
19. R. Shields, The Role of the Virtual in Knowledge-based Economies, Organizations and Localities. *SEED* (4), p. 25-44, Available at http://www.library.utoronto.ca/see/SEED/Vol2-4/shields.html.
20. I am aware of the challenge to modernist epistemology that postmodern thought has brought with it. However, it seems to me that this intellectual revolution has not substantially altered the material political economy of our times. At least not yet.

# IV

# *Lokavidya* and the University

# 24

# Re-inventing the Indian University: Arguing from a *Lokavidya* Standpoint*

*Sunil Sahasrabudhey and Amit Basole*

## 24.1 Introduction

The Indian University is an imitation enterprise. Higher education, including medical and engineering colleges, law and management schools, mass communication and art schools, research establishments and of course the regular university, are not located in Indian history, culture or knowledge traditions. Content, form, styles, methods of work, methods of argument, standards, values, everything is derived from what happened in Europe and what happens now in the United States of America. It is not that the University in the West is particularly well connected with the needs, aspirations or knowledge of the people there, but the imitation product that we have manufactured in India is even further away from our people in all these respects. As a consequence there is a paucity of anything new, creative or innovative in the university here. It is a place of socialization, a place that opens paths to an elite world, almost completely urban. Its connection with any kind of knowledge is very tenuous, the defence, atomic energy and space installations not withstanding. This essay argues that we

---

* This is a revised version of a paper presented by Sunil Sahasrabudhey at a conference on "The Emerging Organization of Knowledge and the Future of Universities," December 2008, 32nd Indian Social Sciences Congress, Jamia Millia Islamia, New Delhi.

have entered an era when it has become possible to change all this and to make the university relevant to the people at large. A period of massive destabilization in the world of knowledge has started creating conditions for radically new initiatives.

The university thus far has been conceived as a place of organized knowledge activity in a sea of ignorance. Walled campuses have been as far away from the people epistemically as the walled palaces of kings used to be from the people with respect to the power they commanded. Re-inventing the university, it is suggested here, requires us to reconceptualize it as a place of organized knowledge activity located in a sea of knowledge. What knowledge? The knowledge possessed by the peasants, artisans, women, artists and variety of others, common people who carry out their daily and specialized activity without the benefit of a university experience. We call this knowledge *lokavidya*, or people's knowledge. The vast majority of Indians organize their lives on the basis of *lokavidya*.

This exercise in reimagination may carry lessons for Europe as well. We observe that the Euro-American University is also in crisis. The ongoing privatization and corporatization of the public university has been hastened as a result of the latest crisis in the global economy. There is unrest in universities across Europe and the USA. The European meeting of university movements called by the Edu-Factory collective in Paris in February 2011 had over 90 organizations from across the world attending. The cry "We Won't Pay for Your Crisis," originally the slogan of the Italian "Anomalous Wave," has resounded in movements everywhere. Most strikingly many of these movements display little nostalgia for the "university of yore" for the way knowledge was produced and distributed in the past. They speak of a new type of university that produces "living knowledge" instead of teaching abstract, dead knowledge. They dream of a fundamental change in the modern university in such a way that it no longer serves as the pillar of capitalist society. However, no clear visions are forthcoming just yet on what a new university might look like.

Drawing upon the work of the *Vidya Ashram* in Varanasi, India, here we put forth a new perspective on knowledge, on what the purpose of the university is, and what its relationship to society should be. While we make the case for an Indian context, we believe that the argument is of relevance to Europe as well.

## 24.2 The World of Higher Education is Becoming More Unequal

A key factor that contributes to the university's distance from Indian society is its narrow social base. The Indian government's own figures indicate that, for a variety of reasons including costs, nationally only some 10 per cent of those who are of college going age actually enrol. Enrolment rates are even lower for rural folks, women, for the backward castes and religious minorities.[1] Some mitigation of this situation is being attempted through affirmative action with the objectives of social justice in mind. This is effected through seats reserved for the backward classes in addition to the already existing reservations for the Scheduled Castes (Dalits) and Scheduled Tribes (indigenous people). However, there is enormous social resistance to such affirmative action from students in advanced and professional colleges, most of whom come from the upper castes. Reservations have been challenged in the courts up to the Supreme Court. The intense battles over a limited number of seats are due to the very high demand for higher education which seems to offer the only pathway for a secure, organized and relatively prosperous life. Of course the rush is for the Engineering colleges, Medical, Law and Business schools, namely for institutions which promise a future. The regular university teaching the sciences, social sciences and the arts is not attractive any more. The obvious reason is that training in these subjects does not lead to employment. But there is perhaps a deeper reason namely, that these sciences and arts no more seem to occupy the apex of the knowledge pyramid. But more on this later.

Globalization has brought in its wake new values in the sphere of education. Utilitarian principles seem to be in the lead, utility being defined by the needs of the market and the large corporations. Across Europe we have seen attempts to corporatize the university, which generally means withdrawing public spending, making education more expensive, tailoring the content according to the needs of corporations, changing the entry rules, tightening the programme and generally taking away the democratic and cultural content of the university. In India, the push towards corporatization has a somewhat different origin. While in Europe privatization is accompanied by a concomitant decrease in public spending on higher education, in India the opposite scenario prevails. Recently, the government has decided to massively increase spending on higher education even as private capital also flows in at unprecedented levels. In July 2009 the government pledged to increase the higher education budget by a dramatic and unprecedented 40 per cent, to $3.1 billion.[2]

However the increased public sector spending is still quite small compared to the private education market which, though estimates vary, may be worth as much as $68 billion by 2012. Private players, domestic and international are eager to cash in on this large potential education market. Slowly but steadily a drift in the private direction can be noticed. By 2006, as much as 63.2 per cent of all educational institutions and 51.5 per cent of the total enrolment were already in the private sector. Particularly in the professional fields (engineering, medicine, management) over 70 per cent of the institutions are in the private sector.[3] Even the very expensive business schools and institutes of technology which have become possible by government financing now openly argue against "government interference" and express a wish for closer collaboration with the corporations.

There is also a strong argument to be made that the products of our higher education apparatus, not counting graduates of a handful of elite institutions, are largely unemployable. This is attributed mainly to absence of quality teachers, which is in turn said to be due to teachers' salaries not being commensurate with salaries in corporations. So the argument goes that salaries of teachers must be increased greatly to attract competence leading to improvement in the quality of teaching, which alone in turn can produce employable graduates with some competence. Due to privatization the increased salaries can come only from the increased fees of students, such an argument inevitably pushes the costs of education upwards, which then demands a credit structure for student loans from financial institutions, from banks and so on. This is an obvious trap for education to be turned into a handmaiden of financial power, as it has already become in the United States and elsewhere.

While increased public spending on higher education has been in the news recently, it should be emphasized that this does not imply a commitment to universal higher education. Rather the increased spending seems intended for only a few "apex" or "elite" institutions. This is another effect of integration into the global market which demands "high and uniform standards" across the world. If India has to keep up in the global race it must have a large number of institutions of very high standard (upgrade old ones and build new ones). This seems to be the most important conclusion of the National Knowledge Commission. It implies that public finance for higher education will largely be cornered by these institutions and the division already present between the elite institutions and the run-of-the-mill, will be deepened. The former will be catered to by public finance to produce graduates and professionals for the new transnational economy and conduct research according the needs of the global market. Whereas, the latter will cater to the multitude, will satisfy the politically correct canons of social justice and keep meeting the popular demand. It will produce service providers and technicians. The current trend is thus clearly towards the setting up of more and more elite institutions (in the name of quality and meritocracy) which will cater to the tiny minority who are already socially privileged, leaving the average student languishing in a decaying state universities public system or at the mercy of private profiteers. The entry of foreign education providers under the General Agreement on Trade in Services (GATS) can be expected to exacerbate this trend. In the entire process education is the chief victim. Knowledge and education assume the status of commodity and resource and the entire sector caters to developing institutions which may aspire to be listed on the stock market.

The increased public spending on apex institutions in some ways dilutes the issue of entry of private capital into higher education and makes it politically complex. Education at the "best institutions" and at the highest level is not the most expensive. For example, the prestigious Indian Institutes of Technology (IITs) still charge around 40,000 INR (less than 1,000 USD) per year.[4] The government has recently opposed increasing this amount. Of course, the extra "coaching" required to enter these IITs is a significant added expense that must be taken into account. On the other hand higher education in engineering, medicine and management for the majority who enroll in less prestigious private institutions is more expensive (upwards of 100,000 INR annually). Then again, fees in public universities for conventional courses (where a very large number of poor students enrol) are quite low (around 5,000 INR per year). This structure of fees in higher education, namely low fees at the bottom, high fees in the middle and again lowering of fees at the very top, seems to create a fees profile which makes it difficult to mobilize large numbers against expensive education. This complexity, coupled with the fact that radical politics has been much more occupied with issues of displacement and dispossession may be why India has not seen an anti-commercialization movement to any significant degree in education.

We believe that given these realities one must look elsewhere for building a politics of education in India. We must connect the politics of education to the politics of knowledge. The moment is ripe for doing this now.

## 24.3 The Information Revolution Presents New Opportunities

The computer and communication revolution has caused unprecedented changes everywhere, including the world of education. The rise of information science and knowledge management is the source of radical changes in the old hierarchies in the world of knowledge. Communication techniques are dislodging the technologies of production from the central place they occupied in human life. Internet and mobile use has started defining the metre of progress which was once made up of production of steel, fertilizer and power. The job market reflects this shift too. The rise of information as science is tending to change humanity's view of itself. There is a tendency developing to see human history in terms of different stages of development of methods of communication and not as it was earlier done in stages of development of technologies of production. There is a new trend in the biological sciences to see the basic cellular processes as information processes, materially given effect to by the chemical and physical processes and not as it was done earlier to see them as chemical processes resulting in information processing. These are massive changes. They make the science we are familiar with, stand on its head. While the world of science consists of things and forces in the ultimate analysis, the philosophy that such new understanding entails may conceptualise the world as mainly consisting of representation and communication, meaning and syntax, receptors and emitters.

With information processes recognised as second to none in importance and with the aid of the terrific connectivity produced by the internet, "knowledge management" emerges as an entirely new element in the world of knowledge. The computer and the internet obfuscate the distinction between knowledge and information, the world of knowledge expands in an unprecedented fashion. First come into existence as a technique of intra-corporation management, knowledge management has been steadily growing in meaning and presence. The result of these changes in the world of knowledge is that the criteria of legitimacy (what is legitimate knowledge and what is not) change and new knowledge hierarchies come into existence.

Thus we observe that the criteria of legitimate knowledge are no more the same as they used to be in the Industrial Age. Scientific method, controlled experiment, reproducibility, cohesive incorporation in the existing world of science, certification by professional bodies and journals no more stand out as requirements to be satisfied for a method, skill or understanding to be accepted as legitimate knowledge. If the piece of information, understanding, technique, skill or practice is usable by the methods of computers and communications, that is if it is organizable by information technology, then it is legitimate knowledge. Such organization leads, or is expected to lead, to greater market competitiveness. The new candidates in the field of knowledge now, therefore, come from people's understandings and practices, what we call *lokavidya*, known in the literature mainly as traditional knowledge. To the new epistemic dispensation it does not matter where and how a piece of knowledge has been produced. Production of knowledge and the methods thereof are not the issue, however important they may be. Thus, information, understanding and practices that were declared unscientific and not proper knowledge have entered the world of knowledge making this world look very different from what it used to be. As a result of this, a fundamental condition that separated the ordinary person and ordinary life from the university has broken down. This is where we shall look for the reconstruction of the Indian university.

In short the global economy and the Internet have created the conditions to use a "market metre" for all knowledge. This is a practical metric and theoretically the new outlook refuses to accept any hierarchy in the world of knowledge, save knowledge management, which sits at the top, declares itself a genuine member of the world of knowledge and proceeds to assume the command. It is now knowledge management that reorders the world of knowledge once ordered by science. When science ruled for centuries, the world of knowledge had developed hierarchies familiar to us all: science at the top, physics within it at the extreme top, life sciences at the lower end, then the social science and then art, performance, communication, representation and what have you, and finally at the very bottom the knowledge deemed "unscientific," "folk," "traditional," etc. University organization reflected this also. Even a cursory look at the university shows that it is no more the case. Departments of commerce, media and communications studies, information technology and management attract more students, command greater prestige than the science departments. There is a new rush for investment banking, law and business schools. And though the rush towards engineering colleges continues unabated, the "best minds" in engineering do not stay with engineering but proceed towards the new disciplines. Places outside the regular university that offer training in information management, communications, etc. as well as in contemporary art forms have multiplied many fold. The new institutions and private universities often dispense with science and social science faculties entirely.

Financial institutions and corporations control the flow of knowledge and resources to their advantage. The idea of truth is a clear victim. The world of knowledge no more has truth seekers of the scientific world. Although *lokavidya* gets a new recognition, it comes with a price. It must take the shape of the new utensils, be organizable by the computer, that is be softwarable. Sitting at the eye of the cyclone in the epistemic world knowledge management sucks in everything of substance into the virtual world. All knowledge that is produced anywhere feeds into it and all knowledge at the site of production stands emaciated and alienated. Knowledge producers thus enter into a fundamental conflict with knowledge managers. This corresponds to the split of the university into the run-of-the mill institutions and the apex institutions. This split is headed to do a great damage to humanity and the struggle against it involves liberating the university from the global trap and relocating it in the society it is a part of. This move for the liberation of the university must come from people outside the university, who are grounded in their own knowledge traditions, the traditions of *lokavidya*.

## 24.4 *Lokavidya*

What is *lokavidya*? Literally translated, it is people's knowledge or knowledge with the people. From the *lokavidya* point of view, the vast majority of Indians who have never entered an institution of higher education appear, not ignorant, but knowledgeable. This knowledge is not merely traditional knowledge or folk wisdom. It fulfils people's needs today, it adapts to changing markets and other life conditions, it is living knowledge, produced not in the institutions of knowledge production, but in life and work of everyday. We contrast this with organized knowledge produced in the present-day university in any domain from performing arts to science and engineering. The universities teach mostly knowledge produced in the West and also some other knowledge, indigenous as well as of other civilizations, but all formatted and canonised according to the frameworks of European "reason" and the scientific paradigm. *Lokavidya* has no such externally imposed constraints other than those that are there in ordinary life. Since, it belongs to ordinary life it embodies a certain type of continuity. Since it belongs to the open society and has an open handed existence it grows with the times, incessantly changes, welcoming the new and rejecting the worn out. It happens through real day-to-day practice in society, it happens guided by the sense of reality, proportion and genius of the people who hold this knowledge and who are at their day-to-day work. *Lokavidya* hardly ever uses theoretical guidelines or arguments to reject something or accept a new practice. Considerations are practical and societal. It apportions no knowledge to the dustbin.

In spite of enormous hurdles through the colonial period, *lokavidya* has remained the source of spiritual engagement with life as well as the source of strategy for material survival. The following four principles encapsulate some of *lokavidya*'s many strengths:

- *Lokavidya* houses the knowledge traditions of this civilization.
- *Lokavidya* is always contemporary knowledge, modified, corrected, changed, improved upon and reconstructed incessantly, daily, according to the experiences, needs and the genius of the people.
- *Lokavidya* belongs to open society. It resides in ordinary life and serves ordinary life.
- All knowledge starts with *lokavidya* and must return to *lokavidya* for its ultimate validation.

The last point requires more elaboration. *Lokavidya* is a kind of "first knowledge." Historically speaking all knowledge originates in *lokavidya*. "High theory" follows practice. As the adage goes, thermodynamics owes more to the steam engine than the steam engine owes to thermodynamics. Several historians of science have pointed out that science and mathematics were once the domain of artisans and manual workers, and that they grew in connection with the solving of practical problems, not divorced from them.[5] Further the contribution of the artisans was not limited to technical knowledge. Medieval India produced many artisan-thinkers. Some prominent examples from the bhakti (devotion) religious tradition are Namdev, the tailor, Gora, the potter, Raidas, the cobbler, and Kabir, the weaver. The ancient relationship between artisanal production and the development of science and technology continued down to the period of the Industrial Revolution in England, where such iconic figures of the new order as James Watt and George Stephenson were also craftsmen. The typical artisan was tied to the scientific and technical knowledge of the time as embodied in the daily practices of craft.[6] *Lokavidya* is also the "last knowledge." Just as science comes from *lokavidya*, conversely all knowledge ultimately must return to *lokavidya* in practice. Knowledge that does not do so turns anti-human, for it loses its human touchstone. Thus for example, by allying with capital science deskills the very people who produce it, it turns artisans into laborers, thereby turning against the people.

Although *lokavidya* is not only limited to technical or economically significant knowledge, we may understand it more concretely by looking at its economic dimension. It takes some obvious forms such as the knowledge of physical materials and processes, of agronomy and ecology possessed by artisans, peasants and other workers who make up the so-called "informal economy." This economy accounts for 90 per cent of the workforce in India. Even without agriculture, it account for over 75 per cent of employment and 50 per cent of output. Its scope is similarly extensive. Small-scale industry produces food products, cotton, wool and silk textiles, wood and paper products, leather and chemical products, metal products, electrical and transport equipment and repair services of various kinds including repair of capital equipment. Knowledge of communities of artisans who produce these articles is dynamic and changes with availability of raw material, changes in demand and technique, and so on. It is the descendant of artisanal science referred to earlier, but today it is invisible.

When seen from the perspective of organized knowledge, all that appears to us is lack or ignorance. For example, the Third Census of Small Scale Industry in India included a question on the source of technical knowledge for the firms surveyed. Table 1 shows that almost 90 per cent of unregistered (i.e. very small, mostly artisanal) firms report no source.

**Table 1: Source of Technical Know-how in the Unregistered Small-scale Industry Sector, [Source: SSI Census, p. 296]**

| Source | % units |
|---|---|
| Abroad | 0.67 |
| Domestic collaborators | 5.58 |
| Domestic R&D None | 4.84 |

What does "none" mean? Surely not that there is no source of technical know-how. We may guess that firms which report no source rely on "in-house" knowledge of their workers, their informal networks, their ability to imitate or adapt formal knowledge to their needs. However this is not a recognized source of know-how, or rather it is so ubiquitous and obvious as to be unworthy of comment. It hides in plain sight. Another striking example of the invisibility of *lokavidya* comes from the nation-wide National Sample Surveys conducted by the Government of India. When asked about the type of skills they possessed only 10 per cent of the respondents in a 1993-94 survey reported having any formal or informal skills. This was despite the fact that "skill" was defined very broadly as "any marketable expertise however acquired, irrespective of whether marketed or not, whether the intention is to market it or not."[7]

Another similar survey conducted in 2004-05 included questions on the type and extent of vocational and/or technical training obtained by the workforce. It found that 89 per cent of the respondents reported having received no technical or vocational training of either the formal or informal kind even though, once again, "informal training" was very broadly defined.[8] This apparent absence of knowledge in the populace at large, as it emerges in national statistics, is all too easily equated with ignorance. For example, on the basis of the 1993 skill data the National Commission on Enterprises in the Unorganized Sector concluded that "nearly 90 per cent of the population above 15 years did not have any skills."[9] This conclusion renders a vast pool of knowledge on the basis of which the majority of the people organize their life, invisible and obviates the need to understand it further. An alternative hypothesis is that work/life and learning being inextricably intertwined questions about training elicit negative responses.

This may be because respondents have a particular image of what constitutes being trained or acquiring a skill. This may include"going to school," receiving a certificate or degree, etc. Our research among the weavers of Varanasi provides some evidence for this view.[10]

The discourse on knowledge is so asymmetric, favouring the economically prosperous and the organized, that when *lokavidya* does deserve a mention it is understood as something which may be about the past, about knowledge that there was. However, this is because the epistemic, economic, political and cultural asymmetries all feed into one-another, reinforcing each other to shape a highly unequal public domain to the complete disadvantage of those who are poor and who have not gone to the school, however knowledgeable they may be. Though university knowledge and *lokavidya* ought to have a friendly dialectic between them in constituting the world of knowledge, the university has stood aloof from *lokavidya*, has considered it an inferior form of knowledge, or not knowledge at all. But *lokavidya* and masters of *lokavidya* do not look at the university as the enemy or the oppressor. This creates the condition for reinventing the Indian university.

## 24.5 *Vidya Ashram*: Towards a People's Knowledge Movement

*Vidya Ashram* (*Vidya* = Knowledge, *Ashram* = Place for learning and reflection) is an autonomous collective with no institutional funding. Its members come from diverse groups in society, men and women, peasants and academics, upper castes and lower castes. The *Ashram* is a political space for organizing and for reflection. It works mainly with ordinary working people (peasants, artisans, small producers and retailers, women and indigenous peoples) and their mass organizations, participating in their existing struggles for livelihoods, against displacement and so on, while bringing the *lokavidya* point of view into discussions with them. As we outline on our website, we believe that a radical intervention in the world of knowledge is a necessary condition for a radical transformation of society. We work towards building a knowledge movement that resides in the existing mass movements of the working people on the other side of the digital divide. We have taken on a critical analysis of the higher education and university system because we believe that the guiding principles of the world of education come from the university. Thus in a fundamental sense, primary schooling is based on university education. Without challenging the university, reform of the school system is partial at best and cosmetic at worst.

The *lokavidya* perspective has emerged out of roughly three decades of work with the peasant movement in India, with women's organizations and with academics working on traditional Indian science and technology. The work of these organizations is outlined in greater detail on our website. Some recent interviews may be helpful to understand the genesis of this idea as well.[11] We attempt to carry the politics of *lokavidya* to international fora such as the World Social Forums as well as other platforms concerned specifically with the politics of knowledge, such as Edu-Factory. We organize Youth Knowledge Camps and Farmers and Artisans Fora in small towns and villages in India. A "*Lokavidya* Research Forum" run from the *Ashram* investigates the dynamics of knowledge in society, its production and transmission, its values, its relationship to the state, the market, the university, etc. This work builds on the work of predecessor organizations such as Nari *Vidya* Sansthan (Women's Knowledge Forum) which brought to light the importance of women's knowledge to society and the economy via interactions with women in the informal economy, such as vegetable vendors, weavers, bead makers, toy makers, and those doing sewing and stitching. A Hindi monthly *Lokavidya Panchayat* is published from the *Ashram* to offer a knowledge perspective on contemporary politics.

We have attempted to create new institutions and spaces where participation, opinions and initiatives of the common people on the question of knowledge become part of the public realm. One such initiative is the "*Gyan panchayat*" (Public Hearing on Knowledge), which is born out of the conviction that if a dialectical, constructive relationship develops between *lokavidya* and the world of alternative thoughts and policy proposals then a world of knowledge free of barriers and divisions can be created. At the first *Gyan panchayat*, organized at *Vidya Ashram* in Varanasi, peasants, artisans, students, NGO workers, activists, researchers and organizers reflected on the theme "Walls of the University Must Come Down." Below are some views that emerged:[12]

- The large-scale tendency to call people ignorant will not break until the walls of the University fall.
- Just as there are brokers of religion in society, there are brokers of knowledge too. Breaking the University's walls means breaking their monopoly.
- The University has created modes of discourse within which *lokavidya*-holders are not able to express themselves fully. Breaking the walls of the University means creating such public modes of expression that allow everyone to participate.
- Knowledge is locked up inside the University and is sold to those who can pay for it. In the informal weaving industry, designers teach students without charging any fees. This presents a new model of education, which stands for equality in society.
- The University is the wall. It divides society and it should come down.
- The rising cost of higher education is making the walls of the University ever higher. Without bringing these walls down disparity in education will never end.

We offer the foregoing as an institutional context for the argument being developed in this essay, in order to show the milieu from which the ideas arise.

## 24.6 Current Trends and the New University

The current trends towards commercialization of higher education for the masses and the setting up of elite publicly funded institutions, discussed in Section 23.2, are two sides of the same coin; the creation of a corporate-oriented workforce. Further, private institutes and colleges, with the promise (mostly unrealized) of well-paying formal sector jobs, are forcing people to spend more and more on education. Even as jobs do not materialize in proportion to the number of people thronging to these institutions higher education itself rapidly becomes an extremely lucrative business. Elite public institutions, though much more affordable remain inaccessible to the vast majority, despite dramatic increases in capacity.

But all these observations and the ensuing debate remain in the domain of the organization of higher education and do not extend necessarily to its content. While we understand that there exists a dialectical relationship between the form and content of education and we do stand opposed to the commercialization of education, our work aims to prepare people's minds for a more fundamental debate on the question of knowledge hierarchies without which the struggle against commercialization cannot be taken to its logical conclusion. The almost axiomatic link between a university or college degree and a decent, respectable livelihood, which is a major driver of demand for higher education (public or private) is built on the denigration and devaluation of *lokavidya*. The mere absence of a formal qualification as we have seen in Section 24.4, makes knowledgeable productive people who satisfy society's needs appear unskilled and ignorant. *Vidya Ashram*'s work and the *lokavidya* standpoint are thus primarily an intervention on content of education and not its organization (i.e. modes of finance, etc).

We close this essay by offering some remarks on the nature of the new university. The foregoing remarks are general, as they must be at this level of abstraction. We have presented a fuller treatment of these ideas elsewhere.[13]

The university is the most prized product of the capitalist age. It is considered to represent the highest achievements of modern culture and to provide the intellectual atmosphere necessary for the preservation of capitalist society via a judicious mixture of consent and dissent. As California's militant student movement puts it, the [modern] university's history is the history of capital itself. Re-imagining, reinventing the university are therefore necessary tasks in the creation of a new society. Unless this is done a new hierarchy will establish itself in place of the old one dominated by science. *Vidya Ashram* insists on a debate on knowledge as a part of the debate on education. Our political programme is motivated by this concern and we believe that the *lokavidya* standpoint can show us the way forward. We suggest that the university be re-conceptualized as a place of organized knowledge activity in a vast bed of *lokavidya*.

Today the holders of *lokavidya* are among the poorest. Thus activity based on this knowledge has no capacity to take risks, to represent itself more imaginatively, more colourfully, in more attractive forms. It lacks articulation in the accepted canons of public discourse. The need is not that it be part of any grand theoretic framework, in fact it defies such frameworks. The need is of facility for artistic expression, for the flowering of all those capacities of people which have found no occasion to flower under the present conditions. We call for a reinvention of the Indian university to do all this, to reflect a creative genius, to be connected with the people and to serve the people. We need such a reconstruction of the socio-epistemic process to solve the problems created by the industrial world, not only social problems, but also the problems of destruction of environment and ecology, disappearing bio-diversity, and climate change.

The university ought to be a place of knowledge activity guided by the genius of the people of the region as expressed in the epistemic finesse of the technical experts, communication experts, artists, spiritual men and women of the region. It should develop methods of expression, articulation, representation, collaboration, cooperation, training and networking with respect to the knowledge in society in that region. The university should not prepare databases of knowledge. It should however, in the natural course have information about who are knowledgeable people in the region. These knowledgeable persons, from all walks of life, should be frequent visitors to the university in both advisory and participatory functions. The university should not be a place of knowledge production. This is done in society by the multitudes in the ordinary course of their lives and also in special circumstances by the specially gifted. Rather it should be one important mode of organization of knowledge in society.

Such a university is naturally rooted in the larger community, it is not a walled campus (public or private). The *lokavidya* standpoint thus demands a constraint on the state, as it does on the market. Respect for *lokavidya* means that the initiative rests with the people and their communities. The university will root itself in the locality via a positive and vibrant relationship with the local market and the institutions of local self-government. The local market will keep the university aware of the actual practices of the people which it can in turn influence through dialogues. Institutions of local self-governance would be expected, through a broad government policy, to support the university, facilitate the task it decides to do. Both the local market and the institutions of self-governance have a natural privilege to influence the university in ways they deem fit and conversely. These are seen as interaction among equals. As can be seen, this university does not have its gaze fixed to the metropole, but rather towards the society of which it is a part.

Needless to say, many concrete details such as the structure of the curriculum, mode of finance, and so on need to be discussed. However, before entering into such details, it is necessary to carry out the epistemic task at hand, which is to challenge the university's current monopolistic claim to knowledge, and to re-imagine a new relationship between the university and *lokavidya*, ultimately to create a new type of university consistent with the demands of social justice.

## REFERENCES

1. *Higher Education in India: Emerging Issues Related to Access, Inclusiveness and Quality*, November 2006 Nehru Memorial Lecture by Sukhdeo Thorat, Chairman, University Grants Commission.
2. India Pushes Higher-Education Expansion With 40% Budget Increase, *Chronicle of Higher Education*, July 7, 2009. Online at: http://chronicle.com/article/India-Pushes-Higher-Education/47844/.
3. Implications of WTO/GATS on Higher Education in India by K.B. Powar in *Implications of WTO/GATS on Higher Education in Asia and the Pacific*, UNESCO Forum Occasional Paper Series Paper No. 9.
4. For rough comparison, incomes in the informal sector (vast majority of the workforce) are around 5,000 INR/month or less, government salaries start at 10,000 INR/month, coveted formal sector jobs pay 50,000 INR/month and more.
5. For example, see E. Zilsel (2003). *The Social Origins of Modern Science*. Springer, B. Farrington (2001). *Head and Hand in Ancient*

*Greece: Four Studies in the Social Relations of Thought*. Spokesman Books, D. Chattopadhyay (1986). *History of Science and Technology in Ancient India*. Firma KLM, C.D. Conner (2005). *People's History of Science: Miners, Midwives and Low Mechanics*. Nation Books.

6. See H. Braverman (1974). *Labour and Monopoly Capital: The Degradation of Work in the Twentieth Century*. Monthly Review Press and D. Landes (1969). *The Unbound Prometheus: Technological Change and Industrial Development in Western Europe from 1750 to the Present*. Cambridge University Press.
7. Government of India (1997). *Employment and Unemployment in India*, 1993-94. NSS 50th Round Report No. 409 [p. 9].
8. Government of India (2006). *Employment and Unemployment Situation in India 2004-05*. NSS 61st Round Report No. 515 [p. 8]."Non-formal vocational training" was defined thus: The expertise in a vocation or trade is sometimes acquired by the succeeding generations from the other members of the households, generally the ancestors, through gradual exposures to such works. The expertise gained through significant 'hands-on' experience enables the individual to take up activities in self-employment capacity or makes him employable. [This] was considered as receiving 'non-formal' vocational training through 'hereditary' sources. 'Non-formal' vocational training received by a person to pursue a vocation different from the trade or occupation of their ancestors, was considered as 'non-formal' vocational training through 'other' sources. The other sources also included the cases where the expertise to carry out the trade or occupation of their ancestors was acquired from sources other than the household members.
9. Sengupta, A., R.S. Srivastava, K.P. Kannan, V.K. Malhotra, B.N.Yugandhar, and T.S.Papola (2009). *The Challenge of Employment in India: An Informal Economy Perspective*. National Commission for Enterprises in the Unorganized Sector, New Delhi, p. 191.
10. A. Basole (2011). *Relations of Production and Modes of Knowledge Appropriation: A Case Study on Weaving in India*. Working Paper.
11. http://vimeo.com/user2920116/videos.
12. The full report is at: http://www.edu-factory.org/wp/walls-of-the-university-must-come-down.
13. The Global Autonomous University by *Vidya Ashram*, in Edu-Factory Collective (eds.), *Towards a Global Autonomous University*, Autonomedia, NY.

# 25

# Eurocentrism, the University, and Multiple Sites of Knowledge Production*

*Amit Basole*

## 25.1 Introduction

The central theme under discussion is "Conflicts in the Production of Knowledge." There are of course many important conflicts to understand and many different ways to understand these conflicts. The one between market-oriented and non-market-oriented teaching and learning (or alternatively between liberal versus vocational/professional education) is one that has been alluded to many times. Similarly the conflicts over greater democratization of the learning process, over open access to research and so on are also important. In my post I would like to take a somewhat different approach. The big questions that I am interested in are:

1. Can the European University (what I mean by this will become clear presently) show us a way forward out of the global socio-ecological crisis of late capitalism?

2. Further, in the context of post-colonial societies such as India, how can the modern university escape or transcend its Eurocentric origins and bounds and become more immediately relevant to society at large?

---

* Originally written in 2007 for an online dialogue on *Conflicts in the Production of Knowledge* conducted by the Edu-Factory Collective (www.edu-factory.org).

Needless to say, these are topics for entire research programmes and here I can offer no more than discussion points (indeed I am not qualified to do much more). Instead of attempting to answer these directly I will raise related issues:

1. What are some of the contradictions/conflicts in the "European University" that stand in the way of it being a force for radical change?
2. In the post-colonial context, how can we think of the university in relation to the other sites where knowledge is produced in society?

## 25.2 The "European University": Contradictions

I realize that there is no such thing as "the University," there are only universities. However, today, as a result of European colonialism, universities in far-flung corners of the earth show some striking similarities. The most likely reason for this is not that, to take one example, economics, sociology, political science, anthropology and history are "natural" ways in which to divide the study of human society. But instead the reason we find these same "disciplines" in universities everywhere is because they are modelled on the "European University," a particular historical entity that arose in early 19th century Germany (Berlin), though of course antecedents are to be found in Paris, Bologna, etc. [Note that this is not to say that "the university is a European idea," an unsurprising Eurocentrism that one often finds in historical accounts of the university, but only to point out that what we call the university today is modelled on an entity that arose in 19th century Europe.] This much is perhaps commonplace. But what causes me to pose the question as above is that today I see the university—particularly in the post-colonial context, but also elsewhere—as a conservative force with a *status quo* bias, rather than as an agent of radical change. Let me explain.

Focusing on two main contradictions in the university, we find that the production of knowledge within the context of the disciplines allows for glaring contradictions of world-view to exist in the same site. There is no over-arching ethical/moral principle that unites all disciplines. Should there be one? This is a matter for debate. I believe that lack of one makes possible the particular types of instrumental rationality that are rampant in science and engineering. Historically (prior to the fact-value separation which is the legacy of the European Enlightenment) this problem was solved by situating knowledge production in the religious context. Modern universities, in contrast either operate under a "knowledge for the sake of knowledge" dictum or even a more naked "knowledge for power" principle. Thus the only thing that unites English, Anthropology, Economics, Ecology and Engineering is that knowledge is produced there. So Anthropology can say we are all different while Economics says we are all the same, or Economics says capitalism can grow forever while Ecology says resources are limited or the English department can say we are all postmodern while Engineering displays all the features of modernist thought and so on. And these contradictions can not only exist, but they can be taught to students who are offered hardly any way to reconcile them (institutionally that is; I am not speaking of exceptions such as individual professors). Of course I am exaggerating the case somewhat to make a rhetorical point. The existence of "ecological economics" for example, shows that disciplinary cross-talk can happen. And such examples can be multiplied. However, the very term inter-disciplinarity tells us what takes primacy (disciplines) and what comes afterwards (inter). As has been pointed out, such fragmentation stands directly in the way of a coherent and holistic understanding of human society, its evils, its impact upon its environment and its likely future trajectory.

The second conflict or contradiction is the oft-repeated one between teaching and research, between knowledge production and dissemination. But still sometimes we forget that a university performs the function, not just of supporting professors and researchers but of training a far greater number of individuals to be something other than professors and researchers (I am referring of course to undergraduate students). Thus the university should be a place where ethically-guided, community-centred individuals are produced, who have acquired a holistic picture of human society and the problems it faces but who at the same time are technically or otherwise adept at their chosen trade or field. In other words engineers, builders and so on who are not instrumentally rational.

Currently we do an excellent job of the technical training and leave the ethics to whoever cares to step up to the challenge. John Henry Newman begins his famous book *The Idea of a University* by defining the University as "a place for teaching universal knowledge." There are several keywords here that are of interest. We can take all of these in turn.

Before we begin, we must clarify of course that Cardinal Newman defends a model of the university that has been termed "pre-modern." Also it is clear that for Cardinal Newman, teaching is a more important function of the university, than what he calls "advancement," (or what we might call production) of knowledge. Why, he asks, would the university have students, if its primary purpose was knowledge production ("scientific and philosophical discovery")? The division of labour between knowledge production and dissemination envisaged by Cardinal Newman (teaching = universities, research = learned societies/academies) is of course no longer true (liberal arts colleges and research institutes represent this strict division of labour today, but the research university of course combines both). The tension between teaching and research embodied in the complaint that teaching leaves little time for research, is an all-too-familiar refrain at least in the natural science departments. But there is an even more significant conflict here. We live in times of super-specialization of disciplines when academic faculty often produce knowledge only for their peers and may even be punished via academic sanctions such as denial of tenure for not producing enough knowledge for specialist consumption (e.g. publishing newspaper articles to shape public opinion, rather than publishing in refereed journals). The more immediate impact upon society at large, of the university may therefore be, not knowledge produced in its research laboratories and its faculty offices, but the knowledge disseminated in its classrooms. In other words, shaping the worldview of students (and future participants in society's debates).

## 25.3 The Multiplicity of Knowledge Production Sites

Finally we come to the operative phrase in Cardinal Newman's sentence, universal knowledge. This conflict that has been mentioned several times on the Edu-factory list in the form of the debate on "multiple universalisms;" however I want to shift the terms of debate slightly and pose it as a question of the "multiplicity of knowledge production sites," the relationship between these sites and the related question of "serious" and "non-serious" knowledge. This is also tangled up (at least in my mind) with the conflict between Eurocentric and non-Eurocentric scholarship. Thus far from serving as an agent of emancipatory change, the university in the post- colonial context has often been an agent of "modernization" and university scholars, often the most "Westernized," have been generally dismissive of the knowledge produced in more "traditional loci" (or subaltern knowledge). The high academy has often slavishly followed European fashions and thinkers (be it deconstruction, post-structuralism, Foucault, Derrida or whatever) for their own sake (or to get published in Western journals). This has been true whether the university was neoliberal or not although things may be changing now. This is not to say that Foucault, to take one example, has nothing interesting to say in the context of India. But that is not a given fact. It needs to be evaluated.

As Rajesh Bhattacharya and I argue in "The Phantom of Liberty" (Kanth 2009), the lamentations often heard (e.g. from post-colonial scholars) that, for better or for worse, we are trapped within the confines of Eurocentric socio-political thought are often a result of the fact that we are taught to regard the academy as the (only?) legitimate site of knowledge production. We further argue that if one looks to other sites of knowledge production, non-Eurocentric analyses of society abound.

Post-colonial thinkers, in so far as they cannot think in their own language, are slaves of the master's discourse—or the master-discourse. What future can such a slave claim for herself? It must be understood that a "free" future for such a slave cannot be claimed solely by "Provincializing Europe" to borrow Dipesh Chakrabarty's phrase. It must also be accompanied by a retrieval of (lost) local wisdom and non-European intellectual traditions, be they elite or subaltern. Not only should the post-colonial scholar historicize and contextualize Marx and Weber, (s)he should be or feel enabled to read Gangesa and Abhinavagupta (two Indian thinkers quoted by Chakrabarty as examples of "inaccessible" authors.) Sadly, Chakrabarty cannot claim such a future. He even finds the project of provincializing Europe an impossibility.

> [S]ince "Europe" cannot after all be provincialized within the institutional site of the university whose knowledge protocols will always take us back to the terrain where all contours follow that of my hyper-real Europe—the project of provincializing Europe must realize within itself its own impossibility. It therefore looks to a history that embodies this politics of despair (Chakrabarty 2000, pp. 45).

Chakrabarty's despair is not only the result of the recognition of a loss in the past but a failure to imagine a "free" future. Hence his despair is a permanent state of being because salvation/redemption/freedom cannot be conceived outside Eurocentric boundaries. We assert that the post-colonial social scientists' failure to retrieve non-European discourses is a measure of their own inadequacy, a corollary of their insertion in the Western academic discourse. In order to be intelligible to the Western audience, in order to publish in Western journals, they necessarily have to speak within the framework circumscribed by Western thought-categories. Thus, the latter understandably becomes the only mode of thought 'available' to them. This has been the case, we argue, with postcolonial studies as well as subaltern studies. Even those who have discovered the original loss of language find it impossible to retrace the steps back to that incidence of momentous discursive violence. This is Thatcher's TINA ("There is no alternative!") in the sphere of social thought.

Further, even critiques of Eurocentrism which are expressed within the confines of the Global Academy, shaped and dominated as it is by the European intellectual tradition described above, are subject to what John Mowitt (2001) has called a "discursive price of admission." That is, even resistance to and protest against Eurocentrism has to be grounded in Western texts and authors so that it can be intelligible to referees of the global publishing circuits.

> Can we hope to publish in an international journal an article that refers primarily to vernacular texts, the majority of which might

> never be translated into major European languages? Even if it gets published, the author will surely be criticized for citing obscure texts. Yet there is a sustained articulation of challenges to European modernity in many vernacular texts—in bad print and cheap jackets—published by small local Third World publishing houses. The "unavailability" of alternative non-European discourses reflects a materiality inherent in the discursive practices and institutions of global academia—a materiality that has the effect of screening out a large set of articulations, utterances, statements and cries as "non-serious" knowledge (Bhattacharya and Basole, 2009).

This brings up my next argument. I have said earlier that Eurocentric categories of thought have colonized our minds to such an extent that the many different processes of reproduction of our life are articulated and understood in the language of European modernity. Yet, resistance to the imperialism of categories exists too and exists everywhere, wherever such imperialism asserts itself, i.e. in all spheres of life. Consequently, counter-discourses emerge at numerous social sites, in the variety of social processes that constitute the postcolonial experience. These sites could provide radical alternatives to Eurocentric thought-categories—other ways of making sense of the world. These constitute an archive of "available" alternatives to European modernity.

Yet, most of us suffer from a fundamental elitism in contemporary social thought, which holds that knowledge is not produced at the site of living, where multiple processes of reproduction of life intersect; rather it is produced where life ceases to be alive, where human experience turns into dead raw materials to be intellectually processed into thought-categories, i.e. at the institutional location of academia. We believe that there are multiple sites of knowledge production in a society, the academy being only one of them. Academic practices constitute a distinct social process. As a specific social process, it has a distinct institutional location or base (university, research institutes, journals and publishing houses), its unique rules of production and dissemination of knowledge statements (papers, conferences, university lectures, participation in the media as experts, etc.) and its particular effect on other social processes (construction of meaning, production of world-outlooks, etc.). But, most importantly, professional academia establishes its social status on the basis of a distinction between knowledge and non-knowledge and by claiming to be the sole site for production of "knowledge."

Perhaps one can allude here to Gramsci's famous quote that while all humans are intellectuals, not all perform the work of (professional) intellectuals. Although of course Gramsci is not concerned with the particular issue that we are dealing with here. Also note that our argument is not that professional intellectuals do not perform an important function in society. Indeed they do, however, that function a) obviously cannot be delinked from the position they occupy in the capitalist world-economy and culture (i.e. there are no universal intellectuals) and b) professional intellectuals (specific or otherwise) are not the only producers of knowledge, nor even "the most important" by whatever criterion.

Here the concept being developed at the *Vidya Ashram* in Varanasi becomes immediately relevant. This is the concept of "Dialogues on Knowledge in Society". The emphasis is not on conflict between the various knowledge production sites (universities, schools, monasteries and mosques, small businesses, ordinary life) which certainly exist, but instead on the possibility of engaging them in dialog with each other.

## 25.4 Bibliography

Bhattacharya, R. and Basole, A. "The Phantom of Liberty: Mo(der)nism and Postcolonial Imaginations in India," in Rajani, K. Kanth (ed) (2009), *The Challenge of Eurocentrism: Global Perspectives, Policy, and Prospects,* Palgrave Macmillan, Basingstoke.

Chakrabarty, D. (2000), *Provincializing Europe: Postocolonial Thought and Historical Difference.* Princeton University Press, Princeton.

Mowitt, J. (2001), "In the Wake of Eurocentrism: An Introduction." *Cultural Critique,* Minneapolis, v. 47.

# 26

# The Autonomous Global University*

*Avinash Jha*

## 26.1 Knowledge Against Society

The 20th century has been a century of knowledge production. It has also been a century of unprecedented violence. The knowledge that we produce is eventually turned against ourselves and against the whole of society. While this was also true of the modern university, knowledge society that is in the making now seems to be singularly designed to appropriate knowledge and turn it against the producers of knowledge in the service of global capital and global machineries of violence.

The university in the modern era was the prime location of knowledge production, which claimed to take society out of the darkness of ignorance into enlightenment and from a regime of scarcity to a condition of abundance. While the university did produce a great deal of knowledge the motion of this knowledge was such that it ended up being a handmaiden of profit and domination. On account of its sole authority in knowledge production, the university became complicit in suppression of society's knowledge. The bargain that the university made offered a space of pure enquiry, of knowledge for knowledge's sake, of pursuit of knowledge without interference from power. The university defended this privilege as much as it could. Now this privilege is being withdrawn.

The university has undergone major transformations in the 20th century. A massive expansion of the university has been

* Originally written in 2008 for an online dialogue conducted by the Edu-Factory Collective (www.edu-factory.org).

going on. Millions have access to higher education. Protocols of knowledge production in the university have been challenged from various directions. Women, blacks, erstwhile colonized, workers, rebels—all have challenged the higher education scenario in the world. But along with these processes of democratization of knowledge, a parallel movement of militarization and industrialization of knowledge production was ushered in with the Manhattan project. These two processes, of democratization and militarization/industrialization, seem to have come to a head in the 1960s, which saw numerous student actions on campuses across the world.

Now the global order is reinventing itself. In the information age, there is not going to be a privileged set of knowledge producers who will be allowed an autonomous space, a safe haven to explore and invent. Knowledge will be harnessed from the whole cultural field and subjected to regimes of cognitive measurement, knowledge management, and information enclosures.

## 26.2 Hierarchies of Knowledge and Labour

Exploitation of labour was the hallmark of industrial society. Exploitation of knowledge is now being added to exploitation of labour to build the foundations of a new capitalist system. Knowledge from all locations—university, Internet, religions, ordinary life—are sought to be harnessed and exploited in the service of the building of this "knowledge society." Technologies of virtuality play an essential role in this management of knowledge. Living knowledge and its exploitation is an essential ingredient of the new production systems unlike the earlier systems, which depended on knowledge embodied in machines and routines. These developments open the way for a self-awareness of workers as bearers and producers of knowledge. There is no contradiction between knowledge and labour, nor is there a gulf between "knowledgeable bodies" and "labouring bodies." Such contradictions stem from the division between mental and physical labour—a relic of the earlier industrial civilization. However, it is now perhaps the time to foreground the human being as an epistemic being.

The category of labor as it was constituted in the older

capitalist system and as deployed even by socialist and communist ideologies of workers' emancipation implies a hierarchy of labor in society—intellectual labour, industrial labour, women's labour, artisanal labour, agricultural labour, primitive labour, the idler and so on. It seems to us that this labour hierarchy is implicitly constructed on the basis of the knowledge hierarchy among the various kinds of knowledge that exist in society. University knowledge and modern science and technology occupied the space of knowledge while women's knowledge, farmers' knowledge, artisanal knowledge, tribal knowledge were considered a product of habit or accident, if not expressions of pure superstition. We reject such descriptions and the resulting hierarchy. Even in the modern era, such knowledge in society that we call *lokavidya* has played an important role in the survival of the people whose knowledge traditions these constitute.

If we grant that there is no hierarchy among various locations of knowledge in society and that all kinds of knowledge have a role to play in the reconstruction of society, the grounds for non-hierarchical solidarities across many boundaries is prepared. Moreover, epistemic recognition of *lokavidya* opens us to a vast realm of living knowledge traditions in society as forms of autonomous knowledge activity. This also creates the condition for people to see their own knowledge traditions as sources of strength, and not only as means of survival.

Unlike the industrial society, the knowledge society does recognize *lokavidya*. But *lokavidya* is recognized only in order to economically benefit from it. In fact, the relation that knowledge society constructs with any knowledge is essentially one of economic exploitation. Knowledge society is built on the integration of any knowledge by economic exploitation. Autonomous Global University (AGU)

The Edu-factory Collective's proposal of the formation of AGU is a bold idea. It has the potential to project a transformative perspective on knowledge society. We support its formation.

To say that AGU is autonomous is to say that the knowledge activity of such a university is free from political interference, economic pressures and military requirements. This requires that it has a political and ideological significance of its own. Autonomy in the context of knowledge in this age of corporatization means above all the regulation of knowledge activities by epistemic norms derived from knowledge activity outside the market. Knowledge activity outside the market relates to a large part of knowledge in society, *lokavidya* and various cultural, political and other expressions and representations which are consciously kept autonomous.

Autonomous Global University (AGU) is not just another site of knowledge production. It is a site of cooperation among knowledge producers and a site of non-cooperation with the global regime of knowledge. It is a university in so far as its stock activity is knowledge activity. We can perhaps think of it as a union of networks and organizations. Of necessity, it will operate mainly through the virtual realm. But it is composed of acts of resistance and acts of organization on the ground.

AGU values all kinds of labour and all kinds of knowledge equally. AGU looks at knowledge as a means of reconstruction of society and individuals. AGU looks at knowledge as a means of liberation, livelihood, culture. AGU thus works for the recognition and representation of all forms of knowledge in society. AGU seeks to step out on the periphery of time and gaze into the future; it seeks to build an imagination of the future society which is not just a variant of global capitalism. Through its activities it seeks to create idioms of global emancipatory transformations.

AGU looks at why our knowledge is turned against ourselves. It seeks to build solidarities across borders of the university and within the universities, solidarity of all bearers and producers of knowledge. It is not a bastion of creativity and production. It is an organ of dialogue, solidarity and organization. It seeks to organize the relatively empowered section of knowledge producers which are located in the university in order to challenge the global mechanisms of exploitation and violence. It seeks to expose the ways and means by which knowledge becomes an instrument of profit and a weapon against society. AGU seeks to emancipate knowledge from this condition.

For this purpose, AGU seeks to spread the virus of non-cooperation to all universities. We have read about the various auto-education initiatives in the earlier round of discussion—in Argentina, Europe, US, India—and about movements of students and precarious workers in Greece and other places. The various auto-education initiatives and movements at the borders of the university and within it can be read as acts of non-cooperation with the institutionalization of a new order of knowledge. This new order of knowledge exploits students, teachers and their knowledge for profit and control. These acts resist the enfeeblement and enslavement of knowledge producers and seek to liberate knowledge from the clutches of dons, managers, and rent seekers.

AGU seeks to link these acts of non-cooperation to create forums and launch activities that direct an uncompromising light on the prevailing order of things. By being a site of dialogues and translations, AGU seeks to sow the seeds of a social movement of knowledge, a *knowledge satyagraha*. Knowledge *satyagraha* means the insistence that knowledge activities be regulated by epistemic norms independent of the market, the insistence that knowledge be linked to values of truth and justice. "Non-cooperation" and *satyagraha* as forms of political action are legacies most notably of the non-violent mass movement against the British Empire during the Indian freedom struggle and the civil rights movement in the US.

AGU seeks to participate in a reconstruction of knowledge and initiate a reconstitution of university. It explores ways and means of building and instituting a new imagination of university that operates in an environment of knowledge abundance. It seeks to reinterpret and reorganize the vast amounts of knowledge that have been generated by the university so far. It challenges the prevailing institutionalized differentiations of knowledge like the one between the sciences and arts. It seeks to reinterpret human sciences by inscribing a human being as an epistemic being at its core. It seeks to develop new principles of integration of knowledge.

We understand that the challenge of actualizing a vision like this is immense. All the tools available in the virtual realm —website, mailing list, wiki, blogs, social networking—will have to be configured and reconfigured. The relation between the virtual life and the ordinary life will also have to be reflected upon, since we are seeking to connect the two. The new institutional form of AGU will have to be elaborated further and its relation with other institutional forms defined. Since this is the first time we are discussing the construction of an autonomous global university, we felt we will try to articulate a possible vision for AGU, rather than try to work out all aspects of it.

## 26.3 *Lokavidya* and AGU

From the point of view of relationship with the market *lokavidya* activity may be divided into three parts. First, *lokavidya* which has been coopted by the global market often through the new techniques brought into existence by the Internet. Secondly, *lokavidya* activity that operates on the margins of the market. This however contributes greatly to the creation of riches by its numbers and vastness. Household production of all types based both on artisanry and farming belong to this category. Thirdly, those *lokavidya* processes that have no immediate economic value attached to them and are therefore outside the market.

Globalization has tried to construct trade routes and linkages for an economic exploitation of all such activity but what gets left out still constitutes large part of social reality, at least in countries like India. A lot of work at home and in remote geographical areas is of this type. Women's work in the house which includes bringing up children, daily healthcare, balanced food, cooking, sanitation and cleanliness, decoration, etc. is work of this type which is definitely based on a steady understanding and knowledge of human beings and their surroundings. To this category also belongs a large part of the activity of tribals and indigenous people in remote areas. They grow food on small plots of land to eat, make and repair implements of their use, build houses, and collect forest produce as food, medicine and fuel. Their life is split into two parts, one constituted by all these knowledge-based activities outside the market and other of work in the market as workers for wages. Similarly, almost all households, including often the very organized urban households too, have these two components, one of women's work outside the market and the other of men and women earning through the market.

So there is this huge expanse of activities of women and tribals and part of the activity of peasants and artisans, which is outside the market and is based on their knowledge that is modified and upgraded regularly and is full of innovations. We would like to further explore, and would like to invite others to explore, what relevance this aspect of *lokavidya* can have in constructing an epistemic frame of reference which may provide the guidelines for knowledge activity of an autonomous university.

### 26.4 *Vidya Ashram*

We end with a brief introduction to some activities and plans of *Vidya Ashram* which bear an affinity with the initiative for the construction of an autonomous global university. *Vidya Ashram* (www.*vidyaashram*.org) was set up three years ago at Sarnath near Varanasi. Sarnath is the place where Buddha first expounded his philosophy of becoming.

Among other activities, we have organized a series of dialogues on Knowledge in Society in various fora associated with the World Social Forum process during the last four years. The dialogues were held at Hyderabad, Mumbai, Karachi, Delhi. We intend to take these dialogues to universities, among computer professionals and generally among people. We hope that these dialogues will lead to the formation of a new academy. This academy, which might possibly be named the *Lokavidya* Academy, will seek to reconfigure relations between different kinds of knowledge in society and between knowledge and society.

Last year *Vidya Ashram* formed an Emancipation of Knowledge Forum. A group of 30 young men and women from the Sarnath region have joined to shape this forum. Attempts to extend it around Varanasi are going on. We hope that this forum can develop as a platform for various organizations and movements to come together to explore the political significance of the knowledge question which might lead to new radical forms of politics.

# V

# LOKAVIDYA JAN ANDOLAN (LJA)

*The pieces in this section were part of an online dialogue conducted in preperation for the First International Conference of the Lokavidya Jan Andolan, held on November 12-14, 2011, in Vidya Ashram, Sarnath, Varanasi, India*

**– Editor**

# 27

# First International Conference, Announcement

## Social Movements and the Knowledge Standpoint

In India displacement of people from their land, their houses and their work has emerged as the single largest concern of the social movements. Movements of peasants against forced acquisition of land and for remunerative prices , movements of *adivasis* (indigenous people) and local communities for local control of natural resources and against ecological and environmental destruction, movements of slum dwellers for civic and social facilities, and the movements of hawkers and artisans against systematic demolition of the local markets and inroads by the corporations and the global market, have all converged to become a single movement against displacement and eviction, though managed and organized separately. Those trying to organize these people are struggling to find pathways to confront the ruling dispensation.

All these people, the displaced, the communities they belong to, have never gone to college and live by the knowledge they possess, called *lokavidya,* which they have acquired from elders, from peers, in the community, at the site of work, through experiments and by their own genius. Displacement alters the conditions of their life in such a way that *lokavidya* is no more able to serve their life needs and thus turns them into sources of cheap labour. It is this severance of *lokavidya* from their lives, which needs to be fought at all costs. In fact *lokavidya,* that is people's knowledge, skills, ways of thinking, values, methods of organization, aesthetic and ethical sensibilities, in short, their world of knowledge as a part of their own world, is the main source of their strength. *Lokavidya* is also what is common to this multitude, which is at the receiving end. It is important to understand that the emancipatory pathways today traverse through the world of knowledge. The *lokavidya* standpoint is the people's standpoint in the Age of Information.

## *Lokavidya*: Knowledge Claim

Peasants and indigenous people the world over are in a new mood of assertion. Expressing, articulating and representing in ways that are their own, these people are staking a claim to their inalienable right to live by their own knowledge, values and belief systems and acquire knowledge that they deem fit for them. Asia, Africa, South America, everywhere a new kind of turmoil is in the making, promising to produce a new unity of the oppressed and the dispossessed, this time based on what is common in their understanding of the world around them, in their relationship with nature, namely based on based on *lokavidya*.

This means that peasants and *adivasis*, artisans and women, pavement retailers and workers need to stake a claim for *lokavidya*. *This is not a claim for survival, this is a claim to build a new world.* They need to claim that a radical challenge to capital and commercialization of knowledge an be posed only by *lokavidya*. They need to also claim that only *lokavidya* provides the knowledge bases for a society based on truth, on social and economic equality. We need to understand that till these claims are staked, we shall remain prisoners of our preconceived notions of radical social change, without effect. Such a *lokavidya* knowledge claim can give birth to a new imagination, new thought in the realm of economics, society, politics and culture. The process of giving shape to such claims is the process of *Lokavidya Jan Andolan*.

## *Lokavidya Jan Andolan*

The global economic and ecological crises have exposed the thought and institutions that have enriched a few by making the majority starve and by bringing nature to the brink of destruction. *Lokavidya Jan Andolan* is a knowledge movement of this majority, that is of those people, who have been dubbed as the ignorant masses by the science establishments, the universities and the modern state. The idea that there is a sea of knowledge outside the university is not alien to most people in the world. Knowledge is widely spread in society and the idea that knowledge is widely spread, has a very wide spread too. That is, people know and they know that they know. And yet neither these people nor the knowledge they possess have dignity in society. Their knowledge has no economic returns, so people are poor. It has no respect in the public domain, so people are culturally marginal. It has no clear relation with people's organizations, therefore people are politically irrelevant. There is a need for a political movement, a space where people can mobilize on the basis of their knowledge. This movement is the *Lokavidya Jan Andolan.*

The conference is an attempt to bring together the organizers of the movements of peasants and artisans, indigenous peoples and small trades people, women and youth on a knowledge platform, which is a platform of their knowledge, *lokavidya*. It is from this platform that the claim can be staked that it is in *lokavidya* that the solution lies.

## Knowledge Movements Worldwide

The world is witnessing a new kind of movement, a people's knowledge movement with entirely new political imaginations. The ideas of *lokavidya* in India, Rights of Mother Earth in Bolivia, Rights of Nature in Ecuador, Food Sovereignty by the International Peasants Movement Via Campesina, and Cognitive Capitalism and the idea of Knowledge Liberation in Europe and America are indications of a churning hitherto unknown to political debates. There is an insistence in all these that people are knowledgeable and that their knowledge and beliefs are not inferior in any way to knowledge doled out in the name of science. There is an understanding that the damage done to people and nature over the past centuries, which is multiplied manifold in this digital era of the New Empire, is correctable only by those who have not been fully subsumed into the systems of modern knowledge.

*Lokavidya Jan Andolan* argues that these and all such struggles worldwide constitute a new fraternity of struggles, building a worldwide knowledge movement of the people, a movement of people's knowledge, a movement of knowledge in society.

# 28

# *Lokavidya Jan Andolan*—Inaugurating a Dialogue

*Amit Basole*

With this post we are starting an online dialogue which, it is hoped, will prepare the ground for the first international conference of the *Lokavidya Jan Andolan* to be held in Varanasi from November 12-14, 2011. During the course of the dialogue, we look forward to hearing from many different people and perspectives. This is not a discussion that is intended to come to a conclusion. Rather, it aims to broaden the voices within the movement and create new avenues for a politics based on *lokavidya*. It is undertaken in the spirit that at this stage of movement-building, breadth of views is to be preferred to cut-and-dry formulations.

In this first post, I address the following questions in brief. What does it mean to stake a claim for *lokavidya* in the public discourse? What could be the content of this claim and why is it a contemporary political statement? The tone of my remarks is assertive but this is only a strategy adopted to make the focus clear. The points made below should be taken as points of debate and departure.

The majority of the people in India and across the world have been told that they are ignorant and in need of education before they can participate fully in society. Politically, even when they constituted the mass-base, they have been sidelined in intellectual terms. And often they ended up fighting someone else's battle. But the people know that they are knowledgeable and that they can construct a new world based on their knowledge. Peasants, *adivasis*, artisans, shopkeepers, students, women, ordinary people are on the move everywhere in struggles and movements across the world. They form not just the mass base of these movements, but also the intellectual base, they supply not only the bodies but also the brains. Gandhiji claimed that before we begin a struggle, we must examine our own sources of strength, which form our starting position. We cannot begin a struggle that moves in our favour if we base it on a foundation which is not ours and that we do not understand. This is Marx's claim also. The *lokavidya* position is that the people's own knowledge is the source of their strength. The *Lokavidya Jan Andolan* (LJA) consists of people rising up to say so.

The various people's struggles against displacement from lands, forests, and livelihoods, struggles for environmental justice and food sovereignty, and many more, are all fraternal struggles which are unified in the yet unspoken claim that across class, caste, tribal, religious and gender divisions, the majority society is coming together to shed the stigma of being "uneducated." LJA is the realization that only if politics is based on the people's own knowledge can it be on their initiative, can it serve their interests. This does not mean that gender, caste or class struggles are unimportant. But it does mean that these struggles must also be based on *lokavidya*, that is they must be driven by people's perspectives on what oppresses them and what the solutions of that oppression are. No longer can "educated" women claim to speak for all women or "educated" workers for all workers.

The time is ripe to put forth such a knowledge claim because the hegemony of Science and the University are being challenged everywhere, creating new opportunities. Disillusionment with capitalism and with the Science-society which have together brought unprecedented suffering to the majority world is strong today. So is disillusionment with the old politics of change. We make no grand claims for a new politics, but we do strive to bring such a politics into existence. No longer is it possible to have the faith in Science and the University that characterized 20$^{th}$ century political thought across the political spectrum. This loss of faith has tangible political manifestations today. Across Europe students have risen to liberate knowledge from the University. Declarations such as the Right of Mother Earth (Bolivia) openly state that the solutions to ecological problems lie not with Science, but with the indigenous peoples of the world.

But the politics of *lokavidya* is not a repetition of the 20th century battle of tradition versus modernity. That battle was lost by tradition and resulted in a pyrrhic victory for modernity. *Lokavidya* is ever-contemporary knowledge of contemporary communities who create and sustain life today. Till the political position is staked that peasants and artisans lay claim to knowledge traditions in no way inferior to any other, struggles against displacement will appear to be resistance to "development." A *Lokavidya Jan Andolan* is born when a people's movement declares that the people's knowledge and way of life is not inferior to those in the cities or in the corporate world. That it does not only fight to save livelihoods, it fights to build a new society.

Finally, does speaking of *lokavidya* mean being "against education" or conspiring to keep the majority out of colleges and universities? No. The *lokavidya* claim is that as long as education is synonymous with the system currently in place, this education can only grant a small number of people a government or corporate job. The others, the vast majority, will forever be kept "in the waiting room of history." But if the claim is staked that knowledge exists with the people too, they too can design education systems, run schools and universities, and absorb any knowledge that benefits them, on their own terms, then the basis of the present system will collapse as will its monopoly on the good life.

The foregoing is intended to stake a few claims, perhaps in provocative and controversial terms, to get a dialogue going. The *lokavidya* perspective eschews political blueprints or general prescriptions. A *lokavidya*-based struggle in Bolivia can and should take shape very differently from the one in India. There is no insistence on a single party, movement or institution.

In the next ten weeks or so, we hope to discuss:

- what is understood by the terms *lokavidya* and *Lokavidya Jan Andolan*,

- what is the significance of taking a knowledge perspective on the struggles presently going on,
- have there been such things as people's knowledge movements in the past,
- can movements over issues of language, identity, caste, be thought of as knowledge movements,
- how do the international struggles over production of knowledge relate to the people's struggles against displacement, etc.
- what should be the strategies of the LJA?

And this is by no means an exhaustive list. We invite you to participate in the dialogue either my commenting on the scheduled posts or contributing your own post.

# 29

# *Lokavidya* and Science

*Avinash Jha*

When speaking of *lokavidya*, and science too, it would be less confusing if we can distinguish between two levels on which we speak. One is the empirical level of description. By *lokavidya*, we refer to knowledge that is spread out in societies, communities and individuals. It may be knowledge of food, farming, health, child rearing, artisanship, mobile phones, steel, art, music and so on. Science also refers empirically to the various sciences. At this level there is a great variety among different kinds of knowledge within *lokavidya* as well as within science. Seen in this manner, *lokavidya* as well as science can be seen constituted by a myriad of knowledge traditions. As knowledge, they are all knowledge, even if with different ontologies, values, methods, etc. What is distinctive of *lokavidya* is that it is carried upon the stream of ordinary life.

In describing the matter in this way, we are already employing a particular perspective on knowledge. *Lokavidya* is also this perspective (presented here as I see it). This is the second level of talk about *lokavidya*. 'Science' (as a perspective on knowledge) described the situation in a completely different way. According to this scientific perspective, society is the hotbed of superstitions, imaginative narratives, and some knowledge acquired through trial and error. In this perspective, the emancipation of humankind lies in slowly replacing all this pseudo-knowledge in society with proper scientific knowledge. It is this perspective, which has shaped the institution that is science and the place of science in society. One important feature of this perspective is that it does not recognize itself as a perspective. The way knowledge is produced in science is considered simply to be the most natural (and rational) way of pursuing knowledge, once we are 'enlightened' and free of all superstitions.

The l*okavidya* perspective is a contemporary perspective on knowledge and politics. It sees in society an abundance of knowledge. All societies are knowledge societies in some way. When this knowledge is denied, all initiative is sucked out of society, as it perhaps happened in more developed societies where any autonomous knowledge activity is seen as disruptive. In the *lokavidya* perspective, there are no impermeable boundaries in knowledge. Knowledge travels both ways. In the 'knowledge society' that is being shaped today in the information age, knowledge travels from fields, farms, homes and workshops to the global network as well as from the labs, networks, etc. to ordinary life. The latter is termed piracy. In the WEB 2.0, social networking that is happening is structured to function on the basis of the knowledge of the people who are contributing. It is building structures to tap knowledge from the people. Science is part of this structure and contemporary scientists are worried that the knowledge they produce is taken away from the domain of the society and put into the hands of the profit-seeking and violence-spawning behemoths.

Science is two-faced, just as the Internet. Noble and the ignoble mix here. Roots of this entrenched ambiguity in matters of knowledge lie at least in part in the scientific perspective which evolved in the 19th and 20th centuries. Even utopian thinkers of the Internet, 'free knowledge' advocates, are unable to extricate themselves from this conundrum.

The *lokavidya* standpoint on knowledge proposes equality in the sphere of knowledge as the basis for the making of an egalitarian society. This equality is posed in terms of locations of knowledge. Prima facie, knowledge at various locations in society, like university, religion, ordinary life, ethnic groups, political and social formations are equal. There cannot be a fiat that knowledge gained in this way or organized in that way only is knowledge. This equality goes beyond the relativism/ absolutism debate. To someone schooled in the 20th century philosophies of knowledge, the assertions of *lokavidya* may seem strangely positivist and plural at the same time.

An important set of questions need to be about how such a standpoint on knowledge (or some other) can translate into a political project by connecting to the struggles of those people who were excluded from the 'developments' of the 20th century and are now again on the verge of being sucked into the global economies of exploitation and violence at massively unequal terms. Can staking a claim for *lokavidya* provide energy and direction for such struggles?

# 30

# *Shudra* of the Modern World and *Lokavidya*

*Lalit Kaul*

The protagonists and the apologists of modern science and technology in our country have had unique habitual indulgence, very tall claims of their own contributions in the realm of science and technology. They love to believe in their claims because it gives them sustenance notwithstanding the naked truth that stares them in their face that there has not been any contribution by them worth the name in the world of science and technology that puts India on its map. Nothing brings out this point more succinctly than the stark fact that India, as a modern state, continues to import technology through the process of either collaborations, one time purchase or business agreement. The situation is so pathetic that from design and manufacture of as simple an item as sewing needle to ink pens, fan blades to any electronic gadget, power plant equipment, any state-of-the-art machinery to the sophisticated medical equipment, etc., nothing, just nothing has a stamp of Indian genius on it. This community has had only tall claims to make to bewilder an outsider to such an extent that these self-styled scientists and technologists are held in awe by everyone.

## The Grand Failure

The National Science & Technology Policy Document, 1975, among other things laid emphasis on self-reliance and self-sufficiency in scientific and technological pursuits. This document was brought out under the leadership of the late

Prime Minister, Indira Priyadrshani (Nehru) Gandhi. Prior to this document were the Five Year Plans that laid the foundations for the pursuit of modern science and technology in our country.

These were not just hollow words, but the intentions were made quite visible by the kind and quantum of spending the respective central governments took upon to help establish premier scientific laboratories, institutions, and infrastructure for pursuing science and technology development. This was done on the basis of the plans submitted by the 'leading scientific minds' of every generation and era ostensibly to fulfil the aims and objectives set forth in the aforesaid mentioned Policy Document and the Five Year Plans.

The resulting outcome was 1) buying of large chunks of real estate at prime locations in premier cities of India that definitely caused displacement of traditionally productive populace and in retrospect, a complete and total halt to any kind of productive activity, 2) building of huge laboratories equipped with the then state-of-the-art equipment and duly air conditioned wherever required, 3) residential accommodation for the 'brilliant' minds who were to put India on the world map of Science & Technology, and 4) clubs and recreation avenues, parks, hospital facilities for healthcare, schools for emerging thinkers, markets and what have you.

The enterprise stopped with large/medium scale recruitment of supporting staff and the scientists, technologists, etc. The biggest question that remained to be answered was: what to do with the established infrastructure and manpower? This question still remains unanswered, even though huge investments continue to be made in 'indigenous' 'research and development' activities.

Unable to relate themselves to the requirements of the Indian state, the manufacturing sector, the health services, the energy requirements for the near and distant future, etc., the natural outcome was a decent, quiet, and deep burial of the 'self-reliant' part of the National Science & Technology Policy.

From now onwards the catch word was to be 'self-sufficiency' and this meant never ending 'assimilation' of collaborated technologies and the so-called R&D centre, big, medium, and small-sized manufacturing units were to only absorb the manufacturing processes and churn out products that were bound to lose quality and market competitiveness and become stale—over the years—because of technological obsolescence. The classic examples are the Ambassador and Premier Padmini cars. The bankruptcy of Indian entrepreneurs was overwhelmingly highlighted when LML Vespa (a two wheeler) was marketed with side indicators. Till then this feature of a two wheeler was incomprehensible to the native 'entrepreneur'.

The affordable units went in for new collaborations, whereas the lesser ones ended winding up their enterprise.

While all this happened before the era of 'Globalization and Liberalization' the engineering and scientific elite in the 'premier' institutions christened as '... of Science & Technology' or 'Engineering' remained as mute spectators to the whole scenario and never was any worthwhile effort made at a purposeful collaboration between Indian enterprise and institutions to tackle the issue of non-upgradation of technology (manufacturing processes) by collective application of minds.

**The Era of Globalization and Liberalization**

This era witnessed over flooding of Indian markets with technologically innovated products. The Indian scientific and engineering community had long lost the race and that tantamount to colossal betrayal of the national aspirations enumerated by the then political leadership in the National Science & Technology Policy Document, 1975.

During the intervening one and a half decades the character of political leadership had also undergone a kind of metamorphosis in that it had no continuity with the leadership of yore. The collaboration between the politicians of the day, the self-proclaimed entrepreneurs and academicians was so innate and expedient that all the pretensions of product-oriented research and development were divorced and the Indian markets were thrown open to multinationals. The Indian scientists, engineers, and technologists by virtue of their deeds over the decades in post-independent India found themselves confined to the dustbin of history with no role to play in the modern ways of economic development except to implement the design of their masters for whatever their labour was priced at. The indentured labour was resurrected, in a seemingly dignified way though.

However, the 'Temples of Modern India' that lay in ruins had to be continued with for the reason that, it generated cheap manpower for the multinationals and their Indian caricatures to tap; its employees constituted a dominant and respectable section in the middle class; and the younger generations continued to aspire to join them as post training they would gain respectability from the society they belonged to. Therefore the character of these institutions underwent a wholesome change in that instead of project-related technical reviews material budget reviews occupied the centre stage because the governments of the day decreed that a basic minimum amount had to be spent on research and development activities. This led to expansions in terms of infrastructure; induction of more manpower, etc. The question "To What Use?" lost relevance as winning the race for spending the allocated funds was the new born aim and it got directly related to tax rebates. This vicious cycle of spending public money and misleading the very public is going on without inhibitions—no questions asked; none answered. The undocumented colossal waste of public money continues unquestioned.

The major and most significant contribution of the era of Globalization and Liberalization lies in the classification of modern societies into two castes: the *Shudra* and the *Brahmin*; the *Brahmin* personifying the knowledge and *Shudra* the multitude of hands to perpetuate the dominance of the *Brahminical* world view. The *Brahmin* originates from Europe and the while the *Shudra* is our own scientist, engineer and technologist.

### *Lokavidya*

Quite contrary to the pampering of 'emerging' scientists, engineers and technologists of modern India by the governments of the day over the last 67 years, the native *Brahmins* (the owners of the knowledge of traditional science and technology) were all through treated as *Shudras* (ignorant, uninformed and steeped in 'superstitions') deserving of contempt and always usable as an available commodity in the service of the new emerging class. What is strikingly remarkable, though, is that the designated *Shudra* (owners of *lokavidya*) has managed to retain his productivity with the help of his *lokavidya* against all odds and hostile conditions, whereas the pampered ones languished in unproductiveness only to be relegated to a *Shudra* in the modern world.

Herein lies the difference between the two in that the owner of *lokavidya* has survived all the onslaughts since the year 1757; has shown the capability to fight (within his means) injustice and oppression meted out to him; and is now trying to regroup to fight the predator in the garb of economic reforms that is threatening to deprive him of all his possessions; whereas the modern *Shudra* remained a rootless entity unable to identify with the modern ways, devoid of any spirit of ownership and therefore ready to capitulate for his survival. While the owner of *lokavidya* draws his strength from his capability for independent enterprise, the modern *Shudra* is dependent on his *Brahmin* for survival.

Whereas, the designated *Shudra* has a valid claim over knowledge production, the modern *Shudra* can afford no such claim because the process of economic reforms has thoroughly exposed him. *Lokavidya* has roots in the soil of this land, whereas the modern *Shudra*'s knowledge system has roots in the alien lands; that is the reason why *lokavidya* is here to stay.

# 31

# Farmers' Movement and LJA

*Girish Sahasrabudhe*

One of the most important movements of the *lokavidyadhar samaj* that LJA seeks continuity with is the farmers' movement. Not only is it the largest non-violent non-political movement in the most recent past, its genesis was in forging of a unity not imaginable within the then existing modes of thought. The lasting nature of this unity is evident, if not in continuation of joint struggles on those scales, then in the continuing perception of identity of interests of all the farmers. Moreover, this perception is today shared by others both within and outside the *lokavidyadhar samaj*. However, this unity can once again blossom only as part of a larger unity of *lokavidyadhar samaj*.

The last quarter of the 20th century was when the farmers' movement in the country arose, spread, peaked and then scattered into segments. Large states spanning the entire length and breadth of the country were engulfed by the movement. The country witnessed huge, determined gatherings of farmers in far-flung areas and state and the national capitals alike, putting forth clear demands. Issues raised ranged over agricultural prices, movement of agricultural produce, farm loans, farm subsidies, policies of import and export of farm produce, and land acquisition from farmers. While the movement started in the so-called green revolution areas, in its later stages it was actually the so-called backward regions which kept it alive. Organizations of farmers in different states differed in their emphases on issues raised and the debate on these never stopped. Yet a national coordination committee of these organizations functioned as a strong and effective body for a fairly long time and directed organization of major agitations.

The most important contribution of the farmers' movement was its assertion that the reasons for rural poverty are external to the rural society. The exploitative mechanisms do not lie within villages but spring from official state policy. This policy sustained and deepened the Bharat-India divide. This understanding of the genesis of poverty stood in direct opposition to the received wisdom of the time, which saw poverty as the result of anything from disparate land holdings to laziness and ignorance of the farmer. It is common wisdom today largely due to the farmers' movement. Moreover, it was clarity on this that made it possible for separate movements led by leaders with widely different personalities and outlooks to forge a loose but strong alliance in the form of a national coordination committee.

The ideological expression of this understanding was the declaration that poverty is artificial, and the active principle, that the farmer is capable of taking care of himself once freed from the clutches of the demon of state policy. By this the movement rejected lock, stock and barrel all theories which put the blame for poverty on forces within rural society. It also declared the farmer as knowledgeable, the community of farmers as capable of organizing their life and society without any external aid. The practical expression of the understanding was the declaration of a non-political creed. By this the movement resisted all tactics and machinations springing forth from these theories of poverty, recognizing them for what they were—attempts at division of rural society and disruption of its unity in struggle.

Globalization proved to be the nemesis of the large unity forged by the farmers' movement. It created pathways of greater opportunities for those in more commercialized forms of agriculture, for those relatively nearer loan, finance and political structures. It also allowed the state leading the globalizing economy to pretend that it is the saviour of the farmer. The more backward regions knew better and the farmers' movement remained strong in these areas for a relatively longer time. The unity forged by the farmers' movement came under fire. Today, after a period of sporadic and separate struggles the movement is again picking up. Two of the important issues are the question of dry-land agriculture and forced land acquisitions.

Even during the peak of the farmers' movement there was no doubt that both in terms of ideological position and intensity of mobilization the question of dry-land agriculture was central to the movement. The dry-land farmer is the farthest removed from benefits of government programmes and subsidies. Most subsidies relate to fertilizers, seeds, insecticides and electricity. These are designed to increase marketable surpluses of food grain and industrial raw material and make no sense for non-irrigated agriculture. With the march of globalization and liberalization and the flight of popular politics from the concerns of responsibility towards rural poverty, it is now impossible to find even isolated measures, which can be claimed to have provided a crucial timely helping hand to the dry-land farmer. That is to say that in a system, which is exploitative for all farmers, the dry-land farmer bears the greatest burden. On the other hand, it is precisely this farmer, who has sustained agriculture in the face of all odds. It is he who devises novel strategies each season, each month and each day in order to face a new calamity and to continue to feed others. It is his *lokavidya* that makes this possible. A *gyan panchayat* held in Nagpur last year formulated this position by resolving to demand that the government must take steps to recognize the dry-land farmer as the first researcher and to re-establish him as the engine of agricultural research. Recently the Punjabrao Deshmukh Krishi Vidyapeeth, one of the two leading agricultural universities in Maharashtra was put under the public scanner for having failed to come up with agricultural strategies, which could have prevented the spate of suicides by Vidarbha farmers. Under pressure, the PKV took a small step in the direction of conceding primacy of research by the farmers. It has announced that it will take steps to recognize 'need-based innovations' by farmers on their fields and that it will organize conferences of such researcher farmers. No doubt this is a small dent in the arrogance of an official-entrenched research establishment. No doubt also that there are any number of ways in which this start can, and probably will, be brought to an end. But it is a vindication of the *lokavidya* of the farmer in the public domain.

The question of land acquisitions has acquired huge dimensions. Restricted earlier to the vicinity of large cities, today the epidemic has spread to widely scattered areas. Witness the displacement of farmers for about a hundred thermal power plants planned for Vidarbha. Here the farmers losing their land are engaged in the struggle for better compensation and other farmers of the region fear loss of water meant for irrigation. Land acquisition is disruptive of all that belongs to the affected, those who are displaced from their land as well as those others in the region who escape this fate. It affects farmers in ways essentially the same as those experienced by other *lokavidyadhar* communities. Even the most lucrative compensations must make the farmer feel like the master stage actor who is asked to leave his stage and audiences and go and perform on the moon because it is so beautiful. In one of the many novel protests that acts of acquisition of land of farmers for power projects has generated, the independent MLA from Amravati District of Vidarbha, Bacchu Kadu threatened *jal samaadhi* with his supporters.

The demands of dry-land farmers do not amount to segregation within the community of farmers. Far from it. Their struggles must be seen from the point of view of forging, and must be taken forward with the aim of consolidating a much larger unity, where all farmers stand together as a large part of the *lokavidyadhar samaj*. Nor can protests against land acquisition be seen as attempts to foist unprofitable backward agriculture on farmers. We must remember that no organization of farmers, engaged as it was against state policies which made agriculture non-remunerative, ever consented to large-scale land acquisitions even if the price is good enough. Surely, this was because these organizations held that consent to sale of land was at best a distress measure on the part of the farmer. Who can be insensitive enough to think that those who hold in their hearts the courage to perform *jal samaadhi* do not know life as they can make it and that they can be led astray either by vain ideals of the glorious past or the virtual reality of the present?

# 32

# A Perspective from the European Students' Movement

*Gigi Roggero*

We are living in a revolutionary situation today. We could reformulate its classical definition in the following way: the governors of global capital cannot live as in the past; the workers, the precarious (informal) workers, the students, the productive multitudes don't want to live as in the past. The recent uprisings and revolts all around Europe (from Greece to France, from Italy to Spain or UK), as well as in other areas of the world, are happening in this context. And the movements in Tunisia, Egypt and North Africa put again the insurrection and revolution on the political agenda, but in a new way: they are definitely beyond and against the borders of the nation-state.

In fact, the context is the double crisis, that is the crisis of the university and the global economic crisis. Or we could say, the crisis of the global university. This term doesn't mean the emergence of a homogeneous or flat world, but the existence of common trends and different forms of translation (as the Bologna Process in Europe). I want to emphasize that to talk of global university and cognitive capitalism doesn't mean to have a Eurocentric point of view, because the traditional dialectic between the centre and periphery is definitely over: in India or in UK, in Brazil or the US, in Australia or China and South Africa, we can see (with different grades of intensity and combination, of course) the whole complex prism of the forms of labour and exploitation, and the new paradigms of the production system. In a stenographic way, I'll point out four of the main trends.

1. The centrality of knowledge in the contemporary forms of labour and production. Talking of knowledge, we have to forget its traditional leftist mythology: in the contemporary capitalism knowledge is a central commodity. In fact, there is no neutrality of knowledge production, it is always a battlefield. But what happens when the knowledge becomes the central source and means of production? Capital cannot manage the social cooperation upstream, and it has to capture it downstream (through intellectual property laws, financialization, etc.). We call living knowledge the new quality of the contemporary living labour. It is the extreme resource and the mortal threat to capital. Since the production is increasingly based on the common cooperation, the crisis becomes permanent.

2. The corporatization of the university. It doesn't mean only the entrance of private funds in the public institutions. Let's take the American and Anglo-Saxon models: the definition of corporate universities doesn't depend on their juridical status, they are both public and private, and both funded by state and corporations' money. Corporate university means that the university itself has to become a corporation, to work on the calculus of cost-benefit, rationality of budget, to be based on profit-rent, to compete in the global education market. It means a university beyond the dialectic between public and private, state and market, because they are two sides of the same capitalist coin. On the point of view of struggles, this means that we have nothing to defend, but what is at stake is the construction of the autonomous and common university. Paraphrasing Marx, the revolution has not to perfect the state machine, but to destroy it.

3. The rise of a new figure of the student. She is no more workforce in apprenticeship, but since she is a producer of knowledge she is immediately a worker, and a precarious (contingent or informal) worker. We could say that there is a continuous overlapping between the education market and labour market (let's think of the "lifelong learning" or the accreditation system). Indeed, the issues of precariousness and devaluation (déclassement) are central in the university

struggles in the last years. Also, it means that the capitalist progressive promises are crashed: the idea of the university as an elevator for the social mobility is definitely over. The precariousness becomes a permanent element.

4. The financialization of education and welfare. In various countries despite the increasing of the fees, there has been an increasing of enrolments as well: how is it possible, in the face of the general precariousness and impoverishment? The answer is, through the system of debt. In the dismantling of the welfare system, the debt was a way to access the social needs (housing, education, healthcare, mobility, etc). We can talk of a financialization of the life. But if we think of the origin of the current crisis, the so-called sub-prime crisis, caused mainly by a proletarian composition who refused to pay back or could not pay back the debt, we see the fragility of the system. We have to claim for a right to bankruptcy for the students and precarious workers, i.e. we have to take the money and not pay back the debt with banks and financial institutions. This is the new level of the struggle to re-appropriate the social richness that we produce in common.

To conclude: a couple of questions for our struggles. On one hand, the space of the struggles and social transformation is no more national, but it is immediately a transnational space. It is impossible to strive against the Bologna Process (process of privatizing and rationalizing universities across Europe) without a European network of struggles. And if we look at Tunisian or North African insurrections, we see a common composition with the European struggles: young people, higher educated, and unemployed or precarious. This networking process at the transnational level is what the Knowledge Liberation Front or the project edu-factory are trying to do. In this common process we have to experiment in a collective way, how to transform the insurrection in revolution, and the destituent power in constituent power. On the other hand, how can we organize the collective autonomy? As mentioned before, the common has a double status: it is what we produce, and what the capital captures; it is the potential of a new social relationship, and what the capital exploits. So the problem is to build up the institutions of the common. They are not happy islands or utopia, but the institutions of the common are the collective organization of our freedom and autonomous cooperation. They have nothing to do with the bureaucracy or the classical idea of institution: on the contrary, they are the destruction of the public and private machine of capitalist capture. How to become an institution of the common? That is to say: how to organize our knowledge production and *lokavidya* not in the marginal spaces, but in the institutions of the common, i.e. in the creation of the new world and social relationship? I think this could be a central question for our initiative.

# 33

# With *Lokavidya* Lies the Solution

*Sunil Sahasrabudhey*

A great fact about *lokavidya* is that it is located in society. Take it away from there and it ceases to be *lokavidya*. Entered into knowledge registers, stored in computers, patented, privatized and reoriented for export or for up market, it turns into a body of information and/or artifacts to be pressed into the advantage of those who are not part of the *lokavidya* world, who do not share the logic, ethics and aesthetics of the world of *lokavidya*, on the contrary, very often look down upon it as something base, primitive, uncivilized. The fish in water when taken out is either eaten away or is kept in an aquarium. The *agaria*, the preservers of the world famous ferrous technology of India, are taken away from the hills of Surguja or the forests of Mandla, either to be turned into the cheapest labour on earth or to be housed with their living art as a show piece in the Indira Gandhi Rashtriya Manav Sangrahalaya in Bhopal. Nothing does greater damage to *lokavidya* than documentation.

Foundations of imperialism and colonialism were laid by the mapping of resources across the world, science providing the knowledge basis to make it possible. It destroyed the economics, politics and society of the people the world over. Now the maps of knowledge. Mapping the knowledge with the people is to provide the foundations of the New Empire, this time based on the knowledge basis provided by the science of information, computers and communication. This is to rob people of the last bastion of strength they still command, namely *lokavidya*. First time as tragedy and second time as farce! Little do they know that this time they have embarked on an enterprise that is doomed to failure.

*Lokavidya* cannot be alienated from the people. There were workers in the city because there were peasants in the countryside, there is the *adivasi* cheap labour on construction sites, because there are *adivasi* communities in the remote areas. The state and the university, the corporations, politicians and the managers of knowledge are up against a mountain which they do not know how to scale, because they do not understand what *lokavidya* is. They see it as traditional knowledge, indigenous knowledge, ethnic knowledge or as community practice. Little do they know that the depth and the variety of the genius of *lokavidya* has kept the world going from day one and shall live as long as humanity does. The new assault is just about two decades old. And we already have the resistances tuned to derive strength from *lokavidya*. The farmers' movement that had started as a movement to secure prices for the farm produce has now moved on to struggles against displacement, to save lands of the farmers and creating new ideas like 'food sovereignty'. The environment movement has moved on to the question of people's control over natural resources and is generating new ideas like the Rights of Mother Earth and Rights of Nature. The celebration of the demise of the trade union movement was barely over when a student movement started taking shape against the 'dead knowledge' of the university and in favour of the 'living knowledge' with the people, their autonomous organizations and the practice of self-education. *Lokavidya* is where all knowledge starts and to which all knowledge must return. Universities may come and go, corporations may come and go, the state may rise and fall.

*Lokavidya Jan Andolan* is the recognition of the fraternity of such struggles across the world. It is to reshape the relations of property, the relations of power and the public discourse, so that people are heard, their initiatives are respected, their knowledge finds a new legitimization to reshape the world. Gandhi is reborn to assure us that the struggles for and by *lokavidya* are indeed the struggles that can deliver mankind from the traps it is in.

# 34

# *Lokavidya* from a Public Health Movement Perspective

*Ritu Priya*

Every society, community, family and individual attempts to understand and grapple with its health problems to minimize them. All attempts to maximize their own health and well-being. Historically, expertise in health emerged with people who keenly observed the experience of health and ill health in their own bodies and of those around them, whether humans, other animal species or even plants. Birthing processes have been one of the natural phenomena requiring support of others and therefore are one of the commonest sites of skill and knowledge accumulation. Childcare, food and nutrition are other similar areas of knowledge development.

As the expertise grows in one area, and expert knowledge gains credence and trust by evidence of its effectiveness, both the expert and the knowledge become seats of special power and dominance. However, the people, who now become 'lay people' in relation to the expert, do retain their own rationality and agency. Besides being socialized into a certain way of life (which includes health-related practices) by their family and community, people add to or modify the practices and knowledge they were socialized into as a result of their own experience and their interaction with the expert system(s). Thereby a third body of knowledge and practice arises that is in consonance with their prevailing social, economic, environmental and cultural context. This is *lokavidya* about health. It is passed on across generations, through oral communication and practice, but is not a static entity. Remaining responsive to the changing context and addition or modifications in available and accessible resources for health, *lokavidya* is a dynamic body of knowledge and practice.

Thus, *lokavidya* about health develops from multiple roots. It is pluralistic in its epistemology and practice. Starting with the traditional or conventional practice in the family or community, people add on new practices according to their perceived needs which the conventional system fails to fulfil. These could be through personal experience of one's own body at the individual level, as in modifications of diets and daily routines. On the other hand, comes new knowledge from sharing of the collective experience and various systems of expert knowledge.

In India, we have textual knowledge and expertise of Allopathy and seven officially recognized other systems—*Ayurveda*, yoga and naturopathy, *Unani*, *Siddha*, Sowa Rigpa and Homeopathy (AYUSH being the official acronym in present use). There is a clear dominance of Allopathy over the AYUSH in the official policy of knowledge generation, knowledge transmission and service delivery. However, informal providers abound, both traditional practitioners and modern forms of them—the dai, the bone-setter, the snake-bite healer, herbalist, the shamans and faith healers, the *Bengali daktar* or Rural Medical Practitioner (RMP). Then there are the traditional home remedies and self-care using modern medication. Finally, there is the *dincharya* and *ritucharya,* that are designed and adopted for promotion of health and well-being, prevention of disease at the collective and individual levels. All these practices have an explanatory knowledge base. So there arises the question—Where is the boundary of *lokavidya*?

Social stratification based on caste, class and gender leads to a wide variation in the nature and context across social and economic sections in any society. While the conventional roots differ because of historical disparities, a body of common knowledge that is similar across the sections is also evident. For instance, the medicinal value of certain plants is found to be widely prevalent across the length and breadth of the country even today. However, the discriminatory caste-based norms have led to differences in health-related knowledge and practice among the *Dalits* and other castes. The extent of exposure to modern medicine, through public health programmes at a mass level and through personal doctors' services being availed, has led to new knowledge and practices reaching even the non-literate, non-school going populations. Some extent of demystification of modern medicine and its diffusion has also happened through paramedical personnel who come from lower socio-economic and rural backgrounds. All this makes the task of defining *lokavidya* in health even more complex.

### *Lokavidya Jan Andolan*

Social movements have historically, addressed issues of health and healing. Gandhiji, subsequent Gandhian organizations, the women's movement both internationally and nationally, have introduced the notion of 'control over one's own body'. Environment-related movements have highlighted the relevance of local ecology and health-related practices. Workers' organizations have raised issues of occupational hazards, safety and healthcare, though not in the same way or to the extent that the workers' own experience and knowledge, i.e. *lokavidya*, require them to. People's science movements tend to 'take science to the people' but not take people's knowledge as legitimate in its own right. However, the People's Health Movement-India chapter (Jan Swasthya Abhiyan) does recognize the value of traditional medicine due to its wider base of political ideologies and because the practice of traditional medicine is so pervasive in our society and has so many textual forms.

The dominant knowledge systems of medicine and public health are beginning to get sensitized to the significance of *lokavidya* as legitimate knowledge, rather than viewing it only as a negative force based on ignorance and superstition, as has been the conventional medical perspective over the past century. This holds true for the industrialized societies, as much as to those such as ours. Modern medicine and public health has two faces, the authoritarian and coercive as well as the progressive, liberative one. So do all the other expert-based systems, as evident by the observation that AYUSH officials generally tend to undermine the LHT (local health traditions). Relevance of *lokavidya* is recognized by the liberative stream of all systems, being viewed as mutually supportive and interlinked, while it tends to be denied by the authoritiarian stream.

Therefore, there is at this juncture, great value in recognizing, strengthening and promoting the health-related dimensions of *lokavidya*. From ensuring agency in the framework of 'personal is political', to rights-based campaigns, to generation of context-specific, decentralized forms of knowledge, *lokavidya* is today of greater significance than ever before.

# 35

# 'Right to Livelihood Based on *Lokavidya*' Act: Concept Note

*B. Krishnarajulu*

## Preamble

The crises of *Lokavidyadhar Samaj* (that vast section of Indian society which bases its life and livelihood on *lokavidya*) is that the (traditional) livelihoods have all but collapsed and the members of this *Samaj*(largely small and medium farmers, argicultural workers, artisans, tribals, small shopkeepers and home-maker women) are forced to live a life sans basic human dignity. They feel completely 'left out' and are at a loss to comprehend life and the future. This 'loss of identity and self-respect' is marked by a great groundswell of agitation (many times violent) by the youth of this *Samaj* all over the country.

In the era of globalization (post-1990) the agitations of farmers all over the country demanding prices, subsidies, etc., the agitation of traders and small shopkeepers against monopoly and entry of big houses into retail trade, the agitation of weavers demanding supply of yarn and market protection, the agitation of artisans of all shades for a protection of their livelihoods and market, the agitation of tribals against appropriation and exploitation of forest wealth to the detriment of the lives and livelihoods, are all pointers to the growing alienation this vast section of society experiences and the continuing exploitation of rampant financial, informational and industrial capitalism. The agitations also find expression against the erosion of societal norms and values, fuelled by crass comsumptive culture of urban India, in agitations for protection of 'culture' and 'identity'. Some of these agitations have led to demands for autonomy, linguistic and regional separatism with the apparent hope that a shared local-identity based polity could deliver economically, socially and politically.

## Inequality and Rural Poverty

Poverty is defined in terms of income, nutrition (number of calories consumed), type of dwelling, access to education, health services and clean environment and facilities for women and children. According to this measure a very large percentage of the population (about 80%) would be poor and most of these (90%) would be rural poor. In other words, almost all rural folk (peasants, artisans and women) and all tribals would fill the ranks of the poor in India. Key to these indicators is gainful employment. Poverty is thus associated, in the main, with lack of gainful employment. For the peasant it translates to non-remunerative price for agricultural produce and low wages for agri-labour. For artisans it means no markets for products of skills and no avenues for practising productive skills. For tribals it is associated with a shrinking 'workplace' and very exploitative terms of trade for tribal produce. For women as a whole it is associated with a continuous fight against all possible odds for survival of self and progeny.

The structure of pre-British society and economics was such that basic life requirements (food, clothing, shelter, work) was within the reach of all. While, social and economic disparities did exist, they were not existence threatening. An individual's work and place in society was defined and governed by *lokavidya* and the internal dynamics of the system allowed for sustenance and growth. The advent of British rule, by all accounts, demarcates the beginning of the collapse of the essential features of the once-stable society—food, work and social security.

## The Right to Livelihood Based on *Lokavidya*

Vast sections of rural society (*Lokavidyadhar Samaj)* share something in common, namely, all they can claim to be truly their own and within their grasp is *lokavidya.* Their lives and livelihoods are largely based on *lokavidya.*This being so, it is imperative that livelihoods based on *lokavidya* be given a constitutional guarantee much like the fundamental right to life, liberty, school education, information, food and reservations in education and employment. This should take the form of a fundamental Right to Livelihood based on *lokavidya* so that *Lokavidyadhar Samaj* can regain its lost momentum and impoverished men, women and children of the *Samaj* rebuild their lives with dignity.

## In Summary

Poverty is associated with lack of gainful employment/jobs, non-remunerative prices for agricultural produce and all livelihood-based services. The British era gave birth to the concept of gainful employment for wages; to meet basic living needs such as food, clothing, shelter, etc. *Lokavidya* livelihoods have ceased to be capable of meeting these basic life requirements.

Employability is now almost entirely dependent on acquired 'modern' skills and/or practices alone.

*Lokavidya* is the knowledge-basis of traditional livelihoods.

De-legitimization of *lokavidya* and destruction of livelihoods has led to low or no incomes and is the basis of inequality and growing poverty.

Activities that have gone to promote urban-industrial-information service livelihoods and lifestyles such as deforestation, land acquisition(agricultural and forest), agricultural policy (crops, major irrigation, fertilizers, pesticides, GM seeds, etc), import policy (cheap industrially produced consumption goods such as cloth, shoes, implementss etc) have all contributed to destroying traditional livelihoods

Right to Livelihood is a corollary of the Right to Life, Liberty and Food.

This fundamental right could take the form of an Act that guarantees The Right to Livelihood based on *lokavidya* and incorporates appropriate provisions to ensure that it is implemented in letter and spirit by making the state accountable as much as it is in case of life and liberty.

## Right to Livelihood Act: Essential Demands

The Act must hold the government accountable to ensure that no man or woman is forced to live a life without dignity because his/her livelihood cannot, by circumstance, support a dignified life.

The Act must place an obligation on the government to encourage *lokavdiya*-based occupations and livelihoods through sustainable and equitable means.

The Act must not abridge but only expand other entitlements such as old age pensions, maternity entitlements and work entitlements under MGNREGA.

The Act must also create new entitlements for those who are excluded from existing schemes, including the elderly and the infirm in need of daily care, migrant workers and their families, bonded labour families, the homeless, and the urban poor.

The Act must create an obligation for governments to prevent and address potential displacement and loss of livelihoods.

The Act must create provisions for governments to deal adequately with natural and human-made disasters and internal displacement, for example, by removing upper limits to person-days of employment in MGNREGA.

The Act must seek to eliminate all social discrimination in work-related matters, including discrimination against Scheduled Castes, Scheduled Tribes, Most Backward Classes and minorities.

The Act must include safeguards against the invasion of corporate interests and private contractors in livelihood policy. Governments must not enter into any partnerships with the private sector where there is a conflict of interests.

The Act must include strong, in-built independent institutions for accountability along with time-bound, grievance redressal provisions (including provisions for criminal prosecution), mandatory penalties for any violation of the Act and compensation for those whose entitlements have been denied. In particular, the Gram Sabha must have effective powers for grievance redressal and monitoring of livelihood-related schemes.

The Act must specify that no laws or policy shall be passed that adversely impact the enabling environment for the Right to Livelihood.

The Act must make it obligatory on the government to protect, preserve and provide infrastructure and resources(land, water, forests, pastures, roads, settlements, electricity, etc) that are essential to the practice of livelihoods.

# 36

# LJA: Engaging the Leftists and the Progressives

*Amit Basole*

Thus far we have paid more attention to "*vidya*" in *lokavidya*, as compared to the "lok." Looking at society from the perspective of knowledge (as opposed to property, income, caste, race, etc) we arrive at a classification that is intimately connected to colonial history. This is because the colonial encounter represented a massive reorganization of the world of knowledge. The knowledge hierarchy is of course related to other hierarchies in society, but it is not simply derivable from them, it is not reducible to any other hierarchy.

Since knowledge has to do with representation and understanding of the world around us, the hierarchy of knowledge is built upon claims of greater understanding or better representation. Because knowledge also has to do with the fulfilment of human needs, knowledge hierarchies are also built upon claims of greater usefulness. Knowledge that is called "scientific" has been deemed to be on top, both because it gives us the most reliable understanding of reality and because it is most useful (because it is the most productive). One claim is epistemological and the other is social/technical, the two are of course related. It is then "common sense" that the more superior kind of knowledge be the basis for the (re)organization of society. Which means that the holders of this knowledge should be given the initiative in shaping society. The *lokavidya* perspective challenges this view. The *Lokavidya Jan Andolan* (LJA) will be the first social movement which publicly and directly questions this view.

Capital sometimes appears to challenge knowledge hierarchies. It appears to support *lokavidya* because capital cares neither about epistemology, nor about usefulness or productivity. It cares about value (in the sense of surplus value). Thus any knowledge, whatever its source or social location, if it can produce value, will be used by capital. Neither epistemological nor technical objections will be raised. Hence the paradox we see today that progressives and the leftist stand opposed to *lokavidya*, while capital appears for it. But the support of capital is fickle. It lasts only as long as the market trend. The immediate problem before us as we embark on the LJA is, how do we speak to progressives and leftists, who are still in the "science mode," about *lokavidya*? To many people the concept of a knowledge hierarchy and knowledge struggle may sound abstract. What is the concrete manifestation of it in society? It may also sound removed from the "bread-and-butter" concerns of jal/jangal/zamin, wages, working conditions, civil liberties, etc. How does the knowledge question relate to these pressing concerns? We will have to address all these issues in a clear manner.

A series of short pamphlets will have to be prepared which take one conventional platform of a social movement (say displacement or civil liberties) and show how they relate to the knowledge question and how they are strengthened by connection with the knowledge issue. If we can do this task adequately, we will be able to build the necessary connections.

What is the "lok" in *lokavidya*? It is not the same as the "working class" or "the poor." It is that majority of society which keeps showing up in government surveys as "uneducated" or lacking in any formal training. These are the "masses" who need experts to organize their lives, because they are deemed incapable of doing it themselves. But this is only a negative definition (such as the definition of a proletarian as one without property). This is the definition one arrives at through conventional leftist thinking. Positively, the "lok" is the subject created through *lokavidya*, through the knowledge it possesses. This is not tautological. A community of scientists not only creates scientific knowledge, but is also in turn created by that knowledge. Its modes of life and thought are shaped by the knowledge it creates. The same goes for the "lok." The "lok" is the vast majority of society whose life and work are organized on the basis of knowledge that is produced in the course of living itsêlf. The lok is that section of society who has living knowledge, knowledge that is tested on the anvil of experience. It is the possessor of specialized knowledge of work, production, the arts, and general knowledge of morals and values. The first contribution of the *lokavidya* perspective is that the lok, the majority, is not defined through lack of knowledge, but the presence of it.

The lok has endured centuries of subjugation and has revolted through those centuries as well. It is the claim of the LJA that the basis of its revolt has been *lokavidya*. Every so often, whether it is via bhakti or via Gandhi, an assertion of *lokavidya* takes place against the pretensions of elite knowledge, be it Brahminism or Science. Even today in its defeated and exploited state, the lok retains this power. Even when it organizes life on a daily basis, in the presence of extreme uncertainty and hardship, the lok is believed to be in need of intervention and guidance from outside. Not an infusion of knowledge as it deems necessary on its own initiative, but rather intervention in a predetermined form, by others who have decided what is good for the lok. Constant schemes, suggestions, projects, programmes and interventions are its lot. Since it is not believed to be capable of thinking for itself.

The lok, defined through *lokavidya* also has many internal divisions and hierarchies that weaken it. Though it constitutes the majority, the minority can keep it subjugated by splitting it along caste/occupation, gender and religious lines. It is deemed incapable of resolving its own problems, although if we look into history, it is the lok and not the elite who has sustained the Hindu-Muslim syncretic culture of North India, it is the lok which has revolted repeatedly against the hierarchies of caste. It still carries the capacity to do so, but it lack the cohesion and organization needed for the task.

This is the task of the *Lokavidya Jan Andolan*. We need progressive people of all colours to join. Initially they may not agree completely with the points laid out above. It is not necessary that they do so. It is only necessary that they see the lok as the possessor of knowledge, and as a class in society which can lay the foundation for a society based on equality. It is only necessary that they reject the urban, university-educated class to be the one which deserves the final word on everything. If they can do this much, they can contribute fruitfully to the LJA.

# Afterword

*Sunil Sahasrabudhey*

Since the November 2011 *Lokavidya Jan Andolan* (LJA) Conference in Varanasi, the LJA has spread through conferences in Darbhanga, Singrauli, Indore and Chirala. These along with Varanasi, have effectively become areas where this Knowledge Movement is programming itself as a people's movement. Demanding employment based on *lokavidya* is emerging as a central issue. The argument is simple. People earn their livelihoods based on what they know and what they do, which is *lokavidya*. So, the surest path to the well-being of the people lies in proper remuneration for what they already know and do. LJA demands that this remuneration be equal to the salary of a government employee. There is a strong internal debate on it. This is for the first time that a demand, like this and an argument like this has been put forth, but this is also for the first time that a movement of the people is attempting to build itself on and around the central idea of *lokavidya*. Social, political and philosophical issues tend to merge into one. Handling such debates is a terse task for the university trained, however those living their lives with *lokavidya darshan* do not seem to find it difficult.

Hand in glove with the LJA, efforts continue to recognize and reconstruct a public domain that would facilitate debates and action towards a new society based on re-legitimization of *lokavidya*. This is *lokavidya tana-bana*. Ideally *lokavidya tana-bana* is the world of relationships among the people not mediated by state, science or capital. Globalization does attempt to mediate every human relation by at least one of these and the resistance to such intrusion reproduces the *lokavidya tana-bana* as an ever new domain of people's activity. It is our understanding that the world of art recognizes *lokavidya tana-bana* and is often able to relate to it. And therefore art that is not a maiden of science needs to put courage together to articulate and represent this *lokavidya tana-bana,* to fill it with a new meaning, this time sufficiently political to tilt the scales. *Vidya Ashram* thus prepares to initiate a new dialogue with the world of art, a dialogue that would encourage the artist to recreate as an ostensive public domain that world of mutual relationships, namely the world of *lokavidya tana-bana,* which already exists as a semi-private, semi-public domain, those of the village, the community and the knowledge *sampradayas.*

It cannot be a forgone conclusion that the world will remain constituted around the city. Since all the debating space is occupied by the university and its advocates, the current debate tends to give the impression that the city has come to stay as the centre forever. Have the Gandhis, Tolstoys and Proudhons lost their battles not to recover ever again? The *lokavidya* movement inaugurates a civilizational movement in the 21st century that would like to argue that there is no civilization where there is no village. The village is the centre of that social imagination which can deliver mankind, a delivery that has always been the undying dream of men and women. It is impossible to realize the Rights of Nature and Mother Earth in a world built around the city. The *lokavidya* movement helps us imagine how the village can recover and rebuild itself as the centre again. So it seems that a *Gaon-Shahar Samvad* (Village-City Dialogue) needs to be developed as a radical knowledge dialogue.

Is this knowledge movement, the *lokavidya* movement, headed towards laying the foundations of a new society, a new public domain to start with, which is not captive to or governed by the state, corporations or the university? Is it headed towards laying the foundations of conceptualizing and building real power that does not draw its spirits from politics, commerce or science? Is this direction of exploration and practice creating a new eye to see the variety of practices across the world today as a growing fraternity? Are these the practices that are attempting to create a spirit of new civilization based on one's own tradition and enriched by the later experiences?

An emancipatory movement is typically the one in which political arguments have strong philosophical undertones and philosophy smacks of political strategy. Let the values and beliefs of the 19th and 20th centuries not hold us back and let us rise with the slogan that everybody is knowledgeable.

# Glossary

| | |
|---|---|
| *acharya kul* | the community (organization) of teachers |
| *adivasi* | indigenous people, tribal, native, forest dwellers |
| *agaria* | a tribe in central India which preserves the tradition of extracting the metal by smelting iron ore in very small furnaces |
| *ahimsa* | non-violence |
| *anchal* | region |
| *ashram* | a place where activists live in an ideologically guided lifestyle |
| *asuri* | satanic |
| *avidya* | what has the appearance of knowledge but is not knowledge |
| *Ayurveda* | healthcare tradition of India |
| *bahishkrit samaj* | the externed, communities or people who do not find a place in the modern structure of opportunities, mainly peasants, *adivasis*, women, artisans and small retailers. |
| *bauddhik satyagraha* | knowledge *satyagraha*, resistance in the world of knowledge from the *lokavidya* perspective |
| *bhaichara* | brotherhood, fraternal relations |
| *brahmin* | traditional Indian priestly and scholarly caste |
| *dalit* | untouchables of traditional Indian society |

| | |
|---|---|
| ***darshan*** | world-view, philosophy |
| ***dharma*** | duty, religion |
| ***dhobi*** | washerman |
| ***dhoti*** | traditional Indian dress worn under the waist |
| ***dincharya-ritucharya*** | regulatory conventions according to seasons for daily life from the point of view of healthcare |
| ***geeta*** | a very important religious-philosophical text of Hindus |
| ***gondi*** | language of Gond people of central India |
| ***gram panchayat*** | village council |
| ***gramodyog*** | village industries |
| ***gurukul*** | a form of traditional Indian school |
| ***gyan andolan*** | knowledge movement |
| ***gyan ki rajniti*** | knowledge politics |
| ***gyan panchayat*** | democratic people's hearing on knowledge |
| ***hakim*** | doctor of *Unani* tradition of medicine |
| ***jal-jangal-zameen*** | water-forest-land |
| ***jal samaadhi*** | giving one's life by immersing oneself in water |
| ***jan andolan*** | people's movement |
| ***jati*** | caste |
| ***karigar*** | artisan |
| ***karigar samaj*** | artisan community |
| ***khadi*** | hand spun cloth |
| ***lassi, pakaudi, chat*** | food items, drinks and snacks, sold by pavement retailers |
| ***lokavidya*** | knowledge in society, people's knowledge including their logic, values, methods of organization. |
| ***lokavidya jan andolan*** | a people's knowledge movement based on *lokavidya* |
| ***lokavidya maha-dhiveshan*** | Third Congress of Traditional Sciences and Technologies of India, organized in Varanasi in 1998. |
| ***lokavidya panchayat*** | a kind of knowledge organization of the |

| | |
|---|---|
| | people, the bearers of *lokavidya*. Also the title of a journal published by *Vidya Ashram*. |
| ***lokavidya pratishtha abhiyan*** | campaign for the dignity of *lokavidya* |
| ***Lokavidya Samvad*** | a journal published by the *lokavidya* group between 1998 and 2008. *Samvad* means dialogue |
| ***lokavidyadhar samaj*** | communities that live by *lokavidya*, by knowledge gained outside the university |
| ***lokakala*** | art with the people |
| ***lokaniti*** | policy that serves the people |
| ***lokashakti*** | strength of the people |
| ***mayavi*** | deceptive, virtual |
| ***mimansa*** | one of the six orthodox systems of Indian philosophy |
| ***mistri*** | technical expert |
| ***mohalla*** | neighbourhood |
| ***nai talim*** | basic education favoured by Gandhi |
| ***navya nyaya*** | a 14th century school of logic in Bengal |
| ***nishad*** | boatmen, fishermen |
| ***nyaya vaisheshika*** | traditional Indian logic and physics |
| ***panchayat*** | council, meeting, often for conflict resolution, traditionally for local governance in India |
| ***pashchimikrit samaj*** | westernized communities |
| ***prayog parivar*** | a network to solve farming problems started by S.A. Dabholkar |
| ***rail roko, rasta roko*** | obstructing the rail and road traffic |
| ***rajniti*** | politics |
| ***rangoli*** | a type of traditional Indian drawing |
| ***samudhayam (samudaya)*** | community |
| ***sangharsh aur nirman*** | struggle and reconstruction |
| ***sankhya*** | one of the earliest schools of Indian philosophy |
| ***satya*** | truth |
| ***satyagraha*** | literally insistence on truth, traditional |

| | |
|---|---|
| | Indian method of struggle (resistance), recreated and popularized by Gandhi in the 20th century. |
| ***shudra*** | name of working castes in Ancient India |
| ***Siddha*** | the healthcare tradition of Kerala |
| ***sloka*** | hymn |
| ***swadeshi*** | what is near you and belongs to your society, one of the political idioms popularized by Gandhi |
| ***swadeshi samaj*** | classes coming down from before the colonial advent |
| ***Swadeshi Vigyan Karyashala*** | the workshop of *swadeshi* science organized at the Gandhian Institute of Studies, Varanasi in October 1993 |
| ***swadharma*** | duty originating in one's own thinking and not guided by alien compulsions and considerations |
| ***swaraj*** | popular Indian term for self-governance, popularized by Gandhi during the Independence Movement |
| ***tana-bana*** | warp and weft, generally used to refer to networks |
| ***vaidyas*** | practitioners of ayurvedic (Indian) medicine |
| ***vedanta*** | the last philosophical part of the Vedas, the supposedly revealed texts of the Hindus |
| ***vidya*** | knowledge inclusive of art, science, logic, skills, values, media competencies, etc. |
| ***vidya ashram*** | a place for knowledge activists |
| ***vidyalaya*** | school |
| ***yoga*** | a method of meditation in Indian tradition |
| ***yoga samhita*** | principles of traditional Indian yoga |
| ***Unani*** | one of the healthcare traditions of the Middle East also popular in India |
| ***zamindari*** | feudal lordship created by the British in India through what has been known as the Permanent Settlement |

# About Vidya Ashram

## Genesis of *Vidya Ashram*

At *Vidya Ashram* in Sarnath, Varanasi (www.*vidyashram*.org), over the course of the past ten years we have arrived at a two-pronged programme to advance the *lokavidya* movement. One is *lokavidya darshan* or advancing the philosophy of *lokavidya*, and the second is *gyan ki rajniti* or the politics of knowledge. Each complements the other, and together they constitute an attempt to forge a new political imagination for the 21st century.

The present volume collects pieces written over the past decade by a variety of associates of the *Ashram*. *Vidya Ashram* was formally established in Sarnath, Varanasi (in Uttar Pradesh) in 2004. In the preceding three decades, the work of three organizations contributed to the *Ashram*'s vision: *Mazdoor Kisan Niti* (Kanpur), a Hindi journal of non-party political discourse and analysis published between 1977 and 1987 successively from Kanpur, Jhansi, and Varanasi. Patriotic and People-oriented Science and Technology (PPST) Foundation (Chennai), a group of scientists who produced a radical critique of modern Science, and Nari Hastakala Udyog Samiti (Varanasi) which developed the concept of *nari vidya* (women's knowledge) while working with women in the unorganized sector. Each of these is described in brief below. In addition, the New Farmers' Movement that started in the 1970s and became a country-wide mass movement in the 1980s, was the crucial *mass political* space within which ideas of several *Vidya Ashram* members were formed.

The Mazdoor Kisan Niti group of students from IIT Kanpur started with left leanings and soon moved on to appreciate

Gandhi and became part of the massive new Farmers' Movement around 1979-80, which over a decade spread in almost all the states from Tamil Nadu to Punjab. They saw this movement in continuity with Gandhi. The journal became a place for developing new Gandhian perspectives and an instrument of coordination in the movement and of taking the new ideas and the message of the movement to the socially concerned educated classes. They saw the farmers' movement as a bearer of a new political consciousness significant for all those who had no place in the modern structure of opportunities. The group engaged in search of the knowledge basis of this consciousness, formulated then as 'living traditions of knowledge', which was later given the name *lokavidya*, now accepted widely. In the process the group developed a conceptual apparatus around the categories of *pashchimikrit samaj-bahishkrit samaj*. *Pashchimikrit samaj* was constituted of people who had by and large found a place in the modern structure of opportunities and in the *bahishkrit samaj* came the large masses of peasants, artisans, *adivasis* and women. The group engaged in the development of a theoretical apparatus for the movement and emancipation of the *bahishkrit samaj*.

The PPST Foundation, started in 1978, was a group of young scientists who took the view that there were valid traditions of knowledge other than modern science. The group engaged in a substantial investigation of the nature of Indian sciences and technologies in earlier periods, at the time of British intervention in the 18th century and during the development of the colonial policy through the 19th century. The work of the group was published in PPST Bulletins, about 20 of which were published between 1979 and 1994. In the early 1990s, PPST launched a movement of Traditional Sciences and Technologies of India, organized through three huge Congresses, each one attended by over a thousand people for five continuous days discussing a great variety of subjects like traditional industries, agriculture, metals and materials, forestry, architecture, health, theoretical sciences and philosophies of sciences. The first congress was held in 1993 in IIT Bombay, the second in Anna University, Chennai in 1995 and the third at the Gandhian Institute of Studies in Varanasi in 1998. This third Congress was called the

*Lokavidya Mahadhiveshan* and distinguished itself by conferences of farmers, artisans and women with *lokavidya* as the focus. This gave it a forward looking creative touch, for *lokavidya* was understood as being renewed every day by people's genius depending on their needs and based on their experiences.

*Nari Hastkala Udyog Samiti* (NHUS) worked from Varanasi between 1992 and 2000. Debates on alternative and rooted traditions of knowledge, movement of farmers seen as movement of the *bahishkrit samaj* and the women's movement of the 1970-80s constituted the backdrop against which the *samiti* had crystallized seeking to answer fundamental questions related to the emancipation of women. The idea of *nari-vidya and* local market was central to it. Strengths of women were seen primarily as flowing from their knowledge, skills, values, methods of organization and communication and the natural disposition characteristic of them. This *Samiti*, a group of women, engaged in both theory and widespread practice to evolve a new standpoint which eventually in collaboration with others emerged in the name of *lokavidya* and *local market.*

*The Lokavidya Mahadhiveshan* marks the beginning of a process of assertion by the subaltern classes in the world of knowledge. It marks the beginning of a claim for equality between various traditions of knowledge, modern science included. It marks the beginning of a new political imagination in which the power of the people flows from their own knowledge, *lokavidya.* It marks the beginning of a knowledge politics that articulates the *lokavidya* standpoint as the standpoint of the people in the Age of Information. This knowledge movement around the idea of *lokavidya* matured further and led to the idea and reality of *Vidya Ashram.*

## *Ashram* Interventions

*Vidya Ashram* is a place where politics and philosophy are not separable. Social and human concern, academy, *darshan* and movement merge into one. The expression lies in attempts to develop a *lokavidya* idiom of discourse through participation in movements, pamphleteering, publishing journals and booklets, organizing conferences, workshops, dialogues and meetings and constructive work in the world of knowledge.

### *Participation in Movements*

Many *Ashram* members come from a background of active participation in the *kisan andolans* (farmers' movements) of the 1980s. A principal means to remain in touch with people's concerns and views has been to make *Vidya Ashram* a resource for the Bharatiya Kisan Union in the eastern part of Uttar Pradesh. This creates a continuous mode of engagement with ongoing struggles against displacement or GM seeds, for prices, electricity and irrigation, and so on. It also creates traffic of *lokavidya*-holders who regularly bring their views to the *Ashram*. The movement is seen as being in continuity with Gandhi. If Gandhi represented the *bahishkrit samaj* of this country, the *kisan andolan* represents the next stage in which the *bahishkrit samaj* is conscious of its *bahishkrit* nature and can assume its own leadership. More recently, *Vidya Ashram* has articulated the view that if the farmers' movements had equipped themselves with the language of *lokavidya*, which all along has been the knowledge basis of this movement, and staked a political claim that farmers possess knowledge on the basis of which they can organize their own societies, the movement could not have been reduced easily to a "pressure group."

The *Ashram* has had a presence in the movements of *adivasis* and farmers against forced land acquisition and consequent displacement in the states of Uttar Pradesh, Madhya Pradesh and Andhra Pradesh, mostly led by local struggle committees and sometimes by national organizations like the Bharatiya Kisan Union or National Alliance of People's Movements (NAPM).

There has also been involvement in the struggles of artisans and roadside retailers against aggressive implementation of State policy by the local administration resulting in disorganization of their economic activity and displacement. In all such engagements the *Ashram* tries to propagate the view that everyone has the right to live by his or her knowledge and that resources necessary for this cannot be just taken away.

### *Dialogues*

Dialogues involving assertion from the *lokavidya* point of view has been a strong mode of interaction both with the ordinary people and with activists and researchers. These dialogues have been carried out extensively by calling meetings at the *Ashram*, by going out into the peasant, *adivasi* and artisan locations and by participating in meetings called by other groups and organizations.

In addition to these dialogues mainly in Hindi and also in Telugu, associates of the *Ashram* have intervened in the English-speaking world via participation in seminars and conferences in the universities and research institutions, and participation in various World Social Forums as well as through engagement with the Edu-Factory network of European Knowledge Activists (www.edu-factory.org). A series of workshops were organized at World Social Forums in Mumbai (2004), Karachi (2006), New Delhi (India Social Forum, 2006), and Nairobi (2007) with the theme Dialogues on Knowledge in Society. Some papers from these workshops are part of the present volume. Some associates of the *Ashram* are members of the edu-factory collective and have contributed to their book, "Towards a Global Autonomous University: Cognitive Labour, the Production of Knowledge, and Exodus from the Education Factory" (Autonomedia, 2009). On the occasion of each workshop in the WSFs, bulletins were published by the titles Dialogues on Knowledge in Society, Virtuality and Knowledge in Society, Knowledge Satyagraha, and Radical Politics and the Knowledge Question.

### Publications

A series of publications in Hindi (some translated into Telugu, Urdu and Marathi) has carried the *lokavidya* view to the social activists, the socially concerned, and generally to the *lokavidyadhar samaj*. A five-booklet series called Knowledge Politics Booklet Series (*Gyan Ki Rajneeti Pustakmala*) was published in Hindi on the following topics: Knowledge Satyagraha, Pro-people Politics and the Knowledge Question, A Call for the Emancipation of Knowledge, Youth Knowledge Camps, and *Lokavidya*. Two Hindi periodicals, *Lokavidya Samvad* and *Lokavidya Panchayat* were also published from Sarnath. Recently the publication of a new periodical, *Karigar Nazariya* (Artisans' View) has been started. From Hyderabad a Telugu journal *Lokavidya Prapancham* is published.

Since 2011 during the preparation and expansion of the *Lokavidya Jan Andolan*, Hindi booklets have been published on the topics of displacement and local market. The Hindi souvenir published on the occasion of the *Lokavidya Jan Andolan* Conference titled *Lokavidya Ki Kitab* (The *Lokavidya* Book) is a concise and particularly telling statement of the *lokavidya* point of view.

### *Programmes*

Programmes of the *Ashram* are in the nature of constructive programmes constitutive of a knowledge movement for, and based on, the knowledge that people possess, namely *lokavidya*. It has been named *Lokavidya Jan Andolan*. The *Ashram*'s participation in various movements and forums, and all its publications broadly speaking contribute to the development of a *lokavidya* knowledge perspective. In addition to these, specific programmes have been developed by the *Ashram* to build this knowledge movement. *Lokavidya BhaicharaVidyalaya*, *Gyan Panchayat*, *Lokavidya Satsang*, *Lokavidya Ashram* and *Lokavidya Tana-bana* are some of these. These are all attempts to construct new types of knowledge locations in society.

*Lokavidya BhaicharaVidyalaya* is a set of evening schools for the children of the poor in the villages attempting to develop competencies for, and inculcate values of removing inequality in society in a strongly interactive mode with its social location, the village. The *Gyan panchayat* attempts through people's hearings to popularize that people's solutions to actual problems need to be taken much more seriously, because their knowledge is not inferior to university knowledge in any sense, and in fact is superior in many respects. *Lokavidya* Satsang is a popular mode of propagating *lokavidya* philosophy, through a claim of an equal place in the world of knowledge, by groups of singers, storytellers and philosophers through the countryside, and the settlements of the urban poor. *Lokavidya Ashrams* are places of *lokavidya* philosophy and a knowledge political discourse, often housing *Bhaichara Vidyalayas* and hosting *Lokavidya Satsang* and *Gyan panchayat*. *Lokavidya Tana-bana* is a dialogue with artists to attract them to pay greater attention to the reality of relationships and connectivity within the *lokavidyadhar samaj*, as the location for imaginative and creative expressions for a new direction to rebuilding this society.

***Lokavidya Jan Andolan (People's Knowledge Movement)***

The interventions by the *Ashram* through participation in movements, and its own programmes and publications, all go towards building a Knowledge Movement called *Lokavidya Jan Andolan* (LJA). The LJA has had its founding conference in Varanasi (November 2011) and regional conferences in Darbhanga (Bihar), Singrauli (Madhya Pradesh) and Chirala (Andhra Pradesh) during 2012. Of particular mention is the spread of LJA in western Madhya Pradesh around Indore. The most appealing idea in this knowledge movement relates to equal status for *lokavidya* with the consequent demand that governments must ensure that those living by *lokavidya* have a stable and regular income of the same order as that of a government employee. As of today this seems to have brought the idea of *Gyan ki Rajneeti* (Politics of Knowledge) to the plane of actual political campaign.